Due Return	Due Return
Date Date	Date Date

MIDDLETON

CHARLES MIDDLETON

The Life
and Times of a
Restoration Politician

by

George Hilton Jones

Caret tibi pectus inani
ambitione? Caret mortis formidine et ira?
Somnia, terrores magicos, miracula, sagas,
nocturnos lemures portentaque Thessala rides?
Natalis grate numeras? Ignoscis amicis?
Horace, *Epistulae*, Book II, No. II, 11. 206–10

UNIVERSITY OF CHICAGO PRESS

Chicago and London

Library of Congress Catalog Card Number 67-25532

The University of Chicago Press, *Chicago & London*
The University of Toronto Press, *Toronto 5, Canada*

To My Mother

PREFACE

This study of the second Earl of Middleton and the foreign policy of King James II of England is intended to serve two functions. First, the career of the earl over the great historical watershed of the Revolution of 1688 illustrates the choosing of sides in that event and the pressures that brought it to pass. Second, the foreign policy of the 1680's, more often remarked upon than studied, receives its first full treatment, chiefly as it affected the "Northern Department."

It may be objected that this study draws too much upon British archives and too little upon those of the continent. Quite apart from the question of time required, I hold that the best material for study of a policy is that which could have affected it and that which recorded it. James and Middleton, that is, formed their notions from the documents available to them, and most of these documents are preserved in the Public Record Office, the British Museum, and the Bodleian Library. The voluminous documentary publications and monographic studies published by continental scholars, on the other hand, supply a corrective where James's information was too far from truth.

I am obliged to many friends and supporters. I could never have broken through the obstacles to research without the leisure afforded by a Guggenheim Fellowship. The Newberry Library, through one of its fellowships, also helped by giving me a pleasant summer among its valuable collections.

Besides these great sources of financial assistance, I acknowledge my debt to the staffs of the libraries and repositories in which I worked. These, besides the Newberry Library, included the Library of the British Museum, the Public Record

Office, the Cambridge University Library, the Cambridge University Archives, the Register House at Edinburgh, the Library of Trinity College, Cambridge, and Dr. Williams' Library, London.

Neville J. Williams, an old friend, has been very helpful in my use of the documents he knows so well; he has also given me much encouragement. Indeed, personal support and encouragement have helped me surmount great problems. D. J. Derx, Robert H. Clarke, C. Leonard Lundin, David Owen, Wallace Notestein, Merton Dillon, Stanley Pargellis, Mrs. David Hornor, Leo Hendrick, and William S. Gray have helped me in one way and another. My family — my mother, my sister Elizabeth, and my brother Philip — have been faithful friends as well as relatives.

A note on calendars: The Julian calendar was still used in England and certain other countries during the seventeenth century, while most continental states used the Gregorian calendar. The difference is that the same day bears a date ten days later in the Gregorian calendar than in the Julian throughout that century, while after February 29 (Julian), 1700, the difference is eleven days. The dates given here are those of the countries in which the events occurred, although both dates are sometimes combined, as January 11/21, 1689. The difference in dating the beginning of the year — that is, between January 1 (as in Rome and France) and March 25 (as in England and Tuscany) — is clarified by a combination of dates falling between the two: for instance, March 11, 1667/68.

A note on translated passages:

Except where otherwise attributed, all translations into English are the work of the author.

G. H. J.

Eastern Illinois University

CONTENTS

CHAPTER I

Father and Son

The English Restoration was formally sealed at Westminster on April 13, 1661, when King Charles II was crowned, anointed, and enthroned. The heir of the Stuart house, having made real concessions and cordial gestures of reconciliation to the vested interests of the Interregnum, recovered the position and most of the power that Charles I had held. Now Charles had three kingdoms — England, Scotland, and Ireland. Because ten years earlier he had been crowned king in Scotland, his coronation in England theoretically was without significance over the northern border, but in fact the English Restoration was of enormous importance to Scotland, and the English coronation day was set aside for Scottish rejoicing.

The Restoration in England had made possible a parallel settlement in Scotland, which had been conquered by Cromwell, and it reestablished the nation's independence. For many years before 1660, Scotland had been governed by England, and swallowed up in a union with it; now old, familiar Scottish civil institutions were revived. Scotsmen governed Scotsmen under Scottish law. Charles was affable; there had been no serious meddling with the religious question, and little retaliation on Scotsmen for past offenses. Many questions remained open, which must some day be taken up and decided, but on coronation day most Scotsmen were content, and malcontents kept their peace.

Edinburgh, the ancient capital, prepared a gala, for the king had authorized extraordinary expense. High officials and private persons displayed their loyalty, patriotism, and means in luxurious dress and lavish entertainment. The center of all this was the king's new lord commissioner to the Scottish parliament, John Middleton, the first Earl of Middleton. To mark the religious character of the celebration, the commissioner and parliament together heard a sermon in the parliament house, which was followed by a grand dinner.

About the middle of dinner, the Lord Commissioner began his majesty's health, of which a signal being given from the terrace, the cannons of the castle were discharged and answered by those from the citadel of Leith, and then the great bonfire in the out court of the Palace was set on fire, about which after dinner the young lords and ladies expressed their joy by several sorts of dances.[1]

There was evidently much drinking; the commissioner, as many in Scotland would soon discover, was fond of the bottle, and this ultimate victory over disasters and frustrations was an occasion for self-indulgence.

At last his party had triumphed. Middleton received princely emoluments, presided over the king's government in Scotland, and enjoyed the universal deference and attention that accompanied his position in the state. His wife, Grizel Durham, was an able and spirited companion, well suited to her new rank and place. His two daughters would be matched with the best-born in Scotland, and his son, Lord Clermont, might expect anything in the king's gift.

Lord Clermont, our subject, who became the second Earl of Middleton, joined in the country dances and the reels, wild with the excitement of coronation day; "so ravished with joy, that if he had not been restrained he had thrown rings, chains, jewels and all that was precious about him into the fire."[2] This was extravagant conduct for a "man of quality," but he was then about eleven years old, and at least a little drunk. The magistrates of Edinburgh drank the king's health that evening upon their knees — as a sign of reverence — at the Mercat Cross. Nobles and gentlemen danced and leaped and drank; the city was filled with the roaring of cannon; the trumpets of the Scottish army sounded back and forth.[3] Warlike,

[1] *The Kingdomes Intelligencer*, April 29–May 6, 1661, No. 18, pp. 270–71.

[2] "Edinburgh's Joy for His Majesties Coronation in England," 1661, reprinted by James Maidment in *Reliquiae Scoticae* (Edinburgh, 1828).

[3] John Nicoll, *Diary of Public Transactions and Other Occurrences . . .*, ed. David Laing (Edinburgh. Bannatyne Club, 1836), Vol. 54, 327–28.

inebriated, happy, Edinburgh followed the lead of the soldier-commissioner in welcoming the return of peace and stability.

The Middleton family prospered. The earl married one of his daughters to the Earl of Morton, the other to the Earl of Kinghorn (and later also the Earl of Strathmore), and lived in Holyrood Palace. He received generous grants and allowances for his table and furniture, and for coaches and liveries. The commissioner was also captain-general in the army of Scotland and captain of Edinburgh Castle. He spent as he got, largely in entertainment, but also in paying old debts. He presumably provided marriage portions for his daughters out of his own pocket, but he was at liberty, within the customary limits, to enrich his family through his official position. Thus one of his sons-in-law, the Earl of Morton, was able to revive his family's interests in Orkney and Zetland, and the young Lord Clermont was spoken of for a commission in the Scottish army. The Earl of Middleton was the greatest man in his country, apparently above attack from any quarter: "The like honor was never conferred upon any former commissioner of Scotland."[4]

He owed his position to his past. After the execution of Charles I, Middleton — who had been a Covenanter and a rebel — changed his political orientation and recognized Charles II as king of Scotland; he became a thorough royalist, and remained one. Having commanded Charles II's horse at Worcester, he was captured after that battle and was imprisoned in the Tower of London, but he obtained permission for his wife to visit him and shortly after (in January, 1652), disguised himself in her clothes, and escaped.[5] He fled to the Continent and associated himself with Sir Edward Hyde, later Earl of Clarendon, Charles II's advisor in exile.[6] In 1653, Middleton engaged in semi-diplomatic negotiations with the States General of

[4] *Ibid.*, p. 383.

[5] Sir James Turner, *Memoirs of My Own Time*, ed. Thomas Thomson (Edinburgh: Bannatyne Club, 1829), Vol. 26, 102; *Calendar of State Papers, Domestic Series* [henceforth cited as *Cal. S. P. Dom.*], *1651–1652* (London, 1877), p. 101.

[6] Charles McCormick (ed.), *The Secret History of the Court and Reign of Charles the Second, by a Member of His Privy Council . . .* (2 vols.; London, 1792), I, 183.

the United (Dutch) Netherlands. After receiving his king's commission to command Scottish royalists in a rising, he took command of a body of men in the Highlands in early 1654 and maintained a kind of warfare against the Cromwellian government until 1655, when he gave up his efforts and returned to Holland. The Protectorate excepted him from a general pardon, and — according to Middleton's testimony years later — his wife and children were condemned to transportation to Barbados,[7] but were apparently beyond the government's reach.

A little later, Middleton was at Cologne, where he renounced his former religion and became an Episcopalian. In 1656 he was with Charles II at Bruges, when his master delegated him to treat with the Jews of Amsterdam for money and authorized him to offer them assurances of protection comparable to those they sought from Cromwell. Middleton was also employed, near Danzig, to recruit Scotsmen deserting from the Swedish army and to raise money from Scottish merchants in Poland. He was accredited to the court of Brandenburg at Berlin, and was at Danzig late in 1656 and in 1657.[8] He may have gone to England on a secret mission in 1659.

These constant services singled Middleton out for promotion even before the Restoration — apparently he was promised an earldom in 1656. When Charles II returned to England in May, 1660, at the invitation of the Convention parliament, Middleton sailed in the king's own ship, the *Charles* (formerly the *Naseby* of Cromwell's fleet), hastily but royally fitted up for the occasion. On October 1 he was enrolled as Earl of Middleton and Lord of Clermont and Fettercairn, in the peerage of Scotland.

Sir George Mackenzie of Rosehaugh, a friend, later described the first earl's character.

He was by his heroic aspect marked out for great things, and was too liberal to be a private person; but this too munificent humour, which made him value the services of those whom he esteemed above all

---

[7] Sir Charles Firth and R. S. Rait (eds.), *Acts and Ordinances of the Interregnum, 1642–1660* (3 vols.; London, 1911), II, 876; British Museum [henceforth cited as B.M.], Add. MS 23,120, fol. 145.

[8] Thomas Birch (ed.), *A Collection of the State Papers of John Thurloe* . . . (7 vols.; London, 1725), VI, 76, 90; B.M., Egerton MS 2,536, fols. 142–43, 176–77, 168–69; Ludwig Bittner *et al.*, *Repertorium der diplomatischen Vertreter aller Länder* (2 vols.; Berlin, 1936, 1950), I, 180.

rewards, made him oftimes disoblige such as were not virtuous enough, by promising to them what he hoped to obtain, though he failed in the undertaking. . . . His natural courage and generosity made him likewise less jealous both of men and events than a great person ought to have been; but his greatest weakness was, that he preferred such to offices of trust as were unfit to serve him in them, regarding therein rather their interest than his own. Nor did he attend his majesty so frequently as was convenient. . . . He was really a man of a manly eloquence as well as aspect; happier in his wit than in his friends; and more pitied after his fall than envied in his prosperity.[9]

Mackenzie should have added that Middleton had a hasty and arbitrary disposition.

Middleton governed in close alliance with the Earl of Clarendon and the dukes of Ormond and Albemarle, a group that represented the rather mixed interests of returned exiles and reconciled rebels. All four members were powerful influences in the king's patronage. Middleton was called upon to vouch for Scotsmen, as Ormond was for Irishmen. They presented a common front to any enemy, and an injury to one was an injury to all. On November 29, 1660, Charles II made Middleton the commissioner to the Scottish parliament, with the power of approving bills in the king's name. Less formally, he had other great powers, and assurances of ample provision for himself not only during his commission but during an expected withdrawal to England afterward.

Already said to be corrupt, the new government had perhaps merely fallen into bad old habits of the days before the civil wars. However that may have been, Charles II instructed Middleton, in March, 1660/61, to inquire about bribery of officials by offenders "cited to the Parliament" for illegal compliance with the usurpers of the Interregnum, ordering that "no private bargains are to be driven to make sale of my grace and mercy."[10] Already Middleton and the Scottish secretary of state, the Earl of Lauderdale, disagreed in their private interests, although the disagreement was not yet public. As another

[9] Sir George Mackenzie, *Memoirs of the Affairs of Scotland from the Restoration of King Charles II*, ed. Thomas Thomson (Edinburgh, 1821), pp. 6–7.

[10] B.M., Add. MS 23,115, fol. 118.

session of parliament approached, Charles II gave Middleton a fresh commission, on January 29, 1662 — for the session that would reestablish episcopal government in the Church of Scotland.[11] Middleton was blamed for that by the Presbyterians and was thereafter regarded as their enemy. He quickly became even more unpopular because of his visitations through various parts of Scotland, turning ministers who refused to submit out of their churches. Thus his position was further weakened at the time of the clash with his rival Lauderdale.

The breach was made public when the Scottish parliament adopted a measure that excluded persons who had been selected by "billeting" (secret ballot) from office under the Scottish Crown. Lauderdale, who had been billeted, complained to Charles II that Middleton was responsible for the enactment and guilty of presumption, neglect of the king's interests, disobedience to orders, persecution of loyal subjects, and other offenses. Because Lauderdale was with the king and Middleton was in Scotland, Sir George Mackenzie wrote the Duke of Richmond and Lenox, one of Middleton's sympathizers: "If he [Middleton] eyed his own interest most he would neglect all and haste up [to Court], but I believe he will neglect that [his own] and regard his master's [interest], this your Grace would show the Chancelor."[12] King Charles, however, did not decide between Lauderdale and Middleton without giving the latter a hearing. The commissioner left Edinburgh for London at the end of 1662, attended, as usual, by a cavalcade of honor, as far as Newcastle-upon-Tyne, a man in power.

On February 5, 1662/63, when the privy council of Scotland met in London, Lauderdale attacked the recent actions of the commissioner and his friends. Middleton was allowed to see and answer the charges. Lauderdale then attacked the defense, and Middleton made a second reply, on April 30.[13] Charles II revoked Middleton's commission on May 29, assign-

[11] Thomas Thomson and Cosmo Innes (eds.), *Acts of the Parliament of Scotland* (11 vols.; Edinburgh, 1811–44), VII, 370. See also Godfrey Davies and P. H. Hardacre, "The Restoration of the Scottish Episcopacy, 1660–1661," *Journal of British Studies*, I (1960), 32–51.

[12] B.M., Add. MS 21,947, fol. 9.

[13] B.M., Add. 23,118, fols. 15–22, 23–24, 9–13; *ibid.*, 23,119, fols. 16–19, 25–35. Charges and Answer were printed by T. Brown in *Miscellanea Aulica* (London, 1702).

ing it to the Earl of Rothes. Although Middleton had naturally called upon his friends — Ormond, Clarendon, and Albemarle — for help, such help as they could give did him no good.

The "cavalier party," nevertheless, took Middleton's cause as its own. One of the Coventry brothers wrote to Ormond: "If he suffer a sudden and apparent disgrace, it will probably put them [the "cavaliers"] much out of humor, and a House of Commons out of humor, seldom puts business into order."[14] Clarendon lamented the coming change; the Earl of Glencairn regretted the accomplished fact. Middleton's friends feared the king would allow Lauderdale to obtain the exclusion of Middleton and the Earl of Newburgh, his close friend, from future trust, and Middleton spoke of leaving the British Isles altogether. No further retaliation was permitted, however; an inquiry into the Act of Billeting laid responsibility firmly on the shoulders of Middleton's friends — with a strong suggestion that Middleton was ultimately responsible — but Middleton suffered nothing worse than loss of office. Living in England, he was now closer to Clarendon than ever; and the king gave him a seat on the English privy council, which he frequently attended.[15] On October 5, 1663, Oxford University — the barometer of court favor — admitted Middleton to an unearned degree of Master of Arts.

The Presbyterians, who hated Middleton for the work he had done for episcopacy, rejoiced in his fall. One wrote: ". . . indeed that man Middleton was raised up of God to work wickedness, and frame mischief by law." This strain of partisan hatred can be traced through the works of William Row, Robert Wodrow, Gilbert Burnet (the Presbyterian bishop), and Thomas Wright to the *Dictionary of National Biography*; but the Presbyterians who did their best to destroy Middleton's reputation suffered so much from Lauderdale's ascendancy that civil war resulted.

Middleton lived in England between 1663 and 1669, appearing at London, Bath, Whitehall, Oxford, and Chichester. Lau-

[14] Bodleian Library [henceforth cited as B.L.], Carte MS 47, fol. 403.
[15] He attended forty-nine meetings in 1664. Public Record Office [henceforth cited as P.R.O.], Privy Council Register (P.C. 2), Vols. 56 and 57. For other records of attendance see Vols. 58–61, *passim*.

derdale followed his movements carefully, but after the first few months Middleton appears to have made no effort to influence public affairs in Scotland. His position was neither glorious nor degraded. He had the revenues of his estates, about a thousand pounds sterling; he also had a pension of a thousand pounds sterling, granted by the king's favor from the Scottish treasury. Because payment of the pension was not prompt, however, and because Middleton was of "a munificent humor," he sometimes needed money. Although James Kirkton, a Presbyterian historian, wrote that Middleton "was constrained to leave the court and spend his time in back lanes among persons obscure and malcontents,"[16] Middleton did not leave the court for any great length of time and he associated with Clarendon and other privy councillors; moreover, he was visited in London by such Scotsmen as Patrick Gordon (later a general in the Russian service) and Archbishop James Sharp. Those, however, were possibly only social visits, for Middleton had transferred his attention to the affairs of England, where he could count upon the support of his friends.

In the end, Middleton made an uneasy peace with Lauderdale. Yet he continued to acquire property in Scotland. On June 3, 1663, through his attorney, he received sasine of the lands and barony of Craiginstoune; on June 29, 1663, sasine of an "annual rent" on the barony of Aberdour; and on November 6, 1665, of another "annual rent" on the lands of Craig, Forfarshire — these transactions were the small change in the life of a Scottish landholder. On June 13, 1666, the Countess of Middleton, acting in her husband's name, contracted for a larger prize, the purchase of Old Montrose from the Marquis of Montrose, who was settling his father's debts. Perhaps the earl intended by these acquisitions to build a basis for eventual return to Scotland.

The Countess of Middleton died in September, 1666 at Cranston, in Lothian — her daughter, the Countess of Morton, had died in March. The earl married again a little more than a year after his first wife's death. The new marriage was appropriate to his rank and convenient to his fortune but otherwise incongruous. Lady Martha Cary, one of the daughters of the

---

[16] Kirkton, *The Secret and True History of the Church of Scotland from the Restoration to the Year 1678* (Edinburgh, 1817), p. 159.

Earl of Monmouth (who had passed the Civil War in literary studies of small distinction), was a tender-hearted but vivacious lady of twenty-five when she was married to the first Earl of Middleton, at St. Andrew's, Holborn, on December 16, 1667. Their unusual marriage contract stipulated that the earl would match his second wife's portion by settling his Scottish estates in trust for her and the male issue of their marriage, in effect disinheriting the son by his first marriage, Lord Clermont. The new disposition of the property caused harsh criticisms when its terms became known.[17]

With the Second Dutch War, Middleton in 1666 resumed his military career. The government feared an invasion of the southeastern counties, and Charles II granted the earl a commission (on June 30) as lieutenant-general of the militia forces of Kent and sent him to Canterbury to hold a general muster. The invasion did not take place. A successful campaign at sea, however, allayed the excitement, and the militia was disbanded before the end of the summer, but, unfortunately for Middleton, his commission was not revoked or superseded. In June, 1667, while negotiations for peace were in progress, the Dutch fleet unexpectedly appeared in English waters, and Middleton again went from London to Kent, as lieutenant-general, to assist his friend, the Duke of Albemarle, who commanded there.

The Earl of Clarendon tells us Middleton so ordered his forces that Albemarle, arriving later, "found Middleton in so good a posture, and so good a body of men, that he had no apprehension of any attempt the Dutch could make at land."[18] Unfortunately, the attack came by sea. Disregarding English shore batteries and breaking easily through a chain which the English had thought would block the Medway, the Dutch sailed up that river and burned several English ships under the eyes of the enraged land forces. Peace was made shortly afterward. It appears that an English defeat was predetermined by inaction, neglect, and corruption among naval officials and the Kentish authorities before Middleton reached his forces. Only three days elapsed between his arrival and the Dutch

[17] B.M., Add. MS 23,132, fols. 56, 61–63.
[18] Clarendon, *Life . . . , Written by Himself* (Oxford, 1759), pp. 419–20.

attack, and the accounts of his conduct give the impression of an able, energetic commander who had insufficient time to reorganize a half-trained militia.[19]

The defeat caused a great popular agitation and a parliamentary inquiry, at which Middleton was a witness. The inquiry vindicated Albemarle's assertion that his orders had not been properly executed, and Commissioner Peter Pett, a naval official, bore a heavy responsibility for the disaster, but his friends attempted to shift the blame to Middleton. Samuel Pepys, who knew the situation as well as anyone, called Pett "a very knave," and indeed the king expressed great satisfaction with Middleton's behavior.[20]

The chief target of popular and parliamentary attack, the Earl of Clarendon, fled the country in December, 1667, bringing down the "system" that had been instituted at the Restoration. Middleton, of course, had already been demoted, and after the end of the Dutch war Albemarle took little part in politics. Ormond alone retained high office, as lord lieutenant of Ireland, but without the support from England which any lord lieutenant needed.

One might have expected Middleton to lose his last vestiges of influence and favor, but he did not. He had made a friend of Henry Bennet, Earl of Arlington, a rising man; and James, Duke of York, the heir presumptive to the crown, supported him as well. Middleton thus not only kept his pension and his seat in the privy council, but in May, 1668 — probably at York's suggestion — obtained the unique English military command in which active service was continuous: the governorship of Tangier and the colonelcy of the Tangier Regiment at that English port in North Africa. Colonial governors sometimes postponed their departure from England to attend to affairs, as did Middleton, but in September, 1669, he sailed from Portsmouth, leaving his wife (who had borne him a daughter) in London. The first Earl of Middleton landed at Tangier in early October and remained there until his death, in 1674.

[19] *Ibid.*; *Cal. S. P. Dom.*, VII, 171; R. P. Cruden, *The History of the Town of Gravesend* . . . (London, 1843), pp. 350–52; H. T. Colenbrander, *Bescheiden uit Vreemde archieven omtrent de groote Nederlandsche zeeoorlogen, 1652–1676* (2 vols.; The Hague, 1919), I, 548–54, 573–81, 595–603.
[20] B.L., Carte MS 35, fol. 478; *ibid.*, 222, fols. 166–67; Pepys, *Diary*, ed. H. B. Wheatley (8 vols. in 3; London, 1928), VII, 252.

Charles Middleton — Lord Clermont, as he was called in his father's lifetime — was a remarkably inconspicuous child before 1669. He was born about 1650[21] and presumably spent at least his first few years with or near his mother. His mother, however, is untraceable during most of the Interregnum. After the Restoration young Clermont may have stayed with his mother at Holyrood and at the family seat at Fettercairn — or, with his father, he may have divided his time between Scotland and Whitehall. In August, 1662, his father rejected the offer of a Scottish captaincy for him. It is not known what school or schools he attended but he certainly attended at least one,[22] for he received good grounding in Latin (his correspondence was strewn with classical allusions and Latin tags), and he may also have learned French at school.

The new settlement of his father's estates was probably a shock to Lord Clermont, who would normally have expected to inherit them, and by 1666 he must have been old enough to know the importance of independent means to a nobleman. The marriage contract, however, had not cut him off absolutely: his father granted his lands in Fettercairn and Old Montrose to trustees "to the use" of the second wife and the eldest son of the marriage, unless the earl purchased and settled on his wife a manor or manors within forty miles of London worth £20,000 sterling.[23] In the latter eventuality, Clermont was to inherit Fettercairn and Old Montrose. He would, of course, inherit the title Earl of Middleton, but he would be forced to make his own way without an adequate income to support his dignity.

The only precedent Scotsmen could recall for such treatment of an heir-at-law was the settlement of the uxorious and perhaps senile Lord Coupar's estates on his wife and any second husband she might choose. But Lord Coupar's heir-at-law was not a son. Both Coupar's and Middleton's settlements were shocking by the standards of the day. At about the same

---

[21] The second Earl of Middleton died at age sixty-nine, in 1719, according to C. E. Lart in *The Parochial Registers of Saint-Germain-en-Laye* (2 vols.; London, 1910–12), II, 100.

[22] B.M., Add. MS 31,257, fol. 179.

[23] The terms of the contract are set forth in a deed: Register House, Edinburgh [henceforth cited as R.H.E.], Registered Books of Council and Session, Mackenzie Office, May 8, 1675.

time that the earl's agents presented his transaction for the registration required by Scottish law, the earl used his influence to obtain a concession for his grandson, Lord Dalkeith, son of the Earl of Morton. The Earl of Tweeddale wrote to Lauderdale of these two actions: "Would the king be more concerned for E. Middleton's grandchild upon the grandfather's pretences than himself is in disinheriting his son whom he has bred up and knows when he never saw the other [?]"[24] Regardless of Scottish opinion, the trustees received sasine, and the fact was registered September 20, 1669.[25] The marriage contract was probably the worst introduction a boy could have to a stepmother, and Clermont was given a more than common interest in the failure of the marriage to produce a son, but the contract did not produce family bitterness and division.

In the spring of 1669, Charles II sent Ralph Montagu (later Duke of Montagu) to Paris as his ambassador. Montagu made careful preparations in France for a magnificent entry into the capital, and Clermont was one of those in his train. Francis Vernon, the older brother of James Vernon, described the entry in a letter.

Thursday last April 25, my lord ambassador went from his house in Rue Richelieu about one o'clock. The master of the horse, Mr. Maginnis, with the lackeys and pages, coaches, and all the preparations for pomp having been ordered before at four o'clock in the morning to go to l'hostel Rambouillet, a villa belonging at present to a president of that name, which is a small distance from Faubourg St. Antoine, which possibly you may remember, though it be not the place from which ambassadors always set out. For ours for the most part begin their entrance from St. Dénis but now the King [of France] appointed this place about two o'clock. Then all were met at the rendezvous of Rambouillet, where there were noble and spacious gardens, with fountains and knots of flowers very suitable to entertain and recreate men's senses and fancies in expecting till all the whole train were gathered together. With my lord, of English gentlemen, the principal were my Lord Rochester, Lord Arlington, the Marquis of Huntly, and Lord Clermont . . . Mr. Bridgemont, Mr. Godolphin, Mr. Murray, Mr. Knatchbull, Mr. O'Hare, Mr. Massam, and others. . . . About 3 o'clock came the Maréchal de Bellefonds and Monsieur Bonoeul to compliment my lord from the King and Queen [of France] and then Monsieur [the Duke of Orleans],

[24] B.M., Add. MS 23,132, fols. 61–63.
[25] R.H.E., General Register of Sasines, 3d series, Vol. 23, fols. 245–52.

Madame [the Duchess of Orleans, Charles II's sister], and all the princes of the blood sent their esquires particularly to congratulate my lord and attend him to their coaches.

The next day the lords and gentlemen were introduced to Louis XIV by Montagu.[26] Thus did Clermont meet the Most Christian King of France, the man who gave his name to the age.

Louis XIV was himself still young. Neglected as a child, he had taken the reins of power on the death of his minister Mazarin (eight years before), and had proved his ambition and his administrative ability. Addicted to glory, he had imposed himself upon his contemporaries by force, by show, and by purchase, in a fashion more Byzantine than Baroque. The spectacle of Montagu's entry into Paris would have pleased Louis, for it reflected his own importance, to which Charles II's expenditure was a kind of tribute. King Louis did not value money for itself but for what it would buy, and in time he would make the mistake of trying to buy the king of England.

The nineteen-year-old Clermont was in impressive company. Lord Huntly bore one of the greatest names in Scotland, and had been under the tutorship of Clermont's father. John Wilmot, Earl of Rochester, a close friend of Charles II, was a poet, wit, and debauchee, and had been sent away from the English court for striking another courtier in his king's presence. Lord Arlington was a member of the ruling clique which has always been known in history as "the Cabal." Sidney Godolphin, later Earl Godolphin, was a young man of good connections with a brilliant future. (We shall meet Godolphin and Rochester again.) "Mr. Bridgemont" was probably one of the sons of Sir Orlando Bridgeman, lord keeper of the great seal. And there was Montagu himself, the ambassador. This was a society that a young snob might cultivate or in which a young man might make useful friendships.

So far as we know, Clermont went to Paris only to see Montagu's entry and the other sights of the capital (*Tartuffe* was in its original run). He returned to England within a few weeks, bearing a letter to Arlington from Montagu (Arlington had returned earlier), and spent the summer in England. A few days

[26] P.R.O., State Papers, Foreign, France (S.P. 78)/126, fol. 144.

before Lord Middleton left Portsmouth for Tangier, Clermont
sailed from Dover to Calais, on September 4, 1669.[27]

This was the beginning of a long journey, the Grand Tour,
or something like it, but Clermont's means were small, and he
was so overshadowed by other British lords and gentlemen
who were traveling at the same time that he is mentioned only
once in the foreign newsletters of the time. He turned up at
Rome in January, 1670.

Her Majesty the late Queen Mother's [Henrietta Maria, widow
of Charles I] funeral [requiem] was Thursday last celebrated in the
English college chapel with a handsome decorum, where assisted
solemnly about thirty prelates, the person of the Duke of Chaulnes,
with most of the French nobility in town, and of his majesty's subjects the Earl of Northumberland, Mr. Molineux, Mr. Boursacy
. . . and of Scots the Earl of Oxfoord, the Lords Napier and
Clermont. . . .[28]

It was a dull time for Rome. A conclave was sitting, but had
already taken a long time in selecting a new pope, "the want
of whom hath plunged the town into a deep melancholy and
put the tramontan strangers [those from beyond the Alps] quite
out of countenance as being deprived of any public recreations
or divertissements."[29] Venice had prohibited some of its usual
frivolities, Florence had an unusually cold winter, and the
foreigners gradually departed — for home or to more amusing
places.

Clermont must have returned home before May, 1671, when
John Luke, Lord Middleton's secretary and Judge Advocate of
Tangier, arrived in London on a business visit. Luke called on
Lord Arlington and the Duke of Ormond and conferred with
Charles II and the "Tangier Committee" about the garrison's
need of money and the extension of the fortifications. Calling
on Lady Middleton, Luke also found Lord Clermont and his
half-sister, Elizabeth, and reported to the governor:

Lady Betty is exceedingly well and the most delicate creature that
I have ever seen: Lord Clermont so happy in his whole conversation
as well as particular behaviour to my lady, that as it is impossible

[27] Cal. S. P. Dom., *1668–1669*, pp. 489, 498.
[28] P.R.O., State Papers, Foreign, Italian States (S.P. 85)/10, fol. 149.
[29] *Ibid.*, fol. 175.

she should treat a son of her own with more affection and kindness, so there is none who know him that have not an esteem for him.[30]

Luke stayed in England through the summer of 1671 and wrote the governor in August:

This vacation . . . I was in the country, some part of the time I employed in waiting on my Lord Clermont at Oxford and Cambridge: In his conversation during that time I had so much honor and satisfaction that it made me forget the trouble of my late solicitations. . . . I am sure his majesty hath not a finer gentleman in his three kingdoms nor a person of his years that is so capable of any undertaking befitting his quality, which I take the boldness to mention not out of flattery, but lest I should be the only one who hath had the honour to be known to him without taking notice of his extraordinary parts, the government of which he wholly submits unto your lordship's determination.[31]

Lord Middleton now planned to have his family join him at Tangier, a move that had the advantage of giving Clermont direct acquaintance with military affairs as a step toward obtaining a commission in the English army; and economy may have been another factor in the decision. At any rate, Lady Middleton and Lord Clermont arrived at Tangier aboard H.M.S. *Dreadnought* in November, 1671.

In the two years since his arrival, Lord Middleton had established himself as an able governor.[32] According to John Luke, the best authority on events at Tangier in this period and a very frank one on the affairs of the Middleton family, Lord Middleton was often ill — as were most Englishmen in the town and garrison, probably from contaminated food and water. Although often "merry" with drink, the governor kept regular hours for business, made and executed plans, and maintained discipline as well as he could in his notoriously riotous post. At

[30] B.M., Sloane MS 3,511, fol. 4; *ibid.*, 3,510, fols. 271–72.
[31] *Ibid.*, fol. 34.
[32] Sir Hugh Cholmley, *An Account of Tangier* . . . (London [privately printed], 1787), p. 291; John Luke, *Tangier at High Tide: The Journal of John Luke*, ed. H. A. Kaufman (Paris and Geneva, 1958) *passim*; B.M., Sloane MS 3,510, fols. 194–95; B.L., Rawlinson MS A 341, fols. 71–72; Sir Palmes Fairborne to Joseph Williamson, Jan. 25 1669/70, P.R.O., Colonial Office, Tangier (C.O. 279)/13. A copy of Cholmley's rare book is in the Newberry Library, Chicago.

four o'clock one morning he arrested a naval officer for breaking the head of another and for taking prize goods without authority. By maintaining good discipline, Middleton intended not only to keep the garrison in a state of efficiency but to improve relations between civilians and soldiers.

Studying the defensibility of the place, Middleton concluded that its fortifications should be extended to take in more ground. Although he had no orders to add to the defenses on any great scale — indeed, he was to restrict expenditure — the military considerations prevailed. The defense lines needed both strengthening and deepening, and because the region was inhabited by a hostile population under rulers who detested the English, attack was a lively possibility. Moreover, the mole that Middleton had orders to build for the protection of the harbor had to be built of stone quarried outside the existing lines. For these reasons Middleton began the extension of the fortifications without waiting for orders and before asking the king and his ministers to provide money to pay for the work.

This was a high-handed action, but the governor set his responsibility for Tangier before everything else. He must have calculated his risks well, for he was vindicated and continued in office, owing largely to the influence of Lord Howard (later Duke of Norfolk), Sir Thomas Allin, Sir Thomas Chicheley, and 'Matthew Wren, all members of the Tangier Committee.[33] These men were well placed to judge Middleton and to impress their opinion upon others: Lord Howard had been ambassador to Morocco in 1669, and Allin and Chicheley were senior naval officers who knew Tangier well as a base. Wren was the secretary of the Duke of York, Lord Admiral of England; and perhaps the duke took Middleton's part with his brother, Charles II. Middleton's decision to extend the lines was approved, but the provision of the necessary money was another thing.

In May, 1673, the garrison was reported to be two and one-half years in arrears of pay. Everyone at Tangier was short of ready money; governor, townsmen, soldiers, and foreigners all lived on credit. Treasury promises were discounted even more sharply than they were in England, but Tangier somehow

[33] Hugh Cholmley to Charles II, Aug. 29, 1670, P.R.O., C.O. 279/13; B.M., Sloane MS 3,510, fol. 271; Luke, *Tangier*, pp. 84–85.

kept up its spirits, thanks largely to Lord Middleton. The governor could be infectiously sanguine, and he was addicted to entertainment — to plays performed by a visiting troupe and by soldiers of the garrison, and to dinners and card parties — and he maintained an unbroken sequence of diversions. He kept open house for the higher officers and officials, and, according to his mood, was touchy and proud or affable and jolly. No doubt he sometimes drank to excess, although the witnesses, men of the Restoration, do not say so. Being "extremely merry" was a privilege of rank.

Clermont, who entered Tangerine society near the top, saw much of John Luke, Sir Hugh Cholmley, his wife Lady Anne, and their niece, Mary Compton (daughter of Sir Francis Compton). Lady Anne, whose husband was the engineer responsible for the construction of the mole, had been a Compton, and did not allow anyone to forget that she was the daughter of an earl. Clermont was twenty-two or thereabouts, and Mary Compton was the only eligible young woman in Tangier.

Within two months Clermont was ardently in love with Mary Compton. On January 9, 1672, Luke wrote in his journal:

Lord Clermont kept his bed, which my lady [Middleton] told me was occasioned by my lord [Middleton]'s having taken notice of his amours to Mrs. Compton and having charged him by her, as he expected any countenance from him, not to make any pretensions there except he really did intend marriage. Upon which my lord [Clermont] hardly knew where to come off from his great profession.[34]

The young man's chagrin was as understandable as his falling in love. He could expect only a small inheritance from his father, because of the property settlement, and Mary Compton had too small a dowry for marriage to a man in his position. Moreover, he seems to have compromised the lady. Lord Middleton might somehow contrive an allowance for his son, but he pled inability and also refused to attempt to secure his commission in the Tangier regiment. Clermont may well have thought his false position was of his father's making. Lady Middleton did her best to help her stepson. On February 9, however, Lady Anne Cholmley and her niece departed from Tangier. In time, Clermont recovered.

[34] Luke, *Tangier*, p. 86.

Life at Tangier was necessarily confined within the lines and
the immediate neighborhood: Moorish nomads made it unsafe
to venture far without a strong escort. One governor, Lord
Teviot, had even so been butchered, with a number of his men,
within sight of the town. Within the lines, the inhabitants were
forced together, whether or not they liked each other's company. Middleton and his predecessors had contrived pleasure
walks and gardens, which were much used by officers, officials,
and merchants. Common soldiers and the lower orders in general resorted to the taverns and brothels of the town. The population was varied and colorful, a gathering of people from
everywhere — Jews, Levantines, Moors, Italians, and others,
besides English. As many of the Portuguese inhabitants had
moved away when Charles II acquired the place, there remained few natives of Tangier itself. Many of the civilians were
socially too "low" for friendship with the governor's family.
Drink, isolation from home, and confinement in a narrow space
shortened tempers so that duels and also scuffles of a less dignified kind were common. Sometimes the irrational conduct and
vindictiveness of residents of long standing bordered on in-
sanity. Lord Middleton, never a patient man, was surely not
improved.

At night his excellency playing at cards [Luke wrote] Mr. Gay
standing near behind him undertook to direct at which his excellency
was angry and bid him begone. But he staying some time longer, his
excellency was very angry and struck him after which his lordship
played again.[35]

He played again, an odd thing to do. Fortunately for everyone,
Middleton did not commonly give in so far to the prevailing
cafard.

Less than two months later, Lord Clermont would also leave
Tangier. The Third Dutch War broke out in early 1672, and
Clermont hoped to find military experience and perhaps win
a commission, but had to wait until April for an English ship
to pass on its way home. On April 3, the eve of his departure
for England, Middleton wrote the Earl of Arlington:

The bearer, my son, will be ready to give you the best account [of
Tangier] he can, if you will please to desire it of him. He has been

[35] Luke, p. 160.

six months in this town but, hearing of action, is desirous to know more of this war than he can learn here. His business for England is to obtain his majesty's permission before he put himself in any service this summer. He will serve in the army without charge [command] the better to enable him to command when occasion offers. If your lordship will recommend him to any of your friends in France (for it is his design to serve there) it will be much to his advantage. . . .[36]

Clermont sailed the next day. He never saw his father again, but the next month Middleton sent a present of Barbary horses after him.

In the war which Lord Clermont now entered, England's main effort was to be at sea, at least until sufficient new regiments had been levied to make a formidable land force. Because the navy was also used to repress piracy, it was maintained between wars, but Charles II had only a small nucleus of an army. His subjects who were impatient to see action on land could do so without delay, however, by enlisting or obtaining commissions in the army of his ally, the king of France; some ten thousand were said to be serving France by March, 1672. Those who were above serving in the ranks and who could not or did not wish to get commissions could serve as "volunteers" with the French army, without command or pay, fighting when possible, and learning the customs and the art of war, but not subject to discipline or forced to do disagreeable work. The French welcomed such foreigners, though many were very young and inexperienced.

On April 15/25, 1672, the Duke of Monmouth, Charles II's eldest natural son, left London for France with a following of almost a hundred, and two hundred went in another group with Lord Dunbar, but Clermont arrived too late to join them. Changing his plans, he decided to join the English fleet, as the Earl of Ossory and Lord Howard had done in January. His family friends easily made the arrangements, and Clermont served as a volunteer aboard H.M.S. *Royal Katherine*, a ship of eighty guns commanded by Sir John Chicheley (who had known Lord Middleton at Tangier), soon finding himself in the thick of the battle of Sole Bay.

[36] P.R.O., C.O. 279/15, fol. 110.

On May 28/June 7, 1672, the English fleet was at anchor in Sole (Southwold) Bay under the immediate command of the Lord Admiral, the Duke of York, and the leading professional naval officer, the Earl of Sandwich. Informed that the Dutch fleet was at the Goree, a haven in South Holland, they were surprised and confused to see it bearing down on them at dawn. By 6:00 A.M. the two fleets were engaged in a battle that lasted all day. *Royal James*, bearing Sandwich's flag, was burned to the water line, and Sandwich was killed. *Royal Katherine*, having tacked forward of the ship of the Dutch vice-admiral, Van Nes, was unable to come to the wind, and the two ships remained together for some time, exchanging boarding parties. Chicheley, on *Royal Katherine*, also fought off an attack by a fireship, but as his starboard portholes were already at water level, he surrendered, and he and some of his officers were taken off. Later, the men who had been confined to the lower decks recovered control of the ship from the prize crew and brought it into an English port.[37]

The Dutch and the English suffered great loss of life. According to a newswriter in Zeeland, "There have been more wounded in this fight, than in any two fights during the last war";[38] but Clermont, who was said to be killed, sustained only minor wounds. It would appear, moreover, that the young man had remained aboard *Royal Katherine* during its recapture, and participated in a naval action that rivaled any in the works of Captain Maryatt. In the midst of one of the most exciting episodes of a battle was exactly the place for a young man who wished to attract notice and help in a martial career, and Clermont's advancement was not long in coming.

On September 25 he was in London, probably recovered from his wounds. Probably also he had heard that his father was taking measures to free the family estates from the disposition made in the contract of the second marriage. The earl had begun to buy up the jointure of Lady Middleton's step-

---

[37] Colenbrander, *Bescheiden* . . . , II, 112–13; *London Gazette*, May 27–30, 1672; Geeraert Brandt, *Vie de Michel de Ruyter* (Amsterdam, 1698), pp. 478–79, 492; B.M., Add. MS 11, 606, fol. 52; Newsletters of June 3/13 and C. de Witt's account of the action, June 8, 1672, P.R.O., State Papers, Newsletters (S.P. 101)/55.

[38] Newsletter of June 3/13, 1672, P.R.O., S.P. 101/55. See also *London Gazette*, June 3–6, 1672.

mother, at an initial cost of a thousand pounds sterling, which was presumably credited against the manor or manors valued at twenty thousand pounds mentioned in the contract. (The countess, though eager for the conclusion of the transaction, was "much troubled" that it be done without taking anything from her stepson.) In October, Middleton gave his son leave to procure the next captaincy that fell vacant. They no doubt based their hopes on Clermont's recent service, the "special kindness" of the Duke of York, and the aid of the Earl of Arlington, an influential friend. By January, 1673, Clermont had obtained a company in a regiment commanded by John Sheffield, Earl of Mulgrave.[39]

If Clermont was to live comfortably, according to his rank, a captain's pay was not enough, and in March, 1673, Lord Middleton appealed to his old rival, Lauderdale, who was now a duke and at the height of his power.

By his majesty's gracious favour I have a thousand pound pension in Scotland; my estate is so inconsiderable that [it] is not worth the naming. I have a son that I have bred to make his own fortune, yet young men without money, let their merits be never so great, will rise but slowly. I have no way to help him but by dividing my pension with him, that he may have the one half in his own name, and the other left to me; this cannot be done but by your grace's extraordinary favor. . . I am most hopeful that the young man may not prove ingrate but own your grace at the maker of his fortune.[40]

If Middleton still felt resentment against Lauderdale, he did not show it; and if he felt humiliation at having to turn to a former enemy for help, he had the comfort of knowing that when he had done so before (in 1668) the appeal had been successful. Quite possibly he felt neither resentment nor humiliation, for since 1663 the two had often sat together as privy councillors and had presumably reached some *modus vivendi*. On this occasion, as before, Middleton got what he asked for, and half of the pension, £500 sterling a year, was transferred to his son, beginning at "Mertimes" (Martinmas), 1673.[41] This,

[39] Luke, *Tangier*, p. 200; Charles Dalton, *English Army Lists and Commission Registers, 1661–1714* (6 vols.; London, 1892–1904), I, 136.

[40] Osmund Airy (ed.), *The Lauderdale Papers* (3 vols.; London, 1884–85), II, 231.

[41] R.H.E., Secretary's Warrant Books (S.P. 57), Vol. 2, 236.

with his captain's pay of £ 145 12s. a year, gave Lord Clermont sufficient income to frequent the court (if he took care to live modestly) or to defray the difference between what he was allowed as an army officer and what his service would cost him.

Although financially independent at last, Middleton's son was hardly in a position to vault into high office. His father was far off, probably unable to help him much more; Lauderdale was in power in Scotland, and he would not welcome Clermont in that field of politics or in the Scottish army. Yet, as a Scotsman, it would be difficult for Clermont to make a career in English office. For the time, he was an officer in the army, and at war.

Lord Mulgrave's regiment was one of nine regiments of foot encamped at Blackheath in the summer of 1673, of which Sir Joseph Player wrote to Sir Joseph Williamson on June 27:

The encamping . . . on Blackheath employs both the tongues and heels of most of the people in London and about it; all persons travel hither to see the new and fine show, and various opinions there are of their being bodied so near London, and some persuade themselves it will not be long before they are disbanded. . . . nothing but rain, which very much incommodes the soldiers at Blackheath; there is not at present above 5,000 men.[42]

On July 14, Mulgrave's and most of the regiments marched to Gravesend, where they would embark for transport and an attack upon the Dutch. There was friction among the higher officers, however, and the Duke of Buckingham resigned his commission because he was not promoted to lieutenant-general. Then the plans were changed, after the men had boarded their transports, because the English fleet was unable to secure command of the sea.

The regiments were landed at Yarmouth a few days later, and they gave trouble.

Monsieur Schomberg complains, it seems, of the great difficulty he has to keep the soldiers at Yarmouth in good order, for want of martial law, the officers thinking it not safe to put the articles lately published in execution on this side of the water; and then besides many of the officers take too great liberty themselves, and by their

[42] W. D. Christie (ed.), *Letters Addressed from London to Sir Joseph Williamson* . . . (2 vols.; London: The Camden Society, 1874), I, 69, 99.

example spoil their soldiers. However, he hopes in a little time to bring them into good discipline.[43]

Schomberg's efforts at discipline caused discontent among the troops; moreover, he and Prince Rupert, who commanded the fleet that year, carried on a feud that was said to prevent getting the troops into action. Clermont's colonel, Mulgrave, was also dissatisfied; although he was governor of Yarmouth, the government neglected his authority in that post. The troops broke camp at Yarmouth in September and never saw action.[44]

A close friendship had developed between Mulgrave and Clermont, probably during the summer of 1673, and this friendship had important effects on Clermont's career in the army. As the war was unpopular and ill-supported by the treasury, there was a retrenchment of forces in January, 1673/74. Part of Mulgrave's regiment was disbanded and part was merged with the Holland Regiment of foot, of which Mulgrave was made colonel. In the following September, his friend Clermont, now second Earl of Middleton, received a commission to be lieutenant-colonel of the Holland Regiment and captain of one of its companies, a promotion that nearly doubled his military pay.

The first Earl of Middleton, at Tangier, had been busier than ever. English ships and squadrons, naval and mercantile, put into port for news, water, food, and fuel even in time of peace, and in war, with Dutch warships and privateers at sea, Tangier was a center of naval intelligence. English naval vessels were stationed there, and prizes taken from the enemy were brought there before being sent to England. The place was comparatively prosperous.

On August 6, 1673, Lady Middleton gave birth to a healthy son, who was christened John. The second family imagined in the marriage contract now existed, portending Clermont's separation from the family estates, but somehow the earl had by that time found most of the money necessary to fulfill the alternative provision of the contract. On October 11/21, 1673, he gave a power of attorney to Thomas Dalmahoy, an old acquaintance from the civil wars, and to Thomas Povey, one

---

[43] In Christie, *Letters*, I, pp. 129, 143.
[44] *Ibid.*, p. 145, and Vol. II, 20; Colenbrander, *Bescheiden* . . . , II, 294.

of the masters of requests, authorizing them to buy the rights of his wife's coheiresses in the manor and lordship of Castle Eden, in the county of Durham, in expectation of the death of Lady St. John, Lady 'Middleton's mother. Once acquired, this property was to be "to the use" of Middleton, Countess Martha, and the heirs of their marriage, with the provision that if Lady Middleton entered into possession of Castle Eden she should surrender, on her stepson's request, the rights in the estates of Fettercairn and Old Montrose. This arrangement was in effect at the time of the first earl's death, July 3, 1674.

His death occurred unexpectedly, the result of an accident. Henry Coventry, a secretary of state and thus a receiver of intelligence from all quarters, gives us the most authoritative full account:

The Earl of Middleton is dead at Tangier, and very unfortunately having been sometime sick of a flux that had weakened him, he had a servant that always watched in his chamber. The earl waking found the candle out, called his servant he being fast asleep heard him not, so he thinking himself neglected, rose himself to call for a candle, when going to the door of the chamber, his servant lay across the door asleep he in the dark stumbled over him broke his arm close by the shoulder, and in two or three days died of the fever, which the pain, and his former weakness caused. . . .[45]

The first earl left his affairs in great confusion. True, he had disposed of his Scottish property in a rational and equitable fashion. On the other hand, he owed money to the king and to Scottish creditors, especially to Sir James Stansfield, while the king owed Middleton repayment of money which the governor had laid out on the garrison and port. It took more than five years to settle the deceased earl's accounts with the Crown. As he had died intestate, the countess dowager applied for letters of administration for such property as remained unsettled. On October 27, 1679, the heirs were at last discharged of £6,534 sterling owing to the treasury. Middleton's arrears were reckoned at £3,345 3s.[46]

The dowager countess returned to England in the autumn of

[45] B.M., Add. MS 25,123, fols. 109–10. A shorter version of this account was printed by George Philips in *The Present State of Tangier* (n. pl., 1676), p. 197. A copy of Philips' rare pamphlet is now in the Newberry Library.

[46] *Calendar of Treasury Books Preserved in the Public Record Office* [henceforth cited as *Cal. T. B.*], (London, 1904–   ), VI, 233–34.

1674. In 1676 she sent to the Anglican Church at Tangier a monument to her husband's memory, an elaborate affair with three coats of arms. It marked the end of the earl's long journey from Fettercairn through Edinburgh, Worcester, London, Oxford, Danzig, Bruges, Amsterdam, and Cologne. One would like to know what the returning Moors made of it and did with it when the English abandoned Tangier a few years later.

CHAPTER II

Young Courtier and Officer

Charles Middleton probably was not aware of his father's death and of his own succession to the title for a month or more, but after the news had spread he immediately began to receive more attention, and we know more about him from this time on. We see him over the next few years as an ambitious man, with a taste for public life such as any courtier must have, and willing to take any chance of improving his position. Thus he had volunteered for the navy, and eventually entered the army, not from an inclination for military life but because that service was open to him on good terms. When other openings occurred, he took advantage of them and brought his army phase to a close. He postponed marriage for better times, when he might make a better match than during the 1670's. He was willing to fight, either in the service or as a second to a friend, but apparently he neither provoked nor issued challenges. For a man in his late twenties, he must have seemed to his contemporaries somewhat cold-blooded in his patience, disillusioned almost before maturity, but he attracted rather than repelled them. In a society of carousers, it is unlikely that young Middleton was a total abstainer. Acquainted with Wycherley, Dryden, and Etherege, he must have known the London playhouses well, besides having a taste for literature.

Owing to his father's disposition of the family property and the huge debt to the Crown, the second earl's financial position was in doubt for several months, but the accounting showed that the first earl had already laid out £15,000 of the £20,000 sterling stipulated in the marriage contract as the alternative settlement of the dowager countess. In consideration of this outlay, no doubt, the countess granted her stepson a five-year tack and lease of the family lands in Fettercairn, Old Montrose, and elsewhere in eastern Scotland for a rent of £300 sterling.[1] The rent represented interest at 6 per cent on the £5,000 not yet used on the countess's behalf. As the average annual revenue of the estate between 1672 and 1674 was about £942 sterling (£11,314 Scots money), the countess's rent left £642 for the upkeep of the estate and for the earl.[2] This income, added to the annual pension of £500 and the £273 he was paid as a lieutenant-colonel and captain, was enough to keep a thrifty man but not lavish for an earl.

This income was, of course, subject to the charge of maintaining the estate, and his army pay was reduced by 5 per cent (which was paid to the paymaster general). One day's pay each year was paid to the commissary general of the musters, besides fees at each muster, which might amount to 12 guineas a year. Officers compensated themselves, however, cheating the treasury by drawing pay for dead men and deserters, cheating their men by scanting them the proper allowance of clothing.[3] There is no reason to believe Middleton was above devices so well recognized by custom. After all deductions and additions, he was better paid than most officers and probably had more private income. Unlike his father, he spent moderately. For the time being, as a bachelor, he could manage on what he had.

His position at court was favorable. The Duke of York and the Earl of Arlington transferred to him the support they had given his father. Lauderdale was not friendly, but he could be relied upon for small favors so long as his rival's son did not interest himself in Scottish public business. Friendship with his colonel, Lord Mulgrave, was an addition of strength at court.

Mulgrave's friendship, however, was costly. Rich and well descended, Mulgrave was also proud and gallant in the seventeenth-century fashion; he was involved in a number of duels, and his close friend could not avoid participation in them. On three occasions Middleton served as Mulgrave's second, in two cases fighting the second of his principal's adversary (a bloodthirsty custom later discarded). The first of these duels took

---

[1] Deed, April 13 and 20, 1675, R.H.E., Registered Books of Council and Session, Mackenzie Office, 8 May, 1675.
[2] "Compt Books," R.H.E., M.P. bundle 280.
[3] Sir John Fortescue, *History of the British Army* (13 vols.; London, 1899–1930), I, 316–19.

place on September 29, 1674, and Sir George Lane gave an account of it.

I will not particularly repeat . . . what happened on Tuesday night last to the Lord Mulgrave: viz. his being seized by a guard of musketeers coming out of a fair lady's lodging; some will have it that it was done by the Duke of Monmouth's orders, but whether it were or no, his grace was confined to his house for a few hours yesterday. And this day the Lord of Mulgrave and Mr. Felton, my Lord Middleton, and Henry Bulkeley fought in the same case . . . at Hyde Park about one of the clock. The two first were principals and the two latter seconds, the Earl of Middleton for the Earl of Mulgrave and Mr. Bulkeley for the other, whose voice his challenger affirmed he heard when he was seized upon by the sentinels and by that concluded him in the plot against him. The greatest hurt was done to the Lord Middleton, who was run into the belly; the chirurgeons cannot judge him till the second dressing; my Lord Middleton's sword broke at the hilt. Harry Bulkeley had a slight wound over his eye and Mr. Felton another in his hand.[4]

Considering the frequent deaths and lingering disablements from belly wounds in the seventeenth century, if for no other reason, it is surprising to find Middleton again seconding Mulgrave, in December of the same year.

On Sunday night last [William Harbord wrote], King being at supper at Trea. [presumably the Lord Treasurer Danby], Harry Saville being very drunk, fell so foully on Lord Mulgrave, that King commanded Saville to be gone out of his presence. However, the next day Mulgrave sent him a challenge by Lord Middleton: Rochester was second to the other side. There was no harm done; but Duke [of York?] hath interested himself and prevailed with King to forbid Saville his presence.[5]

In 1675, Mary Kirke, maid of honor to the Duchess of York, gave birth to a child of unknown paternity in St. James's Palace. The child died, but Mary Kirke was disgraced; and her brother, the fire-eater Percy Kirke, forced Mulgrave to fight him, although Mulgrave took an oath that he was not responsible.

Yet the Earl, with his lieutenant-colonel, the Earl of Middleton, his old accustomed second, who perhaps has undertaken to fight all his

---

[4] B.L., Carte MS 38, fols. 160–61. See also Historical Manuscripts Commission [henceforth cited as H.M.C.] *Rutland MSS*, II, 27.

[5] Osmund Airy (ed.), *The Essex Papers* (Westminster: The Camden Society, 1890 n.s., Vol. 47), I, 281.

colonel's quarrels, met with Mr. Kirke and his second, Captain Charles Godfrey, and fought, in which adventure the Earl of Mulgrave had the ill luck to receive a wound in his shoulder, and as it is said to fall and lose his sword. . . .[6]

In this sequence the duelists were remarkably fortunate, comparatively decent. Middleton took no part in common brawls, but duels that were conducted according to the rules did a young gentleman's reputation no harm; nevertheless, both Mulgrave and Middleton left off dueling as they grew older. Charles II detested the practice and frequently intervened to force challengers and challenged to keep the peace, and, because political and military advancement depended on the king's favor, ambitious courtiers learned to avoid fighting except when absolutely forced to it. (Here, as in other matters, Charles II was better than his time). Middleton was not hot-tempered, and there is no record of his engaging in any duel as a principal.

Association with Mulgrave had advantages quite apart from court favor. Mulgrave was a poet, of small talent but widely acquainted among professional and amateur literary men, and it was probably Mulgrave who introduced Middleton to poets and dramatists of greater reputation. Middleton had known the Earl of Rochester at least slightly since their encounter in Paris in 1669. Lord Buckhurst, later Earl of Dorset and Middlesex, was one of Lady Middleton's trustees. In the 1670's Middleton established friendly relations with Sir George Etherege, William Wycherley, and John Dryden; and if he did not know Samuel Butler, he did know *Hudibras*. Considering his conservative politics, we may be sure that he did not approve the political opinions of John Milton, but he appreciated Milton's poetry sufficiently to subscribe to the lavishly illustrated edition of *Paradise Lost* published in 1688 (after the poet's death). Yet Middleton was a man of literary taste rather than a man of letters; there appears to be no play, essay, or verse that can be assigned to him. When Etherege wrote two verse letters to Middleton from Ratisbon in the 1680's, the earl had the wisdom to ask Dryden to write a reply.

One would like to know more of Middleton's literary friendships, especially those with Dryden and with Rochester, the

[6] Alfred Morrison (ed.), *The Bulstrode Papers* (London [privately printed], 1897), I, 303–5.

Restoration's playboy-poet. Did Middleton patronize the literary professionals, or engage in bouts of wit with the amateurs? Or were his means inadequate for the one pastime and his "parts" for the other? Were the ties that united the "court wits" primarily political, intellectual, or for the pursuit of pleasure? We know that Dryden turned Catholic and conservative in the political struggles of the 1680's, that Etherege depended on employment for his income and curried favor with everyone, that Rochester appears to have taken another course into the radical "Whig" camp shortly before he died in 1680, and that Mulgrave "trimmed" sometimes and at other times showed his true conservative colors. How were they all united in the 1670's? How were they later separated? Unfortunately, we have no convincing answers to any of these questions as yet. Only now are they beginning to be asked.

Middleton could never have planned to earn a living by writing, one of the most difficult professions when authors were pirated and important works were sold to publishers for small lump sums. In the 1670's Middleton depended on his military pay and his private income. His duties were usually not demanding. His company of the Holland Regiment of foot was stationed at Berwick from 1674 to 1678, but he was apparently seldom with it, for we never hear of his going there. As its lieutenant-colonel, he had an interest in the whole regiment, but he relied on influence at court for his promotion as a soldier and spent most of his time there. Apparently he was sometimes called upon, as a senior officer in a small army, to perform special military duties, for in August, 1676, he was a member of a military court that had been formed to try a lieutenant of marines. His colleagues in the court included John Churchill (later Duke of Marlborough), Lord Howard of Escrick, and William, Earl of Craven — three officers who would be important in political affairs.

Middleton was probably also acquainted with most of the other officers who frequented the court of Charles II, such as Sir John Fenwick (cornet in the Horse Guards in 1676), Captain Thomas Tollemache of the Coldstream Guards, Captain Edward Sackville, Captain (later Sir) George Barclay, and Sir Roger Strickland. Those five were involved, in one way or another, in Middleton's activities after the Revolution of 1688; also, Middleton must have known them in the 1670's, for only officers forced by circumstances to remain for long periods at isolated posts could have avoided knowing each other. An officer as skilled as Middleton in advancing himself would have cultivated acquaintance with those who could affect his military prospects. Middleton, moreover, was urbane, clever, sufficiently learned but without pedantry, accomplished without self-assertion, politely skeptical of commonplaces, and inoffensively witty. His duels, or rather those in which he was involved through Mulgrave, showed that he was no poltroon.

Middleton was consistently a conservative in politics, of the cast of mind which would later be called Tory; and this was a very good thing for his prospects at the time. Most of the leading old cavaliers were dead or in retirement, but the Duke of Ormond, after a period of comparative obscurity, in 1677 again became lord lieutenant of Ireland. Lord Arlington was in political eclipse, but still held court office. Younger men of royalist and Anglican sympathies in the middle 1670's rallied behind the lord treasurer, Thomas Osborne, Earl of Danby, the acknowledged leader of the government under the king, and holder of the king's confidence in foreign and domestic policy. His followers, who were to form the "Tory party," shared in Danby's distribution of favors and money, and more or less voted as a group in the two houses of parliament. Agreement in conservative views had as much to do with the formation of a "party" as favors bestowed. In fact, Danby had not the means to reward all his followers (and some had substantial private incomes), but most of them would have supported Danby and the king regardless of financial reward. Thus, no doubt, it was with Middleton.

Mulgrave, also a conservative, was a rich man and somewhat independent in his views. He sat as an English peer in the House of Lords. Middleton sat in neither house, although as a Scottish peer he was eligible to the House of Commons. He was not as wealthy as Mulgrave, nor did he have such extensive English connections. There is no doubt that Middleton wanted wealth and power, for he later obtained a large measure of both and could hardly have done so without design. Although he was not a flatterer or unduly pliant before men in power, he must have seen the king's way as the way to power, and the testimony of his contemporaries is that he chose it and followed it sincerely and with dignity. He was a "king's man" on principle, was known to be so, and was respected for avoidance of much of the harshness and unfairness that blighted the politics of his age.

Middleton's ambitions were not entirely personal; he was the representative of his family connection, which, under the somewhat predatory conditions of Scotland at the time, needed protection and hoped for aggrandizement. The Scottish family was united by blood, obligation, self-defense, religion, and habit. The most important members of this exemplar were Middleton's uncle, Andrew Middleton, and his relations by marriage, the Earls of Morton and Kinghorn. The first Earl of ˙Middleton had done much for the family when he was in power, but later it had suffered from Lauderdale's retaliation. Morton had been deprived of his hereditary rights in Orkney and Zetland, and was so reduced in fortune as to be a political cipher, nor could he obtain payment of the compensation that had been promised for his losses. Kinghorn, better off, was able to help the second Earl of Middleton by giving security for money lent him by Sir Charles Ramsay of Balmaine. Morton and Kinghorn both stood to gain if Middleton rose in favor with the king. So, for that matter, did the Dowager Countess of Middleton, who renewed her generous tack and lease in 1679, on the same terms as in 1675, except that the tack was to run for her life, or for her stepson's (if he predeceased her before he married).[7] The new arrangement helped the earl, but an obligation was conferred by the benefits: young John and Lady Betty must be well married, and John helped to enlarge his fortune. Nothing was put into writing, for no written promise was necessary.

The property settlement, by its very complications, was convenient to the earl as tenant. If he had inherited the Scottish estates he would have been liable for his father's debts; as a mere lessee he was *prima facie* not liable. His stepmother, the possessor, lived in England. The most active creditor, Sir James

[7] R.H.E., Register of Deeds, Mackenzie Office, Vol. 46, 417–20, 410–11.

Stansfield, attempted to show that the second earl had collected
back rents owed to the first earl and was therefore a "vicious
intromittor," who by receiving such benefits from the estates
had subjected himself to the responsibilities of the heir.
Middleton successfully used all the obstructive tactics of Scottish law to resist this contention until he had attained a position
above Stansfield's reach.[8] (Such an evasion of responsibility
may seem unscrupulous, but it was well within the letter of
the law.) Middleton did not take sasine of any part of the family
estates until 1689.[9] By that time the dowager countess had presumably received her £5,000 sterling, or its equivalent, and
Stansfield had probably settled his claims by such compromise
as he could obtain.

From 1674 to 1677 Middleton was at court or in London,
but in the latter year his routine was upset as a result of war
abroad. The king of England had made a separate peace with
the Dutch in 1674, after he had given up hope of obtaining
grants of money from parliament for waging war. The king of
France, however, had continued to fight, with the objects of
conquering the Spanish Netherlands (most of what is now Bel-
gium and Luxemburg) and of forcing the Dutch to recognize
the conquest. Since 1672 the anti-French party that controlled
the United Netherlands had been led by William, Prince of
Orange, nephew of Charles II by his sister Mary. For dynastic
and other reasons, Charles might have wished to side with the
United Netherlands, although this would have been at the risk
of unpopularity among commercial interests in England which
seemed menaced by Dutch rivalry. He might also have wished
to resume the war on the French side, against the opinion of
thoughtful politicians who thought French power was already
too great. Instead, he chose to maintain neutrality, for which
Louis XIV of France rewarded him with a subsidy. Thus
Charles was paid money to do nothing, after parliament had
left him so ill-provided that he could not afford to make war
on either side. Danby and others at court who supported the
king's interests and powers would have preferred another

---

[8] See Stansfield's Information and "Memorandum for Sr. James Stansfield," R.H.E., M.P. bundle 280; Charge to the Earl of Middleton, June 1,
1682, R.H.E., Morton Papers, box 20.
[9] R.H.E., Particular Register of Sasines, Aberdeen, &c., Vol. 13, fols.
341–42.

policy,[10] but parliamentary opponents of royal supremacy were
not satisfied with neutrality because it relieved Charles of some
of his handicaps in dealing with the opposition. They spoke of
the king's duty to help the Dutch against France. Charles's
situation was very delicate.

In the summer of 1677 the Prince of Orange undertook the
siege of Charleroi, a strongly fortified town in French hands.
Rumors of the greatness of his preparations, the strength of
the defense, and the determination of Marshal de Luxembourg,
commanding a French field army, to break up the siege attracted many Englishmen, most of whom encamped with the
Dutch.[11] Although the Duke of Monmouth and the Earl of
Feversham were among the spectators in the French camp, the
disproportion apparently embarrassed the neutral Charles II;
observers in London believed that he deliberately balanced
the observers' representation by sending more Englishmen
to the French side. Lord Mulgrave and a Mr. Stewart, brother
of the Dowager Duchess of Richmond, were two of these; and
when Mulgrave was ready to depart, Lords Middleton and
Lumley suddenly "decided" to do the same. The French minister in London, Courtin, recommended them strongly to the
French marshal, he reported to Louis XIV, "because they have
no gear, and they are very used to take their ease."[12]

Mulgrave evidently wrote to William Wycherley during this
expedition, and Wycherley replied that he had received Mulgrave's letter "with as much satisfaction as my Lord Middleton
would a billet-doux from Mrs. Yard." He begged Mulgrave to
return.

But since, as your lordship says, my Lord Middleton and you are
but one, I must despair of your removal; for though you would jog
on, the Middleton side of you would hang an A——e. For his is the
most invincible laziness in the world; and he could only make it a
military virtue to serve him in the place of ambition, and make him
suffer any thing but motion. I suppose he rides properly like a foot-
officer [in shoes], to avoid the fatigue of pulling on his boots, and
lies rough [in his clothes] rather than take pains to unbutton himself;
and upon a march has always the place of honour in bringing up the

[10] See Danby's memorandum, April 4/14, 1677, B.M., Add. MS 28,042,
fol. 9.
[11] B.M., Add. MS 17,677 DD, fol. 101; *ibid.*, 27,962 W, fols. 213–15.
[12] P.R.O., Transcripts, France (P.R.O. 31/3)/136, fols. 100–102, 106.

rear; and if the whole army were routed would be killed, not to be at the trouble of running away. In fine, if I may quibble, he is of a young one, a very stayed officer, but I shall never think him capable of active fatigue, 'till he writes me as long a letter, as your lordship has done, which, if it were but for the pleasure of sitting still without disturbance, he should do methinks. Well, to say no worse of him, he is properly in the French army no volunteer, and you have pressed him into that service, whilst his inclination would have carried him to his brother lazers, the Spaniards.[13]

This letter is in the high style of Restoration raillery: we need not take it literally; but there was truth in the charge that Middleton was inclined to inaction when the choice was open. Kings were to pour tasks into his hands, and he performed many of them well, but he economized his effort. (The interest Middleton may have had in "Mrs. Yard" is unknown.) We can be sure that Wycherley knew Middleton favored the anti-French side (we must remember it later, when he was officially concerned with foreign affairs), but he followed the king's wish in preference to his own inclination.

The English spectators did not stay long in the Low Countries: the Prince of Orange soon gave up the siege of Charleroi, and the foreigners dispersed. Mulgrave, with the Duke of Monmouth and the Earl of Feversham (and perhaps Middleton), managed to visit Paris before returning to England. The returning English gave good reports, the new French ambassador at London wrote, of the treatment they had received from their hosts.

By the autumn of 1677, Charles II had reached a point at which neutrality was no longer possible. He was urged, not only by his opponents but by his friends, to interpose English force between the two sides so that Louis XIV must make peace on terms reconcilable with the preservation of the balance of power. If he were unsuccessful in such an attempt, Charles II must bring England into the war against France. This pressure arose among members of parliament and others who were alarmed by French success in the war and by the inability of the Spanish forces in the Netherlands to defend the country,

[13] Robert J. Allen, "Two Wycherley Letters," *Times* (London) *Literary Supplement*, April 18, 1935, p. 257.

even with Dutch assistance. The procedure, then, was designed to appear to extend neutrality, so to speak, by forcing Spain and France to agree to a proper peace. Resistance could be expected from both sides: in any realistic settlement, Spain could hardly avoid giving up its claim to some of the territories conquered by France, and France would have to agree to give up its claims to some of the territories it had claimed but not conquered, and surrender part of its gains. Charles II was said to have told Sir William Temple (in July, 1677) that he would never have a quiet parliament while there was war abroad.

That, besides, he saw, the longer it continued the worse it would be for the confederates [especially Spain and the United Netherlands]; and therefore he would fain have the Prince [of Orange] make the peace for them, if they would not do it for themselves; that if he and the prince could fall into the terms of it, he was sure it might be done.[14]

The opening of negotiations for intervention meant a revolution in English foreign policy: the recent Dutch enemy became a friend; the former ally and subsidizing power, France, became a probable enemy. As evidence of the diplomatic shift, William of Orange visited England and was married on November 4/14, 1677, to the Princess 'Mary, elder daughter of the Duke of York and niece of Charles II. This marital alliance, one of the most important in the history of England, foreshadowed a political and military alliance. There were two formal treaties, one concluded at The Hague, on January 10 (N.S.), 1678, the other at London on March 3/13.[15] According to these agreements, Great Britain and the United Netherlands would join to force Spain and France to agree to a peace laid down by the contracting powers.

Preparations for war had already begun. Existing military units were filled up to strength; new companies were added; new regiments were organized: the augmentations amounted

---

[14] Abel Boyer, *Memoirs of the Life and Negotiations of Sir William Temple, Bar.* (London, 1714), p. 279.

[15] The first is printed by Jean Dumont, *Corps universel diplomatique du droit des gens* (8 vols.; Amsterdam, 1726–31), VII, Part 1, pp. 341–42. The second, which was not ratified, is preserved (in French) in P.R.O., S.P., Foreign, Treaties (S.P. 108)/320. I cannot subscribe to Mr. David Ogg's view of these treaties; see, rather, C. L. Grose, "The Anglo-Dutch Alliance of 1678," *E.H.R.*, Vol. XXXIX, 349–72, 526–51.

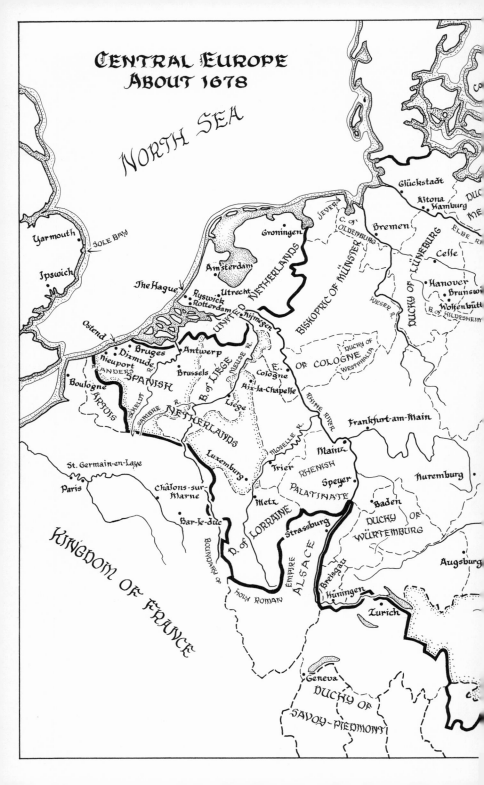

to thirty thousand men. Companies ready to march were concentrated at southeastern ports. The agreements with the Dutch and their "confederates," Spain and some of the German princes, provided that Charles II should send English troops to the Spanish Netherlands, where they could block the French advance. If the French king could be forced to make peace, there would be peace; if not, England would join in the war against France. There was, in fact, little doubt of war.[16]

In January the Holland Regiment was augmented by nine companies, which were formed into a battalion under Middleton's command and ordered to march to Ipswich before February 15. Four of these companies were embarked for Flanders on March 13, and four more on April 7, 1678 (Middleton must have gone with the first four; his own, the lieutenant-colonel's company, did not embark until July 17).[17] The first contingent landed at Ostend and marched thence to Bruges.[18] These hastily raised troops were immediately criticized by foreign observers: "Those English which have arrived at Ostend are poor troops, and beyond that they besides make themselves masters of the places where they are." [19]

As the senior officer present, Middleton commanded the small English force at Bruges for some weeks, but he had hardly settled himself when trouble arose between the English and the townsmen. On April 3, during a procession of the Holy Sacrament — when the utmost reverence evidently was customary — a Dutch officer failed to remove his hat, and someone struck him for his disrespect, although the procession had not yet reached the point at which the officer stood. The officer drew his sword, and there was a fight. A rumor spread that the English had committed a sacrilege, and English soldiers, taken by surprise, were mobbed, although there are no reports that any Englishman had offended anyone. (According to an Ostend newsletter, the English did not draw their swords even when

[16] See, for example, the Duke of York's letter to the Prince of Orange, Jan. 8/18, 1677/8, P.R.O., State Papers, King William's Chest (S.P. 8)/3, part 1.

[17] H. R. Knight, *Historical Records of the Buffs, East Kent Regiment, 3rd Foot* (London, 1905), pp. 194, 195 n, 196; *Cal. S. P. Dom., 1678*, p. 23.

[18] P.R.O., State Papers, Entry Books (S.P. 104)/185, fol. 217; P.R.O., Admiralty, Newsletters (Adm. 77)/1, item 22.

[19] Newsletter, March 25, 1678, P.R.O., S.P. 101/61.

they were attacked.) Fortunately, the Spanish governor of Bruges thought to give a false alarm that the French army was at the gates, and the burghers reported to their posts of defense, where the bishop and clergy calmed them and sent them quietly home. The magistrates offered the English full satisfaction, which included twelve barrels of strong beer for the common soldiers, compensation for the thirty-two who had been wounded, and pensions to the widows of the four or five who had been killed.[20]

Middleton helped compose peace with the civil authorities. On March 26/April 5, two days after the riot, he sent a Captain Fitzpatrick to Charles II with a report on "our Bruges vespers" (an allusion to the medieval Sicilian massacre).

I hope we shall not be reproached with our youth on this occasion, since we took all the care imaginable to prevent the soldiers doing injury, or resenting it; we have to do with an unruly rabble which neither the governor, nor the magistrates can control, we have been extremely obliged to the Marquis d'Osera, and the burgomaster invited us yesterday to the hôtel de ville, where he promised satisfaction for what is past, and security for the future, and though I hope this will not happen again, yet I thought it my duty to inform the king of it, that I might not be condemned for depending on my own judgement in a thing of this consequence. . . .[21]

There was no further trouble. The English force at Bruges was strengthened to four battalions by the middle of April (N.S.), and more were promised.

Neither in England nor abroad did the movement of troops have its expected effects. Henry Coventry observed, in March, that English preparations had not encouraged the Spaniards in Flanders, "who part with their towns [to the French] as if they were afraid that our succours might prevent them." [22] Ralph Montagu wrote from Paris that the chief burden of a war undertaken with such associates would surely fall upon the king of England. If so, Charles II must find more money and men for the war than he had expected or intended — more, indeed, than he could raise.

[20] B.L., Carte MS 222, fol. 225; *London Gazette*, March 28–April 1 (o.s), 1678. Cf. Charles Custis, *Jaer-boecken der stadt Brugge* (2d ed., 3 vols.; Bruges, 1765), III, 278–79; *London Gazette*, April 4–8 (o.s.), 1678.

[21] P.R.O., State Papers, Foreign, Flanders (S.P. 77)/52, fol. 7.

[22] B.M., Add. MS 25,118, fols. 161–62.

Getting money from parliament had from the first been one of Charles's aims in his change of policy. As he had abandoned Louis XIV and the French subsidy and had taken a line known to be popular with the opposition and with many of his best friends in parliament, he expected parliamentary grants of taxation to meet the costs of that line. When parliament assembled, however, the opposition immediately began to attack the royal prerogative by attempting to dictate the terms of his foreign alliances, while it withheld the money. The Duke of York remarked bitterly that this would be "very good news for France"; those "who seemed to be most zealous for a war with France last sessions, are those who obstruct most the giving of supply." [23]

The opposition had its own point of view. The government talked of war, recruited troops and sent them overseas, and spent money it could ill afford; but there were rumors that all this activity was a sham, that Charles II had never intended war with France, and that there would soon be a general peace: money given by parliament to the king for war could then be diverted to other uses. The opposition did not trust Charles, either in war or in peace. Powerful indications that the opposition was wrong about the king's intentions, indications that it should have taken into account, were credible reports that Louis XIV was preparing for war against England,[24] presumably acting on information received from the best intelligence service in Europe. A little later, by allowing word of the former French subsidy to reach the parliamentary opposition, in violation of trust, Louis XIV showed with what alarm he regarded the possible entry of England into the continental war. Did the payments the King of France was then sending to the leaders of the opposition blind them? Or did not the opposition's suspicions that Charles II might be insincere betray it into insincerity? [25]

The garrison at Bruges was quickly built up: the English government was apprehensive that the French might lay siege

[23] P.R.O., S.P. 8/3, part 1, fols. 33, 36. See also Andrew Browning, *Thomas Osborne, Earl of Danby and Duke of Leeds, 1632–1712* (3 vols.; Glasgow, 1951), I, 261–63, 266–70.

[24] Sir Thomas Morgan to Sir Joseph Williamson, Jan. 27/Feb. 6, 1677/78, P.R.O., State Papers, Domestic, Channel Islands (S.P. 47)/1. See also Grose, "Alliance," *E.H.R.*, Vol. XXXIX, 361.

[25] *History of England from the Restoration to the Death of William III, 1660–1702* (London [new impression], 1918), pp. 145–49.

to the city before it had enough men for defense.[26] The larger
force required a senior commander, and Sir Charles Lyttelton
relieved the Earl of Middleton (probably late in April, 1678),
but Middleton remained as a battalion commander. Perhaps as
a reward for duty well done, the king gave him a commission
as colonel of a new regiment, which must have raised him in the
eyes of punctilious Spaniards, but the regiment does not appear
to have been formed. Throughout the spring the English did not
so much as skirmish with the French, though English forces
were also being built up at Nieuport and Dixmude.

In April, Louis XIV condescended to make known his conditions for peace, but his demands for himself and for his allies
were so great that the Dutch, who thought them "offensively
wicked," argued that the French army might compel the acceptance of worse ones if the war continued. The Spanish reply to
this mild recommendation of acceptance was "perfidy"; because
the Holy Roman Emperor and the king of England would supply troops, the French terms might safely be rejected. (In other
words, Spain could and would stand on its pride as long as anyone else could help it.) The Dutch then called attention to the
need for time while English troops were transported to Flanders,
and the Spanish authorities agreed to a six-week suspension of
the conflict.[27]

At the same time, the Duke of York wrote to his son-in-law,
the Prince of Orange, that Charles II might be forced to remain
at peace to avoid "the chief design of the ill people here . . .
to engage the king in a war, that they may the easier ruin him."[28]
Charles, denied money by parliament, except with strict limita-
tions on his freedom to spend it, negotiated for the revival of
French payments and the disbandment of most of the new
English troops, and signed a secret treaty for those objects on
May 17/27.[29]

But the French postponed the suspension of hostilities; in
June, 1678, the Dutch prepared to resume the conflict, and

[26] P.R.O., S.P. 8/3, part 1, fol. 59.

[27] Grose, "Alliance," *E.H.R.*, Vol. XXXIX, 526; B.M., Add. MS 15,898,
fols. 4–5, 6–7, 12–13.

[28] P.R.O., S.P. 8/3, part 1, fol. 69. See Sir George Downing's speech of
May 3, 1678, in Anchitel Grey, *Debates in the House of Commons, 1667–
1694* (10 vols.; London, 1763), V, 308–9.

[29] Grose, "Alliance," *E.H.R.*, Vol. XXXIX, 371–72, 532–35; Browning,
Thomas Osborne, I, 270–72, 277–78.

Charles acknowledged his obligation to help them. He did not ratify the secret treaty of May 17/27, and the Duke of York promised, for his brother and himself: "We shall stand by you for the restoring of the towns in Flanders, and Maestricht, and are a getting ready five [additional] battalions of foot to send to Bruges and Newport, which I hope will have a good effect all ways."[30] Some fresh troops were sent. Although parliament had granted money only for disbandment of most of the army, Charles bound himself to begin war with France if a truce were not concluded within a few weeks,[31] and parliament was alarmed enough to grant the king a new tax on wine and postpone the final payment of the troops. It was planned that the English forces in Flanders would unite (when the time expired) with the army of the confederates, and in July the Duke of Monmouth was sent to command the English contingent. This was a sign of Charles II's sincerity; he would not have exposed his best-loved son to ridicule by sending him on a fool's errand or to danger by giving him an army that would be denied support. The Prince of Orange was satisfied, and would venture battle against the French.

Bruges, a peaceful station since the riot in April, staged a martial celebration of Charles II's birthday in May. In July, French officers invited Middleton, Colonel John Churchill, and others to the French camp, as if there had been no war.

[They] were there nobly treated, but when they had drunk hard a quarrel happened between an English and a French officer, and a challenge followed thereupon, whereof the Duke of Luxembourg having notice, he secured the English officers that night for preventing of mischief which else might have befallen them and the next morning having reconciled the officers he very courteously dismissed the English. . . .[32]

It was an odd code that required officers of different armies to be reconciled before they fought, but the code permitted great barbarity at another level.

When Monmouth arrived in Flanders, he took command of eight English battalions (but not Middleton's) and prepared to

[30] P.R.O., S.P. 8/3, part 1, fol. 91. See also Grose, "Alliance," *E.H.R.*, Vol. XXXIX, 536–37, 539.

[31] Treaty of The Hague, July 26, 1678, in Dumont, *Corps*, VII, part 1, pp. 348–50.

[32] B.L., Carte MS 103, fol. 230. Cf. B.M., Sloane MS 3,929, fol. 7.

move them forward to the confederate camp. The suspension of arms was nearly over, and the two field armies were already maneuvering for battle positions. Before Monmouth's force could join the Prince of Orange, Europe was surprised to learn that the Dutch States General had concluded a separate peace with France, at Nijmegen, on August 10 (N.S.).[33] The Marshal de Luxembourg, commanding the army of Louis XIV, knew of the peace, but this cannot be proved of William of Orange. William offered battle four days after the signature of the treaty, and Luxembourg accepted. The fighting, which took place at St.-Denis, near Mons, cost the two sides several thousand casualties.[34]

Although bloody, the battle had no particular consequence; but the peace forced the Spanish government to follow the Dutch. It also freed Charles II from his obligations to his allies. Under ordinary circumstances, with a will to peace on all sides, these would have been worthwhile achievements; in 1678, however, Louis XIV remained privately determined to obtain all that he had hoped for in the war just ended and to negate all concessions he had made in the treaty of peace. In the meantime, Louis kept the Franche Comté and a number of places on the frontiers of France, such as Ypres, Cambrai, and Valenciennes. The Dutch and Spanish armies were partly disbanded and the English troops eventually withdrawn. The French army, on the other hand, kept most of its strength and was slow in leaving its advanced positions. The former confederates were not only weakened; the sudden capitulation of the Dutch had made them distrustful of each other. Later, when the disastrous results of the peace became obvious, English supporters of an Anglo-Dutch alliance were compelled to defend the separate peace the Dutch had made.

Historians have blamed Charles II for the Dutch action. Leopold von Ranke, for instance, attacked Charles for proposing (through a third party) the "expedient" which Louis XIV used to make the separate peace without losing "honor," and for the ratification of the Anglo-Dutch treaty made in

[33] See Dumont, *Corps*, VII, part 1, pp. 350 f.
[34] For the controversy about this battle, see R. Fruin and W. J. Knoop, *Willem III en de slag van St-Dénis* (The Hague, 1881).

July.[35] The second attack is absurd: the completion of the treaty strengthened the combination against France insofar as the Dutch were willing to carry out its terms, and therefore Charles was probably trying to forestall the treaty of Nijmegen. The "expedient" was only one of a number of suggestions for securing reasonable terms from France made by various persons; had Charles kept quiet, an expedient would certainly have been discovered.

Neither charge is a valid excuse for the Dutch, who had the much better excuse of eagerness to close a long and terrible war. To be sure, the letters William III received from Danby show vacillation,[36] and English vacillation may have helped make the States General overanxious for peace, but the letters appear to have had little or no effect upon William; on the contrary, he has been charged with attempting to prolong the war by precipitating an unnecessary battle. Charles II may have been to blame for William's instability, or for preferring peace to war when Louis XIV did not intend to allow his neighbors the benefits of peace, but the Dutch made the treaty of 1678 and therefore bear the responsibility. There is evidence that the English were much taken aback: just as the States General distrusted the king of England, so Englishmen thereafter distrusted the Dutch.

The English troops remained in Flanders until the French began to execute the terms of the treaty, but—as had been usual with earlier Englishmen on continental service—many fell sick.[37] The sickness, a contagious fever, raged at least a month. Middleton stayed on until September 17/27, when he departed from Brussels for England;[38] his battalion remained at Nieuport. It was disbanded late in 1678.

Middleton had enhanced his reputation. At Bruges he had coped with an ill-trained force and a sensitive population while he commanded the garrison, and he apparently had accepted his supersession by Lyttelton without complaint. He had remained at his post while the soldiers sickened and died, risking his health. Charles II was pleased with his conduct, but Middleton was very possibly depressed by his experience in the Low

[35] Ranke, *History of England, Principally in the Seventeenth Century,* trans. G. W. Kitchin and others (6 vols.; London, 1875), IV, 53–54.
[36] P.R.O., S.P. 8/1, part 1, fols. 41–43, 53–54.
[37] Newsletter, Aug. 30, 1678, P.R.O., S.P. 101/6.
[38] *London Gazette,* Sept. 23–26, 1678.

Countries. His later career would be diplomatic and administrative rather than military. Young men discover their distastes as they mature. Perhaps Middleton had discovered one for military life.

The war was over. Charles II still needed money, however, and he saw no reason why he should not take another French subsidy: "Since the Dutch would have a peace upon the French terms, and France offered money for his consent to what he could not help; he did not know why he should not get the money." [39] At just this time, however, Titus Oates and other informers inflamed the public with the story of a great "Popish plot." Middleton, an undoubted Protestant who held no important office, was fortunate to be spared involvement, but he observed that the poisoned atmosphere of 1679 destroyed any possibility of continuing the foreign policy of 1677–78. The Duke of York was accused of murder and treason; the story of the former French subsidy to Charles II was brought out into the open, and Charles was forced to dismiss and imprison Danby; but the king's concessions to public opinion did him no good.

Parliament accepted the jumble of contradictory accounts of the "plot." Insisting upon its control of the government, it also proposed to exclude the Duke of York from the succession to the throne, but the king would not give in at his brother's expense, and a stalemate resulted. In 1678 the Dutch had made peace (their defenders say) because they doubted Charles II's sincerity, but in 1679 his sincerity was irrelevant: without money from parliament the army could not subsist, and an English alliance was worthless. Sir William Temple, who had never approved of the French subsidy and other features of his king's past policy, was shocked by the possibility that lack of funds would leave Flanders defenseless before the Spaniards were ready to hold it against France.[40] But the English troops were indeed withdrawn and the army retrenched, while for two years the king of England strove to maintain his own powers and the inheritance of his brother.

We know little of Middleton during 1679, but he was proba-

---

[39] B.M., Add. MS 28,054, fols. 188–89; Boyer, *Sir William Temple*, p. 297.
[40] B.M., Add. MS 28,103, fol. 63.

bly more concerned with Scotland than usual. Because his long absence on the continent must have compelled him to postpone the business of his estates, on his return to Great Britain he must have paid at least a short visit to Edinburgh and northeastern Scotland, where he would be out of sight of the London newswriters. Moreover, his father's old rival, the Duke of Lauderdale, was under attack. Lauderdale had for years monopolized power and office for himself and his close friends, and if the king were forced to sacrifice him, Middleton might profit from the redistribution of patronage. At that time a "king's man" might well have thought his prospects better in Scotland, where Charles II ruled almost without check, than in England, where king's men (such as Danby) were in danger of death. In August, 1679, Robert Spencer, Earl of Sunderland, a recently appointed secretary of state in England, was reported to have suggested that Middleton replace Lauderdale as the Scottish secretary of state.[41] As the report came from the Dutch ambassador, and as Sunderland and Middleton became close associates, it was probably correct.

We do not know how Sunderland and Middleton became friends, but they had had many friends in common and had probably known each other long before 1679. Sunderland — clever, unstable, an intriguer, apt to fly to extremes, and addicted to gambling — and Middleton — witty, cool, and fixed to well-known principles — were odd partners. Their association was readily accepted by their contemporaries until the Revolution of 1688. Sunderland took a grave risk in recommending his friend in 1679. Middleton was young, and inexperienced in affairs of state; and Lauderdale, wily and full of lore, had brought down opponents greater than Sunderland then was. It was a sign of Lauderdale's decline that both he and Sunderland kept their places for the time being.

In October, 1679, the Duke of York was sent to govern Scotland for his brother. Unquestionably, he was being removed from the English scene, but in a more honorable way than by his previous exile to Brussels; but he was given very full powers in Scotland, and he used them. The Scots were gratified that the heir to the throne would reside at Holyrood: Edinburgh would have its own court, and Scotsmen would have unusual oppor-

[41] B.M., Add. MS 17,677 EE, fol. 190.

tunities for serving the Stuart family, which might bring them
unusual rewards. Besides, there had been another rebellion in
Scotland, and a show of attachment might therefore be doubly
helpful. "All the Scotch nobility in London are preparing to
go," someone wrote Lord Wharton on October 18; "I do not
hear of one that stays." [42]

Perhaps Middleton was in London in March, 1680, when
Sunderland revived his suggestion for the Scottish secretaryship.
The Duchess of Portsmouth, a royal mistress who was reputed
to have influence in the king's choice of ministers, sided with
Sunderland, but Lauderdale angrily declared he would be secretary for Scotland longer than Sunderland for England. [43] Lauderdale, however, suffered an apoplectic stroke that same
month, and the king gave the secretaryship to the Earl of Moray,
a man of Lauderdale's circle. Sunderland had failed again. But
Middleton did not have long to wait for a valuable preferment.
Perhaps Lauderdale's friends thought Middleton dangerous to
them, at court or in Edinburgh; and perhaps Sunderland thought
himself engaged to do something for Middleton because of his
failure to obtain the secretaryship. As it happened, several
ministers in foreign posts were to be replaced in 1680, and
Middleton was chosen to fill one of the vacancies.

Because the king of France had several times violated the
peace treaties of 1678, it was plain that only force or the threat
of force could compel him to abide by his agreements, but no
European government had the force that was necessary. In the
spring of 1680, Charles II undertook to forge defensive alliances with the rulers of other important states for mutual protection against any aggressor — privately acknowledging that
France was the only probable aggressor under the terms of the
proposed treaties. These treaties would serve instead of, or as a
step toward, a general alliance (such as was later made by
William III), but Charles also intended his policy to please
some of the parliamentary opposition who had attacked his
failure to punish French breaches of the Nijmegen treaty.
Charles hoped that parliament might then give him the money

[42] B.L., letter of Oct. 18, 1679, Carte MS 228.
[43] B.L., Carte MS 39, fol. 127; Gilbert Burnet, "Some Unpublished Letters,"
ed. H. C. Foxcroft, *Camden Society Miscellany* (3d series; London: The
Camden Society, Vol. 11, 1–45), pp. 12–14.

he needed to execute an anti-French policy — and he hoped to distract the House of Commons from its attempts to destroy the Duke of York.

Charles, who had maintained only a few ministers abroad, now appointed ministers to several states where he had had none and replaced some of the ministers he thought unsuited to either the new policy or the new task of negotiating treaties. He accredited Sir Robert Southwell to the electors of Brandenburg and Saxony, Charles Bertie to several other German princes, Sir Gabriel Sylvius to the dukes of Brunswick, Lord Bodmin to Denmark, and Philip Warwick to Sweden.[44] Negotiations with Spain and the United Netherlands were to be carried on directly with their ministers in England, and Charles also wished the emperor to send a representative to England with authority to treat for an alliance.

The Dutch and Spanish treaties were concluded by June. Sunderland, in writing to Henry Savile, Charles II's minister to France, conveyed the king's orders to reply to French inquiries that the alliances were not meant as a threat to France.

Those he [Charles II] desires are all defensive, and designed only to preserve the peace, which he is much concerned to do, or to enable himself and his neighbours to defend themselves the better, if any should go about to disturb the present quiet; and such as the French king does or has solicited in the same places . . . All the world knows that his most Christian Majesty of France may enjoy the present peace as long as he pleases, nobody being in a condition to begin [provoke or declare war] with him. . . .[45]

This could not have been calculated to convince Louis but to deprive him of public arguments. Charles knew how well Louis XIV throve on the helplessness of his neighbors and how little the French king wished to see Spain, for instance, in a defensible state. Moreover, Louis knew that Charles knew it, and Charles knew that Louis knew. The defensive alliances were obviously directed against France, and Louis XIV used all his strength in

---

[44] P.R.O., S.P. 104/57, fols. 38–41, 56–59, 100–110; S.P. 104/153, fol. 78. I disagree with the opinion of Dr. J. R. Jones that these envoys were dispatched "to seek a general alliance on a Protestant basis" (J. R. Jones, *The First Whigs* [London, 1961], p. 123); Spain and the emperor, both Catholic, were to be included.

[45] Sunderland to Savile, June 3, 1680, P.R.O., S.P. 104/19.

the English parliament and at the various princely courts to obstruct them.

The Earl of Middleton was designated in June, 1680, as English envoy extraordinary at the court of the Holy Roman Emperor, Leopold I. His principal task was to persuade the emperor to enter into a treaty similar to that lately concluded with Spain. If the emperor expressed interest, Middleton was to request him to send a plenipotentiary to England to negotiate and sign a treaty. His instructions gave answers to various doubts which he might encounter at the imperial court.

Those that pretend to be jealous or doubtful of us have abundant reason to satisfy themselves if they consider the vigour, the zeal, and the good success wherewith we opposed all the offers that were made, and particularly the alliances that were attempted to be made last winter in The Hague to the prejudice of the general peace, and to the weakening of the alliance we are now in with the States General. . . . As to the parliament, we have the greater confidence in them, that they will stand by us, for that we are now entered into those engagements and have espoused that party, that they by frequent petitions and addresses to us in parliament have besought us to enter into and espouse, as being persuaded nothing could be more agreeable to their interest and security.[46]

The Earl of Shaftesbury, leader of the opposition and founder of the Whig party, disagreed. Advising a correspondent to quit the privy council, Shaftesbury explained his own attitude toward foreign policy.

The Dutch alliance is a thing in itself good and desirable: but as wholesome and nourishing meat, though good in itself, yet to a disordered stomach serves only to add to the disease: so with us if this alliance serve to raise money, men, and ships for our mutual defence under the conduct of his Royal Highness [the Duke of York] it had been much better never made: nothing is good but what tends to set things right at home, in the first place.[47]

In other words, the defense of Europe could go hang unless the king approved the Exclusion Bill.[48]

One would not labor this point had not a number of his-

---

[46] Middleton's Instructions, June 23, 1680, P.R.O., S.P. 104/57, fols. 94–99. For his credentials, see P.R.O., S.P. 104/191, fol. 4.

[47] P.R.O., Shaftesbury Papers (P.R.O. 30/24), fol. 351.

[48] Cf. J. R. Jones, *The First Whigs*, p. 130.

torians insisted on the devotion of the Whigs to the curbing of France, but neither Shaftesbury nor his Whig colleagues renounced any promising maneuver in internal politics for the sake of an international aim. Perhaps Charles II could have obtained his European objective by giving up his brother and some of his own power; it is certain that Charles would have adopted the foreign policy demanded by the Whigs had they let the Duke of York alone and helped the king find the money to pay the cost of that policy. Whiggery, it soon appeared, was isolationism behind a mask of international concern.

CHAPTER III

Envoy and Scottish Secretary

English diplomacy in the seventeenth century was far short of the professionalism of the twentieth. More to the point, it was somewhat behind that of the contemporary diplomatic services of France and the Netherlands; the diplomatic "career" was new to Englishmen. Such professional diplomats as Sir Gabriel Sylvius and Sir William Temple — obvious examples — were exceptional; Middleton's appointment was typical: he had not served an apprenticeship in subordinate diplomatic posts or in the "secretariat" (as we should say) at Whitehall. Thus he learned diplomatic practice only after he had been appointed. He did know French and Latin, the languages essential for diplomacy, and at least a little Italian, which was much used at the imperial court, and had traveled on the continent and knew his own court well. Ordinarily, this was thought sufficient experience for proper performance in a diplomatic post, unless the preparation and signature of an important treaty were called for, and the projected defensive alliance between England and the emperor was to be made in England, by the king, his ministers, and the emperor's envoy, so that Middleton would not be taxed beyond his knowledge.

Foreign policy was part of royal prerogative in the Restoration period. Although the crown had not always succeeded in forbidding parliamentary discussion of a king's relations with other states, it had retained control of policy, and Charles II was determined to retain this prerogative. The secretaries of state who administered foreign policy were appointed by the king, as were ambassadors and other ministers abroad, and the king might or might not take parliamentary politics into account in choosing them. Parliament had not as yet the power of overthrowing a secretary who pleased the king; rather, the king could dismiss one for any reason — although appeasement of parliament might be one reason. A minister abroad did not make policy. (He does not now.) A secretary of state might influence foreign policy, but he did not have great power. Secretaries of state and ministers executed the policy embodied in the king's instructions to the best of their abilities, within the decent bounds of normal diplomatic practice, and obtained and transmitted reliable information on the basis of which a sound policy could be formed and instructions given.

The objects of foreign policy were dynastic, commercial, defensive, and religious. Every ruling family wished to maintain its position and extend its power, and each had its poor relations whose interests it supported. In the 1680's, for instance, the house of Stuart stood protector to the Elector Palatine (a cousin) and the Duke of Modena (the Duke of York's brother-in-law). Dynastic connections and their dominions and rights were taken seriously by men of the seventeenth century, and diplomats were instructed to look after them. Second, the king and his government paid close attention to the foreign trade carried on by English merchants. Charles was much concerned with the protection of those merchants, English shipping, and English merchant seamen while pursuing their lawful commerce abroad. Consuls (unsalaried for the most part) were commissioned in a number of foreign ports for the good of trade, but British commercial interests were often referred by the home government to the accredited resident minister, whose rank and influence at a foreign court were greater than those of a consul.

The defensive services rendered by diplomacy require little explanation. The support of a balance of power, especially among the states near the Narrow Seas, was much in Charles's mind though sometimes beyond his means. In 1678 and 1680 it was the chief motive of his foreign policy and the basis for his appointment of the new ministers, Middleton among them. As for the religious objective of foreign policy, the king of England was the most powerful Protestant monarch in Europe. Lesser Protestant princes expected his assistance when they were threatened with wars of religion. Protestant minorities in Catholic countries, such as France and Savoy, expected and often received diplomatic assistance in times of persecution. In the 1680's, for instance, when the Huguenots of France already felt pressure to accept Catholicism, English ministers at Paris were consistently sympathetic and helpful, as their instructions required them to be.

Success in obtaining all objects of policy depended on a king's prestige, which was also the prestige of his nation. If his subjects were to be safe abroad, his kingdom free from attack, his relations secure in their principalities, and his fellow Protestants unmolested by foreign governments, he had to keep a reputation for strength, will, and sensitivity to challenge by repelling attacks and rebuking affronts. He had to retaliate even for symbolic offences; indeed, the Third Dutch War was caused, in part, by a Dutch refusal of the salute to which English naval vessels were entitled by custom in the Narrow Seas. Diplomacy was conducted accordingly: diplomats were sometimes ordered to bully as well as to persuade. They must not allow derogations of their prestige, which would affect their master's. They often disputed about the order of precedence on formal occasions, appealing to tradition and previous practice, and threatening retribution. Shrewd observers gauged a state's power before they took sides, and one of the indices of power was readiness to assert power. Assertion might be restrained by domestic considerations. England's "mixed monarchy" was peculiar in that parliament had its own idea of the respect which foreign governments should have for England. Charles II was no hector; he despised hectors and hectoring, but he had to contend with a nation and a parliament in which hectors could find a following.

Outward bound, at The Hague, Middleton waited upon the Prince and Princess of Orange on July 4/14, 1680. From Holland he went on to Ratisbon (Regensburg), arriving August 1 (N.S.), and was entertained by Abbot Fleming, of the Scottish Benedictines. Ratisbon was the seat of the imperial diet, to which Louis XIV had accredited a minister, Verjus, and when Middleton departed from Ratisbon for Austria (on August 3), Verjus was reported to have said that the English envoy made haste in his journey but would not make such haste in his business. He offered to wager two thousand crowns that parliament would neither consent to war nor give money for it "before they bring the process against the Duke of York to an end."[1]

Emperor Leopold was not at his plague-ridden capital, Vienna, but at Linz, where Middleton accordingly presented himself. His Francophile predecessor, Bevil Skelton, was at Linz soon after Middleton's arrival, and the new envoy received instruction on court factions and ceremonial, writing afterward: "There is no court in Christendom so full of ceremony as this, yet there is no such officer as a master of ceremonies."[2] Middleton's first official duty was an interview with Count Albert von Zinzendorff, the marshal of the court. Zinzendorff, Middleton reported, agreed that the nations must combine for common defense, and Zinzendorff believed that Charles II was sincere in his proposal, but the great obstacle was the disunion in England.

I said [Middleton wrote] what I could to reassure him, by representing that it was an artifice of some of our neighbours and ill affected persons at home, to make our condition appear much worse than it is, that though we seldom are without heats in matters of religion, yet they did not relate at all to foreign affairs, in which all parties agreed; that it was not to be doubted but the parliament would assist his Majesty with their lives and fortunes in pursuance of such things as by so many humble addresses they had petitioned him to. . . .[3]

Middleton did his best to display parliament's reaction in 1678 as favorable to a European combination against France. Although Charles II might be unable to assist his continental allies immediately, those who might disturb the peace of the Holy Roman Empire would be reluctant to unite the English factions and turn the balance of power against offenders. Despite everything he said, however, the disagreement between Charles II and his parliament remained Middleton's chief hindrance throughout his stay in Austria. Although Count von Thun, who had been designated the imperial envoy, departed for England on September 25, Middleton made no further progress. The debates at home, which were reported at Linz, frustrated all hope for a defensive alliance with the emperor.

[1] *London Gazette*, July 19–22, 1680; Newsletters from Ratisbon, Aug. 8 and Sept. 5, 1680, P.R.O., S.P. 191/35. (The folios of this volume are not numbered.)

[2] B.M., Add. MS 25,362, fol. 20.

[3] Dispatch of Aug. 7/17, 1680, P.R.O., S.P. 80/16, fol. 201.

The king of England had instructed Middleton to associate himself with the Dutch minister at the imperial court and to be on good terms with others. But the Dutch minister was not at Linz — no one knew where he was. The Spanish ambassador could give him no assistance.

In October, however, the Spanish ambassador received instructions to support 'Middleton with his own representations, but he told the English envoy the emperor would not conclude the defensive alliance before he had "an account of the present state of affairs in England." Middleton wrote:

It is plain that the design is to gain time. . . . none of the ministers here have ever taken any notice to me of the [Popish] plot, or the persecution of the papists. . . . but if it should happen hereafter, I shall obey you, in endeavouring to justify the truth of it; though I am sure not to be believed, for if an angel from heaven should tell it them, he would be thought a devil: since they will depend upon the Comte de Thun's relations, the only way will be to possess him with the belief of it. . . . however, I do not think their opinion in this particular of any importance to the main end, for if we can agree amongst ourselves, they will court our friendship upon any terms.[4]

Middleton's instructions called for correspondence with English ministers at other courts, and he exchanged letters with Henry Sidney, Sir Robert Southwell, Lord Bodmin, and Charles Bertie. All had encountered the same problems. Bodmin thought Louis XIV would have the Danes in his camp "at a cheap rate" unless the alliances among the greater powers were quickly arranged; moreover, the Danish court complained of past breaches of faith by Spain and the United Netherlands. Southwell, who could not shake the neutrality of the Elector of Brandenburg, wrote: "But as to England, he [the elector] has told the Prince [of Orange] that if he could once observe an union between the king and people, it would be of encouragement to him to speak plainer than hitherto he could adventure to do."[5] Bertie reported that the Elector of Cologne was too timid to give Louis XIV offense, even though the French had

⁴ Dispatch of Oct. 22/Nov. 1, 1680, P.R.O., S.P. 80/16, fol. 248.
⁵ B.L., Carte MS 104, fols. 44–45. See also Gustave Bulard, *Les Traités de St.-Germain, essai sur l'alliance étroite de Louis XIV et du Grand-Electeur après la guerre de Hollande* (Paris, 1898), 92–94.

already encroached upon his rights; and Bertie feared that the other Rhenish princes would take the same line. [6] The problems of all states near France were grave. Louis XIV observed the terms of the treaty that had been made at Nijmegen (in 1678) only as it suited him to do so, but none of the signatories was powerful enough to force compliance. His army was the largest and most effective in western Europe, and the king of France used not only his own resources but any which he could easily seize upon. In the long war from 1672 to 1678, the French army had followed the customary practice of demanding "contributions" from the civilian population of the occupied territories, and now that the war was over, French troops continued in their positions, making greater and greater demands. Bertie observed in the principalities of Liége (whose prince-bishop was also elector of Cologne) and Jülich "the severe marks of his M[ost] Chr[istian] M[ajesty]s indignation against them, having burnt most of their towns and villages, some for not paying contributions, others for not paying it soon enough, and some could not be exempted, though they paid as soon as demanded." [7] Louis's excuse for his exactions was that the treaties of 1678 had not been promptly ratified. Louis, moreover, claimed the "dependencies" of territories ceded to him by the treaties, then adjudicated the cases in his own courts (the celebrated "chambers of reunion") and sent his troops to occupy the dependencies and force their inhabitants to acknowledge him as their sovereign. The connection between ceded and "dependent" territories was often tenuous or obsolete, but the small states could do nothing against the French army, and the large states could act only in combination.

The great powers concerned were Spain, the Holy Roman Empire, the United Netherlands, and England. Spain was bankrupt and governed by an incompetent king. The emperor was weakened by his involvement in Hungary and anticipation of war with Turkey and was suspected by the greater German princes of designs upon their autonomy. The Dutch (to oversimplify, perhaps) were divided between the faction of the Prince of Orange, who wished to resist the French, and that

[6] B.L., Carte MS 104, fols. 52–53.
[7] *Ibid.* See also A. Levaë, *Essai historique sur les négociations de la trêve de vingt ans conclue à Ratisbonne en 1684* (Brussels, 1844), pp. 5–6.

which feared the prince and wished to give him no more power. The federal constitution of the United Netherlands enabled the factions to stalemate each other. England, of course, was distracted by the disputes between Charles II and his parliament. Thus the "great powers" were not formidable in 1680 and 1681, even in combination.

Middleton's task was hopeless: he could not persuade the emperor to rely on England unless Charles surrendered to parliament, for Leopold insisted on union of Charles with parliament, and parliament would agree to nothing less than surrender. Middleton, nevertheless, learned the trade of diplomacy, and from a good master. In 1680 the imperial court was part of the "province" of the secretary of state for the Northern Department, Sir Leoline Jenkins, who gave Middleton the king's orders and read the envoy's dispatches from Linz. Jenkins suggested weak points in the English arguments which the envoy should avoid and strong ones which he should make count; and the pupil responded eagerly. Explaining his attitude toward a memorial he had submitted to the emperor, Middleton wrote Jenkins:

It will be a very easy thing to criticize upon it, for all arguments cannot be of an equal force, and there [are] some which I know would not hold water in England, yet here appear to be very plausible; if I had gone about to have denied that there were any jealousies in England, I should have persuaded them only that I was a very impudent fellow, and should never have been believed in any thing hereafter; I have taken notice of his Majesty's retrenchments, because I thought I had a good occasion to make advantage of them, by making them appear to be effects of his majesty's prudent foresight, which passed here merely as the effects of his wants; however *valeat quantum valere potest*, for I confess I was unwilling to omit any thing that seemed to favour my cause. . . .[8]

In the age of Louis XIV, an honest diplomat was one who told the truth to his own government.

Linz was a dull provincial town and had little to offer to such a worldling as Middleton. There was little court entertainment (to judge by the dispatches) other than that occasioned by the christening of an archduchess. The imperial court was punctil-

---

[8] Dispatch of Sept. 7, 1680, P.R.O., S.P. 80/16, fol. 224; a copy of the memorial is in B.L., Carte MS 104, fols. 23–24.

ious: a simple meeting between an ambassador and an envoy could lead to disputes over ceremonial trifles which might reflect on their masters' standing. Middleton, an envoy extraordinary — there were no "ordinary" envoys at the imperial court — ranked below ambassadors but above residents and other smaller fry. By another scale, the rank of the acrediting ruler, Middleton was entitled to admission to the antechamber (second of the four chambers at the court) on equal footing with the French envoy. The references to his service at Linz show that Middleton was noted for his courtliness and ability, but he lived quietly and showed great reserve.

Maintaining diplomats abroad was expensive, and Charles II had obviously got no money from parliament. Southwell's recall, in October, 1680, perhaps stimulated Middleton to ask whether he might not also return to England, having no further business to transact. A month later he wrote that he had "several reasons to wish to be quickly recalled" but that he would stay at Linz as long as the king needed him. Early in 1681 he wrote to Jenkins: "I do think it a little severe that I must be forced to continue here, to the ruin of my private affairs at home. . . . I do assure you, sir, I had declined this commission, if I had not had assurances of returning in much less time than I have been here already. . . ."[9] Jenkins did his best, but Middleton was not recalled.

Whatever the state of Middleton's affairs at home, he had exhausted his supply of money in Austria. By March, his pay was six months in arrears, and his Scottish pension was unpaid. At last, on March 22, 1681 (N.S.), Middleton wrote directly to Charles II, explaining his situation at length:

Having entirely devoted my whole life to your majesty's service, I shall in all times, places, and employments most willingly attend it and the only reason I wished to be recalled was, that I foresaw without ready supplies, I could not subsist in such a condition, as suits with your majesty's honour, and service, for this people are much taken with show, and if I could not humour them in it, it might give them a bad impression of the present state of your affairs, sir. I have the misfortune to be destitute of any means of my own, having always lived by your majesty's favour and bounty. . . . Instead of

[9] P.R.O., S.P. 80/16, fol. 276.

appearing as I ought to do, I must pawn the little things I have for bread. . . .[10]

He suggested that the king must know why the Scottish pension had not been paid — no doubt an allusion to Lauderdale — and denied that he himself was to blame, "for it has always been and ever shall be my principle never to engage in any cabals or factions, but to live with a dutiful submission to your will. . . ."[11]

On April 5/15, Lord Conway, who had succeeded Jenkins as secretary for the Northern Department, wrote Middleton that he would be recalled by the next post, that he would be paid a quarter's salary, and that the rest of his arrears would be paid on his arrival in England. "I am sure," Conway wrote, "you will find his majesty very well satisfied with your transaction in all things and ready to express his favour to your lordship. . . ."[12] The letter of recall was written on April 8, and Middleton was in London in July.[13]

In March, 1681, despairing of cooperation from the House of Commons after a very brief session, Charles II suddenly dissolved parliament. The Whigs, as the permanent opposition was now called, had been expected to react with violence, but incidents were few and minor. By summer, the fever generated by the "Popish plot" had lessened, but the Duke of York remained in Scotland; his brother did not yet think it safe to recall him unless he conformed to the Anglican church, which the duke would not do. Danby remained in prison; but the Whigs were dismayed: it was clear that the king controlled the country. That summer Charles committed the Whig leader, Shaftesbury, to prison on a charge of high treason. Shortly afterward, Stephen College, one of the great informers of the time, was convicted of treason and executed. Shaftesbury was released, owing to the refusal of a sympathetic grand jury to indict him, but fled the country in October, 1682, and died abroad. The Whigs were left leaderless.

[10] B.M., Add. MS 18,827, fol. 20.
[11] *Ibid.*, fol. 21.
[12] B.L., Carte MS 104, fol. 63.
[13] *Cal. S. P. Dom., 1680–81*, p. 350. Compare this account with that of Mr. David Ogg, *England in the Reign of Charles II* (2 vols., London, 1934), II, 623, which falsifies the date and cause of Middleton's recall.

The ambitious foreign policy of Charles II had been thwarted by the Whigs and by the reluctance of his prospective allies. *Faute de mieux*, he once more accepted the French subsidy, which helped him carry on the government of England without summoning a parliament. (During the next four years he drew some four hundred thousand pounds "for doing what he himself desired." [14])

After reporting to Charles, Middleton must immediately have gone to Scotland to attend to his private affairs. Because the Scottish parliament was meeting at Edinburgh, and the Duke of York was surrounded by the Scottish nobility, Middleton found it a good time to make himself useful in Scottish affairs. On August 18 he took the oath of allegiance and his seat in the Scottish parliament.[15] He probably remained in Scotland throughout the autumn, for he was made a burgess and guildbrother of Edinburgh on October 19, and in December took part in the trial of the Earl of Argyle.

Argyle's was a political case; he was not accused of an overt act in the usual sense. A test oath had been imposed on Scottish officeholders. Argyle, son of the Marquess of Argyle, executed many years before, had already taken the oath with reservations; when he was appointed to a new office, he came to take the oath a second time, and the Scottish privy council interpreted the reservations in the harshest fashion. With the permission of Charles II, the council had Argyle tried, and the jury found him guilty of treason and other crimes. The Scottish law under which the earl was convicted was harder than the English law, and the jury was carefully chosen for a verdict of guilty.

Scottish Presbyterians have since interpreted the trial as intended to take Argyle's life. One can hardly blame them, as the offenses of which he was convicted were capital, and he was eventually (in 1685) executed on the basis of the conviction, but many Scottish convictions in capital cases were followed by pardons and were probably never meant to result in execution as to life. Argyle himself had been so condemned twenty years before, after the Restoration. In 1681, according

[14] C. L. Grose, "Louis XIV's Financial Relations with Charles II and the English Parliament," *Journal of Modern History*, I (1929), 177–204.
[15] R.H.E., Supplementary Parliamentary Papers, Vol. 11, item 8, fol. 6.

to James II's *Life* (written principally by William Dicconson),
the intention was to deprive Argyle of his great feudal "jurisdictions and superiorities," which were thought "too much for
any one subject," and most people in Scotland believed the
king would extend his mercy to the earl.[16] The Duke of York
has been blamed for Argyle's conviction, but at the time he
wrote that the council had only anticipated action against
Argyle by the Scottish parliament.[17] Argyle certainly had other
enemies. Whether because he feared for his life or because he
wished to preserve his legal title to his feudal rights, he escaped
from prison and fled to the Netherlands. Once he was gone,
he was sentenced to death and proclaimed a traitor; his property
was confiscated. Argyle's son was eventually restored "in
blood," but, on Middleton's advice, his feudal powers were
withheld.[18]

On January 2, 1681/82, Middleton left Edinburgh and
posted to London, apparently as the Duke of York's confi-
dential messenger. The duke had proposed dividing the duties
of the Scottish secretary of state between two men, but the
French ambassador, Barrillon, believed Middleton would obtain the office for himself; Lauderdale, he wrote, had lost all
power in Scotland. A few weeks later the Duke of York, now
supreme in Scotland, was recalled to court, but Middleton was
not promoted until September. Because the reaction against
Whig agitators and Whig-supported informers was at high tide
in 1682, the Catholic duke was cordially received at Yarmouth
and Norwich, and in London the Honourable Artillery Company entertained him at its annual feast. Later in the year, at
the lord mayor's pageant, "loyal songs" replaced the "plotting
Papists litany" that had been sung in 1680. The favor of the
king and the duke was everything to a politician, and Middleton
was in high favor. As it had been decided that the Duke of
York was to live in England, he returned to Scotland on H.M.S.
Gloucester to escort his duchess home, and Middleton was one
of the courtiers on the ship.

Gloucester, as is well known, ran aground on its way north-

[16] J. S. Clarke (ed.), *Life of King James II Collected out of Memoirs Writ
of His Own Hand* (2 vols.; London, 1816), I, 709–10.
[17] Emilia, Marquise Campana de Cavelli, *Les Derniers Stuarts à St.-Ger-
main-en-Laye* (2 vols.; Paris, 1871), I, 380.
[18] Clarke (ed.), *King James II*, I, 712–13.

ward and sank. Gilbert Burnet has vilified the Duke of York's conduct on this occasion, and his remarks have been kept alive by historians who apparently do not believe him.[19] Burnet was not a witness of the wreck and gives no sources for his allegations, but the accounts of witnesses, such as James Dick, contain nothing that would discredit the duke. According to Dick, the duke got off the ship in a "little boat," with the Earl of Wintoun (the president of session in Scotland) and two gentlemen of his bedchamber (Dick entered the "ship's boat," which was apparently larger, with the Earl of Perth). The Earl of Middleton jumped after Dick, from the shrouds, and fell on Dick's shoulders; and other gentlemen and many seamen clambered into the same boat (a third boat was swamped "by the greatness of the sea"). The boat in which Middleton, Perth, and Dick saved themselves was menaced by swimmers who gripped its sides and would have overloaded it, "till they were forced off by several in our boat." A yacht picked up the survivors, but more than two hundred persons had drowned.[20]

The duke did not remain long in Edinburgh, but on May 11, before he returned to London, he saw to the admission of Middleton, the Duke of Hamilton, and the Earl of Tweeddale to the Scottish privy council (all three were in some sense opponents of Lauderdale);[21] and the Earl of Perth was made lord justice general. York and the duchess arrived in London on May 27, and Middleton either accompanied them or made the same journey at about the same time. Middleton profited. His pension, to be sure, was reduced to £300 sterling in July, but when Lauderdale died, in late August, Middleton was compensated with his enemy's place as a gentleman of the bedchamber, which was worth £1,000 sterling a year.[22] On September 26, Charles II commanded the issue of a patent

[19] See, for example, Ogg, *England in the Reign of Charles II*, II, 633.
[20] Henry Ellis (ed.), *Original Letters Illustrative of English History* (2d series, 4 vols.; London, 1827), IV, 67–72. See also *London Gazette*, May 11–15, 1682, and Bevil Higgons, *Historical Works* (2 vols.; London, 1736), II, 234–35.
[21] *Register of the Privy Council of Scotland*, VII, 415–16; Sir John Lauder of Fountainhall, *Historical Notices of Scottish Affairs* (2 vols.; Edinburgh: Bannatyne Club, Vol. 87, 1848), I, 355–56.
[22] Narcissus Luttrell, *A Brief Historical Relation of State Affairs, 1678–1714* (6 vols.; Oxford, 1857), I, 215; Edward Chamberlayne, *Angliae Notitia . . .* (14th ed.; London, 1682), p. 159.

making Charles, Earl of Middleton, conjunct secretary of state in Scotland, sharing the office with the Earl of Moray. The last formality of this promotion was performed on October 23.[23] By an agreement between Middleton and Moray, the latter kept the Scottish secretary's "pension" of £1,000 sterling, but the two shared equally in the fees of the signet and the secretary's office, estimated at £2,000 a year total. The two divided their time in waiting upon the king by alternating fortnights. Neither, therefore, could ordinarily be in Scotland without special leave.

Middleton was now a fully established courtier and official, worth taking into account in public affairs, but he had incurred obligations. The Earl of Aberdeen had helped him with the Duke of York. He had also been helped by Mulgrave, Sunderland, and the Duchess of Portsmouth, but his greatest obligation was to the Duke of York himself. Middleton's service in Scotland, in 1681 and 1682, and the common experience of shipwreck bound the two men together (perhaps the shipwreck was more important; three of the survivors were to be raised to high positions through York's influence: Middleton, Perth, and John, Lord Churchill).

At about this time, Middleton married Lady Catherine Brudenell, third daughter of Robert Brudenell, second Earl of Cardigan. (As his first child was born in November, 1683, the marriage would have occurred between July, 1681 and [say] February, 1683.) Catherine was about Middleton's age, somewhat old for a seventeenth-century bride. Although the Brudenells were a Catholic family, the Earl of Cardigan was rich and "loyal," and he had many useful family connections (an older daughter had disgraced the family by deserting her husband, the Earl of Shrewsbury, to live in concubinage with the Duke of Buckingham, but the scandal had lost its pungency). Lady Middleton was thought a beauty by Restoration gentlemen, who liked their ladies full-bodied, and later attained a reputation for her wit, religious devotion, and political intrigues. Middleton may have been in love with her when they married — he was certainly in love with her later. What was

[23] *Cal. S. P. Dom., 1682*, p. 433; *Register of the Privy Council of Scotland*, VII, 563–64.

more important at the time was that they were well suited to partnership in the advancement of their family.

Middleton applied his influence in helping his relations, as well as himself. The Earl of Morton, Middleton's brother-in-law, had left his title to an uncle, and the king still owed £ 6,000 compensation for the earl's lost rights in Orkney and Zetland; Middleton, the new conjunct secretary of state, on his second day in office, obtained a warrant for the payment of the annual rent of the king's debt. In 1683/84, Middleton's uncle, Andrew, muster master general of Scotland, was granted the escheat of Sir John Falconer of Feisdo; one month later, the king ordered Sir William Sharp to do justice to the Earl of Strathmore, the husband of Lady Helen Middleton, in a legal matter. Two other uncles were gratified by royal favors while the Earl of Middleton was Scottish secretary of state. Middleton, naturally, did not neglect himself. In the seventeenth century, the crown often granted favored persons the fines paid by offenders against the law. Sir John Falconer had been warden of the Scottish mint and was responsible for grave irregularities. Sir John committed suicide, but his son was expected to pay heavy fines, and the two secretaries, Moray and Middleton, obtained a grant of £ 3,000 sterling from these fines, which was to be divided between them. When it was found that the fines did not amount to that sum, Charles II ordered that the difference be made up from the fines of other persons.[24] Middleton needed the money. In March, 1683, John Graham of Claverhouse wrote the Marquis of Queensberry:

I find he [Middleton] has run himself in debt by this marriage and furnishing himself of necessaries for a family to about two thousand pounds; and I think less nor three thousand cannot be offered him [as a gratification]; and seeing the fines are coming in, though he got five, it were well bestowed. . . . it would secure you a friend here [at court] for ever, that has great interest and is a firm and real friend, where he professes it.[25]

The conjunct secretary also followed custom in garnering as much as he could of the crown's gifts; his largest plum as a Scottish official was a grant of the confiscated estates of two members of the Cochrane family. John Cochrane of Watersyde

---

[24] R.H.E., S.P. 57, Vol. 8, 234–35, and Vol. 9, 92–93.
[25] H.M.C., *Report XV*, appendix VIII, pp. 275–76.

and his father, Sir John Cochrane of Ochiltree, were on the
rebel side at the battle of Bothwell Bridge. (The father was
also implicated in the kidnaping conspiracy of 1683, known
as the Rye House Plot.) Their lands afterward fell to the king.
In 1684, Middleton received a gift by royal charter of the lands
of Cochrane of Watersyde and the "liferent escheat" of Cochrane of Ochiltree; he was said to have sold the gift to the Earl
of Dundonald (a Cochrane) for £6,000 sterling.[26]

Greed is never attractive; greed satisfied from the goods of
the persecuted is traditionally odious. Though Middleton may
have been greedy, the Cochranes were not innocent. Bothwell
Bridge was fought to repress rebellion against the only constituted authority in Scotland, and although — according to
law — the lives of rebels were at the king's mercy, yet mercy
as to life was extended in 1685, when the Cochranes were
apprehended after still another rebellion. In the meantime,
their estates had been given to Middleton, who supported the
government. Other suitors for the same kind of gift, many quite
respectable, were numerous. In 1683, for instance, William
Gulston, Bishop of Bristol, asked Charles II to grant to his
notoriously poor see the lands that had formerly belonged to
the late Lord Russell, who had been executed for his share
in the Rye House Plot. Such a grant, moreover, would not
have been the first cession of lands of "traitors and rebels" to
the church.

Middleton began his tenure of office on good terms with
most factions in Scotland: Lauderdale's death ended the last
important quarrel he had inherited from his father, the first
Earl of Middleton. As the second earl had lived in England
or abroad for many years, and still lived in England, he had
made few enemies of his own in Scotland, none of them important, and as secretary he conciliated Lauderdale's connection, cooperating in the settlement of the estate of the late
secretary's nephew and heir.[27] Middleton's closest Scottish associates were the Earl of Aberdeen (chancellor), the Marquis of

[26] Lauder of Fountainhall, *Historical Notices*, II, 554; R.H.E., S.P. 57,
Vol. 8, 434–35, 522–24; Sasine, registered Dec. 15, 1684, R.H.E., General
Register of Sasines, 3d series, Vol. 51; H.M.C., *Report IX*, appendix III,
p. 6.
[27] R.H.E., S.P. 57, Vol. 8, 291.

Queensberry (treasurer), and Sir George Mackenzie of Rose-haugh, and as a fellow opponent of Lauderdale, Middleton presumably found the Earl of Arran (later Duke of Hamilton), the Earl of Tweeddale, the Marquis of Atholl, and John Graham of Claverhouse congenial. James Drummond, Earl of Perth, and John Drummond of Lundin (later Earl of Melfort), Perth's brother, had not yet declared their enmity.

The chief influences in the king's Scottish government were Tory, episcopalian, and conservative, as in England, where the discrediting of the "Popish plot" and the king's firm action had set the Tories in control. According to the Duke of Ormond, a Tory, "where there is any difference of opinion it seems to me to lead to the trimming way. . . . if we have good luck we shall be all Tories, if we have bad we shall not be all Whigs."[28] Agreement on support of the king and of the established church, however, had not removed the jealousies among the Scottish ministers and councillors. They were rivals for grants and for other favors and signs of royal approval, and old family hatreds reappeared from time to time.

While Middleton was Scottish secretary, Aberdeen and Queensberry became estranged. Aberdeen, recently ennobled, had apparently been poor; but Queensberry was rich, ambitious, and a member of a great family, and — with others — resented yielding precedence to Aberdeen, his official superior. Had Aberdeen been conspicuously able, he might successfully have defended his position, but the balance of talent inclined toward Queensberry. Although Middleton had made great professions of friendship to Aberdeen in 1682, he later sided against him, ridiculing him for his "obscure way of living,"[29] and Queensberry enlisted the help of the Duke of York and the Duchess of Portsmouth. Aberdeen was overcome — in June, 1684 — when Queensberry threatened to resign unless the king dismissed his rival. Middleton thereafter continued to be friendly with Queensberry, even when the marquis came into conflict with the Drummonds — after Middleton had relinquished his Scottish office.

The rise of the Drummonds was a challenge to most other in-

---

[28] B.L., Carte MS 219, fol. 417.

[29] Sir John Lauder of Fountainhall, *Historical Observes of Memorable Occurrences in Church and State . . .* , eds. A. Urquhart and David Laing (Edinburgh: Bannatyne Club, Vol. 66, 1840), p. 128.

terests. James Drummond, Earl of Perth, by siding with Queensberry against Aberdeen, secured the chancellorship which Aberdeen lost; and John Drummond of Lundin was treasurer-depute of Scotland under Queensberry but was often at court, from which power emanated. John Drummond evidently approved of Middleton in these years. "You have good reason to be assured of him," he wrote Queensberry, and again, "Lord Middleton does like a hero." Once, at least, Drummond and Middleton took a bottle of wine together, but their contact was rather political than social,[30] and there was no sign of the breach that lay ahead.

Most of Middleton's time "in waiting" as secretary was spent either in social attendance or in administration, particularly in correspondence with Scotland. Originally, the earl corresponded with the Scottish privy council and with other officials, in his own name or as the writer of letters signed by Charles II and countersigned by the secretary responsible. In November, 1683, however, the king formed a secret committee of the Scottish privy council of the councillors then in highest favor (Aberdeen, Queensberry, Atholl, Perth, Drummond of Lundin, and the two Sir George Mackenzies [of Tarbat and Rosehaugh]), which to some extent replaced the privy council in Middleton's work. But there was other official correspondence — with the treasurer about money; with legal officers about prosecutions, litigation, and legal advice; and with the chancellor about the proceedings of his office and the use of the great seal. He countersigned, for instance, the *congé d'élire* to the dean and chapter of the cathedral of Rosse, which permitted them to elect a new bishop. He also countersigned the royal letter of nomination, directing the dean and chapter to choose the then Bishop of Dunblane. He conveyed to Lord Aberdeen the king's wish that Aberdeen recommend George Drummond to the citizens of Edinburgh for election as provost. He countersigned — and presumably drew up — the letter authorizing the secret committee of the privy council, and warrants granting fines (to himself and to others) and ordering a patent that made Perth chancellor of Scotland. The secretary undoubtedly influenced the king, but his official letters express

[30] H.M.C. *Drumlanrig (Buccleuch MSS.)*, II, pp. 39–40, 123, 125, 141.

only the king's will; Middleton had no Scottish policy distinguishable from his master's.

The king's will was sought, and obtained, for extraordinary criminal affairs. Thus Middleton was involved in the problem of Alexander Gordon of Earlston, a Covenanter (and son and grandson of Covenanters) who had been with the rebels at Bothwell Bridge and was captured in Scotland in 1683 when the Rye House Plot was detected. This plot was a very real one for the capture of the king and rebellion against his authority,[31] and it was in the course of things that the council ordered this persistent rebel put to death on the basis of a previous condemnation. The council also tried to discover the details of the plot and the identity of Earlston's associates, and, contrary to the usual practice, ordered Earlston put to the torture of the "boot" although he had already been sentenced to death. One supposes that the king's orders for this treatment, conveyed by Middleton, arose from unusual alarm at court on the disclosure of the plot; but the Scottish privy council temporized, arguing against the use of torture in Earlston's case. In the end, the prisoner was found to be mad, the torture and the death penalty were postponed, and Middleton countersigned Charles II's approval of the postponement.[32]

From September, 1682, to August, 1684, Middleton's duties required that he be either at court or nearby, whether at Whitehall, Newmarket, Windsor, Hampton Court, or Winchester. In talks with the Duke of York and Drummond of Lundin, through his favors and advice to friends and dependents, in his correspondence with the Scottish ministers and privy council — and especially in consultation with, and receiving orders from, the king — Middleton consolidated his position. He must often have thought of the increased power and emoluments he might have if he exchanged his Scottish office for an English one; however, some of his English friends had their own struggles at the time. Sunderland had a conflict with the Marquis of Halifax and had jeopardized his reputation for loyalty during the Exclusion Bill crisis; Mulgrave was in disgrace for pay-

---

[31] There can be no doubt of the reality of this plot, attested to by Lord Howard of Escrick and Colonel John Rumsey. See Ranke, *History of England*, IV, 172–77.

[32] *Register of the Privy Council of Scotland*, VIII, 267.

ing imprudent addresses to Princess Anne, the unmarried
younger daughter of the Duke of York, and Charles had angrily
taken the Holland regiment from him and forbidden him the
court. Middleton may have been responsible for Mulgrave's
return to favor in January, 1684, for he was then more influential than Mulgrave and remained so until the Revolution
of 1688. Charles II recognized Middleton's services and gave
him greater scope when he had the two Scottish secretaries of
state admitted as members of the English privy council on
July 11, 1684.

The English ministry was weak in 1684, and Charles endeavored to strengthen it. Laurence Hyde, Earl of Rochester,
was the first commissioner of the treasury and, in all but name,
lord treasurer of England; using the powers of his post, he
inaugurated a retrenchment of the king's expenditures and thus
made enemies on every side. One of the secretaries of state,
young Godolphin, was inexperienced in diplomacy; and the
other, Lord Sunderland, formerly the ambassador to France,
had lost friends. Some of the candidates for high office were disliked by the king or by the Duke of York, and others were
tarred by accusations made at the time of the "Popish plot."
Charles II heard complaints from all factions, weighed the advantages of this appointment over that, and while rumors of
change spread through the country diverted himself with cock-
fights, tennis, puppet shows, and comedies (performed by the
Prince of Orange's troupe).

In August, 1684, Charles announced his decisions. He removed Rochester, made him lord president of the council, and
gave the first place in the treasury commission to Godolphin —
who proved to be one of the most able government financiers in
Europe. Charles gave Middleton the secretaryship which Godolphin had formerly held, and at the Duke of York's suggestion the vacated Scottish secretaryship was given to John
Drummond of Lundin. At Windsor, on August 25, Middleton
was sworn into his new office.[33]

The reaction to Middleton's appointment was a peculiar

[33] *London Gazette*, Aug. 25–28, 1684. Cf. Ranke, *History of England*, IV,
197–98.

mixture of satisfaction and puzzlement. The Dutch ambassador Van Citters described the new secretary as "a lord of great ability and merit";[34] the Tuscan resident Francesco Terriesi at first refused to believe the news of the changes, but thought Middleton "a very civil gentleman."[35] John Evelyn wrote that the changes were "very unexpected and mysterious."[36] The Earl of Chesterfield was ironic:

'Tis an odd dance among the statesmen; few persons yet know who began it, nor who fiddles to it. . . . I cannot but congratulate the felicity of this age, that affords so many persons equally fit for the treasury, secretaries of state, presidents of the council, or what you please. Formerly 'twas thought these required different talents, studies and educations.[37]

A clerk who had probably served under Godolphin limited his comment to what affected him: "I am like to stick with my Lord of Middleton to receive any of your commands."[38] An anonymous Whig versifier wrote:

> *Scotch* Vermin, *Irish* Frogs, *French* Locusts; all
> That swarm both at *St. James's* and *Whotehall*;
> Though now advanced to all trust, all command,
> All offices enjoy by sea or land,
> Shall, when this sun is set, no more appear
> Within the confines of our hemisphere.[39]

To each writer, in short, the new ministry offered opportunity to express his personality.

The appointment should not have puzzled those who knew the workings of the court. Godolphin, who was consulted about his replacement, wrote:

I did not presume to put him [Charles] in mind of anybody but those that we have to honour to serve him abroad at this time as my Lord Preston [envoy in France], Mr. Chudleigh [in Holland], and Mr.

---

[34] B.M., Add. MS 17,677 GG, fol. 130.
[35] B.M., Add. MS 25,368, fols. 261–62, 285.
[36] Evelyn, *Diary*, ed. E. S. de Beer (6 vols.; Oxford, 1955), IV, 387–88.
[37] Chesterfield, *Letters . . . to Several Celebrated Individuals of the Time of Charles II . . .* (London, 1834), p. 276.
[38] B.M., Add. MS 28,875, fol. 374.
[39] "The Metamorphosis," in *State Poems; Continued . . . to This Present Year 1697* (London [?], 1697), pp. 159–60.

Skelton [at Hamburg]; he seemed not to like any of these, but to incline more to Mr. Blathwayt [secretary of war].[40]

Charles's reasons for rejecting Godolphin's candidates are fairly clear. Preston was "neither of the world nor of the court," as Barrillon had said on his appointment to Paris;[41] Chudleigh was mediocre; Skelton was thought too "French," and had a gift for making enemies; Blathwayt, whom Charles preferred, was a self-made man who would cut a poor figure at court. The field was clear for Middleton. He had the powerful support of the Duke of York and the Duchess of Portsmouth; the Duke of Queensberry was his ally; the Drummonds wanted to make a vacancy for John Drummond of Lundin; Sunderland was his friend; Ormond had been his father's friend; Godolphin, an acquaintance, at least had no objection; and Lord Halifax, who had attacked Rochester, was well satisfied with his rival's loss of power. Middleton attained his position as a man without influential enemies.

"Though it would not have been proper for Lord Middleton to have kept both places," the Duke of York wrote Queensberry in September, "yet shall he be advised with as much as ever in all Scots affairs."[42] Although the Scottish correspondence was conducted by Moray and John Drummond (who was successively made Viscount and Earl of Melfort), Middleton continued to advise the king in Scots affairs — usually in collaboration with Queensberry, the Drummonds, and other Scottish Tories. He thus preserved his own and his family's interests and helped those who shared his political views. The grant of Cochrane of Watersyde's estate was completed after the earl's promotion, and Andrew Middleton's commission as muster master general of Scotland was renewed on the accession of James II.

But Scottish politics became very thorny as time passed. The Drummonds broke with Queensberry, although he had helped them in their rise; then, using Melfort's access to the king, and going over to Catholicism after James II succeeded

[40] Hugh Elliott, *The Life of Sidney, Earl of Godolphin* . . . (London, 1888), pp. 98–99.
[41] P.R.O., P.R.O. 31/3/151, fol. 25.
[42] H.M.C., *Report XV*, appendix VIII, p. 208.

Charles II, they blamed Queensberry for the failure to persuade the Scottish parliament to permit private Catholic worship. When men quarreled with Queensberry — for example, Graham of Claverhouse — the Drummonds took them into their own camp. Using the religious issue freely, they ultimately secured Queensberry's dismissal from most of his offices. Middleton, who stood by Queensberry, came under the Drummonds' attack for a time, but through him the marquis was able to save his commission to the Scottish parliament of 1685.[43]

Middleton preferred — and found it safer — not to meddle with Scotland; as Lauder of Fountainhall wrote, he was "resolved to be an Englishman."[44] He gave a commission to several Scottish trustees for the supervision of his family estates in his absence. His relations did not suffer (Andrew Middleton and Lord Strathmore, for example, appear on a Scottish pension list as late as September, 1686). The Earl of Middleton was not made a knight of the new order of St. Andrew (the Thistle) in 1687, though he must have been considered (perhaps he declined it to avoid expense: the diamond badges of the order were said to have cost each member — including Lord Melfort — seven hundred or eight hundred pounds). A practical man, Middleton preferred to such costly tinsel the real influence and utility that was implied by James II's threat to use him for Scottish correspondence when Melfort was obstructive.[45] He could still "meddle" with Scotland if he wished, but, compared with the affairs of England and the continent of Europe before him, Scottish rivalries and alliances were petty subjects.

[43] Lauder of Fountainhall, *Historical Observes*, pp. 138, 237; C. S. Terry, *John Graham of Claverhouse, Viscount Dundee, 1648–1689* (London, 1905), pp. 169, 182, 186, 213–14.

[44] Lauder, *Historical Notices*, p. 714.

[45] Michael Barrington, *Grahame of Claverhouse, Viscount Dundee* (London, 1911), p. 165.

CHAPTER IV

English Secretary
and Member of Parliament

Middleton, as one of the two English "principal secretaries of state," was used by the king in communicating with his ministers abroad, with foreign ministers resident in England, with local authorities such as borough corporations and justices of the peace, with military and naval commanders, and in a pinch with anyone else whatever. The secretaries kept the king's signets and controlled the office of the signet through which the king's correspondence passed; they countersigned letters signed by the king or sealed with his signet; and one of them was always in attendance upon the king. They had large powers to act, as in the commitment of persons to prison, the seizure of papers, and the administration of oaths. They were, in the seventeenth century, always privy councillors — and usually among the most trusted of them.[1] The secretaries of state were also means of communications between subjects and the king. They received petitions, accusations, testimony on questions under investigation, and the like, and they could do subjects favors by "recommending" them, to the king himself or to other ministers. They were men to whom friendship came unsought.

As secretary, Middleton received £1,850 sterling a year; this we would call salary today. He disposed of £2,000 a year for secret service. As a member of the king's chamber, he also received sixteen shillings a day — £292 a year — for "diet" (a substitute for the table which secretaries had formerly

---

[1] For the office of secretary of state, see F. M. G. Evans [Mrs. C. S. S. Higham], *The Principal Secretary of State* (Manchester, 1923).

kept at the king's expense); and he retained his Scottish pension of £300 sterling. Thus his fixed income, apart from that from his estates, amounted to £4,542 sterling annually, but there is no way of knowing how much additional income Middleton derived from the fees of his office. A new baron, for example, paid £24 to the secretary's clerks as one stage toward the patent that conferred his title; a new duke paid £60, and there were many lesser transactions. Official income was then understood to cover not only the rewards of the officer but the expenses of his office. If Middleton's profit did not exceed £4,000 sterling a year, he was denying himself to a degree unusual in the period. Middleton assumed control of an office which had settled personnel, routines, and methods, formed over a period of some two centuries. There were six men in the office: an office chief (John Cooke); a record keeper, translator, and general assistant (Owen Wynne); three copyists and translators (De Paz, Carne, and Chute); and a writing clerk (Widdows). A son of John Dryden was later added to the staff. The staff was permanent and professional. Its members received both salaries and fees.[2] The office routine was adequate for the work, and Middleton relied upon it.

Middleton's family shared in the secretary's good fortune; his patronage was more valuable than ever before. William Middleton, the earl's uncle, became a lieutenant-colonel in the Scots Brigade that was serving the United Netherlands, and in 1685 a Lieutenant Brudenell, almost certainly a relation of Lady Middleton, was commissioned in the same service. James Middleton, son of William, was reluctantly advanced by the Dutch, but was later broken for sending a challenge. (Middleton refused the young man further help.) In 1686 another Middleton, a clergyman, was recommended to the Archbishop of Canterbury for the curacy of Ash, in Kent, or any other benefice in the archbishop's gift. Such favors were often reciprocal. Count Leslie, a general of the Emperor Leopold, in 1688, wrote Middleton that, "chiefly in regard to your lordship," he was promoting Middleton's cousin Sir Thomas Strachan; in return he asked Middleton to protect the Leslie

[2] F. M. G. Evans, "The Emoluments of the Principal Secretaries of State in the Seventeenth Century," *E.H.R.*, XXXV (1920), 525–26.

family in Scotland.[3] Leslie had a fair way of asking, and Middleton no doubt did as he was asked. In general, his attitude toward patronage was that of his easy-going contemporaries and may be summed up in his own words: "Lord Chamberlain is dead, but the spoil is not yet divided."[4]

As a matter of course Middleton had other posts besides that of secretary of state; he was a privy councillor (we shall see him later as a member and leader of the House of Commons) and also a member of the Board of Trade and Plantations, attending most of its meetings. In this diligence he was almost the equal of such administrators as Sir Joseph Williamson and Sir Leoline Jenkins, and was qualified for this work by virtue of his diplomatic and military experience. At the board, Middleton dealt with colonial policy, usually through proprietors and governors.

In August, 1684, apart from routine administration, two related problems of internal government occupied the secretaries of state: the conspirators of the Rye House Plot must be punished, and other plots and rebellions prevented. The government went to extraordinary lengths to achieve this end. In June, 1684, Sir Thomas Armstrong, brought back in bonds from Holland, went to the scaffold. After Middleton's appointment the quest for fugitives and their political associates continued unabated, in England and abroad, and the government set spies on those who were beyond its reach. The secretaries, as chiefs of intelligence and dispensers of secret-service money, were closely concerned with the detection of wanted men, taking evidence against them, learning their secrets, and arranging for arrests: they also invited suspects to turn king's evidence. This work was very important, because Monmouth and Argyle were living abroad, with knots of followers about them, and were corresponding with Whigs in England and Scotland; furthermore, the Prince of Orange and influential burghers in the Dutch towns were their friends, as were some of the richest English merchants in the Netherlands. The aim of the disaffected appeared to be rebellion, and many of them joined

[3] B.M., Add. MS 41,842, fol. 60.
[4] B.M., Add. MS 41,823, fol. 22.

either Argyle or Monmouth in their unsuccessful rebellions in 1685.

Although Charles II controlled the English central government, local government was dominated by the corporations and magistrates in the towns and cities and by the justices of the peace in the counties. To secure effectual execution of his commands and the election of a friendly House of Commons, Charles set out to control local government more directly than before. The chief obstacle was the borough corporations. These town councils, the custodians of the "liberties" of their boroughs, held charters through which the towns had been constituted legal persons and had been allowed their chief organs of self-government. Under the charters, the boroughs collected their own taxes, held fairs and markets, received tolls, and did many other things. Local cliques or single persons, however, sheltering under the charters, often dominated town affairs and in effect chose the burgesses whom many towns sent to Westminster to represent them in the House of Commons. Charles had learned, in 1679, 1680, and 1681, that for the time being the sum total of these elections by local interests must be expected to be unfavorable to him and to his brother the Duke of York. Being of no mind to yield, he set about changing the local system so that he would have the support of a majority in parliament on all occasions; to do this he must destroy Whig control where it existed and weaken the Whig influence everywhere. He adopted a device that had been used in the thirteenth century to limit the privileges of an aggressive nobility, the *quo warranto* proceeding.

Quo warranto consisted in summoning privileged persons — in this case corporations — to show the legal documents — charters — in which their privileges were set forth. If a borough corporation, say, had exceeded or misused its powers, it could be punished and its charters nullified, or charters could be found void because of defects in form or in the procedure by which they had been issued. Charles II used this device freely in the last years of his reign, although there was strong resistance. The City of London was crucially important: it was richer and more populous, and had better legal advice and more independence of spirit than other town governments; moreover, its title to its privileges seemed incontrovertible. In

1683, however, London lost its case and its charters, and other boroughs and cities found themselves at the king's mercy.

Many made a virtue of necessity and surrendered their charters "voluntarily" to show their loyalty to the king. (Some of these would have done the same if London had won.) At last, in each case, boroughs had no choice but to ask the king for new charters, and on the king's terms. Otherwise, they would lose all that they had accumulated over centuries: their town governments, courts, fairs, markets, and everything else that distinguished them from unprivileged villages and made urban life possible. The king was well pleased to give back most of the things he had taken away, and most of the new charters conformed fairly closely to the old ones, but they excluded from the governing bodies of the towns persons obnoxious to the king, intruded into them the king's most fervent supporters, and established his right to put out in future any he chose and to veto the choice of magistrates.

The policy was used throughout England, even with obsequious boroughs, but its results were unpredictable. In some boroughs the new corporation and magistrates were acceptable both to the king and to local opinion; in others the king had few supporters and therefore little choice, and the reins were entrusted to men of ill repute or little standing; in still others the king was badly informed, so that he gave power to untrustworthy men. Everywhere borough "patrons," who controlled or hoped to control the election of members of parliament, tried to strengthen their influence by getting their friends into town offices and by securing prompt grants of new charters to shorten the interval of confusion — thus the Earl of Gainesborough at Southampton, the Duke of Albemarle at Colchester, the Duke of Norfolk at Lynn, the Earl of Bath at Liskeard, and the Earl of Abingdon at Oxford, among others.

Middleton played his part in the surrender and issue of charters from the time of his appointment as secretary of state. Instructions and advice to the corporations of smaller boroughs, which lacked experience of administrative procedure and the money to retain legal counsel, must have become routine. Members of the corporation of Southampton, after presenting an instrument of surrender and a petition for a new charter, wrote to Owen Wynne (in Middleton's office) to learn what steps they should take to ensure that the new document passed promptly through the several stages and offices without payment of fees. The secretary's office was itself one of the offices through which the new charters passed, and unless the king had commanded otherwise — as he had for Southampton — there were substantial fees to pay. (Wallingford, for example, paid a total of £119 3s. 9d.) One of the secretaries then obtained the king's final signature for each charter. During Charles II's life, Middleton managed the charters of towns as important as Cambridge and Canterbury and as obscure as Holliston; he also managed new charters for several of the companies of the City of London, among them the Merchant Taylors, Grocers, and Fishmongers.

With the boroughs in the hands of his friends, and relieved of the menace of the widespread disorder which might be condoned by hostile local magistrates, Charles could plan to hold parliamentary elections which would return members who were predominantly Anglican and "loyal." Such members would support the king in his internal policy and perhaps supply the money necessary for a foreign policy independent of France. Charles had promised not to call a session unless Louis XIV agreed, but even the French ambassador discounted the promise. Charles would hardly have attacked the boroughs if he had not intended to influence the composition of a future parliament — or have made plans to call a parliament if he had thought his prerogative and his brother's succession would be endangered. He would surely have asked such a parliament, when it sat, for supplies of money. The more Louis XIV used his power of subsidy to limit Charles's freedom of action, the more Charles must have longed to be able to get funds from parliamentary taxation; besides, the subsidy was not large enough to cover his deficits.

Charles did not live to summon parliament. In the morning of February 2/12, 1684/85, he was stricken by apoplexy, and the privy council promptly ordered the ports closed and warships stationed at sea in order to keep the news from Monmouth and other disaffected persons abroad. The dying king lingered for four days. His doctors attempted to deceive him, saying that he was not in grave danger, but the deception broke down. On February 5 he was received into the Roman Catholic church, and on February 6 he died.

With Charles II's death, the Duke of York became King James II. The commissions of all officers and officials were extinguished by the demise of the crown, but within a quarter of an hour James met with the lord keeper, the lord privy seal, the two secretaries of state (Sunderland and Middleton), and others in the council chamber and restored their seals of office. James confirmed these ministers in their posts and announced that the privy council would remain unchanged for the time being; the officials present then took an oath to their new king.[5] James spoke of his sadness on his brother's death, then promised that he would support the laws and would not encroach upon the Protestant religion. The Earl of Rochester, his brother-in-law, a man sure of favor and influence, proposed that James publish these promises in a declaration; with the approval of his councillors, the king resolved to do so. Proclamation of James II's accession was ordered and performed in London that day, with the usual celebration and drinking of the king's health.

As the news spread, the king was proclaimed in all the principal towns. Conduits ran with wine at Oxford, Southampton, and Ludlow; at Portsmouth, the fleet discharged its great guns; the garrison of Hull fired volleys of small arms; there were bonfires and bell ringing everywhere, and "other expressions of joy."[6] All seemed normal and peaceful, even happy. The most unpopular heir to the throne had become a passably popular king. The ports were reopened. After Charles II's funeral, on February 14, the officers of his household signified the end of their duties by breaking their staves of office. There was a flutter of loyal addresses, some certainly inspired by courtiers, and others by the deep-rooted reverence of most Englishmen for the monarchy.

It was known that James II's continuance of King Charles's men was provisional, and as early as February 9/19 Barrillon reported predictions of change. Rochester was to be lord treas-

---

[5] P.R.O., P.R.O. 31/3/160, fol. 43; *London Gazette*, Feb. 5–9, 1684 [/85].

[6] *London Gazette*, Feb. 12–16, 16–19, 19–23, Feb. 26–March 2, 1684 [/85]; B.M., Add. MS 41,803, fol. 138.

urer; Sunderland was in high favor; and the king decided the most secret affairs in conference with Rochester, Sunderland, and Godolphin. James II had announced his intention of summoning parliament, and, by March 5 (Barrillon wrote), a kind of council of Catholic lords had begun to meet, a thing unknown before. Jealousy had already arisen between Sunderland and Rochester. Change was in the air.

James, by 1685, had taken on a firmer mold than he had had earlier. Since his conversion to Catholicism, some years before, he had consistently practiced his religion in the face of popular dismay and threats to his position as heir. It has often been remarked that James became rigid and uncompromising, unwilling to take advice, but much of the advice men offered him appeared to him to lead through dissembling to apostasy. He opposed it with a stern countenance, and even his friends began to think him stubborn and difficult. As he had been vilified by agitators and informers, he came to care little for the public, and secretly distrusted it. He had given his loyalty to his brother, counseling him to stand firm for the royal prerogative and the hereditary succession. His brother had returned his loyalty and had preserved the succession, so that James became king. Opponents attributed Charles II's most arbitrary actions to James's advice, and they were not far wrong. Apparently, James's advice was shrewd as well as unpopular, for Charles's policy was successful.

James's shrewdness in the early 1680's need not surprise us, for it was not new. As lord high admiral he had dealt with matters of national importance, with talent and application. In Scotland he had restored peace, although by harsh means, in the course of two years. That was not a task for every man. James had then seen Charles II through a very difficult time in England. James's courage was well established, and only opponents such as Gilbert Burnet questioned it as early as 1685. He had served in the Second and Third Dutch Wars as a naval commander, and had been praised as a soldier by Marshal de Turenne. Not doubting himself or the rightness of his cause, he conducted himself with dignity; but the man was not without fear, for he was full of suspicion.

He was vulnerable, as his brother had been, to charges of

immorality; he had kept mistresses and had begotten several illegitimate children. At this time of his life he was distressed by thought of his sins, and labored to expiate them and to avoid sin in future, but he also suffered when he denied himself. On his accession he made promises of better behavior, sent away his reigning mistress (the Countess of Dorchester), wavered, and began to visit her again — to the pain and disgust of his queen Maria Beatrice of Modena. It was Middleton, in the end, who went from the king to the countess with a command that she leave the country.[7]

The effect of his bitter experience was that James came to believe he had no one on whom he could rely. One man was indiscreet, another incapable, a third an opportunist; and gradually — if Barrillon is correct — the king came to think all Protestants unworthy of confidence. The result of this distrust was that great pretense was made of secrecy in the king's business, but everything secret came out. James, in fact, took pride in his blunt speech and, even when he was moved to adopt unpopular measures, he made his intentions abundantly clear.

Middleton was the king's servant; clever, urbane, conciliatory, he must have been a very useful one. By degrees, James filled his government with inexperienced Catholic nobles and gentlemen, and with time servers who had found no other way of rising, and drove his best friends into opposition or sullen retirement. Middleton, not a man of religious conviction in the 1680's (perhaps he knew only what he did not believe), resisted the attempts to convert him but (unlike many others) held office to the end. There were reasons for his continued favor. He could not be driven to oppose: his temperament was unsuited to obstruction of his master's will. He had seen the contrast between his father's position before 1663 and that after he had lost the commissionership, and the son was not prepared to give up influence and power because he disagreed with the king. Although most Tories believed — with religious fervor — that subjects must obey a king whom they thought wrong or even unjust, many Tories found their belief untenable under King James and abandoned it. Middleton did not; he consistently obeyed, even when he must have disapproved.

[7] P.R.O., P.R.O. 31/3/164, fols. 256–59.

Because Middleton was rendered vulnerable by the king's distrust of Protestants, it has been said that James instructed his envoys abroad to write to Middleton only of "common news or public transactions," reserving important subjects for Sunderland, who was a partner to James's religious plans.[8] Professor M. A. Thomson has taken these remarks at face value, but they are based on a misconception. Middleton and Sunderland were not rivals; they clashed only on the religious issue, in 1687, and Sunderland won. They were, in fact, old acquaintances, and Sunderland had done Middleton more than one good turn. Powerful attacks on Middleton were made, not by Sunderland, but by the Drummond brothers. But how could Middleton have been denied knowledge of important affairs? He was a secretary of state, he spent secret-service money, and he maintained good relations with courtiers and with the Tories whom James alienated. If James ever intended to keep Middleton in the dark, he must soon have realized that this was impossible and that secrecy would have impeded his undertakings. The many volumes of Middleton papers in the British Museum and official papers in the Public Record Office bear witness that Middleton carried his full share of the responsibilities of the secretaries of state; they are full of secret matters that Professor Thomson appears to have thought had been kept from the secretary. Only the common preference for the accessible narrative source can have made ignorance of the facts possible.

Sunderland, the senior secretary, was willing to sacrifice his religious opinions in order to keep the king's favor, and he did so, reaching a pinnacle of unpopularity not often reached in English history. He corresponded with envoys responsible to Middleton, but Middleton corresponded regularly with envoys in Sunderland's department — particularly with Sir Richard Bulstrode at Brussels. No rule forbade such correspondence, which had been a common practice with other secretaries before the reign of James II, but the information given to Sunderland by his correspondents in Middleton's province was usually given much more fully to Middleton. The envoys seem

[8] Clarke (ed.), *Life of King James the Second*, II, 99–100; P.R.O., P.R.O. 31/3/167, fol. 49.

to have wished to make friends of both secretaries for protection of their interests at home.[9]

There is only one exception to the rule that Middleton knew what was going on as early as anyone else at court; he did not take part in discussions of religious subjects in the "Catholic council" or in the Ecclesiastical Commission, and Sunderland did. Thus the king must have decided on steps favoring Catholics of which Middleton, for a time, did not know, but the interval was probably short. The king was indiscreet, and when he began to carry out a decision he needed the work of both secretaries, so that Middleton had to know what James had decided. The Ecclesiastical Commission's government of the Church of England could also have been no secret to a secretary of state, and Middleton must have intentionally excluded himself from its membership. In 1688, Middleton could show the new government a clear record on the religious issue.

Middleton's willingness to obey, although he refused conversion, had other things to commend it. Protestants who were revolted by Sunderland's cheapness naturally preferred to approach the king through Middleton; in this way, Middleton was useful to them and, whether James knew it or not, also useful to the royal cause. This was one of many advantages James threw away, but he did not lose it entirely by dismissing Middleton from his service. The junior secretary of state remained in service, and eventually replaced Sunderland as the senior.

Although Sunderland was a member of the commission set up to prepare for James's coronation ceremony and celebrations, Middleton appears to have no part in it. Two other privy councillors who were not English peers marched in the procession, but Middleton did not — perhaps to avoid having too many Scotsmen about. Presumably at Whitehall during most

---

[9] See, e.g., Sir George Etherege's letter to Sunderland, cited by Professor Thomson to support his contention. Etherege, *Letterbook*, ed. Sybil Rosenfeld (London, 1928), p. 58. Etherege refers Sunderland to Middleton for full news in other letters (*ibid.*, pp. 103, 134–35). A more convincing but untenable argument could have been made from Skelton to Sunderland (June 13/23, 1685, P.R.O., S.P. 84/220, fol. 5). In April, 1685, Skelton wrote to Middleton asking approval for having written directly to the king (B.M., Add. MS 41,812, fols. 22–23).

of the festivities, attending to business, Middleton missed the omens of the reign.[10] The horse of the king's champion "broke loose and run into the church up to the very chancel"; the canopy broke over the king's head "at the church door, as he was coming out"; the fireworks "succeeded but pitifully, drooping all aside." [11]

There was plenty of business to do that spring of 1685; while Monmouth and Argyle moved in Holland and discontented persons in England circulated libels, the king ordered the issuance of writs for the election of a new parliament, so that there was also election work to do. Middleton, as a Scotsman, had neither hereditary nor acquired electoral influence, and therefore little direct contact with the king's efforts to obtain the choice of Tories in the counties and boroughs, but he seems to have played a role in winning over members once they had been chosen. The management of elections was done by others in royal favor: by Sunderland and by such borough patrons as the Duke of Albemarle and the earls of Bath and Yarmouth; the Marquis of Halifax (whose position at court was tottering) still used his influence for court candidates.[12] But there were limits to the king's control of elections, and James must also have concluded understandings with some men who would have been elected solely through their own interest.

It was to the king's advantage to have one of his secretaries of state in the House of Commons. Sunderland, as an English peer, was ineligible, but several Scottish peers had sat in the house since 1620, and it was therefore possible and desirable for Middleton to secure election. James, rather than ask a borough patron for a safe seat for his candidate, or enter Middleton in a doubtful race, used a tradition of the Cinque Ports. Each of these ancient and privileged towns returned two members, and it had long been the custom that each choose as one of its members a man nominated by the Lord Warden of the Cinque Ports; in effect, these members were crown nominees. On James II's accession the mayors, bailiffs, and other persons of the Cinque Ports had jointly acknowledged the lord warden's

[10] B.M., Add. MS 41,823, fols. 11–13.

[11] R. B. Weldon, "Course & Rough First Draught . . . ," B.M., Add. MS 10,118, fol. 117.

[12] J. P. Kenyon, *Robert Spencer, Earl of Sunderland, 1641–1702* (London, 1958), p. 114 n.

"right of recommendation,"[13] and Middleton was probably nominated by the king to a seat for Winchelsea, which elected him on April 11, 1685. An expression of the king's will was enough to elect Middleton; the new member of parliament had probably not even visited the town as a candidate.

Not all of the elections were so easily won (the Earl of Danby's son was rejected by Buckingham, in spite of his father's advice, which he presumably followed, to threaten the town with loss of its town house or assizes). On the whole, the king was fortunate: besides Middleton, two senior privy councillors (Sir Leoline Jenkins and Sir Thomas Chicheley) were chosen, and the rank and file of the new House of Commons were predominantly Tory. A member on whom the king especially relied was Richard Graham, Viscount Preston, his envoy to France and a new privy councillor. As Sir Richard Graham, Preston had been a member of several parliaments since 1675 and had defended the hereditary succession during the Exclusion Bill crisis. Of Scottish ancestry, and a peer of Scotland, he had been an enemy of Lauderdale[14] and had distinguished himself by his support of Charles II in the Scottish parliament.

James gave the responsibility of managing the House of Commons to Middleton and Preston jointly, an unusual arrangement in two respects: both leaders were Scots, and Middleton was a new member. Talk of "Scotch vermin" must have grown intense among the Whigs, but there was no open expression of disgruntlement. Middleton and Preston were lucky: both had resided in England for many years and both had many English friends. (Preston had the additional advantage that his parents had lived in England many years before his birth.) The House of Commons accepted its leaders without a murmur; they had the king's favor, patronage, and wrath at their disposal, and they were of the majority party. As individuals, both were acceptable to the house, and the opposition had no plan for organized resistance to the king's proposals or his managers. Disaffection among the "electing classes" of England had been subdued, if not destroyed.

The House of Commons assembled in the morning of

[13] Address of March 31, in *London Gazette*, April 13–16, 1685.
[14] Anchitel Grey, *Debates in the House of Commons, 1667–1694* (10 vols.; London, 1763), VII, 408–9; V, 358, 381; VII, 188–89.

May 19/29, 1685. The Duke of Ormond, the lord high steward, administered the statutory oaths of allegiance and supremacy to some of the members, who then did the same for others. Many had taken the oaths when the members were summoned to the House of Lords to hear the king open parliament; they returned afterwards to their own meeting place. Middleton then informed the house that the king directed that it elect Sir John Trevor Speaker. The house unanimously approved the king's choice, and Middleton and Henry Savile conducted Trevor to the speaker's chair. In the afternoon the house presented Trevor to the king, who approved the election and granted the commons its customary privileges. (It was observed that Trevor read a prepared speech of thanks to the king, contrary to custom.)[15] The house then returned to its oath taking; it did not begin business until May 22.

The secretary of state and joint leader was busy, insuring at the last minute his master's control of the house. At the end of the day, May 19, Middleton wrote Bevil Skelton at The Hague: "I was never so weary in my life."[16] But to the Prince of Orange he wrote of his satisfaction with the members: "I cannot doubt of their dutiful compliance with his majesty's desires, which will be a great disappointment to the rebels [Monmouth and his friends abroad] in the meantime; all necessary orders are given to prevent their attempts."[17]

On May 22, when the members had been sworn, the king summoned the house once more, to hear his speech in the House of Lords. In a conciliatory message James declared his intention to "defend and support" the Church of England, to "preserve this government, both in church and state, as it is now by law established, . . . never [to] depart from the just rights and prerogative of the crown, [and] never to invade any man's property." He desired that parliament settle the revenue and use him well.[18] According to the Modenese resident in London, the speech was several times interrupted by "applause

---

[15] Journals of the House of Commons [henceforth *J.H.C.*], Vol. 9, *1667–1687* (London, 1803), 713; Cambridge University Library [henceforth C.U.L.], MS Mm. 1. 51, fol. 102.

[16] B.M., Add. MS 41,823, fol. 16.

[17] Letter of May 19, *ibid.*

[18] *J.H.C.*, p. 714. Kenyon interprets this request as "truculent" (p. 117). The parliament did not. Cf. Ranke, *History of England*, IV, 234–35.

and acclamations."[19] In closing, James also told the houses that
the Earl of Argyle had landed in the western islands of Scotland and had begun a rebellion against the government. The
commons withdrew, voted thanks to the king for his speech,
and — after deliberation in a committee of the whole house —
ordered the preparation of a bill for settling the king's revenue.

Edward Seymour, however, a former speaker, raised opposition. According to the fullest report,

Mr. Seymour . . . spoke to this purpose, that though he had heard
many in that house apprehend great danger of popery, he was never
afraid of it while the elections of parliament kept its true channel, but
now they had by their new charters altered the old way and chosen
representatives themselves, without the knowledge and against
the wills of the inhabitants that they represent in very many parts of
the kingdom, even to the number of 2 or 300 members. Therefore
he desired that none who were come in upon controverted elections
upon new charters might be of the committee for elections to judge of
others' right to sit there, when they had none of their own.[20]

This went too far: many members would have been affected
by such a prejudged verdict and others were unwilling to make
enemies. Seymour won no support for his position.

On May 23 the House of Commons received petitions concerning disputed elections and referred them to the committee
of elections and privileges, of which Middleton and Preston
were members. In the midst of this tedious work Middleton
received from the king a copy of a declaration issued by Argyle,
which contained this inflammatory paragraph:

I have now, with God's strength, suffered patiently my unjust sentence and banishment three years and a half, and have never offered
to make any uproar or defence by arms, to disturb the peace, upon
my private concern: but the king [Charles II] being now dead, and
the Duke of York having taken off his mask and having abandoned
and invaded our religion and liberties, resolving to enter into the
government, and exercises contrary to law, I think it not only just,

[19] C.U.L., Add. MS 4,836, fol. 17.
[20] Dr. Williams' Library, Morrice MS P., fol. 462; Giacomo Ronchi to
the Duke of Modena, June 22, 1685, Archivio di Stato, Modena, Cancelleria
Ducale, Oratori e Ambasciatori, Inghilterra [henceforth cited as A.S.M.],
Busta IV.

but my duty to God and my country, to use my utmost endeavours to oppose and repress his usurpation and tyranny.[21]

Argyle thus denied James II's right to rule but did not say where the true right lay—although members of parliament thought of Monmouth. The house resolved, without opposition, to "stand by, and assist his majesty with their lives and fortunes against *Archibald Campbell* [Earl of Argyle] . . . and all rebels and traitors."[22] The house then returned to its election petitions, until it was time to attend King James for the purpose of giving him its resolution and receiving his answer—a happy one:

I could not expect less from a House of Commons so composed as (God be thanked) you are.

I rely on the assurances you have given me, which are the natural effects of your being monarchical and Church of *England* men. I will stand by all such: and, so supported, have no reason to fear any rebels or enemies I have, or may have.[23]

The Tory members were satisfied with this reply. "All things seemed now to look very auspicious." Sir John Reresby wrote later, "The king not giving the least token to change the religion, but much the contrary."[24] A bill to give James II for life the same revenue his brother had received was introduced earlier that same day and soon was passed by both houses. (James had been collecting the customs and excise duties since February without legal sanction.) By the end of May he had the parliamentary grant he needed.[25]

On May 26, an incident which is not recorded in the Journals of the House of Commons but became generally known occurred. When someone (we would like to know who) began a motion to "set a discriminating mark" on the members who in previous parliaments had supported the Exclusion Bill, "the Lord Middleton stood up and said he had command from his majesty to acquaint them that, as he had forgiven, so he would forget all things that had been acted there against him as Duke

[21] *J.H.C.*, pp. 715–17; *London Gazette*, May 21–25, 1685.
[22] *J.H.C.*, p. 717.
[23] *Ibid.*, p. 718.
[24] Reresby, *Memoirs*, ed. A. Browning (Glasgow, 1936), p. 367.
[25] *J.H.C.*, pp. 716, 718, 719; *London Gazette*, May 28–June 1, 1685.

of York."[26] The motion got no further; the house instead ordered that votes against the king — while he had been Duke of York — should be expunged from its journals by a committee.

A proposal to address the king to put into execution the laws against all dissenters (including Catholic recusants) seems to have been put forward by the opposition, but the house — not yet distrustful of the king — decided to offer James an address expressing its satisfaction with his promise to support and defend the Church of England.[27]

On May 30 the king assented to the bill for settling his revenue. Thanking the two houses he asked for a supply of money for the navy and for the suppression of the rebellion in Scotland. The two Sir John Lowthers again tried to raise objection to seating members elected by remodeled corporations, but the house resolved in favor of a supply and ordered that a suitable bill be brought in on June 1. The bill was brought in, taxes to provide the money were approved, and the House of Lords concurred on the bill on June 5.

The king had received his supply of money in unusually short time. More than one contemporary thought the procedure irregular — that voting on a motion of supply on the same day it had been proposed was a breach of rules. Sir John Bramston also thought the procedure in settling the revenue incorrect,

such was the eagerness of the house to comply with the crown, and such was the ignorance (shall I say, or non-acquaintance rather) of the managers which appeared, I mean the Earl of Middleton and the Lord Preston, who put these country gentlemen on the motion (and yet the Lord Preston and Mr. Strangways had served long in former parliaments).[28]   .

A good House of Commons man might well say so, looking back on James II's reign. But Middleton and Preston were working for the king, not for the house; their duty was to get

[26] P.R.O., Adm. 78/2, p. 91; Lauder, *Historical Observes*, p. 172; B.M., Add. MS 10,118, fol. 140; B.M., Add. MS 17,677 GG, fol. 294.

[27] *J.H.C.*, pp. 719, 721; Dr. Williams' Library, Morrice MS P, fols. 462–64.

[28] Bramston, *Autobiography* (London: The Camden Society, XXXII, 1845), p. 199. Was the procedure irregular? See Browning, *Danby*, I, 262.

money quickly and with as few conditions as possible, and from this point of view their management was superb.[29] The critics, by the way, said nothing of the rules when it would have made any difference to do so. (During this period of harmony, both houses approved reversal of the judgment against Viscount Stafford, who had suffered death during the "Popish plot" frenzy. The only recorded resistance was made in the House of Lords.)

On June 13, after a bill to enable Protestant aliens to practice trades in certain places had been scheduled for another reading,

the Earl of *Middleton* acquainted the house . . . that his majesty had this morning received advice, as well by letter from the Mayor of *Lyme in Dorsetshire*, as by two messengers come from thence . . . that the Duke of *Monmouth*, with the late [attainted] Lord *Grey*, was landed in a hostile manner, with many men and arms. . . .[30]

The House of Commons returned its thanks to James for the notification, resolved it would stand by him, and set up a committee (whose members included Middleton and Preston) to prepare a bill of attainder against Monmouth. It then returned to bills for the regulation of hackney coaches and to prevent the importation of foreign buttons.

The bill of attainder was read for the first time on June 15. Bills imposing a duty on sugars and tobacco, to make up the king's supply, were passed, and the lords concurred on June 16. Another supply bill began its legislative course on June 17, and the king gave his assent on June 27. On June 22, Middleton reported the capture of the Earl of Argyle.

The session was now inconvenient to the government. A number of members were officers, either in the regular army or in the militia, and others, as leading loyalists, should be at home giving support to the government during the crisis. The king gave notice, on June 18, that he would adjourn parliament after the second supply had been granted, and on July 2 he ordered adjournment until August 4.

[29] Cf. Thomson: "The only task of importance committed to Middleton was the management of the Commons during the short Parliament of 1685, and this task he performed none too well" (*Secretaries of State*, p. 5). Thomson appears to have thought that the king's management was in opposition to the king.

[30] *J.H.C.*, p. 735. Cf. the fragment of a parliamentary report, P.R.O., Adm. 77/2, item 142.

Middleton had been taxed to the limit of his strength during this six-week session — in the house, in committees, and in the secretary's office. On June 10, for instance, Lord Moray reported to the Marquis of Queensberry that Middleton had been detained so late in parliament that he had missed a meeting with the king about Scottish affairs. Moray wrote again, on June 13: "I have not had three minutes time to speak with E. Middleton this week past, he is still taken up attending the House of Commons, and tells me he can not get time to eat or sleep." [31] The rebellions added greatly to his urgent correspondence; he could hardly pose as a lazy man.

Despite many distractions, James II's first session of parliament was a success; the two managers deserved much credit for it. The king himself had lent a hand in the work, for without the benevolent expressions in James's speeches, Middleton and Preston could have done nothing.

[31] H.M.C., *Drumlanrig (Buccleuch MSS)*, II, 77.

CHAPTER V

Monmouth's Rebellion
and Its Aftermath

The landings of Argyle and Monmouth did not completely surprise the government; it was aware that the Whigs were desperate and that they had been collecting arms for just such
attempts. Monmouth had gone abroad after the detection of
the Rye House Plot, in disgrace because though professedly
repentant he had refused to break with the other conspirators
by openly informing on them. Nevertheless Charles II had
hoped his beloved natural son would eventually reverse his
course. In the meantime Charles took special care of Monmouth's deserted wife. To the government's alarm, the Rye
House Plot fugitives and other malcontents flocked about the
duke wherever he went, and, to its disgust, the authorities of
the Dutch republic and the Spanish Netherlands gave Monmouth official countenance in his travels through their territories.

The death of Charles II changed Monmouth's position.
William of Orange, who could not afford to quarrel with the
new king of England, submitted to James II's wishes and left
Monmouth alone, at least in public. Persons designated as
obnoxious by the English government lost their commissions
in the Dutch service,[1] and the Dutch States General took other
steps to compel the dissidents from England to avoid giving
offense to James. The conspirators were therefore forced to
attack James and stir up rebellion at once or to abandon their
hopes and sue for mercy. Some of them would have died

[1] B.M., Add. MS 41,810, fol. 266.

rather than ask pardon; others feared that pardon would be denied them.

Even before Charles II's death, Middleton had received word that some of the fugitives at Groningen had "erected a tribunal amongst themselves, inquired into his majesty's [Charles's] rights, and afterwards very formally deposed him declaring all persons traitors that should adhere to him."[2] These could not have been primarily supporters of Monmouth, who believed he was Charles II's heir. (Perhaps they were republicans.) Others openly treated Monmouth as the king's legitimate son; some recognized James II as rightful king but reserved their right to rebel against him. Still others were little better than criminals, with no special theory but a sharp eye for pardons and rewards from Monmouth. These men of very diverse beliefs and intentions were Monmouth's supporters abroad.

The privy council had stopped the ports during Charles II's last illness, had secured control of the army, and had proclaimed James II throughout the country. These measures, followed by the king's promises to the Church of England and his prompt summons and assembly of parliament, had taken the wind out of the malcontents' sails. There could be a rebellion only if Monmouth went to England and, as neither Monmouth nor Argyle hoped to make peace with James, they decided to venture their lives by landing in Great Britain.[3] Their supporters, meanwhile, dispersed written matter and spread rumors, playing on James's Catholicism, and there were many conferences at the plotters' principal centers, especially Rotterdam.

The government used every resource to learn their intentions. On April 10/20, Bevil Skelton, the English envoy at The Hague, wrote Middleton that he had heard a landing was to be made in the west of England and that emissaries had already gone to prepare the way. The next week he reported that the conspirators had been invited by persons in "the highlands and other parts of Scotland" to send a leader for a rising there.[4] Despite Skelton's efforts to prevent it, Argyle got off

---

[2] Newsletter, Jan. 24, 1684/85, B.M., Add. MS 41,803, fol. 115.
[3] Monmouth was extremely slow in making up his mind; see W. R. Emerson, *Monmouth's Rebellion* (New Haven, 1951), pp. 10–18.
[4] B.M., Add. MS 41,812, fol. 16, 26–27.

from Holland in early May.[5] Middleton conveyed the king's orders that Skelton press the Prince of Orange for the expulsion of disloyal English from Dutch territory and to stop a frigate and two other ships said to be fitted out at Amsterdam, with arms for the Scottish rising. Action was urgent, and Middleton instructed Skelton to make it clear to the prince that James II "will not be paid with words."[6]

When Argyle's ships touched at the Orkneys on their way to western Scotland, two of his men who went ashore were captured and tortured by the authorities (under Scottish law) to make them decipher Argyle's intercepted letters. Anticipating possible need, Middleton signified the king's desire to have the regiments of his subjects in the Dutch service sent over to help suppress rebellion at home; this request may also have been a test of Dutch sincerity after the failure, perhaps refusal, to prevent embarkations for Scotland. Some believed the Dutch government was helping Argyle and Monmouth, contrary to understandings with James II; on the other hand, the Tuscan resident reported that "adherents of Spain" believed France was defraying the cost of the rebels' preparations in Holland.[7] The country was oversupplied with rumors until May 23, when the first word of Argyle's landing reached London; thereafter, his movements were followed by the authorities in Scotland, and reported to the king, and accounts were published in the *London Gazette*.

Reports of Monmouth's intentions and actions, however, were vague, until Gregory Alford, the mayor of Lyme, wrote Middleton on June 11, 1685, "near 12 at night," to tell him that Monmouth had landed with 300 men west of Lyme on the coast of Dorsetshire.[8] (Probably on the basis of later information, the *London Gazette* halved the number of men in its report.) Monmouth actually brought only eighty men to fight for him. Three deputy lieutenants of western counties forwarded to Middleton a copy of Monmouth's declaration to

---

[5] Emerson (pp. 35–44) has accepted the charge that William of Orange allowed Monmouth and Argyle to depart so as to play them off against James, and manuscript evidence which Emerson did not see supports his opinion; viz., B.M., Add. MS 41,812, fols. 47–48, 57–60; Add. MS 41,822, fols. 258–59, 262–63; P.R.D., S.P. 84/220, fol. 5.

[6] B.M., Add. MS 41,823, fol. 11.

[7] B.M., Add. MS 25,370, fol. 115.

[8] B.M., Add. MS 41,803, fols. 292–93.

the people; militia officers described their efforts to recruit and train their men for active service, local officials their steps to apprehend suspected rebels.[9] Although the militia was inexperienced, and some of its members were unreliable, Lord Lumley, who had been in the Low Countries with Middleton in 1677, was pleasantly surprised with the conduct of the men of his command, who were "all very willing, and more orderly than I expected from such a sort of people."[10]

As the rebellion sped on toward disaster, suspects became anxious to clear themselves: Colonel Richard Norton, who wrote Middleton that he had known the secretary's father well, maintained he had been loyal "since [James II] came to the throne."[11] Middleton was beseiged by such people, and by informers as well, and was harried by officials who demanded orders or instructions. He was also concerned for the king and for himself, until the Earl of Argyle was captured in Scotland, and until Monmouth's disorderly army was defeated at Sedgemoor on July 5. Monmouth fled from the field, disguised in a carter's frock, but the king's men captured him at Horton, in Dorsetshire, on the morning of July 8 and recognized him by his Garter ribbon and emblem. The king's friends were elated.

Monmouth and his friend and fellow rebel Lord Grey were then taken to London. Monmouth's attainder by parliament had cleared the way for execution without trial. (Trial would have done the duke little good.) Monmouth threw himself on James II's mercy and appealed for a personal interview. James had to choose between being condemned for refusing an interview and being condemned for granting an interview and raising hopes when he had already decided that Monmouth must die. Pardon was truly impossible. Monmouth had been James's rival for several years, and in 1683 had conspired against James's liberty; he had assumed the royal title during the rebellion and had made war on the king; now he begged for family feeling, having shown none. He was willing to bind himself not to rebel again, but he was so indiscreet and unstable that James could not rely on his promise; moreover, he was

[9] *Ibid.*, fols. 301–2, 318, 329–30.
[10] *Ibid.*, fols. 333–34.
[11] *Ibid.*, fols. 335–36.

responsible for the deaths of hundreds of the king's subjects.

James gave the interview, with both secretaries of state present and taking down all that Monmouth had to say. Pardon was denied, and the prisoner was sent to the Tower of London. On the eve of the execution, Middleton wrote that the duke was "more dejected than ever woman was . . . [but] you may guess we are merrily disposed, and sure people never had more reason to be so. . . ."[12] He recorded Monmouth's words on the scaffold without sentiment.

At his death he showed as little judgment as in his life; he declared he died of the Church of England, and yet maintained opinions, not only contrary to hers, but contradictory in themselves he said he was sorry for the invasion, but would not call it a rebellion; he would not acknowledge that it was unlawful to resist authority, he would not own the Duchess of Monmouth to be his only wife, nor would he deny his being married to Lady H[enrietta] Wentworth [the duke's mistress], he talked of nothing so willingly as her praises; he said he had led so innocent a life these last two years that he had nothing to repent of, and concluded with that fanatical illusion, that he had a full assurance of his salvation; and this seeming contradiction may truly be observed of him, that none ever showed a greater desire of life nor less fear of death.[13]

Unsentimental is the best word for the punishment of the rebels in 1685. The king's soldiers cut down many in the battle and the pursuit — as Monmouth's rustic rebels would have cut down the soldiers had the battle gone the other way. We hear of hanging without trial at that time, but the evidence of it is vague; perhaps one day it will be cleared up for us. Many captives lived to be tried.

No one now would call the trials of 1685 either fair or merciful — Justice Jeffreys, later Lord Chancellor and Lord Jeffreys of Wem, was by all accounts a brute on the bench — but most of the prisoners were guilty, as proof went in the seventeenth century, and the king pardoned many. Years later, the pamphleteer, Charles Hornby, wrote:

I have sometimes thought, that in Jeffreys his western circuit, justice went too far before mercy was remembered, though there

[12] B.M., Add. MS 41,823, fols. 20–21.
[13] *Ibid.*, fols. 21–22.

was not above a fourth part executed of what were convicted; but when I considered in what manner several of those lives then spared were afterwards spent, as may be instanced in their late scribbler *Tutchin*, and many others, I cannot but think a little more hemp might have been usefully employed on that occasion.[14]

Hornby might also have mentioned Lord Grey, who lived on by benefit of James II's mercy, to be one of the worst enemies of the government.

There were certainly many pardons, and the king granted to courtiers the money paid by petitioners for their pardon — just as he granted away fines.[15] Except in a few cases, the guilt of the petitioner was clear; nevertheless, many of them were pardoned — and might have thought themselves fortunate that they or their families were only mulcted by the king's allies. It was indeed unfair that examples were made from among the poor and friendless, while the wealthy and well connected were usually pardoned; one may condemn the social system of the time with its assumption of "class justice," but James did not make the system, and surely Lords Grey and Delamere (who escaped punishment) would have been the last to complain of the social inequality that saved them.

Middleton appears to have had no share in the payments made by any English prisoner. The Cochrane family, however, accused him of taking a bribe from its head, the Earl of Dundonald. Sir John Cochrane of Ochiltree and his son John Cochrane of Watersyde had returned from abroad to take part in the rebellion and the authorities had captured them. They got off, according to the family's story, because Dundonald bought Watersyde's property back from Middleton for three times its market price. The charge is serious, but there is more plausible reason why the Cochranes escaped the legal punishment appropriate to their actions. Sir John Cochrane had been in correspondence with one of Charles II's secretaries of state in the autumn of 1683; after he had fled his country, in custody in 1685, he and his son confessed their offenses and gave the

[14] Charles Hornby, *A Second Part of the Caveat against the Whiggs, &c,* (2d ed.; London, 1712), p. 22.

[15] David Ogg attacked the whole Stuart family for a lack of clemency on one page and recorded the sums paid for pardon on another: Ogg, *England in the Reigns of James II and William III* (Oxford, 1955), pp. 149–53.

government valuable information.[16] Apparently, Dundonald bought Watersyde's property to keep it in the family, and Middleton sold it because the price was good. Had Middleton wanted a bribe, he could easily have had it, and the property as well.

Many rebels — such as the Cochranes — betrayed their friends; and other persons proved their loyalty by denouncing their neighbors. Two witnesses, for instance, accused a Mrs. Lee of having furnished the money for printing Monmouth's declaration, but the woman had the good sense to surrender herself on hearing of the charge; as Sir Charles Sedley, the rakish poet, wrote to Middleton on her behalf, she may have been able to exculpate herself. A person or persons unknown denounced Alderman Elcock of York, but the king ordered him discharged, taking into account "his demeanour in the said city at the time his majesty past by into Scotland, and also . . . his great age."[17] Several witnesses offered testimony about events of this period in Middleton's presence. His office collected news for several months, directing the pursuit of the rebels and suspects who were still at large. Those who escaped abroad later became one of the great problems of James II's foreign policy, but, for the time being, James apparently sat secure on his throne, celebrating his birthday on October 14, with fireworks, artillery salutes, bonfires, and a ball.

Although parliament had been adjourned until August 4, the king had not intended that it would meet on that day, because he did not expect the country to be settled. As the houses began to assemble, they received the message of further adjournment, until November 9, 1685. By November, the "Bloody Assizes" of Judge Jeffreys were concluded and most of those who had been condemned had been pardoned, executed, or transported. The nation was settled, but signs of dissatisfaction were appearing among the king's friends.

As early as July, the Tuscan resident had noticed that the

---

[16] B.L., Rawlinson MS A. 266, pp. 29, 38; B.M., Add. MS 41,809, fols. 138–46; B.M., Add. MS 10,118, fols. 122, 127. Cf. Morrice MS P, pp. 491, 535 (Dr. Williams' Library).

[17] B.M., Add. MS 41,823, fol. 120.

employment of Catholic officers in the hastily expanded army gave offense to Protestants.[18] (James had always intended to reward the leading Catholics of the country for their loyalty, at the same time showing Protestants that they could become Catholics and still be promoted to public office.) At the onset of the rebellion, the king had employed Catholics only as volunteers, because the legal requirement of oaths disqualified them for commissions, but he later dispensed with the law for these men. It remains to this day a vexed question whether, in 1685, he had a constitutional power to do so. If he had not, this was his first serious breach of law, as Lord Halifax pointed out in the privy council during the summer. We cannot know why he began the career of blunders which culminated in the Revolution of 1688. Perhaps the opportunity afforded by the military crisis tempted him; perhaps the friendly disposition of parliament during its first session blinded him to the assumptions upon which its apparent good will was based; perhaps the quick success of his army made him confident that he could deal with any opposition. Whatever his reasoning, James did not take into account the fears awakened in England by the growing religious persecution in France, in which military power played an important part.

Parliament assembled on November 9. James II spoke to the two houses, thanking God for the restoration of peace, but tactlessly referring to the inadequacy of the militia for the defense of the country (many members held commissions in the militia). He said that he felt compelled to keep a larger standing army thereafter, for which he would need more money. He did not doubt that parliament would cheerfully supply him.

Let no man take exception, that there are some officers in the army, not qualified, according to the late tests, for their employments: the gentlemen, I must tell you, are most of them well known to me: and, having formerly served with me on several occasions, and always approved the loyalty of their principles by their practice, I think fit now to be employed under me: and I will deal plainly with you, that after having had the benefit of their service in such time of need and danger, I will neither expose them to disgrace, nor myself to the want of them, if there should be another rebellion to make them necessary to me.

[18] B.M., Add. MS 25,370, fol. 259.

James offered his certain belief that there would be no quarrel between parliament and himself on this subject, assured parliament of his kindness for it, and declared his "resolution to venture even my own life in the defence of the true interest of this kingdom."[19]

James must have thought out that speech carefully, and its reasoning is sound — as far as it goes. Many agreed that the militia was generally of poor quality; the Catholic officers had Protestant friends in both houses, and no one seriously doubted their loyalty to the king; parliament had already given money for the fleet and for the suppression of the rebellion and might well have given more for a larger army. James did not foresee that members of the houses would be excited to opposition by his cool suspension of the test acts; he certainly gave his Protestant friends no reassurance.

After the commons had withdrawn to its meeting place, Middleton seized the stage to move that the house immediately return thanks to the king for his speech "and also proceed to the consideration of answering the ends therein mentioned." His proposal was too sudden, and the house, after "some debate," resolved instead to consider the speech in a committee of the whole house. Sir Edward Jennings and Sir Thomas Clarges are reported to have led the opposition, an interesting partnership, for Jennings was a friend of Danby and Clarges a friend of Halifax.[20]

Deliberations in committee took place on November 12, when Middleton, more cautious after his first check, moved that the speech be considered by paragraphs, so that supply of money would have priority over the question of the Catholic officers. Anchitel Grey gives a fairly full account of what was said. The staunch Tory, Sir Winston Churchill, favored the supply; Lord Preston argued for an increase in the regular army, pointing out the need of troops "for preservation of ourselves and Flanders" and the good effects of the king's military strength in foreign affairs; the Earl of Ranelagh also took the king's side. Sir Thomas Clarges was the first recorded speaker against a supply, contending that the militia had done "con-

[19] *J.H.C.*, pp. 755–56.
[20] *J.H.C.*, p. 756; Grey, *Debates in the House of Commons, 1667–1674*, VIII, 354; Dr. Williams' Library, Morrice MS P, pp. 493, 496.

siderable service in the late rebellion." Clarges reckoned that parliament had already given four million pounds, and that the king's revenue exceeded his expenses by as much as six hundred thousand pounds a year. He professed affliction that Catholics could secure public employment contrary to the law of the land, and he urged the house to resolve "that a standing army is destructive to the country." Sir John Ernley, a privy councillor, replied that standing forces were necessary "to aid and help the militia" and that parliament ought to give the king half the cost; indeed, a tax on "commodities" for that purpose might improve the balance of trade.

Two members defended the militia: one of these, strangely, dreaded a standing army but favored a supply. The discussion then became general; King Henry V, the yeomen of the guard, the natural indolence of soldiers, and the powers of lords lieutenant were brought into it. Members avoided attacking the king and instead argued principle. Sir Richard Temple took a practical line: "We have already made an ample supply for the government. It is for kings to come to the house, from time to time, on extraordinary occasions; and if this army be provided for by law, they will never more come to this house." [21]

Nevertheless, after the committee session, the house resolved, without a contrary voice, that the king should have a supply and that a bill should be brought in for the improvement of the militia. The House of Commons was still tractable and willing to compromise, and it was expected to become even more friendly to the king, for some absent supporters of the court were due to arrive shortly.

The next day, November 13, the house — on Middleton's motion — again considered the king's speech in a committee of the whole; commons had to decide "whether to go on with supply or proceed to the next paragraph" — the Catholic officers. According to a manuscript account written for the Modenese resident, Sir Edward Seymour, who had attempted to foment opposition in the first session, attacked the employment of Catholics and argued that the house should give no money to the king before the Protestant religion was made secure. Seymour was supported by Lord Falkland, the treasurer of the

[21] Anchitel Grey, *Debates*, VIII, 355–59. Cf. B.M., Harleian MS 4,187, fol. 161.

navy. Sixteen supposed adherents of the court absented themselves, and seven or eight who held valuable offices voted
against a motion to proceed with supply before dealing with
the Catholic officers. The motion failed by one vote, 182 to
183. Lord Preston, Bramston says, used a devious parliamentary maneuver to delay consideration of the Catholic officers
until the next day.[22]

That evening James feared complete defeat in the House
of Commons. He told Sir John Reresby, a late arrival, that
he was sorry Reresby had not come before, and that his defeat
was "hard, and the more so because he lost it by his own officers."[23] The leaders attempted to rally the officeholders to vote
with the court; Macaulay tells of Middleton's encounter with
Captain James Kendall, member for West Looe. " 'Sir,' said
Middleton, 'have you not a troop of horse in his majesty's
service?' 'Yes, my Lord,' answered Kendall, 'but my elder
brother is just dead, and has left me seven hundred a year.' "[24]

On November 14, however, the house was still not in determined opposition, and there was doubt as to the wisdom of
any address to James II on the Catholic officers. "Some seemed
to doubt his majesty's compliance. Others that it was not to be
doubted, when addressed by such a house."[25] Some members
recognized that the case of the Catholic officers as individuals
was a hard one and proposed such compromises as giving
them pensions, permitting those already serving to continue
if no more were added, or allowing the king a limited number
of Catholic officers. Others — "very many," according to the
Modenese resident's account — wished to get rid of all the
Catholic officers with no more ado. Sir Thomas Clarges, Sir
Edmund Jennings, and Richard Hampden led the opposition
in this debate. The Committee of the Whole House recommended an address to the king for the dismissal of the Catholic
officers coupled with a bill to indemnify them for serving while
unqualified. The house softened these recommendations, asking James "to give such directions, that no apprehensions or

[22] Sir John Bramston, *Autobiography*, p. 213.

[23] C.U.L., Add. MS 4,880, fol. 217; Sir John Reresby, *Memoirs*, p. 395.

[24] T. B. Macaulay, *History of England from the Accession of James II*,
ed. C. H. Firth (6 vols.; London, 1913–15), II, 687; see also Dr. Williams'
Library, Morrice MS P, p. 505.

[25] Grey, *Debates*, VIII, 361; B.M., Harleian MS 4,187, fol. 162.

jealousies may remain in the hearts of his majesty's good and faithful subjects."[26] Middleton, Preston, Clarges, Seymour, Jennings, Hampden, Falkland, Pepys, and Williamson were members of the committee that prepared the address.

The committee submitted a draft to the House of Commons on November 16; as a concession to Clarges and his supporters, it asserted that the disabilities of Catholics could be removed only by an act of parliament. The house approved the draft and ordered the privy councillors who were also members of the house to arrange a time for the delivery of the address. Debate on a grant of money followed: lines were quickly drawn, not between a supply and no supply, but between a large supply and a small one. Clarges said, "Let us give little now, to have opportunity to give more another time," that is, so that the king would continue to hold parliaments; Lord Camden, Sir Edmund Jennings, and others sided with Clarges. Lord Preston argued cogently that a revenue that had been grossly inadequate for Charles II would not suffice for James II; Preston proposed a grant of £1,200,000, in addition to the sums already approved (estimated at £6,000,000), to be paid over several years. Sir Winston Churchill — or perhaps Sir William Clifton — supported Preston tersely: "Soldiers move not without pay. No penny, no paternoster." The terrors of a brutal and licentious soldiery were conjured up by Thomas Coningsby. Defending court policy, Colonel Edward Ashton predicted, "Were not these forces standing, to prevent a rebellion, you would have one in a few days." William Blathwayt, secretary at war, assured the house that all neighboring states had proportionately larger armies, but Clarges replied that England's power was in its navy. In the end, the House of Commons resolved to give a supply "not exceeding the sum of seven hundred thousand pounds."[27]

The House of Commons presented its address on Catholic officers to King James on November 17, in the Presence Chamber at Whitehall. Having heard it, the king reproached the house:

[26] *J.H.C.*, p. 757; Grey, *Debates*, VIII, 361; Bramston, *Autobiography*, p. 214.

[27] Grey, *Debates*, VIII, 364–67; *J.H.C.*, p. 788; Bramston, *Autobiography*, pp. 214–15; Reresby, *Memoirs*, p. 396; B.M., Harleian MS 4,187, fols. 164–65; B.M., Lansdowne MS 253, fols. 47–53.

I did not expect such an address from the house of commons, having so lately recommended to your consideration the great advantages a good understanding between us had produced in a very short time, and given you warning of fears and jealousies amongst ourselves.

I had reason to hope, that the reputation God hath blessed me with in this world, would have created and confirmed a greater confidence in you of me, and of all that I say to you: but however you proceed on your part, I will be steady in all my promises I have made to you, and be very just to my word in this, and all my other speeches.[28]

This answer, cold but restrained, was communicated to the house by the speaker on November 18, but before a day could be fixed for its consideration, John Cooke, member for Derby, exploded: "We are all Englishmen; and we ought not to be frighted out of our duty by a few high words."[29] The house was instantly alarmed. When Preston asked Cooke to explain his words, Cooke said "he intended no ill" but that he could not remember what he had said — although the clerk had set down his words and several other witnesses confirmed them. Cooke withdrew until the house decided what to do about him.

The hot-headed member had clearly reflected upon the king, Sir Joseph Treadenham remarked, and Mr. Ashburnham said that to let the matter pass would be a reflection upon the house itself. Sir Hugh Cholmley and others vouched for Cooke's loyalty, but did not excuse his words; and Preston proposed sending Cooke to the Tower. Middleton supported Preston in a speech which was either inaccurately reported or comically incoherent.

The meaning of this seems like an incendiary. The Tower! This needs no aggravation. A reprimand for an offence to this house might do; but this does not end there; and it is a question whether it be in the power of this house to pass it by, the offense being to the king as well as you: I am for calling him to the bar in the first place.[30]

[28] Thus Grey, *Debates*, VIII, 369. *J.H.C.* (p. 759) omits several words in the second paragraph. Reresby, *Memoirs* (p. 397) supports Grey.

[29] *J.H.C.*, p. 760; Reresby, *Memoirs*, p. 398; Grey, *Debates*, VIII, 364; Bramston, *Autobiography*, p. 216.

[30] Grey, *Debates*, VIII, 369–70; B.M., Harleian MS 4,187, fol. 166; *J.H.C.*, p. 760; *Faithful Register*, pp. 27–28. The *Register* errs in attributing Cooke's speech to a Mr. Coventry. There was an interesting parallel to this case in

Cooke was sent to the Tower; the house thus dissociated itself from its most refractory member; it also deliberately or otherwise failed to name a day to discuss the king's answer to the address. (Cooke submitted to the king and went free later in the month.)

Election petitions were considered by the House of Commons on November 18. Its members were apparently quiet, but there were great debates in the House of Lords on the employment of the Catholic officers. Ranke has summarized the lords' debate in his *History of England,* but he seems to have missed the account of Ronchi.

The upper house yesterday moved the affair of the test, or of the Catholics who hold places in the army, which they [the lords] do not wish for their own ends (which tend always to the ill service of his majesty), and some lords spoke warmly and with concern, in order to move the others to follow them. Among the first was the Earl [actually Marquis] of Halifax, formerly president [of the council], who so as not to seem piqued but reasonable and dispassionate, had not yet opposed anything, reserving himself to do so in this case in which he encountered opposition. After the Bishop of London had also seconded the said earl in the name of all the bishops of the kingdom, the business was postponed to next Monday, but the king this morning came to parliament, and, complaining of their behavior, gave order to the Lord Chancellor, who prorogued it [parliament]. . . .[31]

Thus it was the debate in the House of Lords that made the king decide to prorogue parliament.[32] On November 20, when the king decided on this step, the House of Commons was making progress with the supply. Parliament was to meet again on February 10, 1685/6.

Some members, Sir John Reresby wrote later, conjectured that "the king had so good a revenue and was so good a man-

---

the Scottish parliament of 1681, so close that it proves Middleton was present on the earlier occasion; see *London Gazette,* Sept. 5–8, 1681. Ogg (*England in the Reigns of James II and William III,* p. 161) sees the 1685 incident as "interference with freedom of debate." It was obviously discipline by the House of Commons of one of its members, a cherished privilege.

[31] Ronchi's dispatch of Nov. 20/30, 1685, A.S.M., Busta IV. (In translating this passage I have broken down one very long sentence into three shorter ones.)

[32] Cf. F. C. Turner, *James II* (London, 1948), p. 196, and J. P. Kenyon, *Robert Spencer, Earl of Sunderland, 1641–1702,* p. 126.

ager that he would be able to subsist . . . without more money. . . . Others were of the opinion that the houses would meet again at the time," and that the king would somehow satisfy parliament in its objection to the Catholic officers.[33] Probably both notions were in the king's mind. There had been a great retrenchment early in the reign, and James continued to retrench in spite of the irritation of some of his friends. The French ambassador, Barrillon, calculated that James II would have the money to pay the cost of a larger army; indeed, an estimate of revenue and expenditures (made in 1687), shows that James achieved a surplus of nearly £300,000 after having paid a little more than £600,000 as the cost of "near 19,000 officers and soldiers."[34] On the other hand, James's subsequent attempts to secure control of borough corporations show well enough that he meant eventually to call a parliament, but one which would repeal the Test Act and make moot the question of the Catholic officers.

Middleton must have learned much from his experience in the House of Commons. In the first session, the leaders were conspicuously successful; in the second, the king's stubbornness undermined their work, but there was no revolt against them. Both leaders spoke frequently and with authority, but their influence must have been greater behind the scenes, where they used patronage, cajolery, flattery, and implied threats of the king's displeasure. They were apparently effective managers. Even in the second session they could leave the king's interests to friends who were less obviously interested, as is shown by the fact that they spoke less frequently than they had in the first session. It was the undemocratic House of Lords which stood against the king's growing power in 1685.

[33] Reresby, *Memoirs*, p. 399.
[34] P.R.O., S.P. 31/3, fols. 37–38.

CHAPTER VI

The Slippery Path of a Secretary

James II, from the prorogation onward, tried to bring the "electing classes" to heel. One of his first plans was rapidly carried out — the dismissal of officers and officials who had voted with the opposition. This was of course a punishment that Walpole was to use later; it was intended to warn others against deviating from support of the king. A more far-reaching decision was to "remodel" the corporations even further. Something quite new was the canvassing of justices of the peace, lords lieutenant, and deputy lieutenants on repeal of the penal laws and the Test Act.

Charles II had reconstituted many of the borough corporations, as we have seen. King James remodeled some of those which his brother had left alone, but he also reconsidered the composition of the new Anglican corporations recently installed and broke many of them so as to include Catholics and dissenters. Strong opposition might be expected from Anglicans, for any concessions to Catholics would encroach upon Anglican vested interests, and Anglicans were sincerely convinced that concessions to Catholics were dangerous to state and church. Some Anglicans, to be sure, would follow the king in anything he proposed, but the November session of parliament suggested that they were not numerous enough to carry the necessary legislation and to block embarrassing resolutions, and the king would be satisfied with nothing less. Whether or not James needed money from parliament, he needed control of its statute-making power: Catholics whom he favored and appointed to office might be ruined after his death, unless he secured repeal of the penal laws and the Test Act, and those who were disposed to conversion might be held back by fear of the penal laws, to the destruction of their souls.

James was much concerned for his subjects' souls and quite sure what was good for them. He held there was no salvation outside the Roman communion, and in his eyes the conversion of his people was his highest duty; indeed, it was for this work that God had made him king, against so much opposition, and had preserved him through shipwreck and rebellion. James never doubted divine support in converting the heretic; he thought he had only to act boldly to succeed. He had already taken the first step by dispensing with the anti-Catholic laws in particular cases, and he continued to do so, but a greater achievement would be the legal establishment of a toleration for Catholics — which to appear at all fair must be also a toleration of all Protestant dissenters who were not inimical to his government.[1] When waverers were relieved of fear of punishment, with God's help they would choose the Catholic religion. Those influenced by worldly motives would observe the king's preference for Catholics and would fall into the arms of their Savior from a love of loaves and fishes.[2] The first few converts would be followed by more, until at last the Protestant ranks were emptied: *Magna est veritas et praevalebit.* A king less sure of his mission and less sure what was truth might not have expected the maxim to be made good in the short days of one man or one generation.

James did not, it seems, provide in his plans for the "invincibly ignorant" or the merely stubborn, the Protestants who would resist conversion to the grave. He may not have admitted to himself that the problem existed. There was evidence that it did; the flight of Huguenots from Louis XIV's kind provisions for their salvation should have suggested that many Englishmen and Scotsmen might also resist the attractions of the Roman church. Would toleration of Catholics be followed by a persecution of hardened and impenitent Protestants? There is no proof of such a plan, but there are plenty of hints that in the long run James would have excluded Protestants from his household and from offices of state. In the short run, the

---

[1] In 1686, according to Burnet, several bishops of the Church of Scotland offered support for toleration of Catholics, provided the laws against Presbyterians remained in force. Middleton advised Bishop Paterson that such an address would be used to make the established church odious.

[2] P.R., P.R.O. 31/3/162, fol. 209.

Protestants who continued in place were those who were useful to his plans.

Thus the changes James made in borough corporations and other bodies had the object of securing control for those who would elect members of parliament pledged to the establishment of religious toleration; and some of the men put in by Charles II now had to be put out by James II. Middleton again played his part in the issue of new charters.[3] As before, some boroughs surrendered their charters willingly, and a few so satisfied the king that their offers to surrender charters were declined. In some boroughs it was difficult to man a willing corporation for the new policy; Hull, for instance, had been reconstituted in 1684 and was twice remodeled in 1688. After each act showing favor to Catholics, some of the king's Protestant supporters fell away or became unreliable, and James had to act drastically: he felt compelled to remove three mayors of Buckingham in three months of 1687 and four times removed whole corporations in single orders.

A concerted effort was made in late 1687 to learn the opinions of lords lieutenant, their deputies, and justices of the peace on three questions posed by the king.

1. Will you, if returned to parliament, vote for the repeal of the penal laws and the Test?
2. Will you support candidates who are in favour of such a measure?
3. Will you live neighbourly and friendly with those of a contrary religion?[4]

The inquiry began with the lords lieutenant. Instructions, dated October 26, were delivered to the Duke of Beaufort, who held several western lieutenancies, at a cabinet meeting in Lord Sunderland's office. Sunderland, Middleton, and Lords Jeffreys, Godolphin, and Dartmouth were present; and similar papers were given, at about the same time, to the Duke of Norfolk, the Earl of Bath, and Lords Preston and Waldegrave. According to these instructions, the lords lieutenant were to

---

[3] H.M.C., *Report XII*, appendix VI, pp. 298–99.
[4] Ogg, *England in the Reigns of James II and William III*, p. 188. Cf. H.M.C., *Report XII*, appendix VII, p. 208.

put the three questions to their deputies and the justices of their shires, besides answering for themselves. They were also to report on the possibility of securing the election of compliant members of parliament and to suggest the names of Catholics and dissenters who were fit for service as deputy lieutenants and justices of the peace.[5]

Beaufort and most other lords lieutenant carried out their instructions, gathering opinions by interviews or by letter, but their reports to the king were generally discouraging:[6] a common and probably agreed answer to the first question was that the respondent must first hear arguments on both sides in parliament. The king thereafter put men into corporations and the commission of the peace on the recommendations contained in these reports and on the advice of local "regulators," but it does not appear that he profited by the changes. Because his hold on the electoral machinery remained weak, James was never ready to hold elections and meet a parliament, and when at last he thought he was ready, he was on the brink of ruin. James probably thought his alienation of the Tories and his diminishing strength among the political classes was only temporary, and he continued on his course without caution, anxious to emancipate Catholics before the succession of a Protestant could break down all their hopes.

Without awaiting the repeal of the Test Act, James II promoted Catholics and prospective converts to posts for which they could not qualify, using his dispensing power freely. Neville Payne became a receiver of fines in the Court of Common Pleas; Lords Dover, Belasyse, and Arundel of Wardour were elevated to the privy council; Andrew Popham was admitted as a pensioner at the Charterhouse. The fellows of Sidney Sussex College, Cambridge, declined to choose a royal nominee as master; it was said that the college lands would revert to the donors (the Sidney family) if a Catholic ever became master.[7] As James had expected, there were conversions: Count d'Adda, the papal emissary in England, reported that

[5] H.M.C., *Report XII*, appendix IX, p. 91.

[6] They were printed by Sir George Duckett in *Penal Laws and Test Act* (2 vols.; London and Kendal, 1882–83).

[7] B.M., Add. MS 29,561, fols. 446–47.

the Catholic Bishop Leyburn had confirmed nearly three hundred converts in one day of 1686.[8]

Middleton was not often concerned with James II's actions in favor of individual Catholics. In the Cambridge University Archives, for instance, among a number of James's mandates directing the grant of degrees and other actions, Sunderland countersigned ten and Middleton only three. Again, an abstract of the dispensations from the anti-Catholic laws shows that Middleton managed only one, which constituted Sir John Peake and other commissioners of the lieutenancy of the City of London.[9] It is impossible to be as sure of Middleton's part in bestowing ecclesiastical preferment upon Anglican ministers who were thinking of becoming Catholics. In the mass of ecclesiastical business handled by his office, many persons benefiting from royal patronage are not classifiable by religion, and some, such as Peter Mew, who was made Bishop of Winchester, were unimpeachable Protestants. It is quite possible that a Middleton who was made a demy or scholar of Magdalen College, Oxford, in November, 1687 — one of several who might be called the "demies of the crown" — was a relation of the secretary of state, but Middleton took no direct part in the struggle for Magdalen College. The evidence tends to show that the king did not use him in such affairs because, as a French diplomat remarked, "He can hardly conceal that he does not approve what is done for the advancement of the Catholic religion."[10] Indeed, the governors of Charterhouse, when ordered in 1687 to admit an unqualified Catholic pensioner, turned to Middleton for intercession with the king.

The great exception to this rule occurred when the king attempted to secure the choice of the subservient Lord Jeffreys as chancellor of Oxford University in July, 1688; the first Duke of Ormond's death had created a vacancy. The university quickly elected the second Duke of Ormond, grandson of the

---

[8] B.M., Add. MS 15,395, fols. 360–61; see also Ronchi's dispatch of June 16, 1687, A.S.M., Busta IV.

[9] H.M.C., *Report XII*, appendix VI (Lords MSS), pp. 300–304.

[10] P.R.O., P.R.O. 31/3/174, sheet 137. In expelling fellows, James II did no more than Leopold Finch, warden of All Souls, who struck off the books a fellow of his college who had voted against Finch in an election for the Camden professorship. Thomas Newley, who reported the incident, said that it appeared "a little too hot" (B.M., Add. MS 36,707, fol. 201).

first, before the king could nominate a candidate. The day after the election, Middleton countersigned a royal mandate to the university to elect Jeffreys. On hearing that Ormond had already been elected, the king had Middleton write to the Earl of Rochester, desiring the earl to "acquaint his grace (Ormond) that it is his [the king's] pleasure he should not accept of that office of chancellor of Oxford, and in case he had already accepted that he should forthwith resign it," sending his written refusal to the king. The pretext for demanding the resignation was that the young duke "probably may not appear in public for some time." Ormond, who heard of this letter while he was on his way to court at Windsor, turned about and went home, but two days later the mandate for Jeffreys' election was communicated to Ormond directly.[11] Ormond did not resign; he continued as chancellor of the university until 1715, when he declared himself a Jacobite.

By July, 1688, James had evidently begun to feel the risk entailed by his high-handed policy. Middleton cannot have enjoyed bullying the grandson of his father's old friend in such a cause.

The king's measures for the protection and promotion of Catholicism and Middleton's disapproval of them caused speculation that the secretary would be dismissed, for one Protestant after another lost his post, voluntarily retired, or suffered neglect.

Several factions shared favor at James's court in 1685. At the beginning of the reign, the Protestant factions were disunited, and even later they disagreed, although some of the highly placed Protestants suspended their old grudges under the king's pressure for toleration of Catholics. To Catholics — and also to some confused historians — the Protestant "interest" appeared, deceptively, to be indivisible, and its symbol was Laurence Hyde, Earl of Rochester, the king's brother-in-law. Rochester had a spotless record of loyalty to the hereditary succession, to the royal prerogative, and to Anglicanism. James

[11] B.M., Add. MS 41,823, fol. 125, and Add. MS 41,805, fol. 34. Lord Clarendon unconsciously makes this letter harsher than it was (*State Letters . . . During the Reign of K. James the Second: And His Lordship's Diary . . .* [2 vols.; Oxford, 1765], II, 212, 449); B.L., Carte MS 217, fol. 277.

made him lord high treasurer early in the reign. Initially, Protestants who had similar records, such as his brother, the Earl of Clarendon, were Rochester's supporters. Danby, who had emerged from the Tower after several years of unjust imprisonment, was still supported by many Tories who remembered his past services and patronage but was not close to James. Lord Halifax, another Protestant, with a reputation of "trimming" between Whigs and Tories, held under James the not very powerful position of lord president of the council; his followers were perhaps not numerous, but he had influence with other factions through his vein of common sense. Sunderland, Middleton's closest political associate at this time, was an opportunist. Middleton, although detached from Sunderland on the religious issue, was too strong a supporter of the king to give ear to any voices of opposition.

Halifax was dismissed by James after the parliamentary session of 1685, in which Halifax's part had been far from satisfactory to the king. Danby's alienation was caused by exclusion from office under James; it became more serious as James began to favor Catholics. As the king turned away from other Protestant leaders, Rochester rose in influence, and the other Protestants in high office were lumped — often erroneously — with his friends. Sunderland, in particular, although he did not change his religion for three years, dissociated himself from Rochester very early to seek the Catholic side.

There were also at court at least two Catholic factions. According to Barrillon, rich and well-established Catholics counseled moderation, wishing to preserve themselves and their property in the event of a reaction. Catholics who inclined toward a Spanish (i.e., anti-French) policy also wished to reconcile various factions (presumably Protestant and Catholic) and argued that the king could depend on parliament and the people if he opposed the ambitions of Louis XIV; but other Catholics (Barrillon named Lords Arundel of Wardour, Powis, Castlemaine, and Dover) joined with the Jesuits on the French side. The "Spanish" faction hoped for a fresh parliament in which the king would show himself independent of France, but Barrillon, of course, sided with the Francophiles and reported that this faction stood higher in the king's trust than its rivals. These divisions never ceased throughout the reign.

The royalist Protestant group, of which Rochester was called the chief, had a difficult course to pursue. First, it was divided between staunch defenders of the Anglican church, in all its privileges, and firm Protestants who would have consented to the repeal of the Test Act and the penal laws; second, it had to deal with a king who was intent on the improvement of the Catholic position, and it learned by experience that the king was most pleased by those who advised precipitate action — which many tolerant Protestants could neither advise nor approve. Third, some of them feared that their king intended to force them to abandon the Anglican establishment, cross the gentle vale of tolerance, and clamber into the dizzy abyss of Catholicism after only the briefest interval of preparation — a fear that was even stronger outside the court. Whatever the king's final intentions, Protestants knew that an increasing number of household and administrative positions would be reserved for Catholics.

In the seventeenth century, contention for office was constant, but at most times, rivals were agreed on six questions in seven. The introduction of Catholics into places in the king's gift created new and greater rivalries, in which agreement was less frequent, and misunderstanding distorted motives. Former favorites were resentful of their exclusion from lucrative and honorable service, and especially at seeing their replacements attend mass and kiss the Catholic bishops' rings. So it was with Danby, and eventually with Rochester.

Middleton avoided exclusion. His office was desirable to rivals, certainly, and he also labored under a disadvantage. When the court was at Windsor or elsewhere, he usually remained at Whitehall to perform the duties which required a resident secretary of state. During the king's stay at Windsor, in August, 1685, Middleton went to court only once a week, for council meetings.[12] He was thus removed from the king's presence much of the time and sometimes missed important items of information. "If I were at Windsor, I cannot doubt but his majesty would communicate to me the matters contained in his letter, since it cannot be imagined that whilst he is pleased to continue me in this office, that he would conceal

---

[12] B.M., Add. MS 41,823, fols, 25–26.

matters that really belong to it. . . ."[13] This complaint is unique; as we have seen, he was ordinarily well informed.

It was rumored, in the following October, that Middleton would be removed as secretary of state and be sent to Scotland as commissioner.[14] The quarrel between Queensberry and the Drummonds was near its climax, and the former was in danger of losing his commission to the Scottish parliament; perhaps James intended at one time that Middleton serve "as an indifferent man" between the two sides, but in fact he temporarily saved the job for Queensberry. According to Sir John Lauder, it was this check to the Drummonds that decided Perth to "pull off the mask" and declare himself a Catholic, "from which time his favor and court increased."[15] In February, 1686, the king chose Lord Moray to replace Queensberry, who thus lost his last important post. Middleton, who could hardly have preferred any Scottish position to the English secretaryship, apparently stood too well with the king in the autumn of 1685 to be forced to accept a transfer.[16] Middleton was again menaced with removal in July, 1686, a correspondent wrote John Ellis. The king was planning a westward progress,

to go and let all his good friends of Bristol and Taunton [where Monmouth had recruited many of his men] and the towns about see him and judge how decent an attendance 4000 men at arms are. The chancellor of Scotland [Perth] stays here to take Lord Middleton down with him president of the council of the kingdom; poor Middleton hangs an arse, thinking of Cleveland's judgment of Cain's doom. The chief reason is to admit Lord Montague in his room who is come in with the Jesuits, and will be secretary.[17]

Once more, however, rumor ran beyond fact.

In January, 1687, Lord Rochester was dismissed from the treasury. Other dismissals followed; and again there was talk

---

[13] *Ibid.*, fol. 29.

[14] B.M., Add. 22,910, fol. 247; P.R.O., Powis Papers, P.R.O. 30/53/8, fol. 16.

[15] Lauder of Fountainhall, *Historical Observes of Memorable Occurrents in Church and State, from Oct. 1680 to April 1686*, pp. 237–39.

[16] B.M., Add. MS 25,371, fol. 88.

[17] B.M., Add. MS 4,194, fol. 81. "Cain's doom" is an allusion to John Cleveland's "The Rebel Scot":

Had Cain been Scot, God would have changed his doom,
Not forced him wander but confined him home.

of Middleton's fall. Perhaps Middleton was pressed to change his religion, as Rochester had been. Burnet tells of a conversation which may have taken place at this time.

The earl of Middleton had married into a popish family, and was a man of great parts and a generous temper, but of loose principles in religion. So a priest was sent to instruct him. He began with transubstantiation, of which he said he would convince him immediately: and began thus, "You believe the Trinity." Middleton stopped him, and said, "Who told you so?" At which he stood amazed. So the earl said, he expected he should convince him of his belief, but not question him of his own. With this the priest was so disordered, that he could proceed no further.

Burnet was not in England, and we do not know where he got the story, but if such talk was forced upon Middleton (it probably was), he must have stood off would-be proselyters, for he was still a Protestant at the time of the Revolution of 1688. Protestants, however, believing that James II would not keep a Protestant secretary, said in February that Lord Melfort was "outing" Middleton; indeed, when the king ordered the payment of arrears on the earl's Scottish pension, some Scotsmen "construed [it] as a preliminary to his dismissing." [18] Queensberry had fallen; Perth and Melfort, both Catholics, were entrenched in Scotland by the authority of James II; and Scotsmen presumably knew of secret intrigues.

Somehow, Middleton preserved himself. Our only hints of his methods — aside from his prompt obedience to orders — come from Barrillon and from another French emissary, the Sieur de Bonrepaus. Barrillon reported that the Protestants at court were increasingly driven together by attacks upon their position, and he rapidly came to believe that Rochester was one of a "cabal for the Prince of Orange," which Barrillon wrote of as early as October, 1685. [19] He also reported that Rochester favored Huguenot refugees in England and that the king did not like him for it. (Barrillon disliked Rochester. In 1686, explaining this grudge to the Marquis de Seignelay, the French secretary of state for the navy, Bonrepaus said Barrillon

[18] B.M., Add. MS 4,194, fols. 144–45; R.H.E., S.P. 57/11, pp. 565–66; Lauder of Fountainhall, *Historical Notices*, II, 784.
[19] P.R.O., P.R.O. 31/3/162, fol. 150.

and Rochester had been on opposite sides when Charles II was alive.)

In September, 1686, Barrillon described the remaining Protestant officeholders as supporters of Rochester.

> There are still some courtiers who believe that the lord treasurer [Rochester] will last, and who remain attached to him, such as Lord Feversham, Lord Dartmouth, Lord Middleton, the Duke of Ormond, Lord Preston, and all the others who wish to be thought good Protestants: the other party, which is that of the Catholics, has all favor and credit; Lord Sunderland is at its head, and Father Petre without showing himself has as much trust as anyone. The queen is also of that party and appears to be in great esteem and to know all that passes.[20]

Some oversimplification is evident here. What has become of the rival Catholic factions? Especially, where are the Catholic moderates? Did the Catholics truly accept Sunderland as their leader when he was still nominally a Protestant? Bishop Leyburn, Lord Belasyse, the nuncio d'Adda, and the queen herself were said at that very time to oppose the "French," "Jesuitical" faction.[21] Was it true? Historians who use Barrillon's dispatches as their sole source will never know; those who are willing to use other evidence will do well to inquire into the matter.

Bonrepaus, who returned to England after Rochester's fall, informed Seignelay that Sunderland was the chief minister.

> Monsieur Middleton, who is the other secretary of state, having found himself on the point of being involved in the disgrace of the Earl of Rochester with whom he had great ties, submitted himself to Monsieur Sunderland to maintain himself, and as besides he is lazy, although he has wit, the other has made himself master of business.

But Sunderland's power was precarious. Bonrepaus wrote that the king knew the earl to be an unprincipled opportunist, but he used him because he would help establish the Catholic religion. Father Petre, on whom Sunderland had relied, would be free to drive Sunderland out at any time, now that Rochester was no longer a threat to the Catholics. Later, Bonrepaus wrote that Middleton did only what Sunderland did not want

---

[20] *Ibid.*, bundle 167, fol. 48.
[21] Dr. Williams' Library, Morrice MS P, p. 628.

to do, and was accordingly thought to be of no importance.[22] So it no doubt appeared to a man who saw Sunderland often, and who does not seem to have had much to do with Middleton. That Middleton did not want to do what Sunderland had to do might otherwise have occurred to Bonrepaus, who was certainly no fool.

The evidence does not show how far Middleton "submitted" to Sunderland. If Sunderland in fact suggested all or most of James's measures in 1687 and 1688, and overcame Middleton and others who doubted their advisability, he bore a grave responsibility. But there is a danger of underestimating the king in accepting the idea of Sunderland's overwhelming predominance. Sunderland, according to a recent biography by J. P. Kenyon, was always striving with rivals, always urging extreme measures for fear that those rivals might secure and control the royal favor, until he could not face a reckoning with James's enemies. At last, after the Revolution of 1688, he made such a humiliating recantation as few men could have survived and thereafter borne any share in public affairs. By comparison, Middleton followed a safe and dignified path; obeying orders, he avoided many thorny tasks by letting the impulsive Sunderland manage them and take responsibility. Sunderland may have thought, for instance, that countersigning the royal mandate to Cambridge University for the grant of the degree of master of arts to the Benedictine Alban Francis meant he was in the king's good graces and the most important man in the government. Middleton, more reflective, was probably happy to be left out of a business so full of risk. Thus it was that the revolutioners of 1688 could compile grave charges against Sunderland and never mention Middleton. F. M. G. Evans has said that secretarial history is sadly lacking in heroes, and Middleton was in this a typical secretary.

Possibly Bonrepaus, who had been absent from England when Rochester fell, meant no more than that Middleton had renewed his alliance with Sunderland. The two must have divided for a time, through Sunderland's cultivation of the king at the cost of his own religion, but there could have been no breach of relations. For a time, perhaps, Middleton sup-

---

[22] Dispatch of July 11/21, P.R.O., P.R.O. 31/3/171.

ported Rochester, as did other "loyal" Protestants, but afterward a few friendly words would have been enough for a reconciliation. Besides, with Father Petre rising in the king's esteem, Sunderland needed a friend as much as Middleton did.

It would be a mistake to assume that Middleton, or any other official, was exclusively concerned with the "great affairs" that absorb political historians. He and his office attended to a great mass of routine business, which administrative historians have taught us not to scorn, but this business is difficult to describe. A few illustrations of the working of the office under Middleton would be better than an attempt to repeat earlier studies. The secretaries of state were administratively connected with the postal service and were its most constant patrons, for the posts had first been established to facilitate the king's communications (the public was a comparatively late sharer in its benefits). Lord Rochester was postmaster general from 1685 to 1687; after his fall, Philip Frowde was governor of the Post Office until the Revolution of 1688. Although the posts were less frequent and towns served were fewer than in later times, the Post Office had a good deal of business and required efficient coordination, prompt handling of mail, loyalty, and honesty.

One of the most important duties of postmasters was the forwarding of news of events in their own parts which might be useful to the government. In 1688, for example, they fully reported the motions of the Prince of Orange, when mayors, justices of the peace, and lords lieutenant were deserting to William.[23] Middleton took an interest in the efficiency of the system and at least once used his power of arrest to further it. Frowde, in August, 1685, asked a correspondent to complain to Middleton of the dilatory postmaster of Southwark: "Pray tell my lord I beg him to let him [the postmaster] be kept two or three days in custody for example sake, or I shall not be able to make the letters come in in time."[24] Acting on this suggestion, the earl sent a messenger with a warrant to take the postmaster into his keeping, "him to bring before me to answer to such contempts and neglects in the execution of his said

[23] See B.M., Add. MS 41,805, fols. 168–69.
[24] B.M., Add. MS 41,804, fols. 83–84.

office of postmaster (to the great prejudice of his majesty's service) as shall be objected to him."[25] Thereafter, the letters of Southwark and other towns probably "came in in time."

The power of arrest was often used, as when a messenger bearing a warrant from Middleton sought Hugh Wickstead, "lately escaped out of custody" and suspected of "treasonable and dangerous practices."[26] Middleton also signed warrants for release — as for Archibald Campbell, Lord Lorne, in October, 1685. On the king's orders, he signed warrants for the preparation of pardons, such as that of Thomas Culpeper, for attacking the Earl of Devonshire in the "verge of court" in 1685. The secretary's pen was a key to the great locks of state.

Besides the secret-service money, which he spent without accounting, Middleton was concerned in certain payments from the treasury, particularly the pay, allowances, and extraordinary expenses of English diplomats. Middleton would inspect bills of extraordinaries, question some items, and refer them to Lord Treasurer Rochester, a procedure that was routine but not perfunctory. Before a diplomat could draw his salary and allowances, the secretary of state of his department (northern or southern) certified the date of his departure, at which his pay began; he similarly certified the date of his return. In his allowance of extraordinaries, Middleton was as a rule much less lenient than the lord treasurer and the commissioners of the treasury. It appears that Middleton sometimes also took part in the procedure for paying the royal messengers through the king's chamber.[27]

Reports of riots and other disorders were frequently made by local officials to the secretaries of state. In May, 1686, Middleton commended the mayor of Coventry for his prompt suppression of a riotous meeting "at its first beginning."[28] When the Lord Mayor of London failed to take prompt action in the dark days of November, 1688, to protect the house of Mr. Hills, the king's printer, Middleton ordered the lord mayor, in the king's name, to have "a sufficient guard . . . placed

[25] P.R.O., S.P. 44/54, p. 316.
[26] *Ibid.*, p. 397.
[27] *Cal. T. B.*, VIII, 571.
[28] B.M., Add. MS 41,823, fol. 122.

about his house this night to prevent any further damage." [29]
Throughout the reign, James II's enemies distributed libels
against him, his religion, and his government. The mayor of
Manchester sent Middleton a libel found by the local constable
in 1686, and the Dean of York, as a justice of the peace, sealed
up others delivered to a York bookseller, pending orders for
their disposal, in August, 1687.

Middleton signed passes for Englishmen going abroad, warrants for the admission of the king's officials to their posts,
and certain commissions. He authorized the Lieutenant of
Dover Castle to swear Edward Sudell as gunner of the castle
and signed Samuel Francklyn's commission to be the king's
procurator. His office also registered caveats, forbidding specified actions without prior advice to a specified person. Samuel
Pepys secured a caveat in 1685 at James II's command.

That no new grant be hereafter passed, or old renewed, to any
maritime city or corporation or to any private person whatsoever,
wherein any of the powers, rights, or jurisdictions appertaining to
the office of our High Admiral of England shall be concerned
before the secretary of our Admiralty [at that time Pepys] shall
be advised of and heard thereto by us. [30]

The mayor and aldermen of Thetford secured another caveat
"that no warrant pass for a new charter to that borough, till
notice be first given to Sir Joseph Williamson, their recorder
. . . or to the mayor." [31]

Middleton's almost continuous residence at Whitehall, even
when the king was elsewhere, seems to have meant that the
routine during the king's absence fell chiefly upon him. When
the court was at Windsor he went there once a week for meetings of the cabinet council; in 1687 he and Godolphin attended
court at Windsor Saturday and Sunday, but when the court
was further away, business was sometimes impeded. In September, 1685, the king (at Winchester) signed a warrant addressed
to the High Sheriff of Nottinghamshire for the postponement
of the execution of one Daniel Carr; Middleton countersigned
it when it was brought to him at Whitehall. The urgency in

[29] P.R.O., S.P. 44/97, p. 15.
[30] P.R.O., S.P. 29/359, p. 195.
[31] P.R.O., S.P. 44/73, p. 1.

this case was clear, but the procedure was irregular and note was made of it.

Middleton's administration as secretary was criticized by contemporaries only for his failure to reply promptly to requests for instructions. Lord Clarendon, when he was lord lieutenant of Ireland, complained to his brother, Rochester, that although he had sent a very civil letter to Middleton with a report on the desirability of having a Dutch consul at Dublin, he had received no response: "As to the business, it is nothing to me. . . . But his lordship might have afforded me the civility of an answer . . . I believe, being a secretary of state makes a man forget to write."[32] On the foreign side, Sir Gabriel Sylvius twice begged Middleton to correspond regularly and frequently — to no avail.[33] There can be no doubt that Middleton neglected these and other correspondents, but the volume of business he transacted shows well enough that he was usually available and quick in his decisions. Unfortunately, he was forced to refer many subjects to the king, and the king showed an increasing tendency to postpone consideration of subjects which had nothing to do with his centralizing policy or the encouragement of Catholicism. Sometimes Middleton wrote even though he had no instructions to give, but he ordinarily thought such correspondence pointless.

He rarely took a holiday. In July and August, 1687, he was granted leave for ten or twelve days to visit an estate in the country, and in the spring of 1688 he was forced by illness to keep to his house for several weeks. Except at such times, he did the king's business, often at the king's side. He had accepted the limits imposed upon him. He was growing rich and wielding influence.

The office itself was not much changed until February, 1688, when "a clerk belonging to the office of . . . the Earl of Middleton . . . being discovered to have used some unfair practices, is both put out of his place, and prohibited the court."[34] Early in March, a newswriter published these details:

[32] Clarendon, *State Letters*, II, 17.
[33] See B.M., Add. MS 41,828, fols. 28, 46–47.
[34] *Publick Occurrences Truely Stated* (Feb. 28, 1687/88); see also N. Japikse, *Correspondentie van Willem III en van Hans Willem Bentinck, Eersten Graaf van Portland* (5 vols.; The Hague, 1927–37), IV, 5.

De Paz, one of the clerks from before the time of Middleton's appointment, "some weeks since dismissed from that employment, as it was said for discovering the secrets of the council into Holland, hath now been lately seen at the Brill [in South Holland] and a report is of further matter against him." [35] De Paz was a native of Holland who had translated out of modern languages; presumably he was the Samuel De Paz who had a few years before projected a scheme for procuring intelligence for the navy. Not long after his flight he desired a pass to return to England, where his wife had property, and stayed at or near The Hague for several months, asking help of the English minister, the Marquis of Albeville, and protesting that his only wish was to do King James further service. [36]

The seriousness of this treason can hardly be exaggerated. How long De Paz had been a Dutch agent we do not know, although Barrillon heard a rumor of betrayal as early as July, 1685; nor do we know how De Paz was detected, or whether he was an agent of the States General or of the Prince of Orange. The Dutch ambassador does not refer to him in his dispatches, so that it is possible that the clerk dealt directly only with persons in Holland. A spy could hardly have occupied a place more dangerous to the English government; dispatches from ministers abroad, spies' reports, newsletters which were almost spies' reports, informations by British subjects, all accumulated in the secretary's office. If De Paz did not know everything, he did know much, and adroit use of his knowledge may have meant the escape of suspects, anticipation by the Dutch of the king's foreign and military policy, the capture and punishment of English secret agents abroad, loss of the trust of secret informants at home — in short, a thorough snarling of the king's plans. Strangely, the detection of this agent has never been mentioned by historians of the quarrel between James II and William of Orange.

When Sunderland was dismissed, in October, 1688, and Middleton assumed the duties of the Southern Department, there were changes among the clerks. Philip Madox wrote, on November 10, that Mr. Bridgeman and Dr. Owen Wynne were then in Middleton's office, a Mr. Warre and Fergus Graham

[35] B.M., Sloane MS 3,929 fol. 34.
[36] B.M., Add. MS 41,815, fols. 176–77; Add. MS 41,816, fol. 173.

in Lord Preston's, and that a Mr. Tempest cared for "my Lord Preston's private affairs in the office."[37] The new arrangement lasted so short a time, and business was in such confusion, that nothing more is known of it. When Middleton left his secretary-ship in December, apparently, Owen Wynne carried off his official papers (which are now in the British Museum Library). Until the menace of revolution so disordered England that no office could have coped with it, Middleton's office handled not only routine business but the execution of extraordinary matters fairly well. Its weaknesses — particularly the secretary's dila-toriness in some of his correspondence — were fewer than one might expect in a bureau charged with duties in which neither chief nor staff could believe.

No part of the nation was so much affected by the religious policy of King James as the clergy of the Church of England. If James were successful, their exclusive privileges would (at least) be shared, and even their endowments might be reduced, or utterly taken away. Furthermore, the Anglican clergy ob-served with horror that Catholicism now flourished in the land as the wicked or as the green bay tree. Resistance was predict-able when the danger of their position was gradually brought home to them. Resistance was long in coming, however, for it was a leading Anglican doctrine that even a wicked king must be obeyed.

James, who found his title of supreme governor of the Angli-can church an embarrassment, delegated his authority to a group of Anglicans, the Ecclesiastical Commission, a body that subsequently acted as the king's disciplinary agency for the clergy. Middleton avoided assignment to the commission, for-tunately for him, but Sunderland became a commissioner and threw himself into the unpopular work, largely the curbing of anti-Catholic utterances by the Anglican clergy. (A junior fel-low of Jesus College, Cambridge, forced to recant reflections on Catholicism, went mad.)[38] Some of the criticisms were cer-tainly strong: Sunderland reported Elby, the minister of Chis-

---

[37] *Letters Written during the Years 1686, 1687, 1688, and Addressed to John Ellis,* II, 287.

[38] Arthur Gray and Frederick Brittain, *A History of Jesus College, Cambridge* (London, 1960), p. 100.

wick, for preaching that "papists are liars and hypocrites, and none ought to give any credit to what they say."[39] The Ecclesiastical Commission suspended Henry Compton, Bishop of London, for refusing to take action against such a preacher, but Compton's noncompliance was exceptional in the first two years of the reign. George Hickes, Dean of Worcester, expressed the typical attitude: "I hope the insolence of R[oman] C[atholics] everywhere will in the end do them no service; we must pray, and be loyal, and patient, and God will preserve us in our apostolical, and true worship of himself."[40]

Serious trouble began with the issue of the Declaration of Indulgence, on April 4, 1687. The Anglican clergy was gravely disturbed that Catholics and Dissenters were to be free to worship in public and were no longer subject to the restrictions of the test acts. Many, both clerics and laymen, were distressed and resentful at the suspension of parliamentary laws for the benefit of unpopular minorities, and James's reassurances to the Church of England seemed hypocritical. Some Protestant Dissenters did not avail themselves of the declaration or give public approval to it because of its constitutional implications, and addresses of gratitude, except from the beneficiaries of the new toleration, were unusual. Most Anglicans stood silent, or complained in private of the subversion of their church.

When the Declaration of Indulgence was revised and reissued on April 7, 1688, James and his ecclesiastical commission were determined to secure the widest circulation for this version — and the adherence of the clergy of the Church of England. Bishops were commanded to direct the clergy of their dioceses to read the declaration to their congregations. Some bishops complied; others hesitated; and the Bishop of Rochester, having obeyed the command, resigned his seat in the commission when it resolved to punish those who had not.

In May, seven bishops consulted with Lord Clarendon, deliberated among themselves, and resolved to petition the king against the distribution and compulsory reading of the declaration. In the evening of May 18,

[39] B.L., Tanner MS 31, fols. 178–79.
[40] B.L., Ballard MS 12, fol. 8.

all the subscribers (except the Archbishop [of Canterbury], who had been forbidden the court almost two years before) went over to Whitehall to deliver it to the king. In order thereto the Bishop of S. Asaph went first to the Earl of Middleton (principal secretary) in the name of all the rest to desire his assistance for the introducing [them] to his majesty; but he had been sick for a fortnight before, and so confined to his chamber. Then S. Asaph (his brethren staying at the Earl of Dartmouth's house) went, and made the like application to the Earl of Sunderland.[41]

Sunderland refused to do more for the bishops than to announce their arrival. Middleton's illness, which is well attested by other sources, was a stroke of bad luck for the bishops. (Middleton had formerly served as a channel of access for Archbishop Sancroft, and during the autumn of 1688 he was to do so again.)[42]

The king was very angry with the petitioners. He may have been encouraged in his anger by Sunderland, who on May 27 signed an order that Archbishop Sancroft appear before the king and council on June 8. The offending bishops appeared on that day, and the council ordered the Lieutenant of the Tower to take them into custody. Middleton had evidently recovered, for he was one of several Protestants of the council who signed the orders for their arrest and prosecution. The charge was that the petition, which had somehow become public, was a seditious libel. Unquestionably, action against the bishops was unpalatable to Middleton, but it would have been taken even if the secretary had not signed the order. Unquestionably also — as Ranke says — James "was by nature fond of political danger; he felt at home in the midst of it,"[43] and counsels of delay or leniency would not have helped.

The bishops had strong support; according to a report that reached the Dutch ambassador, even the Catholic lords advised the king to be moderate. The defendants carefully prepared for the trial, in the court of king's bench. Parliamentary privilege and the legality of the dispensing power were brought

[41] Ranke, IV, 346–50; B.L., Tanner MS 28, fol. 38.

[42] George D'Oyly, *The Life of William Sancroft, Archbishop of Canterbury* (2d ed.; London, 1840), pp. 144–46; [John Gutch,] *Collectanea Curiosa; or Miscellaneous Tracts, Relating to the History and Antiquities of England and Ireland . . .* (2 vols.; Oxford, 1781), I, 426.

[43] Ranke, IV, 354.

out in the trial, for the bishops were peers and members of the House of Lords, and if the dispensing power was illegal the bishops had committed no offense when they protested against it. Apparently, the bishops asked for, and were granted, parliamentary papers obtained through Middleton's office. The proceedings were fair, even overbalanced in favor of the accused.[44] (The bishops were ably represented by Heneage Finch, later Earl of Aylesford, and others). The jury found the defendants not guilty on June 30, 1688, and the bishops' release was greeted by the people with an outburst of jubilation.

Laymen had showed discontent before the leading clergymen did so. Popular opinion had been excited early in the reign by Louis XIV's revocation of the Edict of Nantes. Huguenot refugees had fled to England for some time before the revocation; afterwards, they could not return to France. Reports of maltreatment — of torture, executions, and long terms in the French galleys — were purveyed in printed accounts written by embittered Huguenots. English Protestants resident in France were harassed, especially those whose wives were French Protestants. James II's toleration was regarded as the first step toward just such forced conversions as were being made in France. Gilbert Burnet, meanwhile, living safely in Holland, published letters that circulated in England, casting aspersions on the government and its policy.

James endeavored to show tolerance toward the French Protestants living in England; he asked Englishmen to give them alms, and he constituted a committee (of which Middleton was a member) to collect and distribute money. He permitted them to worship according to their custom and to build "one temple or tabernacle" in Spitalfields, for which Middleton countersigned a warrant. Rochester, and no doubt other supporters of Protestantism, favored the refugees.

Unfortunately, the king did not like the Huguenots — or so he told the Frenchman Barrillon, who was naturally very glad to hear it. James spoke of them as "very evil-minded," saying he would prevent the distribution of money to "seditious people" and to those who refused to conform to the Church of England. Although he tried to keep his opinion from the

[44] Cf. F. C. Turner, *James II*, p. 403.

public,[45] he did not succeed in doing so. Nevertheless, in 1686/87, a new collection for the Huguenots was permitted, which raised a good deal of money. (Altogether, more than £67,000 were received for French Protestants in these collections authorized by King James.)[46] French Protestant services were in fact performed. The French church in the Savoy conformed, and its treasurer's recommendations account for most of the disbursements from the funds. Perhaps the refugees made less distinction among themselves than the government would have liked; perhaps not. Whatever James thought of them, the Huguenots enjoyed more religious freedom than they had had for years. In June, 1688, the Dutch ambassador reported that they had addressed the king to thank him for "his gracious protection and helpfulness in their great need, and for the enjoyment of their free liberty of conscience in the use of their divine worship. . . ."[47]

Nameless persons, who did not dwell on the treatment accorded the refugees, played with the fears of the leading English Protestants. On January 28, 1687/88, Lord Danby received a letter warning him that he had not many days to live if he did not make his peace with the king, and other men received similar letters. Agitators may have incited the riots that occurred with increasing frequency throughout the country in 1688. The discontented wrote letters of veiled meaning, such as this from Thomas Walker to Lord Hatton: "I have sent your lordship the declaration which tells us when the parliament shall meet; and what it is the king designs, which we all pretty well knew before: he tells us that he has a pretty good army and will have a bigger, if occasion require. Which is a great comfort to us all."[48] Seditious papers were secretly distributed. It was reported from Barnstaple that the quarters of some of Monmouth's supporters, which had been displayed as an example to the rebellious, had been secretly taken down.[49] The names of some dissidents were well known to the king.

[45] P.R.O., P.R.O. 31/3/164, fols. 261, 271.
[46] W. A. Shaw, "The English Government and the Relief of Protestant Refugees," (*E.H.R.*, Vol. 9, 1894), pp. 663–65.
[47] B.M., Add. MS 17,677 UUU, fol. 568.
[48] B.M., Add. MS 29,563, fol. 130.
[49] P.R.O., S.P., Foreign, Holland (S.P. 84/)220, fols. 33–34.

We do not have lists made by his officials, but we have the names Barrillon reported to Louis XIV.

> The heads of the opposition in the upper house are the Marquis of Halifax, the Earl of Devonshire, the Earl of Danby, and the Earl of Nottingham. . . . They have their secret relations in Holland and confer often with those of the same party who are Anglicans, of whom the greater number have been members of the lower house in earlier parliaments.[50]

Bonrepaus gives us two more names. "Lord Churchill, liked and loaded with benefits by the king his master, stands more than anyone in favor of the Prince of Orange. Lord Godolphin, who is in all the secret councils, opposes nothing, but he plays the good Protestant and keeps always a back door to the Prince of Orange."[51] Everyone knew, Bonrepaus wrote, that the king's ministers had their eyes on his successor — everyone, that is, except the king. By July, 1688, the Modenese resident Giacomo Ronchi had heard that "the great men at court and in the army have made an association, of which his majesty has been given word, but he does not appear to believe anything about it."[52]

English Catholics, according to several observers, were influenced in two directions by the consideration that the heir to the throne was a Protestant, Mary, Princess of Orange (James's daughter). Some pressed James to take steps to legitimate their holding office during his reign, to forestall punishment later; they urged the repeal of the Test Act and the anti-Catholic penal laws by parliament. Other Catholics, fearing that any action might later be treated as criminal, cautiously avoided taking advantage of their opportunities under James.[53] Both groups, however, hoped and prayed for the birth of a male heir to James and his queen, Maria Beatrice of Modena — an heir who would grow up as a Catholic and take precedence over his half-sisters, Mary and Anne. The frequent pregnancies of Maria Beatrice had not produced a child healthy enough to reach maturity, but she was not yet beyond the age of childbearing.

[50] P.R.O., P.R.O. 31/3/173, fol. 309.
[51] Bonrepaus to Seignelay, July 11/21, 1687, *ibid.*, bundle 171.
[52] C.U.L., Add. MS 4,836, fol. 256.
[53] B.M., Add. MS 15,396, fol. 20; Add. MS 38,493, fols. 15–16; Add. MS 25,374, fol. 65.

In the autumn of 1687, rumors spread that the queen was again pregnant. The Modenese resident notified his master (the queen's brother) of this on November 13; on November 24, Barrillon wrote Louis XIV that there was no longer any doubt of her condition.

It did not suit the members of the opposition that James II should have a legitimate son. When Maria Beatrice had been pregnant in 1682, they had said that she was pretending; the attitude of disbelief was dropped on that occasion when a daughter was born. In 1688 the charge of fakery was again made — in the form of the myth that a male child had been smuggled into the confinement chamber in a warming pan. Lady Middleton, according to Barrillon, was one of the first to be mentioned as a possible governess,[54] but she had many rivals, and many Catholics were opposed to her on the ground that her husband was a Protestant. She stood high in the queen's favor, nevertheless, and in April it was common talk that she would be governess and that Lady Carteret would be the royal nurse.[55]

Protestants, meanwhile, looked to the Prince and Princess of Orange; a Catholic heir would overthrow all their hopes for a comfortable and peaceful resumption of power and privilege after James II's time. A justice, returned from circuit in March, 1688, reported that the grand jury of Surrey had rejected a proposal for a congratulatory address to the king, and, in Kent, Sir Thomas Taylor had spoken against an address on the hope for the birth of a prince of Wales, saying he favored a request that the king would have any prince born brought up as a Protestant.[56]

In early June, the queen decided that her quarters in Whitehall were too cramped and hot and ordered St. James's Palace made ready for her confinement: A bed of state was set up, and a cradle of state for the reception of the child, "both being exceeding rich." On June 10/20 the queen gave birth to a "well-shaped prince." According to custom, the confinement chamber was crowded by witnesses — privy councillors, peers, officials, and their wives. There was no doubt in the mind of

[54] P.R.O., P.R.O. 31/3/175, fols. 384, 390.
[55] B.M., Sloane MS 3,929, fol. 44.
[56] B.L., Ballard MS 11, fols. 183–84.

anyone present that the Prince of Wales, christened James
Francis Edward, was the son of Maria Beatrice; even so, because everyone had heard the mockery of pregnancy, Middleton — as he later deposed — went nearer to the bed of state
than he would otherwise have done, so that he could give a
circumstantial report of the appearance of the newborn child.
He could not, he said, see the midwife take it from the bed,
but he saw it just afterwards, still in a foul state.[57] (Middleton
was attacked for this testimony after the revolution.)

The privy council immediately notified the lords lieutenant,
and through them all local officials, the colonels of the army,
and the ship commanders of the fleet, in order that they might
join in "solemn thanksgiving" and "public rejoicing."[58] Vilifi-
cation of the birth began, at home and abroad: the Prince of
Wales was a bastard, a son of Sir Theophilus Oglethorpe, anybody, a nobody. What he must not be was a royal Stuart, born
in wedlock with dozens of witnesses to attest there had been
no possibility of the introduction of a young impostor. Other
families have fallen through extinction; the Stuarts fell through
the renewal of their male line.

[57] See *Revolution Politicks: Being a Compleat Collection of All the Reports, Lyes, and Stories . . . in 1688 . . .* (London, 1733), pp. 24–25, or
Depositions on the Birth of the Prince of Wales, printed without title (London, 1688), pp. 27–28.

[58] See, e.g., B.M., Add. MS 27,448, fol. 342; P.R.O., W.O. 4/1, p. 823;
P.R.O., Adm. 1/5139, p. 1223.

CHAPTER VII

Greedy Merchants and a Greedy King

As foreign policy was the king's, and as Middleton did not boast of his influence in this field, it is difficult to say which of James's decisions in foreign relations were the results of Middleton's advice — although the earl was fully responsible for and cognizant of the events of his Northern Department as a secretary usually was. The relations of James II with individual states are interesting in detachment, and an account of foreign relations could be written so, but the foreign states were never considered separately at the time. In every international dispute, the king of England had to deal with all the other great powers.

It is more profitable here to describe the principal problems in Middleton's province, taking into account the involvements of other powers, whether within that province or not. This and the next three chapters will examine seven problems of foreign relations: disputes between the English and the Dutch East India companies, French encroachments upon the Holy Roman Empire, Danish threats to Hamburg and Holstein-Gottorp, English relations with Russia and Poland, fugitives from Great Britain in the Dutch Netherlands, depredations of Algerine corsairs upon Dutch commerce, and the personal relations between James II and William of Orange. Other problems might also be treated — for one, the disputes with Denmark and Sweden about English trade — but are not included here for lack of space. Our material nevertheless makes it possible for the reader to understand the foreign policy of James II so far as it affected northern Europe.

The East India companies of England and the Netherlands were old rivals for the hugely valuable trade of the Indian

Ocean. Earlier in the century, trade rivalry had produced the "Amboyna massacre," which plagued Anglo-Dutch relations for many years. In 1682 a new dispute arose from the overthrow of a sultan of Bantam by his son, supported by the Dutch, and the confiscation of the English company's "factory," or trading place.

According to the English company's account, on March 14, 1681/82, a Dutch force of ships and "prowes" intervened in a war between the sultan and his son: the Dutch attempted to land men at Bantam but were beaten off by the defenders; then, with reinforcements from Batavia, the Dutch commander, Martin, made a successful effort on March 28, captured the sultan and the town and castle of Bantam, and put up Dutch flags in various places. The next day the Dutch resident led armed men to the English company's factory and closed it. Despite protests by the English that they had been neutral, officers of the "young king" ordered the English to leave Bantam. The English account made the "young king" a puppet of the Dutch. As the English began to load their goods onto boats for transport to their ships, the Dutch threatened to fire upon them, saying they were acting on the orders of the "young king." The English factory was ransacked by the Dutch on April 11. The evacuating English left their flag flying over the factory, but on April 12 they observed that it had been taken down and that a Dutch flag had been raised in its place.[1]

It took several months for the news of the expulsion to reach England, at which time English East India company "actions" (shares) are reported to have fallen to less than half of their former value. About March, 1682/83, the English company submitted a petition to its government protesting against the "injurious and subtle practices" of its Dutch competitor, and the business was duly taken up by the diplomats. In May, the English envoy at The Hague, Chudleigh, requested redress from the States General in the name of Charles II. "His majesty is confident that you will give without delay the necessary orders for having your arms entirely withdrawn from Bantam, and having fully compensated the damages which his sub-

---

[1] B.M., Add. MS 41,822, fols. 7–10; B. H. M. Vlekke, *Nusantara: A History of the East Indian Archipelago* (Cambridge, Mass., 1944), pp. 160–61.

jects have suffered there."[2] (The Danish envoy joined with
Chudleigh, protesting against similar aggression against the
Danes at Bantam.) An agreement was made for the restoration
of English rights, and plans for recovering the Bantam factory
by force were canceled. In 1683/84, however, the Dutch expelled the young king and assumed the government and trade
of the port and its dependencies. The English were again removed.[3]

New attempts to settle the dispute progressed very slowly.
Under the existing commercial treaties the incident called for
the delegation of commissioners by the two companies, and,
if the commissioners failed to reach agreement, the problem
must be negotiated by the King of England and the States
General. Not until March, 1684/85, after the accession of
James II, were the preparatory arrangements for the commissioners finished. The Dutch delegation, which was to treat with
its counterpart in England, arrived in May. The conferences
were preceded by assurances of close friendship — appropriate
at a time when the defensive alliance of 1678 was near the
point of renewal (it was renewed on August 17)[4] — but the
commissioners represented interests so directly opposed that
the negotiations soon foundered. Recommendations of speed
produced no effect, and in October a newswriter in The Hague
reported that the Bantam negotiations had made no progress.

A good share of the blame must be borne by the English.
When the lord keeper, one of the English commissioners, fell
ill, his replacement was delayed, and when the commissioners
wished to select an arbitrator, Middleton postponed the se-
lection.[5] The most important hindrance, however, was the composition of the English commission — Middleton, Sunderland,
Rochester, and Lord Guilford (after his death Lord Chancellor
Jeffreys). Each of these men held at least one high office and
had many other affairs to preoccupy him. The Dutch representatives, on the other hand, were away from home and chafed
in idleness. Besides, the English East India company was labor-

[2] B.M., Add. MS 41,822, fols. 19–20.
[3] John Bruce, *Annals of the Honorable East-India Company* (3 vols.;
London, 1810), II, 503, 519–20.
[4] For a Latin copy of the treaty, see P.R.O., S.P. 103/50.
[5] B.M., Add. MS 17,677 UUU, fol. 206; Add. MS 17,677 GG, fol. 520.

ing against an easy settlement. In March, 1685/86, the commissioners, having failed to agree on an arbitrator, decided to leave the settlement in the hands of the two governments. The Dutch commissioners went home, and the English responsibility was transferred to Bevil Skelton, the envoy at The Hague, who received express orders to inform the States General that James demanded justice in the name of friendship and equity. Skelton attempted to interest the Prince of Orange in the English company's case, but William refused to intervene.

The English position, stated by Sunderland and restated by Middleton, was that the *status quo ante* must be restored. "That is that all things be put in the same condition that they were in before the late revolution there: that in order to that they [the Dutch] would at least withdraw their land and sea forces from thence without which their pretended King of Bantam could never have expelled us from thence." The young king had been "a mere property to serve their turn." [6] The Dutch view of the case, however, was that the young king had attained his position through the intervention of Dutch troops and had, in return, granted the Dutch exclusive trading privileges, to continue until they had reimbursed themselves. Dutch forces had been in Bantam because the young king could not have remained in power without them, a judgment that was confirmed by the overthrow of the young king by the Dutch. [7]

The disagreement was obviously on the question of the engagements that bound the Dutch company in its East Indian operations. The English contended that Dutch regulation of English trade in their conquests and puppet states should accord with the Anglo-Dutch treaties. The Dutch held simply that its company was a free agent and was empowered to conclude the best bargain for itself, and that no one else had the right to complain of its actions.

The controversy was complicated by the growth of other differences between England and the United Netherlands, especially over the presence of English rebels and conspirators in Holland. (As early as November, 1686, a newswriter at The Hague predicted a rupture between the two nations as a result of Bantam and the refugees.) Bantam was neglected, for a

---

[6] B.M., Add. MS 17,677 UUU, fol. 225; Add. MS 41,823, fol. 42.
[7] B.M., Add. MS 41,822, fol. 161; Bruce, *Annals*, II, 519.

time, but in June, 1687, Middleton instructed Sir Ignatius White, Marquis of Albeville in the Holy Roman Empire and English envoy at The Hague, succeeding Skelton, as follows.

I suppose it may be time to move in the Bantam affair, though I fear with as little success; if there were ground for a treaty his majesty would treat, but when a man takes my cloak I am to ask for it again; and they are deceived if they think the king will accept of any expedient; and to say that the King of Bantam is master there and not they is to use us like children, and so a new affront. . . .[8]

Albeville accordingly submitted a memorial to the States General to the effect that the King of Great Britain expected satisfaction for the English East India Company without delay.

Word of further Dutch aggression reached London at this time,

viz. upon the coast of Coromandel, pretending a war against the King of Golconda. They have seized upon Masulipatam after the same manner they did Bantam, and have forbid your majesty's subjects, after eight weeks, to trade there, notwithstanding your majesty's East India company has had a residence and factory there about eighty or ninety years, which factory was built by the company and the ground whereon it stands was purchased by them.

Moreover, Sir Josiah Child wrote that the Dutch had assailed the English company's fort at Batancapas, on the western coast of Sumatra, had taken it by force, had pulled down and destroyed the flag, and had robbed the company's people.[9] King James's immediate reaction was bitter. "The Hollanders disgust everybody everywhere," he said to the Dutch ambassador.[10]

Middleton passed on these new complaints to Albeville in June, 1687, commanding him to tell the States General "that as his majesty is willing to believe, that these things were done without their knowledge, so he cannot doubt, but they will disapprove of them. . . ."[11] In reply, the States General professed its willingness to enter into a conference with Albeville, and in August, Albeville submitted a documented protest against the Masulipatam and Batancapas incidents.

[8] B.M., Add. MS 41,823, fol. 52.
[9] B.M., Add. MS 41,822, fol. 107.
[10] B.M., Add. MS 25,374, fols. 102–3.
[11] B.M., Add. MS 41,823, fols. 54–55.

The Dutch company gave a very detailed defense to the States General. The prohibition at Masulipatam was a temporary war measure; the Dutch had allowed the English several weeks' warning; the King of Golconda had made peace, and the Dutch had restored the town to him; and trade now proceeded according to treaty, as it had before the incident. The interruption of trade during the war had cost the Dutch company much more than it could gain by excluding English trade; the company asked nothing better for itself than the treatment it had given the English company during recent Dutch wars with Persia and Golconda. Moreover, the right of a conqueror to forbid trade and navigation to others within a conquest was sanctioned by English, French, Spanish, and Portuguese precedents, so that the Dutch had the right to forbid English trade at Masulipatam while they occupied it. Nor should the English complain, for they continued to trade at Madras and Fort St. George, which were English possessions in the neighborhood of Masulipatam. (This argument weakened the Dutch case, as Madras and Fort St. George were not near Masulipatam.) The incident at Batancapas, the Dutch company said, had resulted from an encroachment by the English upon territory in which the Dutch company was sovereign and upon a pepper monopoly which the Dutch held by treaty. After a rebellion supported by the English, the local "peace party" which suppressed the rebellion, took possession of the fort, and it was the Dutch present who prevented the killing of English captives.[12]

The multiplied East Indian disputes dragged on. In December, Middleton directed Albeville to request the States General — not the Dutch East India company — to empower commissioners to treat at London with commissioners who would be named by James II. The States General expressed a preference for negotiations at The Hague, and the English government agreed to this in February, 1688. By then Anglo-Dutch relations were rapidly deteriorating. Nevertheless James reaffirmed his willingness to treat as late as September, when Dutch preparations for the invasion of England were already far advanced.

No English political dominion had been challenged by the Dutch — the East Indian disputes were purely commercial.

---

[12] B.M., Add. MS 41,822, fols. 135–36, 158–73.

Engaged in aggressive warfare for the protection and extension of its commercial interests, the Dutch consolidated their advances through political dominance, as in Sumatra, or through native puppets, as at Bantam. English interest was in the way, and the Dutch struck it down as wars afforded opportunity.

The role of the English government, on the other hand, was consistently defensive of the English interest. It neglected only two further steps: reprisal and war. Pressing for heavy compensation during the Anglo-Dutch conferences and the deliberations of the English ministers was the English East India company, itself aggressive and resentful. Yet James II and his secretary persisted in their efforts to reach an accommodation by peaceful means.

The Dutch were hardly helpful. They pointed out that if their merchants traded with Barbados, Virginia, or Jamaica, they would surely be arrested. The Dutch regarded their new acquisitions as conferring exclusive privileges parallel to older ones. The English government labored in vain to protect rights that had been secured from earlier East Indian rulers, but the Dutch company felt free to repudiate the agreements or to treat them as having expired. At that time, we should remember, leadership in the transfer of the East to European hegemony was in the hands of the Dutch.

The Holy Roman Empire presented a feeble front to France in the 1670's and 1680's; since 1648, it had consisted of several hundred states of various sizes, sovereign in most respects. Emperor Leopold I, head of the Austrian branch of the Habsburg family, was the titular superior of the Empire's eight electors and its numerous dukes, margraves, counts, petty free lords, and imperial free cities. His position gave him at least some moral support from such states as had conservative rulers who honored the tradition of law. Many of the small states looked to the emperor for protection against the more powerful, and the states in general looked to him for leadership against foreign invasion.

At this juncture, the empire was endangered on two sides. To the southeast, the Sultan of Turkey, who already governed the Balkans, had waged long and bloody wars against the Habsburgs for the possession of Hungary, but since 1664 there had been a fragile peace. The sultan was in the hands of a "dynasty" of viziers, one of whom, Kara Mustapha, had ambitions for a conquest not only of Hungary, but of Austria and Germany as well. Kara Mustapha came to power in 1676 and created a general European crisis in the early 1680's. The eastern problem was not a simple one of Turk against Christian: Protestant Hungarians enjoyed toleration under the Ottomans, and Catholic opponents of the Habsburgs sometimes fought on the side of Moslems. Transylvania, a Christian dependency of Hungary, struck out for political independence. The Turks were divided by the internal politics of their court.

On the empire's western boundary was France, the second enemy. Cardinal Richelieu and his successor, Mazarin, as a result of the Thirty Years' War and a long Franco-Spanish war afterward, had made conquests that had been confirmed by treaties in 1648 and 1659 — eroding the area nominally subject to the emperor. The King of France thus acquired much of Alsace, the three bishoprics of Metz, Verdun and Toul, the county of Artois, and other lands on the borders of the Low Countries. He bought the "right" of succession to Lorraine from its duke in 1662 and drove out the legitimate heir in 1670; in 1672 he annexed the ten imperial cities of Alsace. As opportunity presented itself, he made claims to other territories; he also reached an understanding with Hungarian rebels, whom he supplied with money, and cooperated less explicitly with Kara Mustapha.

The emperor was greatly embarrassed by simultaneous threats from east and west. His hereditary dominions were menaced by the Turks, while his cousin of Spain, Leopold's vassals, and Leopold himself (in Hither Austria) were bullied and robbed by the French. The pope, Innocent XI, urged Leopold to give first attention to the infidels, but prudence continually reminded the emperor of the rapacity of the Most Christian king of France. The claims for restitution of Duke Charles V, excluded from Lorraine by Louis XIV, could not be ignored. Protests that the peace was violated were blandly answered by Louis XIV and his ministers, but no compensation or correction was offered. Leopold was forced to recognize the Turkish threat as closer and more dangerous, however, and in 1683 distributed his forces accordingly.

The emperor could not protect the western portions of the Empire. In 1680, when Charles II of England offered him a defensive alliance (through Middleton), Leopold, seeing that the English parliament was unwilling to grant money for an enlarged English army, dismissed the project as futile.

Louis XIV, made bold by Leopold's weakness, applied his policy of "reuniting" former "dependencies" with places which he had acquired to German lands as well as to the Spanish Netherlands; in 1681, for example, his army threatened to seize the imperial city of Strasbourg as a dependency of Alsace. Strasbourg capitulated on the best terms it could make for itself.

Louis used the jealousy of the German princes against the emperor, as well as intimidation, and his ministers concluded treaties with several of the important. The Archbishop-Elector of Cologne, Prince Maximilian Henry of Bavaria, usually supported the French side, and in the 1670's the French had been allied with Charles XI of Sweden, who possessed several northern German principalities. After the peace of Nijmegen, the King of Sweden withdrew from the French alliance. The Elector John George of Saxony joined the French camp in 1679, impelled by his fear of Brandenburg;[13] in the same year France seized upon Brandenburg's isolation to conclude a treaty with Elector Frederick William III.[14] Louis cemented these and other alliances with money and presents — far more liberal than the princes' sincerity warranted. For the time being, the Empire was disunited.

Although willing to renew the peace with the Turks in 1681, Leopold managed only to delay hostilities. He had made concessions to his Hungarian subjects, including freedom of religion, but the Ottoman court, knowing that Hungary was in disorder and that France exerted unremitting pressure in the west, made such demands that Leopold was forced to refuse peace. With Transylvanians and Hungarian rebels for allies, the Turks declared war in 1683 and moved rapidly through

[13] See Bertrand Auerbach, *La Diplomatic française et la cour de Saxe, 1648–1680* (Paris, 1887), p. 476.

[14] Gustave Bulard, *Les Traités de St.-Germain, Essai sur l'alliance étroite de Louis XIV et du Grand-Électeur après la guerre de Hollande* (Paris, 1898), pp. 73–75, 78, 81–82, 92–93.

Hungary and into Austria. The emperor fled Vienna on July 7, and the invaders besieged the city for more than two months, while all Europe — except France — waited in alarm. At last, on September 12, the combined efforts of imperialists and a Polish army under King John Sobieski defeated the Turks and forced them to retire.

During this time the emperor sought help from neighboring monarchs and from the states of the Holy Roman Empire. It was clear that if the emperor fell the rest of Germany was exposed. Various German states furnished money and troops for the common defense. Volunteers from other nations served the emperor in large numbers. When the siege was broken up, celebrations in most capitals of Europe testify to the tension of the crisis and to the relief at its relaxation. But the crisis was not over; the Turks were not yet subdued. Until the capture of Buda in 1686, the empire was not safe; the Elector of Bavaria, for instance, refused to send his forces to the Rhine in May, 1684.

France, meanwhile, took advantage of the opening in the imperial defenses to resume war with Spain in 1683 and 1684. The truce of Ratisbon ended the war in 1684, but its terms were favorable to France because of the danger to the emperor in his hereditary dominions. Louis XIV retained in his possession all that he had taken from Spain during the previous twenty years, without prejudice to the final settlement; he sought in 1687 to convert the truce into a peace, and thus acquire permanent dominion over his temporary conquests.[15] But he went on to menace the peace in four ways.

Having no intention of yielding his conquests at any future time, he erected defensive works to hold them. In 1686 he strengthened his position in Alsace and the Breisgau by building and garrisoning a fortified bridgehead opposite Hüningen, near Basle, on the land he held and said he had paid for, but

---

[15] According to Wilhelm Fraknói, the proposal to convert the truce into a peace originated with Cardinal Buonvisi, whose preoccupation was the successful prosecution of the emperor's Turkish war. *Papst Innocenz XI (Benedikt Odescalchi) und Ungarn's Befreiung des Türken Herrschaft*, trans. into German by Peter Jekel (Freiburg-in-Breisgau, 1902), p. 237 n. Barrillon told James II that the pope approved of the conversion. D'Adda was instructed from Rome to undeceive James and Sunderland on this point. B.M., Add. MS 15,396, fol. 268.

the Margrave of Baden protested his right to fortify it.[16] The bridgehead, which could be used either for the defense of Louis XIV's conquests or for launching further attacks on southern Germany — for instance against Baden-Durlach — seems to have been undertaken by the Marquis de Louvois without the knowledge even of the French foreign minister.[17] Once built, it remained in spite of all protests, and in 1687, the right to build such works was one of those reserved by France in agreeing to the English guarantee of the truce of Ratisbon. That same year, the French began construction of a fortification called Mont Royal at Trarbach on the Moselle, in the dominions of the Elector of Trier, where they had no right to be at all, though the French war minister Louvois furnished falsified documents tending to show the opposite.[18] The Elector of Saxony, for one, offered to join the emperor in pressing Louis XIV to desist.[19]

The fortification of Trarbach was a symptom of another imperial affliction: the king of France was continuing to annex German territory. Early in 1687, Peter Wyche wrote to Middleton that France had annexed 200 parishes in the baillage of Agein, between Metz and Mainz, that an abbot in the city of Trier itself had done homage to Louis XIV, and that the Chamber of Reunion at Metz showed signs of renewed activity.[20]

Claims were not invariably based on forged titles. In 1685, when the ruling house of the Palatinate became extinct, two related branches of the Wittelsbach family — those of Neuburg and Veldenz — laid claim to it. Prince Philip William of Neuburg had obtained designation by his predecessor and approval by the emperor; he entered into possession. There was another claim, more dangerous to Germany: Elisabeth-Charlotte, Duchess of Orleans and sister-in-law to Louis XIV, was a daughter of a former elector palatine. "Madame," as she was called, had no desire to put herself forward, but Louis XIV demanded for her son (the later Regent of France) not only

---

[16] B.M., Add. MS 41,826, fol. 4.

[17] Onno Klopp, *Der Fall des Hauses Stuart und die Succession des Hauses Hannover in Gross-Britannien und Irland* (14 vols.; Vienna, 1875–88), III, 215–16.

[18] Klopp, *Der Fall*, III, 344–45.

[19] B.M., Add. MS 41,841, fol. 44.

[20] B.M., Add. MS 41,826, fol. 60.

the movables of the deceased elector, but all his allodial possessions and all the property acquired by electors palatine since
1356.[21] It was a large claim even by a narrow interpretation,
and would have made near-enclaves of parts of other German
states; besides, it would have reduced an elector to impotence
and penury. But Louis XIV had never taken a narrow interpretation of any claim he chose to make. Legally, at all events,
there was no principle of female succession in such a case in
the Holy Roman Empire: if France could assert it in this case,
it could assert it as well in any other. The Elector of Brandenburg was reported to have offered James II 20,000 men for
the protection of the Palatinate.[22]

Although the king of France was tempted to take the prize
by force, he accepted instead the offer of Innocent XI to serve
as arbitrator; the parties arrived at a compromise about the
movable property.[23] As the relations between France and the
pope worsened, however, the arbitration project was forgotten;
also for once Leopold's stubbornness seemed likely to equal
that of Louis XIV.

The king of France was not content with the German allies
whose cooperation he thought he had purchased and an elector
palatine subject to his will; he also hoped to name a subservient
Archbishop-Elector of Cologne.

Prince William of Fürstenberg, younger son of a ruling
family in southern Germany, had long been the chief French
agent in Germany, influencing (among others) Elector Maximilian Henry of Cologne. He was an ecclesiastic, and French
influence had already procured for him the bishopric of Strasbourg and a cardinal's hat. He was also a member of the
cathedral chapter of Cologne, and he aspired to that arch-
bishopric.

Maximilian Henry had no serious objection to French and
anti-imperialist leanings; he himself concluded an offensive

        [21] Richard Fester, *Die Augsburger Allianz von 1686* (Munich, 1893), pp.
8–9, 25.
        [22] J., Count d'Avaux, *Négociations . . . en Hollande, depuis 1679, jusqu'en
1688* (6 vols.; Paris, 1752–53), III, 75–76.
        [23] Fester, *Augsburger Allianz*, p. 28; Dumont, *Corps universel du droit des
gens*, vol. VII, Part 1, pp. 148–49; Innocent XI, *Epistolae ad principes*, ed.
I. I. Berthier (2 vols.; Rome, 1891–95), II, 286.

alliance with Louis XIV in June, 1687.[24] In the autumn of the same year, when he announced that he needed a coadjutor in his see, several candidates presented themselves — Fürstenberg, Prince Joseph Clement of Bavaria, and a palatine prince who was Bishop of Breslau. The cathedral chapter, which had the responsibility of election, and made up largely of members of German princely and noble families, secular in outlook, disregarded the pope's command to postpone the election. In January, seventeen or eighteen members voted for Fürstenberg, who had spent French money freely.[25] This election to the coadjutorship was naturally alarming to princes who feared France. Frederick William III of Brandenburg disdained even to answer the formal notification of the results of the election.

The more powerful rulers of Germany — Leopold, the king of Sweden, the Elector of Bavaria, and others — were now organized, after a fashion, for resistance to French attack. In his concern for the Turkish war, Leopold had hoped for the stabilization of western Europe; he had wished Charles II of England to guarantee the truce of Ratisbon when it was concluded and had wished the truce to include all his allies.[26] Though Leopold's ordinary irresolution was well known, he did not strip his western possessions of troops.

The princes of the empire and the neighboring states were gradually drawing together as the truce was proved to be an illusion. There were a number of treaties and conventions in 1685 and 1686, culminating in the League of Augsburg, comprising the emperor, the kings of Spain and Sweden, the Elector of Bavaria, three of the imperial circles (political regions), and various princes.[27] This league, made in July, 1686, was designed for the preservation of the truce of Ratisbon and the public security of the Holy Roman Empire and its states. The contribution to be made by each member in the event of breach

---

[24] Leonard Ennen, *Frankreich und der Niederrhein, oder Geschichte von Stadt und Kurstaat Köln* . . . (2 vols.; Cologne and Neuss, 1855–56), I, 467. On the Cologne election of 1688, see also Ernst Böhmlander, "Die Wahl des Herzogs Joseph Clemens von Bayern zum Erzbischof von Köln 1688," *Oberbayerisches Archiv für vaterländische Geschichte. Zugleich Forschungen zur Geschichte Bayerns*, LVI (1912), 173–247; LVII (1913), 224–84.
[25] Ennen, *Frankreich und der Niederrhein*, I, 471, 473–75, 480–81.
[26] B.M., Add. MS 41,806, fols. 83–84; P.R.O., P.R.O. 31/3/158, fol. 280.
[27] Dumont, *Corps*, VII, Part 1, 131–38. For the formation of the league, see Fester, *Die Augsburger Allianz*.

of the peace was set forth. The probable enemy of the league, though not named, was France. The French minister at Ratisbon declared that the league was in itself a breach of the truce.[28]

This League of Augsburg still lacked the power for a sustained struggle with the formidable French armies. The king of England was not a member, nor the Dutch Netherlands, nor some of the more important German states. The adherence of all or most of these must be gained. The king of France set about breaking the alliance as soon as it was made, for instance by encouraging Denmark to "alarm" the Circle of Lower Saxony. In reply, it was said, the Dutch urged Sweden on by means of subsidies. Leopold's purpose, however, was strengthened by the Elector of Brandenburg and other princes, who urged him to make peace with Turkey and turn to the protection of the western parts of the Holy Roman Empire.[29] On the other hand, German unity was easily disturbed: the Elector of Mainz and the great imperial city of Frankfurt-am-Main engaged in a petty dispute as late as the spring of 1688.

The long-expected clash with France came when the Elector of Cologne died, on June 3, 1688. The Elector John George of Saxony, with the approval of the Elector of Bavaria, the Elector Palatine, and Emperor Leopold, prepared to make a party in the chapter at Cologne against the election of Fürstenberg.[30] The stakes were enormous — besides Cologne, the bishoprics of Liége, Münster, and Hildesheim, each a principality, all vacant by the death of Maximilian Henry. Neither France nor the German states could neglect such prizes. Sir Richard Bulstrode wrote from Brussels:

This incident is like to occasion great factions and parties and to give a great *Embaras* in those parts, if it go no farther; and in all appearance it will hasten the treaty at Aix betwixt the states of Holland, the Elector of Saxony, the Landgrave of Hesse-Cassel with some other Protestant princes whose territories border upon those bishoprics; but it is not yet known whether the Elector of Brandenburg will engage therein. . . .

[28] B.M., Add. MS 41,826, fols. 54, 58, 60.
[29] *Ibid.*, fol. 62; Bertrand Auerbach, *La France et le Saint Empire Romain Germanique depuis la paix de Westphalie jusqu' à la révolution française* (Paris, 1912), 235–36.
[30] B.M., Add. MS 41,833, fol. 124.

French troops began to move: between the Sambre and the Meuse, they advanced on Liége in the middle of June; from the Saar, they approached the electorate of Cologne — in both cases pressure for the election of Fürstenberg — and Bulstrode thought the election at Cologne would certainly give the French candidate a victory.[31] Spanish troops countered the French by marching to Namur, and the Spanish governor-general at Brussels sent an agent to Düsseldorf to "promote the pretensions" of one of the other candidates.[32] The emperor favored Prince Joseph Clement of Bavaria, Bishop of Freising, and declared Fürstenberg ineligible because, though a German by birth, he was French by interest and naturalization. Those charges Fürstenberg denied. Kaunitz, the imperial minister at Cologne, threatened that if the French candidate were chosen, the electoral vote of the archbishop would be transferred to another prince.[33]

The pope gave Joseph Clement an advantage. The rule was that the holder of another bishopric must be "postulated" by two-thirds of the members of the chapter. Dispensing with the requirement in Joseph Clement's case, the pope ruled that he might be elected by a simple majority vote, making no exception for Fürstenberg. Thus the Bavarian prince needed only thirteen votes of the twenty-four, while the French candidate needed sixteen. The election took place on July 19 with inconclusive results. Fürstenberg received thirteen votes, while Joseph Clement had nine, with two for minor candidates. No one was elected, although Fürstenberg said he was, and the matter was referred to Rome. On September 15, a consistory declared Joseph Clement elected: Louis XIV gave this election as a ground for war against the emperor on September 24.[34]

The election at Liége was held in the interval. Bulstrode reported on June 15 that a Prince of Neuburg had only a small interest; and the Grand Dean of Liége, the Baron Jean-Louis d'Elderen, had a strong one, but if Elderen and the Neuburg prince joined forces, Fürstenberg's prospects were doubtful.

[31] B.M., Add. MS 41,832, fols. 234, 236.
[32] *Ibid.*, fol. 238.
[33] Ennen, *Frankreich und der Niederrhein*, I, 488–91.
[34] *Ibid.*, 491–92, 493, 496; Jo. Lytcot to Sunderland, Rome, June 26, 1688, P.R.O., S.P. 98/17.

The Spanish governor-general, the Marquis of Gastañaga, said to have little influence, opposed Fürstenberg. After the vote at Cologne, the French candidate went to Liége to conduct his own campaign. The rival interests united against him in support of the Grand Dean.[35] Elderen was elected on August 17; and his election was in due course recognized by the pope, although (Bulstrode wrote) the Spanish governor-general had bought six votes for the successful candidate.

We are told [Bulstrode went on] the Prince [= Bishop] of Liége, being of a very quiet temper, will spend most of his time in devotion and leave the care of the government in the hands of those who are good imperialists; the like care will be taken at Cologne, till Prince Clement [then seventeen years old] be able to govern, so that by these two elections, we are like to continue in peace, which is necessary for preservation of these provinces, and for the great good of Christendom.[36]

At Münster and Hildesheim, two other German candidates were chosen, breaking up the over-great agglomeration of states once held by the Elector Maximilian Henry.

Bulstrode was mistaken about the results of the election. War broke out in September, French troops overran both Liége and Cologne, and the pacific Bishop of Liége joined the coalition against France contrary to expectation. His capital was burned. Joseph Clement lost control of most of his electorate, and a French army occupied and devastated the Palatinate of the Rhine.

The War of the League of Augsburg thus arose quite naturally from German immediate causes. Because the French armies were concentrated in the Rhineland, the Dutch in 1688 were free to employ their troops in the invasion of England.

English policy on Germany varied, affected by the interests and the dynasties involved. Charles II had shown solicitude toward Charles V of Lorraine, whose homeless condition resembled that of the young Stuart exile during the Interregnum. In 1676, for instance, after congratulating the French ambassador on his master's successes in war, Charles told the ambassador,

---

[35] B.M., Add. MS 41,832, fols. 258–59.
[36] P.R.O., S.P. 77/55, fol. 480.

that he would hope with all his heart that the advantage which you [Louis XIV] have just gained over your enemies could persuade your majesty that it would not now be contrary to your glory to accord the title of Duke of Lorraine to Prince Charles; and that in doing so your majesty would receive the same praises as you received nearly two years ago when, after your arms had driven the Germans beyond the Rhine after several defeats, you were pleased to give concessions as to the interests of Prince William of Fürstenberg, which you had until then always refused.[37]

On the other hand, Charles II regarded the annexation of Strasbourg as inevitable and irremediable, as did the emperor.[38]

James II continued his brother's diplomatic support of the Duke of Lorraine, perhaps more strongly than Charles, because James regarded the Austro-Turkish war, in which the duke was a general, as one of vital importance to Christendom. In 1685 he instructed Sir William Trumbull, his envoy at Paris, to add his representations to those of Count von Lobkowitz, the imperial envoy, for a settlement of the duke's affairs. The English efforts were apparently serious, for Charles V later thanked James for his protection: "If I perceive some change in the inclinations of the Most Christian King, I ought to attribute it to the kindness of your majesty."[39]

Charles II and James II also took special care of the elector palatine, Philip William, who as Count of Neuburg had rendered friendly, but futile, service to the Stuarts during the interregnum. James also undertook to protect the elector at the court of France. One of Philip William's first actions when the Palatinate was actually attacked (in September, 1688), was to beg James for help.[40]

Another appellant was Louis Antony of Neuburg, Grand Master of the Teutonic Order, when, in the autumn of 1685, Louis XIV commanded the seizure of the order's property in Alsace and Lorraine. Louis Antony appealed to James through Count Hamilton, the palatine envoy at London,[41] but James

[37] P.R.O., P.R.O. 31/3/131, fol. 150.
[38] *Ibid.*, bundle 150, fol. 283.
[39] P.R.O., S.P. 78/150, fol. 15.
[40] C. Brinkmann, "The Relations between England and Germany, 1660–1688," *E.H.R.*, XXIV (1909), 247–77, 448–69, esp. 467; B.M., Add. MS 41,808, fol. 115.
[41] *Ibid.*, fols. 11–16.

was cold — perhaps because the grand master was supported by Emperor Leopold.[42]

James II's relations with Leopold had certainly been friendly when the emperor had been the Christian defender. The imperial envoy, Count Sigismund von Thun, hardly a model diplomat, was the only diplomatic contact with Vienna until the arrival of Count Andreas Kaunitz, in January, 1687.

Kaunitz went to England by way of The Hague, where William of Orange gave him an interview. While there he heard from Pensionary Fagel of Holland a flat assertion that Louis XIV and James II had a secret understanding.[43] This James denied and the agents of Louis took care to repeat. For James to admit it, as Lord Chandos reflected, would be to say that "our master is withdrawn from his inestimable post of neutrality, whereby his majesty was sure always of the advantage and benediction of the peacemaker between most Christian princes, and therein also the mighty conveniency of being on all sides embraced for the great arbitrator and almost lawgiver to Europe. . . ."[44] There was truth in what he said. There was no Anglo-French alliance; James was courted by foreign rulers; and he did contribute to the peace of Europe, if only in the short run.

It was convenient for William and Fagel, who had their own ends, to believe and disseminate these reports of an Anglo-French alliance. James, who knew this well, also knew that Kaunitz had been prejudiced by his visit to Holland. Furthermore, the makers of the new Augsburg alliance had been reported to James as spreading the same story, and he was afraid of the growth of a Protestant league against Catholics, particularly against himself.[45] As to peace, his resident at Ratisbon, Sir George Etherege, doubted that Leopold would long observe the truce of 1684.[46] The emperor appeared to be turning away from the Turkish war to a useless war in western Europe. James admitted, however, that the fortification opposite Hüningen was a violation of the truce and he spoke of such a fortifi-

[42] Brinkmann, "Relations," *E.H.R.*, XXIV, 467.
[43] Klopp, *Der Fall*, III, 273–75.
[44] P.R.O., S.P. 97/20, fol. 63.
[45] B.M., Add. MS 41,836, fol. 219; P.R.O., P.R.O. 31/3/162, fol. 219; *ibid.*, bundle 163, fol. 251; d'Avaux, *Négociations*, V, 276–77.
[46] Etherege, *Letterbook*, p. 138.

cation (to Barrillon, in October, 1686) as a thing to be avoided by the king of France, who should "anticipate the designs of those who would like to see the war begin again." Barrillon replied that as the works were finished and no enemy would attack them, the Hüningen affair would simply be another grievance of the Austrian party — whether a justifiable grievance Barrillon evidently did not care. At that time, some persons about the English court thought that King James's efforts would settle the problem of Hüningen.[47]

By the spring of 1687, James's views were changing. In May, Count Andreas Kaunitz, the new imperial envoy, made a serious proposal for an English guarantee of the truce of 1684. The king of France, Kaunitz said, would have no objection to such a guarantee if he were peacefully inclined. James replied that he was laboring for the security of the Catholic religion and for his own domestic concerns, in order to be able to do more in future for the common good. (But nearly at the same time he declined to urge the Duke of Lorraine's claims further.)

D'Adda and Ronquillo, the papal nuncio and the Spanish minister, supported Kaunitz in parallel memorials submitted to James, but to no effect, and James thereafter neglected German affairs. He refused his guarantee of the truce, which Kaunitz had requested in the emperor's name. He declined the renewal of an alliance with the Elector of Brandenburg, who, he thought, had been associated with Monmouth.[48] He feared and disliked the League of Augsburg and its association with his increasingly disobedient son-in-law William of Orange. He thought any event that strengthened the anti-French coalition was dangerous — to him, to Catholicism, and to the British monarchy — and Barrillon, the French ambassador, encouraged him in these views. Louis XIV's support of Fürstenberg after the election was acceptable to him. When the Dutch were distracted by continental dangers, he thought, they could not disturb his plans for England. As Middleton wrote Albeville, on June 5/15, 1688, "I might have imagined that the people where you are [at The Hague], might have had their heads so full of the bishops of Cologne, Liége, and Mün-

---

[47] P.R.O., P.R.O. 31/3/167, fols. 65–66; B.M., Add. 25,373, fol. 10.
[48] Brinkmann, "Relations," *E.H.R.*, XXIV, 465–66.

ster that they could not have thought of ours, who are to appear
before his majesty in council next Friday. . . ."[49] The defeat
of Fürstenberg at Liége gave an advantage to the Dutch, James
told d'Adda, and the Dutch were the enemies James most
feared. Indeed, they were preparing their invasion when he
spoke. Apparently, even the Duke of Lorraine and the elector
palatine were associated in the king's mind with the threat to
his own safety, for the instructions to Lord Waldegrave, going
to France as envoy in November, 1688, omit any mention of
protection to be extended to them, though such mention had
formerly been inserted as a matter of course.[50]

The complexity of the situation rendered the empire almost
indefensible without very large contributions from foreign
allies. Because James could not make these contributions early
in his reign, he had to rely on a diplomacy in which his only
counters were his disposable military forces and his potential
association with the anti-French side in some future, favorable,
parliament. All things considered, his diplomacy was fairly
successful. In the Spanish Netherlands, Spain was restrained
from entering a war it could not win; on the other hand, the
French found it wiser not to seize Namur, as they once came
near doing. In Germany, French aggression did not proceed
as far as the German states had feared. In 1687, however, a
change in English policy was apparent, and French progress
became more open and ambitious. Louis XIV began a campaign to dominate the German Rhineland; when it failed, in
the summer of 1688, he made the war that James II had earlier
tried to avoid. But by that time James's wishes were imma-
terial: England was faced with an invasion.

Although the states affected by the encroachments of Louis
XIV lay in the Northern Department, the aggressor belonged
to Sunderland's province; thus the pressure exerted by James II
upon his French cousin was not Middleton's responsibility.
Middleton, however, collected the information from various
sources to shape James's foreign policy.

England was almost directly affected by the course of events

[49] B.M., Add. MS 41,823, fol. 68.
[50] Instructions of Nov. 8, 1688, P.R.O., S.P. 104/19. Compare with instructions to Trumbull, Sept. 21, 1685, and to Bevil Skelton, Nov. 8, 1686,
ibid.

in Germany, which alarmed Amsterdam so much that it fell in with the plans of William III. Those events also committed the French armies to such a campaign as made counterattack on the Dutch republic impossible during the invasion of England.

CHAPTER VIII

The Drawn Sword Blind as Fortune

On February 4, 1678/79, Sir Joseph Williamson wrote to Sir Peter Wyche, English envoy to the Hanse towns, acknowledging receipt of a dispatch.

The enclosed from a Duke of Holstein shall be carefully delivered [to the king], but we cannot at all find out which Duke of Holstein it is; I see it is dated at Frenzhagen, but where that is, we must pray you to inform yourself. [And also to supply the] alliances and genealogies for two or three descents, but especially the present one of all the branches of that House of Holstein, which is run into so many various branches.[1]

We may judge from this that previous contact between England and Holstein had left little trace in the secretary's office.

Probably the duke whose identity eluded Williamson was Christian Albert, Duke of Holstein-Gottorp, who held lands in Schleswig and Holstein, most important of the rulers in the region next to the Danish King Christian V. Neighborhood and kinship connected the families of the king and the duke, but the two branches had been enemies for several generations. King Christian also held parts of Schleswig and Holstein, intermingled with those of the duke in a complicated fashion, and as princes of Holstein the king and the duke were members of the Holy Roman Empire. Until 1683, the king of England had no interest in Holstein worth mention.

Adjoining the ducal and royal portions of Holstein, in the lower valley of the Elbe River, lay the rich Hanse city of Hamburg, one of the great marts of the North Sea region, where merchants of many nations traded, and where some grew rich.

---

[1] Williamson to Wyche, Feb. 4, 1678/9, P.R.O., S.P. 104/56.

Although Hamburg was an imperial free city, under its own government, the rulers of Holstein had in the past asserted a vague superiority over it. Other neighbors, the Dukes of Brunswick, also coveted the city. Because the English Company of Merchant Adventurers had its German base and enjoyed many privileges at Hamburg, and the company was influential in the City of London and at court, the fortunes of Hamburg greatly interested the English government.

In the 1680's the enviable success of the king of France aroused emulation in Christian V. Denmark was not a great power, but in northern Germany it had few rivals, and Christian hoped to make permanent additions to his German dominions while the empire was distracted by French encroachments and the Turkish war. Louis XIV was a natural ally: the king of Sweden had drifted away from his alliance with France, eventually aligning himself with the anti-French states in the League of Augsburg, and Louis could use Denmark to counter Sweden and to threaten the German states in the North, distracting them from resistance to France. In March, 1682, France and Denmark contracted a defensive alliance, and on November 6/16, 1683, Louis XIV concluded a further treaty of alliance and subsidy with Christian V.

King Christian had clashed with and overcome Christian Albert, and had imposed hard terms upon him. The duke had protested the terms and had sought diplomatic intervention by the United Netherlands, Sweden, France, and England. Lord Preston, who was at Paris in September, 1682, had signified to the French foreign minister, Croissy, that Charles II desired Louis XIV's interposition in the affair. Croissy answered that his master had great consideration for the King of England but would not interpose.

The proceedings of the Duke of Holstein had been something extraordinary, and his carriage towards him [Louis], and the King of Denmark of late by no means obliging. He [Croissy] said further that he [the duke] had been very forward in sending his proportion of men to the troops of the circles for the defense of the Empire, and so shewed his great inclination to begin a war in Germany; that upon that account he [the duke] could not expect any great favour or assistance from this court; but that he would advise him to change his measures, and to endeavour to live well with the King of Denmark, which was his true and most safe interest. . . .[2]

Thus Louis XIV was at once helping Denmark and punishing a too faithful defender of Germany. In January, 1683, Charles II also refused to meddle with the duke's affairs, saying that he might do more harm than good at that time. Nor were the Dutch willing to seem sympathetic, for they would enter into a treaty with Holstein-Gottorp only as a cosignatory with several members of the Circle of Lower Saxony. The English envoy at The Hague, Chudleigh, attributed this attitude to fear of war.[3]

England's connection with the differences between the king and the duke was altered, however, by the marriage (later in 1683) of Prince George of Denmark and the Princess Anne, the younger daughter of the Duke of York. To some observers, this dynastic connection appeared to foreshadow an alliance with an ally of France, if not with France and Denmark both. In the smaller affairs of Holstein-Gottorp, the marriage may have seemed to Christian Albert a savage blow of fate. Early in 1684, when Danish troops occupied the duke's lands in Schleswig, the dispossessed ruler moved to Hamburg.

He did not, perhaps could not, give up hope of English assistance. He wrote Charles II, in the summer of 1684, that the king of Denmark had occupied his domains in Schleswig and most of those in Holstein, and that quarters and other exactions for a Danish army had been levied on his subjects for more than two years. King Christian, who intended by these means to compel the duke to renounce his rights under several treaties, had revoked his concessions to Christian Albert, including his recognition of the duke's sovereignty in his portion of Schleswig. Christian relied on French support to protect him from the consequences.[4] Sweden, Brandenburg, and Emperor Leopold tried to help, and, in October, Count von Thun conveyed hopes that Charles II would also use diplomatic pressure for the duke,[5] but diplomatic work at this early

---

[2] P.R.O., S.P. 78/144, fols. 99, 119; see also B.M., Add. MS 17,677 TT, fol. 294.

[3] B.M., Add. MS 41,809, fol. 66.

[4] B.M., Add. MS 41,807, fols. 94–95; Ranke, *History of England, Principally in the Seventeenth Century*, IV, 380.

[5] B.M., Add. MS 41,840, fol. 9; Add. MS 41,806, fols. 85–86.

stage was futile. The king of Denmark retained what he had seized, and no one appeared willing to proceed to actions that might lead to war, although Charles XI of Sweden talked fiercely.[6]

Hamburg's riches had long tempted Denmark, and Christian V, in 1679, had threatened the city for refusing him an oath of fealty. Charles II, on the request of the city, had then asked the United Netherlands for cooperation in preserving Hamburg's independence, and the city had been saved. The Brunswick dukes were also concerned, for the States General avowed that it had acted "more out of kindness to the house of Brunswick, than to the town."[7]

Alliance with the Brunswick house was part of Charles II's policy of 1680. There were then three princes of the family who were worth taking into account: the Dukes of Celle, Hanover, and Wolfenbüttel. Sir Gabriel Sylvius set out to attract them into alliance with England at almost the same time as Middleton went to Linz. The danger to Hamburg passed, and for some years there were no more Danish menaces. But English relations with Celle and Hanover worsened: in September, 1684, the Brunswick dukes were actually sheltering English political offenders.[8] Celle and Hanover were forming agreements nearer home in the 1680's, with Sweden, the emperor, and the Prince of Orange, so that these two dukes and the Duke of Holstein-Gottorp were indirectly allied through Sweden. Moreover, the marriage of George of Denmark with Princess Anne made Hamburg anxious lest English protection be withdrawn.[9]

The citizens of Hamburg were divided into factions, some favoring the Brunswick dukes, others the king of Denmark. The "Danish" or popular party was in power and oppressing its enemies, the city's merchant oligarchy, when Hamburg got into trouble again in 1685. Duke George William of Celle was

[6] B.M., Add. MS 41,831, fol. 51; *Urkunden und Aktenstücke zur Geschichte des Kurfürsten Friedrich Wilhelm von Brandenburg* (Berlin, 23 vols., 1884–1930), XIX, ed. F. Hirsch, 690.

[7] Jenkins to Sylvius, June 1, 1680, P.R.O., S.P. 104/189.

[8] P.R.O., S.P. 82/16, fol. 298.

[9] *Urkunden und Aktenstücke*, XIX, p. 445; B.M., Add. MS 41,809, fols. 74–77.

ordered by the emperor to intervene in these disputes, settle them, and punish certain of the citizens, but the senate of the city regarded George William as an enemy, and refused to allow him to execute his commission; moreover, it forbade commerce between Hamburg and the lands of Celle and eventually seized the duke's subjects in Hamburg in June, 1685. The emperor threatened the city with the ban of the empire, and the senate thereupon proposed a compromise through the mediation of the Elector of Brandenburg. The "Danish" faction, however, continued to look to Christian V for the preservation of the city's liberties.[10]

The Elector of Brandenburg, Frederick William III, was deeply concerned about the outcome of the dispute: in February, 1685, one of his agents discussed the matter with Middleton, who assured him that James II would have intervened in any case, but that the elector's offices made the occasion a better one. England could not permit the city on which its German trade depended to be oppressed, even had the Duke of Celle not given offense by protecting the rebel, Colonel Waller. Thus James was very willing to use diplomatic methods to succor Hamburg when threatened by the house of Brunswick.

The English trade in Germany was, as Middleton suggested, in hazard. The Hamburg commerce in woolens was interrupted, and the position of British subjects was at first unsettled. The Duke of Celle offered the Company of Merchant Adventurers free passage through his territories in August, 1685, but Wyche, the English representative at Hamburg, thought that Duke George William meant to divide the company from the citizens by this discriminatory treatment.[11] Resentment so created would last, and the merchants of the company might be regarded as enemies of the city.

At just that time, Sir Gabriel Sylvius was negotiating for a defensive alliance between England and Denmark, similar to a rather loose one of 1670. Denmark's alliance with the United Netherlands had expired, leaving Christian V exposed to a possible coalition of Sweden, Brandenburg, and his former

[10] B.M., Add. MS 41,824, fols. 193, 247, 270; Fester, *Augsburger Allianz*, p. 88.
[11] B.M., Add. MS 41,825, fol. 7.

ally, and the renewal of the treaties between England and the Netherlands in 1685 had also made a stir. But the alliance offered by Sylvius to Christian V was unsatisfactory: the Danish king wanted a closer alliance in the event of a northern coalition, while James was more interested in a commercial treaty than in a tight political alliance that might involve him in war. He did not respond favorably to Danish representations on the subject.[12]

Hamburg, having been subjected to severe diplomatic pressure, was now less recalcitrant. The city showed its sympathy for the emperor's side in the Turkish war by holding a solemn thanksgiving for his series of victories, "though they are to be led in the triumph, nothing being to be foreseen but they must at last undergo what shall be enjoined them by the Emperor. . . ." The Elector of Brandenburg was at the same time reported to be renewing his good offices with the Duke of Celle.[13]

The dispute came near settlement in October, 1685, and trade was unofficially reopened. A division arose, however, between the Senate, which would have accepted the terms offered by George William of Celle, and a popular committee, called "the Thirty," which resisted the return of the estate of an obnoxious former burgomaster, one Meurer, which George William demanded. The King of Denmark chose this time to make a progress through Holstein. Representatives of the two sides in the city waited upon him, and no doubt as a result of Danish assurances, the Thirty refused in December to yield to the emperor and the Duke of Celle.[14]

Early in 1685/86, the forces of Celle invaded the territory of Hamburg, and Christian V immediately gave marching orders to several of his battalions nearby.[15] The Duke of Holstein-Gottorp left the city, which professed itself ready "to repel force by force." The English company there offered the lives and estates of its members in the common cause. Wyche thought the senate ready to make peace with the emperor and fearful of Denmark. As for the Thirty,

[12] B.M., Add. MS 41,828, fols. 20, 24–25, 30, 40; Add. MS 41,825, fol. 16.
[13] B.M., Add. MS 41,825, fol. 16.
[14] B.M., Add. MS 41,825, fols. 41, 72–73.
[15] B.M., Add. MS 41,828, fols. 62–63.

This hot-headed junto (who have been soothed and cajoled by Danish emissaries ever since they had any power) are suspected to be inclinable to call to their assistance and protection that king, when the whole will be in danger, and this place is to do all things precariously at his pleasure; thus are we *inter sacrum saxumque* [between the knife and the victim]. . . .[16]

Those most endangered were of course the merchant adventurers, who asked James II (on February 6/16, 1685/86) for directions and protection in securing their property from damage if the Danes should attack. While the Elector of Brandenburg made further efforts for peace, the troops of Celle entrenched themselves near the city, and the Danish ones found quarters on the remaining property of the Duke of Holstein-Gottorp. Wyche wrote Middleton, indeed, that Hamburg's neighbors were "glad of fresh quarters," which would cost the city more than submission to the emperor would have done.[17]

Again the English situation was difficult. Within the city were the goods and persons of English merchants; outside it, the king of Denmark seized two bailiwicks (*baillages*) belonging to the Duke of Holstein, on which Prince George of Denmark had a mortgage.[18] Wyche conveyed to deputies of the senate his master's advice to reach an accommodation with the emperor: "I let them know, that the Senate offering any particular wherein his majesty might in their behalf interpose his royal offices, he would . . . most willingly and earnestly do it. . . ." The senate wisely refrained from calling in the king of Denmark, despite his offers of help; it proposed, rather, that the troops of Celle should withdraw, after which the two sides would come to an understanding through the mediation of the Elector of Brandenburg.[19] Sir George Etherege reported that the elector had offered Hamburg 2,000 of his foot, "but they have refused them — they are jealous (not without cause) all their neighbours have a mind to 'em and it is happy for 'em so many have a longing, the number of the rivals only hinder the rape. . . . it is generally thought here, the Lüneburgers

[16] B.M., Add. MS 41,825, fols. 84–86. The Latin allusion is to Plautus, *Captivi*, Act iii, scene 4.
[17] B.M., Add. MS 41,825, fols. 96, 98–99.
[18] B.M., Add. MS 41,828, fol. 64.
[19] B.M., Add. MS 41,825, fols. 106–7.

[the troops of Celle] will draw off, as soon as honorably they can." [20]

In March, the senate accepted the mediation of the king of Sweden, an ally of the Duke of Celle. The duke also accepted and withdrew his troops in early April, under pressure from Christian V and the Emperor Leopold (whose commission he held), but the Danish forces remained in Holstein, close by.

Hamburg's troubles were only beginning. The counts of Holstein had long ago claimed the homage of the city; after the last crisis with Denmark, this homage had been decently shelved under the Treaty of Pinneberg, in 1679. Having taken the duke's portion of Holstein, Christian V reclaimed the homage. Wyche wrote on July 20/30:

The King of Denmark being assured by his ministers he hath here, that he hath a considerable party in this place, renews his pretensions of having homage done him by this magistracy, which point to obtain, he came before this city six years since, when with a good sum of money paid him, the homage was either to be decided by a fair treaty, or by the chamber at Speyer.

The Danes were in 1686 uncommonly strong near Hamburg, and the city was seriously alarmed. [21]

A month later, Sir Gabriel Sylvius wrote from the town of Schleswig that the king of Denmark had assembled twelve thousand or fourteen thousand soldiers for the capture of Hamburg with the collusion of the Thirty. The mask was now off. Christian V told Sylvius that he wanted only simple homage, and that he intended nothing against the town's liberties; but if he did not receive homage, he would take it as a right, by force. The merchant adventurers need fear no harm, he said. Sylvius thought that this plot had been undertaken without French foreknowledge. [22]

Within the city, the Danish faction "disappeared"; the Thirty were "laid aside"; and the senate assumed full control, resolved to defend Hamburg against the Danish demands, and appealed to James II for protection, saying that it already had promises

[20] B.M., Add. MS 41,836, fol. 60.
[21] B.M., Add. MS 41,825, fol. 207.
[22] B.M., Add. MS 41,825, fol. 200; Add. MS 41,828, fols. 109, 114–15; P.R.O., S.P. 82/116, fol. 293.

of support from the Brunswick dukes. It was recalled that, a few years before, Charles II had promised to send ships to the Elbe to protect Hamburg against Denmark. Wyche reported that the Duke of Celle was already popular because of assurances he made to the city.[23] On August 21 (o.s.) the Danes made their first onslaught, fighting and plundering under the city walls. The citizens were united at last, and a Brandenburg envoy went to warn Christian V that Frederick William III would resent a bombardment of Hamburg as though it were one of Berlin.[24]

The merchant adventurers had already expressed their fears through Wyche, "That such a trade of our nation may run such a risk. . . ."[25] Middleton queried Wyche in return. James II, he said, could not "be thought to approve of their standing too stiffly upon things that are not only insignificant in themselves, but such as may help to increase rather than to quench that flame which is broke out." But what were these matters which the king of Denmark pretended against Hamburg? Upon what were they founded? What was the history of the subject?[26] Still, on September 2, 1686, James wrote Christian V "a very pressing letter in favor of the city of Hamburg as well as of his subjects there."[27]

The king of Denmark was slow in presenting his side of the question to James II, because of the secrecy required by his plans. He never succeeded in convincing the king of England that his claims were just.

At the outbreak of fighting, both Wyche and Sylvius became active participants in smoothing over the quarrel. Both were on the scene — Wyche in Hamburg and Sylvius in the Danish camp — and they were apparently allowed free movement by both sides. Each tended to support the government to which he was accredited. (When the senate asked Christian V to withdraw his forces to a safe distance, Sylvius called the request "this haughty and disrespectful answer.")[28] But they worked for the same master, whose policy required a peaceful settle-

[23] B.M., Add. MS 41,825, fol. 236.
[24] *Ibid.*, fols. 238–39.
[25] P.R.O., S.P. 82/16, fol. 293.
[26] B.M., Add. MS 41,823, fols. 88–89.
[27] *Ibid.*; P.R.O., S.P. 104/2, fol. 96.
[28] B.M., Add. MS 41,828, fol. 117.

ment. Sylvius did his best to persuade the Danish king not to bombard Hamburg because a bombardment would endanger British residents, ruin the city, and make an agreement impossible.

It was suspected that French influence, as well as French example, had inspired King Christian's proceedings: "There are whispers that his Most Christian Majesty seems only to disapprove the Danish design on this place, because 'tis too unsuccessful for his reputation to be seen in. . . ."[29] However, the French Envoy to Wolfenbüttel, Rébenac, joined Sylvius in his peace-making mission.[30]

Middleton, in September, sent letters to Sylvius for delivery to the two sides, with instructions to secure a Danish safe conduct for English merchants and their goods at Hamburg. Sylvius on this occasion superseded Wyche in a large part of the latter's commission, and Wyche complained of it, though Sylvius said that he informed Wyche fully and only saw the magistrates of the city in his presence. English efforts were chiefly to persuade the magistrates to make concessions to satisfy the king of Denmark.[31]

The merchant adventurers in Hamburg again cast their lot with the city by voting without a contrary voice against asking a safe conduct of the king of Denmark. Wyche therefore informed them only of James II's letter to Christian V in favor of the city, "and gave them assurances of his majesty's constant good offices and protection. . . ."[32] Hamburg was determined to resist. Two of the former Thirty were beheaded.

Christian V, under pressure from too many sides, did not push his attack home or bombard the city. Gradually, the two parties in the conflict were brought to arrange preliminaries to an agreement, with the Emperor Leopold and the electors of Brandenburg and Saxony serving as mediators. The Danish troops fell back from the environs of the city on September 24 and 25, and the senate sent the king of Denmark a letter of thanks and respect. Trade with Altona (in Danish hands) recommenced. The Danes also released Hamburg ships that had

[29] B.M., Add. MS 41,825, fol. 270.
[30] B.M., Add. MS 41,828, fol. 121.
[31] B.M., Add. MS 41,825, fol. 261; Add. MS 41,828, fols. 129–30.
[32] B.M., Add. MS 41,825, fol. 265.

been arrested at Glückstadt. The deputies of the senate com-
plimented Wyche on his services in making peace, Wyche said.
He closed his dispatch of October 19, "Wishing his majesty
the perfect fruition of his power, and of his own, and his ministers' prudence, that he may, as here, hold the balance everywhere, and give peace to the Christian princes. . . ."[33] Christian V issued a declaration of his friendship for Hamburg, and
on October 22, Brandenburg and Celle troops marched off.
Shortly after, the former burgomaster Meurer reentered the
city.[34] This last concession to Celle counterbalanced the conciliation of Denmark and helped to satisfy the emperor, who
had made Meurer an Aulic Councillor. The dispute, as between
Hamburg and Denmark, was completely settled, the Tuscan
Terriesi wrote from London on October 25/November 4.

Throughout the crisis the support the French king might
give his ally had been a subject of urgent and anxious discussion. Some fears remained that Louis XIV might incite the
Danish court to trouble the new League of Augsburg by renewing the Hamburg dispute.[35] In the United Netherlands, the
Prince of Orange hoped to use the disturbance of the peace
as an excuse for securing a larger war establishment, while the
anti-Orange party of Amsterdam feared that the crisis would
facilitate an alliance of Sweden, Brandenburg, and the Brunswick dukes, which would force a general war. That party
showed little sympathy with Hamburg, though not much more
for Denmark. They and many others throughout Europe hoped
that both sides could be made to desist from obstinacy which
might ignite a conflagration.[36]

While Hamburg was menaced, James II had lent support
to his son-in-law, George of Denmark, against Holstein-
Gottorp. According to the Danes, Christian Albert of Holstein had owed money to Christian V, and Christian V had assigned the debt to Prince George, his brother. The king also used
the debt as an excuse for the occupation of certain bailiwicks in

---

[33] B.M., Add. MS 41,826, fols. 3–4; Fester, *Augsburger Allianz,* p. 94.
[34] B.M., Add. MS 41,826, fols. 5–6, 11; Dumont, VII, Part 2, 140–41.
[35] Duke of Montalto, "Cartas . . . à Don Pedro Ronquillo," (*Colleccion de documentos inéditos para la historia de España,* LXXIX, 299–475), p. 374.
[36] D'Avaux, *Négociations,* V, 314–17.

ducal Holstein. James sent a letter to Ratisbon on the subject, accepting the Danish account, and Sir George Etherege conveyed the letter to the imperial diet on July 10/20, 1686.[37]

The Duke of Holstein-Gottorp mustered his own argument and wrote to James from Nuremberg on August 4/14. The debt, so called, amounted to fifty thousand crowns, part of the arrears of "contributions" demanded of him by the king of Denmark. (These demands, he said, were a violation of the Treaty of Fontainebleau in 1679.)[38] The duke had had to accept responsibility for payment of three hundred thousand crowns, on which interest at 4 per cent was payable. The king had wished to assign all of this debt to Prince George, but the duke had refused. As security, the duke had pledged the island of Fehmarn. He was to pay the principal over a period of six years. The first installment, due in 1682, had been assigned by the king to Prince George, but the duke, unable to pay because his estates were exhausted and his subjects impoverished, agreed to give George an "obligation" for fifty thousand crowns, at interest of 5 per cent, pledging his bailiwicks of Tremsbüttel and Steinhorst in Holstein. At the end of 1682, Christian V again demanded "quarters" and contributions in the ducal lands, so that the duke could barely subsist; nevertheless, he paid George the first year's interest in 1683. When he was in effect driven out of his dominions in 1684, the duke held that the peace had been broken, and he refused to pay the second instalment of fifty thousand crowns, which the king assigned also to Prince George. Danish troops then seized Fehmarn. The duke threw himself for protection upon the emperor and the empire, of which he was a member: the emperor dispensed with payment for a period of five years. The king of Denmark's reply was to take Tremsbüttel and Steinhorst in Prince George's name.[39]

The Duke of Holstein-Gottorp had the tact in writing to James to acquit Prince George of responsibility for these hard dealings. The duke himself had been accused of bad faith, he said, because an untrustworthy agent had failed to mention

[37] Etherege, *Letterbook*, pp. 95–96.
[38] Actually, a separate "Acte concernant Monsieur le Duc de Slesvik-Holstein-Gottorp," Fontainebleau, Sept. 2, 1679. Dumont, VII, Part 1, 422.
[39] B.M., Add. MS 41,807, fols. 101–3.

a prior mortgage on the two bailiwicks when they had been pledged for the fifty thousand crowns. The duke said that he had publicly condemned the agent, but that the two places were ample security for both mortgages. Even since the seizure he had offered to pay further interest on the "debt" for which they had been pledged; besides, Prince George was well endowed in other ways. The duke also reminded King James that the king of England was a guarantor of the Peace of Nijmegen, and that Charles II had given the duke a guarantee under the great seal.[40]

At the end of 1686, the parties concerned agreed to meet at Altona, near Hamburg, and deal with the Duke of Holstein's difficulties. The emperor nominated the Brunswick dukes as mediators, but Christian V refused them. Eventually all the parties were induced to accept mediation by the emperor, the Elector of Brandenburg, and the United Netherlands. A peaceful outcome was by no means assured, because, as Wyche wrote, Louis XIV was well known to intend the breaking of the League of Augsburg. "Therefore 'tis not to be doubted by the remises which have lately come thick out of France into Denmark, and the 80,000 crowns newly remitted, are to enable that crown so to alarm this Lower [Saxon] Circle, as to keep it perpetually in arms, that the princes of it may neither spare men nor money to the common guaranty. . . ." For that reason those allies chose the king of Sweden to watch over Norway, and Holstein to prevent the distraction of another attempt on Hamburg. The Dutch, Wyche wrote a little later, subsidized Sweden, which in turn subsidized Hamburg.[41]

The Congress of Altona did not convene until near the end of 1687. At first the king of Denmark was so stubborn that men said his minister had no authority to negotiate on the restitution of Holstein-Gottorp.[42]

A rumor had run about during the summer of 1687 that England was allied with France and Denmark — doubtless a variant of the general rumor of the Anglo-French alliance, current at the same time, traceable to French sources, and probably intended to strengthen the French side. On the other

[40] *Ibid.*, fols. 103–4.
[41] B.M., Add. MS 41,826, fols. 54, 58.
[42] B.M., Add. MS 41,831, fol. 165.

hand, the king of Sweden and the Elector of Brandenburg were said to be so closely agreed that the former could insist on the satisfaction of the Duke of Holstein.[43]

James denied with truth that he was allied with France; and his negotiations with Denmark had never been intended to lead to a close alliance. He appears to have been chiefly concerned for Prince George, his son-in-law; however, he used only diplomatic means to assist the prince. When the duke had returned to Hamburg, Middleton wrote Wyche, on December 23/January 2, 1687/88, to remonstrate with the duke. Christian Albert had been proceeding in the Chamber of Speyer for the remedy of his grievances, and he had actually secured a mandate from that court on October 12. James thought this legal course strange, Middleton wrote: the duke knew very well that Tremsbüttel and Steinhorst were properly mortgaged, but if he would pay the 50,000 crowns, Prince George would give them up, and the King of England would be pleased by such a conclusion. He would also be pleased to see further proceedings in the Chamber of Speyer stopped. The duke would not suffer by his patience. "You may further observe to the Duke of Holstein that in all probability, if the treaty at Altona comes to any conclusion, this matter will of course be comprehended therein." [44] The Dutch ambassador at London, Van Citters, reported that James had written to the emperor about the mandate. Here he was acting to protect the reputation of a member of his own family.

The Danish envoy at London, Christian von Lente, submitted a memorial to Middleton in January, 1688, requesting the king of England to press upon Sweden and Holstein-Gottorp an easy agreement with Denmark.[45] Middleton did write to Wyche at Hamburg and Poley at Stockholm, recommending moderation of demands as the "easiest, shortest, and surest way for the duke to recover his country again"; if the conferences at Altona broke down for any other reason, the rupture would not then be blamed on Charles XI and Christian Albert.[46]

The duke's actual demands were for the most part limited

[43] *Ibid.*, fol. 170.
[44] B.M., Add. MS 41,823, fol. 99.
[45] B.M., Add. MS 41,806, fols. 119–20.
[46] B.M., Add. 41,823, fol. 100.

to the restoration of the *status quo ante*. The duke said to
Wyche that except for his title of duke and his duchies of
Schleswig and Holstein, all subjects were "treatable." He might
quit his claims for compensation for damages, and the union
of the two branches of the family might be renewed.[47] Poley
wrote from Stockholm that Count Oxenstierna, who was reported as favoring war, insisted on the justice of the duke's
claims, as did King Charles XI of Sweden; Charles XI, however, said that he would be glad of peace if King Christian
would restore the Duke of Holstein and abide by his treaties.
The rumor of an English alliance with Denmark and France
had evidently reached Sweden, for, Poley wrote, "I do find
in some of this court so great a jealousy of England that I was
the more willing to remove all occasions of it." [48]

Prince George, living in England, exposed to the wishes of
King James, was apparently acting independently of his brother
Christian V, who wished to yield nothing. Owen Wynne, writing for Middleton during some indisposition, told Wyche that
the prince would have Wyche do nothing more in writing
(presumably for secrecy). He was only to let the Duke of Holstein know that James II would be content if the duke either
paid Prince George or left George's agents in undisturbed
possession of Steinhorst and Tremsbüttel. Indeed, the prince
was willing to accept payment of the duke's debt by anyone.[49]

Louis XIV had stood by his Danish ally so far; he had also
tried to get the king of England to associate himself with
Danish resistance to pressure. The French envoy at Altona in
mid-February, 1687/88, desired Wyche to make joint instances to the duke and, if necessary, to threaten him. Wyche
pleaded that he had no orders to do so and requested Middleton
to instruct him.

Christian V was now forced by the strong combination
against him to offer something to the Duke of Holstein, but he
meant to keep the ducal portion of Schleswig, which disrupted
the unity of his own territories. The obvious device was the
substitution of an "equivalent," but the king had difficulty

[47] B.M., Add. 41,826, fols. 252–53.
[48] B.M., Add. MS 41,831, fols. 181–82.
[49] B.M., Add. MS 41,823, fol. 101.

in finding one and never persuaded Christian Albert to accept a substitution.

The Danish commissioners at Altona proposed in February that the duke exchange his lands in Schleswig for one of the king's German lordships — Oldenburg or Delmenhorst. The duke declined to be ejected from part of his inheritance for the convenience of the king of Denmark. The Danes retorted that the duke had once treated for just such an exchange and was (they said) manifestly an enemy to Danish security.[50]

Wyche assured the Duke of Holstein of James II's friendly feelings, but observed that nothing had so far been settled, and if war resulted, "the drawn sword (blind as Fortune) does not always open the path of justice" — a certainty was better than an uncertainty. On this remark, Wyche reported, he saw "some alteration in the duke." Christian Albert said that to claim his patrimony was not cause for war, nor could he begin a war, "but must leave it to those princes who might think themselves concerned to see the northern treaties observed; by all which he was undisturbedly to be restored. . . ." Wyche made no headway by dwelling on obstacles and hazards, but the duke afterwards asked him to dinner, Wyche accepted, and the host was merry.[51]

In March, 1688, Christian V made another offer in exchange for ducal Schleswig: both Oldenburg and Delmenhorst, the principality of "Geuvre" (Jever), payment of the duke's debt to Prince George, restoration of Tremsbüttel and Steinhorst, and lands and rights in Holstein, free of any "contributions." "On the whole, [Sylvius wrote] it is believed that altogether the offers which the king makes constitute a good equivalent and that it is not doubted here, that it will be found very reasonable and very just, by all disinterested persons, and even by the mediators. . . ."[52] Indeed, the duke would have remained an important prince if he had accepted this exchange, but he would have altered his family's long-established position. Furthermore, Jever only belonged to Christian V by virtue of investment by the king of France acting as the Duke of

[50] B.M., Add. MS 41,826, fol. 271.
[51] *Ibid.*, fols. 272–74.
[52] B.M., Add. MS 41,828, fol. 242.

Burgundy. The house of Anhalt, which had formerly possessed Jever, might challenge the right of the king of Denmark to give it away; so that the Duke of Holstein might find part of his equivalent illusory. A Danish commissioner, Ehrenschild, tried to persuade Wyche to say that James II approved of the equivalent, but the English envoy refused to do so without orders from home — orders he was not likely to receive. James had called the Danish occupation of the duke's domains "the usurpation of the king of Denmark upon the Duke of Holstein," and was unwilling to give it support; on April 22, Barrillon wrote that he saw no signs that the king of England would succor Denmark.[53]

The Danes fell back upon another line. As the duke would not accept an equivalent for ducal Schleswig in Oldenburg and Delmenhorst, other Holstein princelings might be transplanted to make room for compensation to the duke in Holstein. France now wanted a quick settlement: Croissy was said to have had "a long and cool conference" with the Danish envoy in France, "to the great mortification of the latter."[54] The duke's commissioners at Altona continued to insist that the "equivalent" was neither equal in value to ducal Schleswig nor defensible in conjunction with the ducal portion of Holstein. Although Wyche believed that an equivalent in Holstein would be acceptable, the duke's commissioners seemed bent on a real restitution: the duke, they said, was not simply "peevish" in preferring the recovery of his patrimony. Christian Albert appeased the king of England by refraining from publishing the decree which he had obtained from the Chamber at Speyer.[55]

King Christian V had stirred up a powerful combination of states against himself, and could not rely on effectual French support if war broke out. As he had failed to find other allies on whom he could rely, he was already defeated. His opponents knew that they could compel him to abide by existing treaties and to agree to another one; they need not yield to him on any important point. Thus, when Charles XI (or his minister Oxen-

[53] P.R.O., S.P. 31/3/175, fol. 393; A.E., Corr. Pol. Ang. 165, fol. 251.
[54] B.M., Add. MS 41,827, fol. 5.
[55] *Ibid.*, fol. 7.

stierna) said that "he would rather hazard his crown, than advise the Duke of Holstein to part with any thing of the Duchy of Schleswig etc.," he knew that he took no great risk in the event of war, while war would be such a risk as Christian V dared not contemplate.

On the other hand, Sweden was not so rich, nor the alliances of the north so reliable, that Charles XI would begin a war without deriving some advantage from it. He certainly did not wish to alienate England or the German princes by giving an aggressive impression. Instead, he took his stand on the treaties of Roeskilde, Copenhagen, and Lund. Poley wrote, "They seem to declare this crown [*i.e.*, of Sweden] as a safeguard to all such whom time and the necessity of their affairs may bring into their party, and surely the present condition of Germany does afford such a kind of project as this."[56] That is to say, the condition of Germany was driving states into the League of Augsburg or any other shelter.

The Danes could not be expected to like their defeat: Lente in London complained that Swedish support had made the Duke of Holstein-Gottorp bold enough to reject offers of revenues and privileges which he had never had before.[57] All that Christian V secured from Louis XIV was the last (paper) measure of devotion, a guarantee. The French envoy at Altona told Wyche that his master was determined "should the King of Denmark (by the rupture of this treaty) by attacked or molested on any pretensions of the duke's, he should be bound to assist him with all his force. . . ."[58]

In May, 1688, the Danish king offered a recess to last as long as the truce of Ratisbon, with concessions to the duke during the interval. This the mediators rejected. The Dutch agent was said to be "fostering the duke's resolutions of standing fast"; while, regardless of the guarantee, the French minister was complaining of Danish stiffness. "All the northern ministers advise from Paris that his Most Christian Majesty is very desirous an adjustment should be made," Wyche wrote.[59]

The Danish affair was now a burden to Louis XIV: he did

[56] B.M., Add. MS 41,831, fols. 195–96.
[57] B.M., Add. MS 41,806, fols. 130–31.
[58] B.M., Add. 41,827, fol. 15.
[59] *Ibid.*, fol. 19.

not wish to confess weakness by an open desertion of Denmark, but he also did not wish to involve himself in a war in the north when he might soon need his forces in Flanders and the Rhineland. Although his envoy at Copenhagen assured the Danes that the treaties of alliance would be observed, he made proposals for the restoration of the Duke of Holstein-Gottorp in his domains. Sylvius wrote Middleton that in his own opinion such a restitution was the only way to preserve the peace. He would try to induce the Danish court to it but held out little hope of success.[60]

The death of the Elector of Cologne, the controverted election, and the war in the Rhineland finally destroyed Christian V's position. By the Treaty of Altona, on June 20, 1689, he conceded the restoration of the duke's dominions, including ducal Schleswig, Fehmarn, Tremsbüttel, and Steinhorst. He was indemnified for exactions paid during the occupation, and the mediators took upon themselves the settlement of Prince George's claim.

What remains to be said of James II's part in the disputes about Hamburg and Holstein? Unquestionably the English intervention helped the Duke of Celle to decide to remove his troops from the territory of Hamburg. James's real concern was more for English trade and the general peace than for Hamburg's rights. (He advised the city to compromise both with Celle and with Denmark.) His treatment of Christian V, which was also governed by the dangers of a general war, gave rise to a real fear in the north, strengthened by false reports, that he had a secret alliance with Denmark. In fact, the English proposal for an alliance was so carefully hedged that in January, 1687/88, Sylvius thought that the Danish court, dissatisfied, was turning toward a renewed alliance with the Dutch Netherlands.[61] Sylvius was right. Preliminaries for settlement of differences between Denmark and the United Provinces were signed on July 6, 1688, and an alliance between Christian V and William III of England (formerly William of Orange) on August 15, 1689. Louis XIV's disappointed northern partner in this way joined the allies of Augsburg. Nevertheless, he stood neutral in the war then in progress, for he was

---

[60] B.M., Add. MS 41,828, fols. 250–51.
[61] *Ibid.*, fols. 230–31.

seeking protection, not against France, as were so many members of the coalition, but rather against the enemies of France around him.

James II had no sympathy with Danish aggression and offered no protection against its consequences. He declined to keep his fleet at sea in 1688 to support Denmark, although he decided to do so for another reason — the hostile attitude of the Prince of Orange and the States General of the United Netherlands. His chief intention was to keep the peace, and he disliked any action by anyone which might cause a general war. He had counselled all sides to moderation and abstention from force, but offenses against the peace at a distance sank into insignificance beside those of the Prince of Orange nearer home. James's attention turned toward his son-in-law in the Netherlands with fear, suspicion, and (eventually) hatred.

CHAPTER IX

Comedy and Severity

The Turkish war of Emperor Leopold alarmed the states of eastern Europe. King John Sobieski of Poland, who intervened in the war and whose army helped to break up the siege of Vienna, fought on after 1683, but with little success for Poland, although the emperor made important conquests.

On April 14, 1686, King John concluded a treaty with the two tsars of Russia, Peter and Ivan, young half brothers then under the regency of the Princess Sophia. (The two had come to the throne as colleagues on the death of Tsar Feodor in 1682. Peter was better known later, when he ruled alone, as Peter the Great.) The treaty provided among other things for an alliance between Poland and Russia against Turkey. One of its clauses obliged the tsars to send ambassadors to France, England, Denmark, and the Dutch Netherlands, to procure help from those powers. This would mean reopening diplomatic relations between Russia and England for the first time since 1682.

The tsars were in no hurry to send the ambassadors: only on February 16, 1687, was Vassili Timofeivich Postnikov accredited to England. The regent, in the name of the young tsars, equipped him with a letter to James II, explaining that Russia and Poland were now allied against the Turks and Tartars; Postnikov, the new envoy, was to congratulate James on his accession and to establish a correspondence and an understanding with him.

Before Postnikov's arrival, England was teased with reports of Russian doings at other courts. Poley, for instance, wrote to Middleton from Stockholm on June 26/July 6:

It is thought the king [Charles XI] will be away three weeks, unless the coming of a Muscovite envoy who is already in the river . . .

should occasion his returning sooner. It is the custom to entertain Muscovite envoys, all the time of their stay, at the expense of the king, and it is said the king will endeavour to receive him the sooner, that he may the sooner dispatch him.[1]

Russian envoys had a bad reputation. In May, 1685, Lord Preston had written to Sunderland from Paris: "A Muscovite ambassador is now at St. Dénis, and is to make his entry into this city on Thursday. I am afraid you will be troubled with him in England."[2] The French diarist, Marquis de Dangeau, noted with relief that these ambassadors were well born; ordinarily, he said, the Russians sent only wretches whom they wished to earn money, or who even paid the tsar to have the embassy, because their expenses were paid and they could engage in trade. The audience of these ambassadors went very well, and Dangeau observed that they played chess so well as to find good French players mediocre.

In September, 1687, Postnikov sailed from Holland to England, with a retinue of thirty persons. It soon became apparent that he was as venal as the ordinary envoy described by Dangeau. The English court was in the country, and the ministers could temporarily give no orders as to Postnikov's reception. The envoy remained aboard his ship, "not wishing to let himself be persuaded to go to lodge in an inn," Terriesi wrote. Although assured that King James would pay his charges, the envoy wished to retain until the last moment the financial support of the Dutch government, which would cease when he landed. (In Holland, as in Paris and Stockholm, Russian envoys did not pay their own way.) At last, with all difficulties removed, Postnikov went ashore and was met by a royal carriage. The king of England allowed him fifty pounds sterling a week for subsistence, and paid five pounds a week for the rest of the envoy's house. "But he cries out that the allowance is too scanty, and wants to have more," Terriesi wrote again, sighing, no doubt, that the Grand Duke of Tuscany did not allow so much.[3] Postnikov was successful at least in securing payment of subsistence for his eleven days on shipboard.[4]

[1] B.M., Add. MS 41,831, fol. 121.
[2] P.R.O., S.P. 78/148, fols. 60–63.
[3] B.M., Add. MS 25,374, pp. 284, 298, 307.
[4] P.R.O., S.P. 104/119, fols. 45–46.

It was evident that the Russian envoy was greedy. He also proved to be so oddly behaved as to retard his mission. Terriesi took a particular interest in him, because he was to go on to Tuscany after completing the mission in England. The Dutch ambassador told the Tuscan resident that Postnikov's "extravagances" had been such and so many at The Hague that the States General had been compelled to complain through the Dutch minister at Moscow. Apparently, Postnikov's difficult conduct in England was intended to prolong the time before the envoy's audience with King James, so that he could have the allowance as long as possible. Perhaps Postnikov took it for granted that James would give no assistance to the Russo-Polish alliance; at all events, he did his best to disgust the king and prejudice him against giving any. He made difficulties about delivering his credentials before the royal audience, as custom required; and when an appointment had been made for the audience, he broke up the arrangements by demanding that James II rise and lift his hat on asking the health of the tsars and on receiving the credentials. He said that he would risk his head if he did not insist on this point. James then let it be known that the envoy could leave if he liked, but without pay or transport to his next (lucrative) port of call.[5]

That argument was convincing, for on November 27/December 7, 1687, Postnikov at last had his audience and asked for assistance to his masters in the form of a large sum of money. For himself he desired a ship to carry him to Leghorn.[6] In reply, James applauded the alliance against Turks and Tartars, reciprocated the tsars' expressions of friendship, and remarked that "the renewing of the ancient privileges" of English merchants in Russian trade would have a favorable effect upon relations between the two countries. He could not furnish the money requested, but he would order a vessel to carry the envoy to Leghorn.[7] James granted recredential letters to Postnikov in which he repeated his remarks, closing with a notification that in future Russian and English ambassadors would be paid by their own governments. The ship was hired for the Leghorn voyage through Samuel Pepys at a cost of six hundred

---

[5] B.M., Add. MS 25,374, fols. 330–31; 334–35.
[6] B.M., Add. MS 17,677 HH, fol. 244; P.R.O., S.P. 104/119, fol. 46.
[7] P.R.O., S.P. 104/119, fol. 46.

"weighty dollars," and the envoy's allowance was paid for three weeks after his audience of leave, to help him make preparations for his journey.[8]

Postnikov was an ill-chosen envoy, and his instructions (especially as to hats) foolish in the extreme. If James was not cordial, he was generous and very patient. The mission, however, was probably hopeless before Postnikov ever saw England. James could give no money without supplies from parliament, bearing, as he did, the costs of an enlarged army. He used the opportunity to suggest the renewal of the old trading privileges which English merchants had had before 1649[9] — indeed, trade was the only serious concern which Englishmen then had in Russia.

Already the Russian government had approached General Patrick Gordon, a Scotsman in its service, asking whether the king of England would send a minister to represent him in Moscow. Gordon gave his own opinion that some things might be redressed or rectified if such a person were present. Middleton replied almost immediately that James II had decided to make Gordon envoy extraordinary to Russia and that instructions and credentials would shortly be sent to him by way of Riga. Gordon recorded in his diary, "With this letter I was much surprised."[10] He could hardly be an effective representative, for he was on active military duty, usually away from Moscow; moreover, he was unwilling to remain in Russia, from which he had been refused permission to retire. And the Regent Sophia preferred sending an envoy to the west. Gordon's chief service was to send word ahead of Postnikov's mission, with advice that the privileges of English merchants must be the basis of Anglo-Russian friendship, that they were valuable, and that the tsars ought not to deny them.[11] No record tells whether Gordon demanded pay from the regent for his subsistence.

[8] *Ibid.*, fols. 47–49.

[9] I. Liubimenko, *Les Relations . . . l'Angleterre avec la Russie avant Pierre le Grand* (Paris: *Bibliothèque de l'École des Hautes Etudes*, fasc. 261, 1933), pp. 251–52, 257. Mme Liubimenko missed much of the material cited here in preparing the relevant portion of her study.

[10] B.M., Add. MS 41,842, fols. 148–49; Add. MS 41,823, fol. 89; Gordon, p. 161.

[11] B.M., Add. MS 41,842, fols. 154–55.

Russia's ally King John Sobieski of Poland was generally approved of in England as the champion of Christendom, but one of his actions as champion gave rise to bad feeling between King John and King James. Late in 1686, *St. John,* a French "privateer" with a Polish commission, attacked and searched *Jerusalem,* an English merchant vessel, a hundred miles from Alexandria. The captain of the privateer, the Marquis of Flory, deposed at Malta on November 16 that he had found on board the Pasha of Tripoli and other "Turks," who had been traveling as passengers. These and their goods had been removed and were inventoried at Malta.[12]

To King John this encounter was part of the war with Tripoli's Turkish suzerain, but to Englishmen it was a violation of the rights of the English flag. The French "nation" at Malta, one of the knights wrote, supported the English, while the Spaniards, Germans, and Italians did not. The French could boast that their king enforced French immunity from search by such corsairs. Thus English prestige was at stake. "It would seem to the whole world, if the capture by the Marquis de Flory were found good, that the English flag would be quite inferior to that of France. . . ."[13] This consideration and the safety of commerce must have influenced the English consul at Naples when he acted firmly to have Flory excluded from that port.

Word reached John Sobieski, apparently in May or early June, 1687, that Flory was in trouble with the English. King John protested that the marquis had made war under the Polish flag against the enemy of the Christian name, "non piraticam, sed militiam sacram exercens." This message must have taken some months to reach James II, who replied on May 3, 1688, that Flory had been very indiscriminate in his commerce raiding. "Christianos plerunque magis quam Turcas insecutus est."[14]

The pasha of Tripoli had long before been released to go on his way, and the goods taken had been secured by the knights of Malta. Owing to the extraordinary difficulty of communication between England, Poland, and Malta, the case

---

[12] P.R.O., State Papers Foreign, Malta (S.P. 86/)2, fols. 5–12, 19.
[13] *Ibid.,* fols. 21–22.
[14] B.M., Add. MS 41,808, fol. 254; P.R.O., S.P. 104/119, fol. 52.

remained unsettled at the revolution in England; apparently Flory was still at large. Probably the knights found their own solution. The new English government of 1689, however, could hardly have taken a different line on search of English vessels by foreign privateers.

From the Restoration of 1660 onward, the whereabouts and activities of English rebels and malcontents abroad were a continuing concern of the Stuart monarchs, and there was no break between the pursuit of veterans of the civil wars and Interregnum and the pursuit of Whigs, Rye House conspirators, and supporters of Monmouth's rebellion. How one was bridged over to the other is suggested by a letter from Sir Joseph Williamson to a Mr. Meredith in January, 1676/77.

His Majesty is informed of a pernicious book, of that late villain Milton's, now about to be printed at Leyden; I am commanded to signify to you, that you immediately apply yourself, to find out by the best means you may, if there be any such, who is the printer, and by what order he is set on work. There is one Skinner, a young scholar of Cambridge, that some time since did own to have had such a thing in his intentions . . . I know not whether this may be the same thing and whether it came from his hand or some others. . . .[15]

Another connection between the older and younger generations was made by the English groups resident in foreign cities — often well-established merchants — who from fellow-feeling offered shelter to political fugitives of the 1680's.

Because the harboring of fugitives seemed to the English government a menace, English diplomats often complained of it, at The Hague and other places, keeping under surveillance Englishmen and Scots in the Brunswick states, in Denmark, and in the Hanse city of Bremen. (Sir William Waller, a particularly obnoxious person since the Interregnum, was for a time commander of Bremen's "military forces" and proposed to manufacture woolens there in competition with English-made goods. Bremen expelled Waller when Charles II protested, but the Duke of Brunswick-Celle protected Waller after his expulsion and thus gave great offense to Charles.)[16]

[15] P.R.O., S.P. 104/66, fol. 120.
[16] P.R.O., S.P. 82/16, fols. 298, 300; S.P. 104/2, fols. 64, 67; S.P. 104/58,

Sympathy for the persecuted sometimes obscured the fact that protecting conspiratorial subjects of a friendly state was (and is) a hostile act. Duchess Sophia of Hanover wrote to Skelton at Hamburg (in September, 1684) to smooth over Charles II's displeasure with the Duke of Brunswick-Celle; the duke, she said, would prevent fugitives in his territories from harming the king of England. She reported that all of these men denied plotting, that they had only fled political enemies; Catholics who had taken refuge from the "Popish plot" prosecutions had never caused any noise. All these factions did the English nation harm. "In my opinion, [she wrote] the king would have done better to grant liberty of conscience as he had permitted it to the Presbyterians, who restored him to the throne, as Spinoza thinks good; there is only one Anglican church in the world; it is not reasonable to make all the others enemies. . . ."[17]

Skelton gave a blistering reply. The Catholic fugitives had been wrongly accused, and the king knew it, as one of the duchess's servants could testify. On the other hand, Waller's "life and conversation [were] so well known by the whole kingdom that even those of his party have no confidence in him." Any man who rose against his king or his government was a dishonest man and a rebel. The Presbyterians had not restored Charles II, Skelton wrote, and the king's attempts to allow them freedom of religion had shown that they misused it.[18]

The legal right and wrong of the question was uncertain: states had often allowed asylum to fugitives from other states with which they had no alliance. Treaties of alliance sometimes specifically forbade asylum in one contracting state to rebels and traitors of the other. England and the United Netherlands were allies after 1678, and the two powers renewed their alliance in 1685, but the treaties did not stipulate the treatment of rebels and traitors; nevertheless, the implications of an alliance of any kind were opposed to harboring fugitives who continued from asylum attacks on the government of their country. As recently as 1960, the government of Switzerland

---

fol. 328; Carl Brinkmann, "England and the Hanse under Charles II" (*E.H.R.*, vol. XXIII, pp. 683–708), p. 708; B.M., Add. MS 41,807, fols. 193–94.

[17] P.R.O., S.P. 82/16, fol. 298.

[18] *Ibid.*, fol. 300.

expelled a French national who had been condemned in a
French court for assisting Algerian nationalists; Switzerland
and France were not even allied at that time.

Sympathy with misfortune cannot be left out of consideration; some of the fugitives were poor, even destitute, and chari-
table persons overlooked political and other offenses in eagerness to relieve human suffering. Some runaways asserted —
with or without reason — that they suffered for the sake of
the Protestant religion; therefore, foreign Protestants were
doubly engaged by charity and by religious sympathy. Ardent
Dutch republicans felt kinship with some fugitives of anti-
monarchical tendencies, and enemies of the family of Stuart
were greeted as friends by enemies of the family of Orange.

Had the States General tried to placate Charles II and the
Duke of York when fugitive Whigs first went to Holland in
large numbers, it would have had two choices: to deport them
to England, or to move them on beyond the Dutch frontiers.
The first choice would certainly have meant rapid trial and
execution for some of the deported; after the Rye House Plot
the Stuart kings had both motive and opportunity to demand
the full penalties of the law. The other choice, less drastic,
would have turned the refugees into wanderers, always fearful
of persecution, deportation, seizure, and death — unless they
were prepared to leave western Europe altogether. Such a
doom their Dutch sympathizers refused to contemplate.

The fugitives might of course have settled in Holland and
discontinued their plotting. Some may have done so; but asylum
often was less important than their determination to weaken
the English monarchy and to secure Protestantism from the
dangers they believed menaced it. Many Dutchmen shared
this feeling: a weaker monarchy in England could give William
of Orange little help, and Dutchmen, like Englishmen, were
convinced that international Protestantism was in peril.

The reader will observe that the Dutch republicans, William's opponents in Dutch affairs, were James II's logical
enemies on the refugees. William might have taken his father-
in-law's side, but James's measures gave William both an opportunity to make himself king and the means of conciliating the
anti-Orangist party by joining in its resistance to James's pressure for the expulsion of his foes. Without serious inconsistency

or loss of prestige, William built up support for his English
expedition and also for the war against France, which gave his
life its meaning.

The fugitives made little trouble before 1683. Shaftesbury,
to be sure, had left England in 1682, and had died abroad, but
his return had not been demanded. It was the revelation of
the Rye House Plot, in the summer of 1683, that sent a number of Whigs into exile and that hardened Charles II against
them, both at home and abroad. Charles had already instructed
Chudleigh, his envoy in the Netherlands, to "find emissaries
to go among the fanatical Whig party of our own countrymen
at Amsterdam or elsewhere by whom you may get better intelligence of their designs and contrivances, I mean in our
country, than we can here."[19] In September, 1683, Chudleigh
reported, among other things, "that several of that sort of people
have talked that neither the king nor the duke must expect to
live long. . . ."[20] This dangerous talk became more intense
and more plausible when Monmouth joined the conspirators
in the Netherlands later that year, and Charles was irritated
that his disobedient son was hospitably entertained by William
of Orange and by the governor-general of the Spanish Netherlands, not once but many times. When Chudleigh protested to
William, the prince lost his temper and was so rude that the
envoy feared a permanent estrangement. Even worse, Colonel
Wauchope reported to a friend that Monmouth's recommendation was essential to English and Scottish officers aspiring to
promotion in the Dutch service.[21]

The death of Charles II ended William's high favor toward
Monmouth, and the duke then embarked on the rebellion in
the west; but some of the fugitives remained in Holland, and
others fled to the Low Countries after Monmouth's defeat.
There they tarried, bitter, destructive, and (for the most part)
poor.

To this time, the Dutch authorities had usually allowed the
refugees protection. Although Sir Thomas Armstrong had been
deported to England in 1684 *pede legato* and had been executed, there had been no other surrenders of English malcon-

[19] B.M., Add. MS 35,104, fol. 53.
[20] B.M., Add. MS 41,809, fol. 112.
[21] B.M., Add. MS 41,811, fol. 234.

tents by the Dutch. Middleton, in December, 1684, had given Chudleigh Charles II's direction to protest to the States General about libels emanating from Holland, "for no stoic could with patience suffer those indignities." Middleton did not doubt that the States General would act properly; proper action apparently meant punishment of the sellers of the obnoxious libels.[22]

On his accession, James II, however, demanded more: he required William of Orange to "cashier such officers of his subjects there as his majesty shall name" — apparently those who had been friendly to Monmouth and hostile to James. In addition, Middleton wrote to William, at the end of April, 1685, the king expected the banishment of the rebels and other fugitives. "This I look upon as the happy opportunity I have always wished for, by which your highness may express your concern for his majesty's interest, which is equally yours, since these villains drive not only at the kings sacred person, but the confusion of all the royal line and the subversion of this monarchy. . . ."[23] As to any pity William might feel for Monmouth, the Earl of Rochester reassured the prince (before the rebellion):

I do not believe the king hath the intention of driving him from country to country, and to make all places uneasy to him, but on the other hand it is not at all necessary, nor in truth decent, considering the circumstances he hath put himself in, that he should be hovering just over against England, and as it were always in a readiness to transport himself. . . .[24]

After the rebellion had begun, Middleton stated the hope that *Heldrenberg*, a ship used by the rebels, would be confiscated by the States General and its captain hanged. The ship was confiscated in November.

Although the States General was not implicated in Monmouth's preparations, it was clear that neither he nor Argyle could have embarked without the connivance of Dutch officials. James II demanded better behavior in future. He had some success in the Spanish Netherlands. Skelton obtained the

[22] B.M., Add. MS 41,823, fols. 2, 4.
[23] *Ibid.*, fol. 12.
[24] P.R.O., S.P. 8/1, part 2, fol. 5.

seizure of a rebel named Tiliard or Tyler at Malines; and in
1686 Bulstrode persuaded the Spanish authorities to punish
the publishers and printers of a "scandalous print" at Brussels.[25]
In November, 1685, Middleton urged that at least some of the
rebels in the Dutch Netherlands might be delivered to the English authorities. "I wish for the Prince of Orange's service as well
as his majesty's that he would concern himself a little warmly
in this matter, for nothing could endear him more to the king." [26]
English agents abroad naturally kept watch on the malcontents.
Under surveillance and other pressure, some gave way. Joshua
Locke professed "great penitence" and desire for pardon, and
promised to put a stop to woolen manufactures at Leeuwarden
and Lüneburg. (Those at the latter place were the creation of
Sir William Waller. Bevil Skelton dwelt on the damage which
these factories might do to the English trade in woolens.) [27]

For some months the Dutch did nothing toward deportation
or expulsion of the fugitive rebels. On May 10, 1686, Skelton
presented a memorial to the States General asking that English
rebels be banished.[28] On May 20, the states resolved that those
excepted from James II's general pardon and act of indemnity
be required to leave the United Provinces, and a proclamation
was ordered to that effect. The rebels were very frightened by
this, and several of them, including Sir Robert Peyton and
Slingsby Bethel, asked for pardon; Bethel, indeed, appealed
to the mercy of a king "that hath acquired the addition of James
the Just." [29]

Middleton wrote to Skelton, however, that King James observed that the resolution of the States General still had to be
confirmed by the provincial states (or assemblies), and there
was no penalty for failure to comply. "This his majesty would
have you seriously represent to the principal men there. . . .
I wonder that when men intend to do a thing they should do it
with such ill grace as to forfeit the thanks." [30] The States General responded to these comments by resolving that rebels who
did not withdraw from the United Provinces within fifteen days

[25] P.R.O., S.P. 104/187, fols. 185, 234.
[26] B.M., Add. MS 41,823, fol. 33.
[27] B.M., Add. MS 41,813, fols. 96, 110.
[28] B.M., Add. MS 41,806, fols. 263–65.
[29] B.M., Add. MS 41,819, fols. 45–46, 51–52, 69–70, 93–94.
[30] B.M., Add. MS 41,823, fol. 40.

would suffer loss of life and goods, and a second proclamation was issued.[31] Middleton remarked that it was promulgated "par manière d'aquitte" and "caulks no sheers." He was right, for Friesland and the city of Amsterdam would not honor the decree of banishment.[32] A newswriter reported, on August 22, that these two jurisdictions had yielded — "It is the positive and secret order of the Prince of Orange which has compelled them to it";[33] but a month later Skelton wrote from Amsterdam that the rebels appeared in public and lived and ate in the same places without fear. He said he got no satisfaction from the town authorities. By the autumn of 1686, Skelton's patience had worn thin.

On October 12/22, as the envoy was preparing to return to England from Rotterdam on an English yacht sent over for the purpose, Captain Solomon Slater, an English officer in the Dutch service, encountered Sir Robert Peyton, a prominent refugee. Slater and other officers seized Peyton and attempted to force him to board the yacht, but Peyton cried out in the street that he was being taken to England to be murdered, and a mob formed quickly. The officers took their captive indoors, while thousands of townspeople assembled outside. Apparently, Peyton was beaten with a cane and his papers were taken from him. The *Schout* (bailiff) of the city appeared and took Peyton to the "town house." Skelton, who had received Peyton's papers, returned all but those that might be of "some service," but the city magistrates indignantly complained of this violence. Thus wrote Skelton.[34]

The Dutch envoy, Van Citters, took the matter up with James II in December. Peyton, it appeared, had been made a burgher of Amsterdam, and Skelton had never complained against him; further, officers in the service of the states had been used in this disorderly affair. The States General expressed its sense of insult and demanded that James disavow the action and give satisfaction.[35]

Some of the accused officers — including Middleton's kins-

[31] B.M., Add. MS 41,806, fols. 269, 273–74.
[32] B.M., Add. MS 41,823, fol. 41; B.M., Add. MS 41,813, fol. 212. "Caulks no sheers" means "to chalk the cloth is not cutting it."
[33] B.M., Add. MS 41,819, fol. 244.
[34] B.M., Add. MS 41,814 fol. 48; see also Add. MS 41,842, fols. 209–10.
[35] B.M., Add. MS 41,806, fols. 176–77.

man Lieutenant-Colonel William Middleton — exculpated themselves; others withdrew to England in the yacht that carried Skelton home. Four apparently remained: two lieutenant-colonels and two captains.[36] James disavowed their action as unauthorized, and Middleton informed Van Citters that, if Skelton had not already been recalled, the king would certainly have recalled him because of his part in the Peyton affair.[37]

James, however, could not permit officers who had offended out of loyalty to be punished by his and their enemies; prestige was involved, and the safety of loyal British subjects in the Netherlands. Sir James Kennedy, who was charged with the protection of Scottish privileges in Holland, wrote to Skelton: "The truth is we are all like so many outlaws here at present, and not a man, that's not known to be a Whig, secure of his life." Solomon Slater fled to Paris and resigned his Dutch commission because he dared not return, but other offending officers, who were still in Dutch custody, were worse off: Lieutenant-Colonel John Hales wrote to Kennedy, from a prison where he awaited trial, to say that he had no bed and no fire, and that there was an abominable stink in his cell. Could Kennedy, he asked, use the king's influence to procure better treatment?[38] Hale's letter reached Middleton, who on January 11, 1686/87, ordered the Marquis of Albeville, the new English envoy at The Hague, to use his best endeavors with the Prince and Princess of Orange, the Grand Pensionary of Holland, Caspar Fagel, and deputies of the States General to obtain the release of the officers. Peyton, meanwhile, had petitioned James II for pardon, alleging that he had made no complaint against his assailants.[39] Fagel, for one, was very cordial to Albeville: he even promised to help in the capture of fugitives if it could be effected in open country, outside Amsterdam.[40]

Albeville's work, and no doubt Middleton's conversations with Van Citters, bore fruit in the announcement (March 23) that the imprisoned officers would be sent to the king of Eng-

---

[36] B.M., Add. MS 41,820, fols. 33–34; B.M., Add. MS 41,814, fols. 105–6.
[37] B.M., Add. MS 17,677 GG, fol. 739; Sunderland to Skelton, Jan. 3, 1686/87, P.R.O., S.P. 104/19. (Skelton, having been transferred to Paris, was then in Sunderland's province.)
[38] B.M., Add. MS 41,820, fols. 112–13.
[39] B.M., Add. MS 41,823, fols. 45–46; P.R.O., S.P. 31/3, fol. 59.
[40] B.M., Add. MS 41,814, fol. 136.

land for his free disposal. In April, Terriesi wrote to the Tuscan government of their homecoming.

The English officers, four in number escorted by twenty-five soldiers and a provost, arrived from Holland. The Dutch return them into the hands of his majesty the king instead of the death penalty with which they had wished to punish [them] for the outrages which they made at Rotterdam, wishing to carry off from there the Cavaliere Peyton. . . .[41]

The whole affair had worsened Anglo-Dutch relations. The fugitives remained, at first frightened by the attack on Peyton, later emboldened by its failure and the imprisonment of the officers. The Dutch authorities were unsympathetic to Albeville's demands for expulsions. In May, Albeville learned that some British officers had surrounded a Monmouth rebel named Parson at a house in The Hague. He informed the bailiff and the burgermaster of the town, but they would not arrest Parson, and the Prince of Orange said he could do nothing. Albeville ordered the officers to withdraw, because he believed that if they seized their man the Dutch would slaughter them. He complained later to the pensionary Fagel and the deputies of Holland.[42]

The English government could hardly ignore its enemies openly walking the streets of Dutch cities or that its loyal subjects, while visiting Holland, fell in with them and were sometimes dissuaded from their allegiance. Moreover, some of the fugitives were active pamphleteers against James II, and Dr. Gilbert Burnet, the most obnoxious of them, had attached himself to the Princess of Orange. Both the prince and the princess testified to Albeville that Burnet expressed "great esteem and loyalty for his majesty," but Albeville thought his professions hypocritical. In 1687, Burnet addressed three letters to the Earl of Middleton, threatening to print them and "justify" himself. If so, he would be forced to "mention a vast number of particulars which I am afraid will be displeasing to his majesty." [43] This attempt at blackmail failed: Burnet printed the letters. He avenged himself on Albeville in his *History*, calling the envoy

[41] B.M., Add. MS 25,374, fol. 51.
[42] B.M., Add. MS 41,814, fols. 223–26.
[43] B.M., Add. MS 41,823, fol. 54; Helen Foxcroft and T.E.S. Clarke, *Life of Gilbert Burnet* (Cambridge, 1907), p. xxix.

"a most contemptible and ridiculous man, who had not the common appearances either of decency or of truth." [44]

The States General's answer to Albeville's protests against Burnet's presence was unsatisfactory to King James. Middleton remarked that it seemed to vindicate Burnet. Even though the doctor had not been officially a fugitive when he entered Holland, he had been proclaimed one since; Middleton asserted that the king asked only that the Dutch do what they had "particularly bound themselves to do." [45]

Not all scribblers went unpunished. Albeville reported that two newswriters who had reflected too freely on the Electress of Brandenburg had been arrested and kept close prisoners. Burnet, however, was safe, in spite of Albeville's memorials, and Bulstrode heard in Brussels that the States General would rather risk war than give up the pamphleteer. [46]

The king of England was aggrieved. Foreign cities were havens for his malcontents and rebels, and foreign governments were unreliable and untrustworthy. In October, 1687, James II wrote to Sir Thomas Jeffreys, consul-general at Valencia, forbidding British subjects "to discourse of or concern themselves in any matters relating to our government or state, and if any shall discourse seditiously or otherwise to the prejudice of our service, you are to secure such person or persons, and send them into our kingdom of England, on board some of our ships. . . ." [47] How many such letters were sent we do not know, but such a person appears to have been repatriated in April, 1684, aboard H.M.S. *Virgin*, where he was allowed no "private conference" with anyone. [48] It is possible that a few unfortunates were so treated under James II.

As relations between King James and the Dutch worsened, a struggle arose for the control of the British troops in the Dutch service. These troops had been on foot since the 1670's and were a valued part of the Dutch armed forces. The custom had been for commissions and promotions in these regiments to be given by agreement between the Prince of Orange and the king

[44] Gilbert Burnet, *History of My Own Time*, ed. O. Airy (2 vols., Oxford, 1897), II, 708–9.

[45] B.M., Add. MS 41,823, fol. 60.

[46] P.R.O., S.P. 77/55, fol. 366; B.M., Add. MS 41,823, fol. 60.

[47] P.R.O., S.P. 104/187, fols. 265–66.

[48] P.R.O., S.P. 104/192, fol. 128 [unnumbered].

of England; thus each could prevent the appointment of an enemy. James had requested the return of the regiments during the rebellion of 1685, and they had arrived in England but had not been needed for suppressing the rebellion. James then released them to the Dutch once more. Apparently, he had the right to recall them as seemed good to him. This precedent confirmed that of British troops in the French service, recalled by Charles II in 1678. Late in 1687 James II revolved the idea of recalling these units from the Low Countries, but Barrillon's dispatch of January 1, 1688, which makes the first allusion to it, mentions that the principal Roman Catholics — specifically Lords Arundel and Powis — were opposed to recalling the troops before the assembly of a new parliament. The reason which James gave for the recall was that he had found the soldiers ill affected in 1685, and that he now wished to dismiss them "in order to take away from the factious a support and a resource of which they thought themselves assured." Louis XIV, as a mark of friendship, offered to help James to maintain two thousand of these men, no doubt the more loyal portion.[49]

Albeville, who apparently had been instructed to approach the pensionary Fagel and the Prince of Orange about the recall, was told that the States General was not obliged to send the regiments back on James's summons. Albeville alleged that there was a treaty obligation to do so. Evidently, word of this approach and the refusal was passed on to the troops.

My Lord Coott [Albeville wrote], and several others of that stamp, do triumph now; some in their garrisons speak not only licentiously, but rebelliously; of which I complained this morning to the prince, whose answer was, that it was impossible to bridle men's tongues: some of these villains, have clapped into prison some sergeants and soldiers who preached loyalty to their comrades.[50]

On January 17, Middleton wrote to Albeville and enclosed a letter from the king to the prince and the States General that demanded the return of the troops to England "as a matter of right, that cannot be denied."[51] The prince replied that he "was desirous to know what moved his majesty to take this resolution; and to know if they were to continue there, always or for a

[49] P.R.O., P.R.O. 31/3/175, fols. 352, 354, 376.
[50] B.M., Add. MS 41,815, fols. 128, 130–31.
[51] B.M., Add. MS 41,823, fols. 58–59; Add. MS 17,677 HH, fol. 306.

time"; wrote Albeville, "I could not satisfy his curiosity." [52]
James was already preparing transportation for the troops and
their families.

The Dutch authorities insisted that they were not bound to
send the troops home when England was at peace, but Fagel
said that he thought those who wished to return would be allowed to do so, if James would permit the others to remain.
Some deputies said the prince was afraid that the German princes might also recall their troops, "and so leave the states without a man." [53] The governor general of the Spanish Netherlands
was surprised when he heard the news of the refusal, "fearing
it may have a very bad effect." Bulstrode, questioned at Brussels, said he

knew nothing further than that the states' comportment towards his
majesty had been of late very extraordinary, in not giving satisfaction to the king's just and reasonable demands, and in particular
for protecting Dr. Burnet, and for delaying to give satisfaction in
the affair of Bantam etc., and that I supposed his majesty had
given them this mortification to show his resentment of their proceedings.[54]

Some of the officers, such as Hugh Mackay, were unwilling to
return. Mackay wrote to Middleton as to an old patron, pleading that he had a tender conscience and might meet with difficulties in the king's service and professing that he would be
grieved to displease the king, whom he would ever reverence.[55]
(Mackay, after the revolution, campaigned in Scotland for
William against James.)

The States General wrote James, on February 9/19, 1688,
that it had considered all existing treaties and conventions and
had found no requirement that it send the troops to the king
of England on his demand, but it offered to show its good will
by permitting the officers who wished to return to do so. Albeville privately instructed loyal officers to go to their posts, teach
their soldiers loyalty, and await the king's commands.[56] Middleton, almost simultaneously, instructed Albeville to

[52] B.M., Add. MS 41,815, fol. 134.
[53] B.M., Add. MS 41,815, fols. 136–39.
[54] P.R.O., S.P. 77/55, fol. 352.
[55] B.M., Add. MS 41,815, fols. 147–48.
[56] B.M., Add. MS 41,822, fols. 202–3; B.M., Add. MS 41,815, fol. 152.

press that all of them, both officers and soldiers, may have leave to come away, for though they are not bound by any treaty to send them over, yet to hinder subjects from going into the service of their natural prince, when he requires it, is a thing unheard of . . . by the countenance they there show to rogues, and the restraint they would lay upon honest men, one wound think they studied to provoke the king, which was never thought to be the interest of that state.[57]

When Middleton received Albeville's report of the recalcitrance of the States General, he told the envoy to encourage the officers to leave without delay. "From that day, they are to be in the king's pay, according to the several capacities they are now in. . . ." Albeville was to promise them money to clear them of their private debts, up to the limit that could be repaid by deductions from pay in a reasonable time. Sunderland directed Bulstrode to assist any of these officers or soldiers who might return by way of the Spanish provinces.[58] Albeville continued to argue for the release of the men, and about sixty were reported to have arrived in England by the middle of March. Although James received this loyal remnant "benignly," Middleton warned Albeville "that his majesty would not have you press any to come over, who show any unwillingness to it, not being desirous to harbour any such snakes in his bosom." [59]

The English government had up to this time conceded that no treaty regulated the matter, founding its argument for the return of the troops on the duty of a subject to his own sovereign, but officials meanwhile made a search of all the known treaties. Middleton did not think the States General was bound by a capitulation that had been made by the Prince of Orange on his own authority in 1678, but its terms were exactly what was wanted: the prince had clearly promised that the troops would be returned upon the king's request.[60] The capitulation had only recently been discovered. Middleton evidently subdued his doubts: he instructed Albeville to say that the capitulation was binding even without ratification.[61] A few days later, he sent

[57] B.M., Add. MS 41,823, fol. 61.
[58] *Ibid.*, fol. 62; P.R.O., S.P. 104/187, fol. 275.
[59] B.M., Add. MS 41,823, fols. 64–65.
[60] P.R.O., S.P. 84/220, fol. 35; B.M., Add. MS 41,822, fols. 184–86.
[61] B.M., Add. MS 41,823, fol. 65.

copies of a proclamation for distribution to the king's subjects in their garrisons. Even the Dutch ambassador, he wrote, was surprised that his masters the States General refused to allow the common soldiers the release already granted to the officers.[62] Albeville presented a memorial and a copy of the capitulation on April 5. The request for release was refused on the ground that circumstances required the States General to retain the soldiers who had been brought into its service at great expense.[63]

Relations thereafter rapidly deteriorated. While Burnet was busy at propaganda, the Dutch demanded punishment of the author of the anti-Dutch tract *Parliamentum pacificum*. J. Cutts could write to Middleton, from the shelter of the Netherlands, that he would obey the king, "were not the present measures of state visibly opposite to the principles, and interest of that religion, which is dearer to me than all things in this world; or than life itself." [64] The Bantam negotiations had failed, and the Dutch had not secured the redress they had claimed for alleged English assistance to Algerine corsairs in the English Channel. Albeville wrote, on April 2, that the Princess of Orange "grows daily more and more subject to the will of the prince: his sentiments of all affairs are become hers," and the prince wanted war in the coming summer. A few weeks later the English envoy wrote that formerly he had seen and conversed with everyone, even intimately with the prince, "but now it is a crime to come at me, or visit me; a man is looked upon as a very disaffected man that is seen to converse with any of my domestics. . . ." [65] In England, Middleton compared the current negotiations with the Dutch to "talking to the deaf, and holding a light to the blind." [66]

In spite of Dutch orders to the contrary, a trickle of English, Irish, and Scots went home. The governor general of the Spanish Netherlands allowed them free passage, saying "the king [of England] was hardly used to have his subjects kept from his service." Some who were stopped at Ostend were released and permitted to embark.[67] A Jesuit at Antwerp, Father Visconti,

[62] *Ibid.*, fol. 66.
[63] James Ferguson (ed.), *Papers Illustrating the History of the Scots Brigade* (3 vols.; Edinburgh: Scottish History Society, 1899–1901), I, 564.
[64] B.M., Add. MS 41,805, fols. 23–24.
[65] B.M., Add. MS 41,815, fol. 243.
[66] B.M., Add. MS 41,823, fol. 67.
[67] P.R.O., S.P. 77/55, fol. 396.

helped such deserters as he heard of, and the English government sent him passports and money. (The Dutch actually sent pursuit parties into Antwerp for one fugitive in March, but did not find him.) Visconti, who received James II's thanks, helped at least twelve deserters in May; Bulstrode sent on at least five in May, eleven in July; and in October, on the eve of the invasion of England, he was harboring three deserters.[68] How many more there may have been is impossible to say, but those who reached Bulstrode reported that many others wished to go home. Their continued presence was not voluntary: as early as April 30 the officers who remained in the British regiments forbade their men even to ask for their release, "under pain of being put into chains." [69]

Thus the pursuit of British fugitives by James II ended in another pursuit by the officers of William of Orange. After the Revolution of 1688, William III's diplomats would follow the example of their predecessors in dealing with the problem posed by the Jacobites: arguments which had been used against Whigs in Amsterdam were used also against supporters of James II at St.-Germain-en-Laye.

---

[68] *Ibid.*, fols. 409–10, 421–22, 425, 469, 472, 493; P.R.O., S.P. 104/187, fols. 278–79.

[69] P.R.O., S.P. 77/55, fol. 469; B.M., Add. MS 41,815, fol. 251.

CHAPTER X

The Breaking Point

Piracy in the Narrow Seas was a recurrent problem in the seventeenth century, a problem that each European nation usually dealt with in its own way. Admiral Arthur Herbert had made peace between England and the state of Algiers in 1682, as the first Earl of Middleton had done with Morocco. Such treaties had often been concluded, but it was difficult to persuade or force the Moslem states (in which governments were sometimes suddenly changed) to keep their bargains. Under James II, however, a different aspect of Christian-Moslem relations was exposed. Could one Christian nation respectably maintain neutrality when another was attacked by Barbary "pirates"?

In the summer of 1686, when corsairs belonging to Algiers appeared in the English Channel and attacked Dutch shipping, Van Citters brought the subject to James II's attention, the privy council discussed it in early July, and James promised Van Citters he would "use his endeavours that they should abstain from coming for the future." [1] One Algerine ship later took shelter beneath Landguard Fort and would not leave it for fear of two Dutch men-of-war waiting offshore. Sir R. Manley, at Landguard, was concerned to prevent acts of war within English waters, and, late in October, two English frigates escorted the "Turk" out to sea. The Dutch were disgusted that they had been deprived of their prey; also, it was said that English merchants and courtiers had bought prize goods and ships from the Algerines.[2]

In the autumn of 1686 James, however, did act in accord

[1] B.M., Add. MS 17,677 GG, fol. 631; B.M., Add. MS 41,823, fol. 53.
[2] B.M., Add. MS 38,694, fols. 78–79, 82–83; B.M., Add. MS 41,827, fol. 200.

with his promise to Van Citters, sending a squadron of English ships, under Sir Roger Strickland, to overawe Algiers and force confirmation of an article of the treaty of 1682 that forbade "the Algerines to cruise near or in sight of any of his majesty's roads, havens, or ports, towns, and places, nor any way disturb the peace and commerce of the same, which the Algerines then promised punctually to perform."[3] Regardless of treaty provisions, four Algerine ships were in the Channel in May, 1687. (The turbulent people of Algiers had overthrown their government and put in a new one.) The raiders took one Danish and one Dutch vessel before May 11. The king of England (Barrillon wrote) was much displeased. James gave orders that denied the corsairs entry to English ports or approach to the coasts;[4] apparently this order was executed in most places, and the Algerines, who had a healthy respect for the English navy in English waters, gave no provocation.

Thus of this foray into the Narrow Seas, Middleton reported that "they have not had any encouragement or connivance from his majesty, nor have they in the least touched at any of his ports nor insulted any of his friends [e.g., the Dutch] where, by treaty or the customs of the Seas they are forbid to do it."[5]

James was in a difficult position. On the one hand, as long as the treaty endured, he was bound to extend ordinary and decent treatment to a state "in peace and amity with him" though it be Algiers; on the other, his relations with the Dutch and the solidarity of Christendom required that he deny help to these Moslems. Middleton instructed Albeville that the king would extend the corsairs nothing beyond what was stipulated in the treaty and would comply in all respects with the Anglo-Dutch treaties then in force.

The Dutch were not satisfied by such neutral stuff. Van Citters presented a memorial to James (on July 8/18) laboring the indiscriminate damage done by the Algerines and complaining that a Dutch ship they had taken was then in Falmouth harbor. (This ship, *Schermerhorn*, was presumably the one referred to by Middleton a month before as having been "brought into Falmouth by reason of its being very leaky.") Van Citters

[3] B.M., Add. MS 41,823, fol. 53.
[4] P.R.O., P.R.O. 31/3/169, fols. 209–10.
[5] B.M., Add. MS 41,823, fol. 53.

requested restitution of the ship, under Article 29 of the Treaty of Breda, and suggested that, as the Algerines were pirates, they should be barred from English ports, under Article 12 of the same treaty. Even if they were not pirates, it was argued, the Anglo-Dutch defensive alliance of March, 1677/78, bound James II to give assistance against them.[6]

Middleton referred the case to Sir Richard Raines, who was learned in admiralty law, for consideration of legal points. Pending a report, Van Citters appealed to James II under the treaty of defensive alliance for twenty ships of war for use against the Algerines. James, in reply, asked for twenty Dutch ships for use against the puppet king of Bantam. Bonrepaus wrote that Van Citters was "much stung by this jest" but that the States General was said to incline toward satisfying James in the Bantam affair.[7]

Raines' reply, when it came, was trenchant: he ruled out the terms of the treaty with Algiers as irrelevant; James II could properly allow the Algerines any privileges which did not contravene provisions of treaties with the States General. Article 12 of the Treaty of Breda did not apply to the Algerines, but only to English subjects or residents of England, and the Dutch, who had also made treaties with Algiers, could not object to James II's observance of treaties he had made. The admission of captured Dutch ships into English ports was not a hostile act against the Dutch; it would be unreasonable to expect England never to be neutral in a war between the United Netherlands and another state also bound by treaty with England. The treatment of the prize *Schermerhorn* had been correct: its sale at Falmouth had not been allowed; and its captors had been permitted to sell only a portion of its cargo, in order to provision the ship for its journey to Algiers. Certainly, if the treaty between England and Algiers were to be maintained, James II could not regard the corsairs as pirates or punish them as such. "I do suppose," wrote Raines, "the States General would not have offered this consideration [that the Algerines were pirates], in case the Algerines had not broke with them." The treaty of March, 1677/78, applied only to "the preservation of the lands, rights and liberties of navigation and commerce, which either

[6] B.M., Add. MS 41,806, fols. 182–84.
[7] Dispatch of Sept. 8 [1687], P.R.O., P.R.O. 31/3/172.

party have, or ought to have by common right, or by treaties with other princes and states, jointly and unanimously made." Raines could not see that such a question had arisen; if one had, then *pari passu* the States General had owed help to England in a recent dispute with Sallee, in Morocco. Raines therefore disallowed all of the Dutch complaints in his opinion.[8]

Middleton and the king were convinced by his reasoning. On November 15, the earl replied to Van Citters that English actions in the *Schermerhorn* case were justified by the laws of nations and by English treaties with the States General. The king was sure a mature examination of the matter would show that a demand for restitution was not warranted.[9]

The merchants of Holland were, of course, not satisfied. In the summer of 1688, d'Avaux reported to Louis XIV that the "Messrs. d'Amsterdam," with whom he had previously been on good terms, were weakening in their opposition to William of Orange, because they believed the kings of France and England were resolved to destroy their religion "and above all, their commerce." [10] Many instances may have been in their minds — the East Indian disputes, French restrictions on foreign trade, and English neutrality toward the Algerines.

The last allusion to the dispute occurred on the eve of William's sailing, when James received Van Citters at Windsor. It had been said that the Dutch armament was for the purpose of disciplining the Algerines. James rebutted allegation of an Anglo-French alliance, deduced by the States General from Louis XIV's recent statement that he would regard an attack on England as a hostile act against France. James also told the Dutch ambassador that the naval preparations in Holland were too great to be merely defensive and that to send such a force against the Algerines would be a joke. The Algerine use of English ports, he said, had already caused as much discussion as the subject deserved.[11]

After the Revolution of 1688, Jean-Antoine de Mesmes, Count d'Avaux, one of the ablest of Louis XIV's diplomats, wrote an account of James II's difficulties.

---

[8] B.M., Add. MS 41,806, fols. 191–95; see also P.R.O., S.P. 71/3, fol. 185.
[9] B.M., Add. MS 41,806, fol. 196.
[10] D'Avaux, *Négociations . . . en Hollande*, VI, 175.
[11] B.M., Add. MS 41,823, fols. 71–72.

The King of England will be seen from this time on to work diligently for his own ruin; one will see him deliver himself entirely to the Prince of Orange, after all that he had known of his plans, and make new treaties with the States General; abandon the interests of the king [of France] who alone could support him in the designs which he had for the Catholic religion: make known to the States General the resolution which he had taken to have absolutely no tie with the king of France, to make no alliance with him.[12]

D'Avaux was in a position to know a great deal: during the whole of James's reign he was the French representative at The Hague. His statement is one of many that suggest an investigation of the relations between James and William.

Before the death of Charles II, William had displeased James by showing favor to Monmouth. The accession of the new king had forced the prince to change his conduct. In February, 1684/85, William sent over his relative and supporter Hendrik van Nassau-Ouwerkerk (called by Englishmen Overkirk) to England with a letter that Middleton described as "full of submission." In response to Ouwerkerk's offer of an oral *carte blanche*, James required of William three things: a breach with Monmouth, the cashiering of the British officers in the Dutch service whom James should name, and "that for the future he should observe and follow the same measures that his majesty shall think fit to take as to the public concerns of our neighbours."[13] Ouwerkerk had apparently been empowered to yield to these demands, for the king wrote on March 6/16, "I am fully satisfied,"[14] and a full reconciliation was attempted, or pretended. Middleton, who had known the prince for years, joined in the happy chorus of concord: "Now . . . his present majesty is happily seated in the throne, knowing his goodness, and your highness's great prudence; I never doubted but all mistakes would be quickly cleared, as they are now to my unexpressible joy. . . ." The earl also said he hoped the union would continue, and asked for Williams' protection, which he would endeavor to earn (a ceremonial expression).[15]

In this mood, both sides made concessions. The prince, for

[12] D'Avaux, *Négociations*, IV, 7–8.
[13] B.M., Add. MS 41,823, fol. 5; cf. P.R.O., P.R.O. 31/3/160, fol. 67.
[14] P.R.O., S.P. 8/3, part 2, fol. 241.
[15] P.R.O., S.P. 8/1, part 2, fol. 1.

the time being, set his face against disloyal Englishmen; the king decided against urging the promotion of a Scottish officer (Colonel Canon) in the Dutch service until the prince was satisfied with his behavior; and three Scottish regiments were returned to England to help suppress Monmouth's rebellion. On August 17, 1685, Dutch and English commissioners signed a treaty renewing several previous treaties between the States General and the king of England, one of which was the defensive alliance of March 3, 1677/78. Middleton, Rochester, Halifax, and Sunderland were the British signers of the treaty of renewal.

But could this mood last? Although Monmouth and the officers seem to have meant little to William, a promise to follow James II's foreign policy must have sat very ill with the prince. James had given no particular sign of joining France, but suspicion filled the gaps in the evidence. In October, when Louis XIV was known to have referred the Palatine succession to the pope for arbitration, the Dutch ambassadors in London feared the step had been concerted between Louis and James with evil intent. Although the ratifications of the new treaty were then on the point of being exchanged, Middleton's congratulatory letter to the States General on the success of the negotiation must have seemed hollow to the recipients, in spite of Middleton's reputation of detachment from France.[16]

The Prince of Orange had his reasons for attempting to maintain public friendship with his father-in-law: good relations would make for his wife's easy succession to the English throne, and at this stage the friendship of the king of England would strengthen William's position in the Netherlands. Thus in April, 1685, William urged Skelton to inform the burgermasters of Amsterdam that the breach had been mended and to suggest that they would do well "no longer to oppose the sentiments of the Prince of Orange with so much obstinacy." Skelton apparently did so.[17] In May, d'Avaux informed Louis XIV that if the king of England pressed the Dutch to form an alliance, the French minister could no longer use his accustomed threats to prevent it. Formerly, he wrote, the Dutch had been afraid of the war that might arise from a league with England, but now

---

[16] B.M., Add. MS 41,823, fol. 29; d'Avaux, *Négociations*, V, 59.
[17] D'Avaux, IV, 346; V, 39.

they were not. Although the leaders of Amsterdam would probably have been happy to see the project collapse, the alliance was renewed, as we have seen.

James, who knew of and opposed Louis XIV's intention to possess the Spanish Netherlands, feared an imminent violation of the truce of 1684;[18] the Palatine succession also threatened the peace, James knew. On these subjects, James acted independently of Louis XIV; Skelton had secret talks at The Hague with the Brandenburg envoy Fuchs;[19] and d'Avaux learned that the king of England had notified William by Middleton's chief clerk that James "saw clearly that France was not acting toward him [James] as it should; that he knew well what measures he should take; but that it was not the time to let anything show, because if he ceased to pretend the same confidence in your majesty [King Louis], he might ruin himself." [20]

James naturally expected William's cooperation in dealing with his enemies in the Low Countries. As a newswriter tells us, the influence of the prince presumably reinforced that of Fagel and Dijckvelt in obtaining the decrees banishing English rebels and traitors from the United Netherlands.[21] The Amsterdam authorities, on the other hand, were close to d'Avaux and disliked William. They asked d'Avaux in January, 1686, to confirm or deny reports that James had intervened in the interest of the Prince of Orange at the court of France. If James had done so, they hoped it had been only a gesture. (James had indeed supported the prince by diplomacy in connection with his principality of Orange.) [22]

Rumors of a Protestant league against Catholics, which would include the United Netherlands, disturbed King James. He wrote to William strongly warning against oppression of Dutch Catholics. The nuncio d'Adda wrote to Rome that Skelton had been ordered to Rotterdam, where there had apparently been

---

[18] For James's intervention in the affair of Namur, e.g., see Klopp, *Der Fall des Hauses Stuart*, III, 264; Montalto, "Cartas . . . á Don Pedro Ronquillo," *Colección de Documentos Inéditos para la Historia de España*, LXXIX, 374; Dumont, *Corps universel diplomatique du droit des gens*, VII, Part 1, 144.

[19] D'Avaux, *Négociations*, V, 43–44.

[20] *Ibid.*, 83–84.

[21] B.M., Add. MS 41,823, fol. 33; B.M., Add. MS 41,819, fol. 244.

[22] D'Avaux, *Négociations*, V, 227–28; P.R.O., S.P. 78/148, fol. 157.

anti-Catholic disturbances.[23] An English shipmaster was tortured, whipped, and imprisoned at Dort (Dordrecht) on suspicion that he had cheated and deserted French Protestants who had trusted him to carry them out of France. In May, 1686, also, James II received fresh information on William's former relations with Monmouth and expressed displeasure to Van Citters, who told the States General. This angered William and weakened his hold on the States General, and some Dutchmen feared there would be war with England in the next campaign season.[24] Although the Amsterdam opposition insisted on a reduction of the size of the Dutch forces on foot, d'Avaux thought the prince was sure of support for his plan to enlarge them.[25]

The unpopular and Francophile Bevil Skelton was recalled late in 1686, and his successor, Sir Ignatius White, Marquis of Albeville, arrived in Holland in the middle of January, 1687. If this was an attempt to improve relations between James and William, it was a complete failure. Albeville was a Catholic seeker of fortune, who had been raised to noble rank by the Holy Roman Emperor. (Middleton's letters consistently addressed him as "Sir" rather than "My Lord.") His reputation was not good, and he lived up (or down) to it. Barrillon gave the marquis money before he left England, but d'Avaux disliked and distrusted him, considering him a double agent, for sale to the highest bidder.

In England, the States General maintained the uxorious, indolent, and hot-headed Van Citters. In February, 1687, Van Citters reported that predictions of war between England and the United Netherlands, such as he had heard in 1686, were no longer made; those Englishmen who had been most bellicose were saying "that England could enjoy no rest so long as it was at odds with Holland. . . ."[26]

Albeville's first action on reaching Holland was to call upon the Prince and Princess of Orange, who professed all honor and service to James II, as did the pensionary Fagel. Albeville also reported that Everard van Weede van Dijckvelt would shortly be sent to England as envoy extraordinary; it was unusual, he

[23] D'Avaux, *Négociations*, V, 234; B.M., Add. MS 15,395, fol. 431.
[24] D'Avaux, *Négociations*, V, 276–77.
[25] *Ibid.*, 311–12; 314–15.
[26] P.R.O., S.P. 84/220, fol. 30; B.M., Add. MS 41,814, fols. 135–37.

said, for Holland to consent to the employment of a man from another province (in this case Utrecht) or of a confidant of the prince in such a capacity, but for whatever reason, Dijckvelt was accredited on January 20, 1687.

The French reaction to Dijckvelt's mission was unfavorable. Skelton observed in Paris: "Monsieur de Croissi took notice to me of Monsieur Dyckvelt's going into England, and I find it is not approved of here, fearing he does not design any good to his majesty and they hope that the king will give him a short answer and speedy dismission." [27] D'Avaux, at The Hague, found Albeville suggestible and hinted that the mission was an affront to the English envoy and that it probably arose from secret motives contrary to King James's interests. D'Avaux hoped James would express surprise that Dijckvelt had been sent to England, when Albeville was fully authorized to satisfy the Dutch on the points which had caused them alarm. Thus if Dijckvelt, who would have no excuse for a long stay in England, delayed his return, James might learn by it the evil intentions of the Prince of Orange. Writing later, d'Avaux added that such precautions might have "turned aside that storm which the Lord Dijckvelt raised in the sojourn he made in England." [28] When Albeville testified to the friendly feeling Dijckvelt had for James II and for his late brother, d'Avaux was convinced that Albeville had been bribed. [29]

Although James II had now become angry over the continued presence of his enemies in the Low Countries, not only William but Fagel and other officials now pretended they could do nothing. Dijckvelt's mission therefore produced only small results: English diplomatic intervention for the release of the president of the Parlement at Orange and of five Protestant ministers there. [30] James told Dijckvelt in the end that he was resolved not to meddle further with the principality of Orange, which was then under French occupation. Dijckvelt, after consulting Anglican leaders, declared his opposition to the removal of the tests, which balanced the score. [31]

[27] P.R.O., S.P. 78/151, fol. 12.

[28] D'Avaux, *Négociations*, VI, 31–33; B.M., Add. MS 41,827, fols. 25–26.

[29] D'Avaux, *Négociations*, VI, 40–41.

[30] Sunderland to Skelton, April 25, 1687, P.R.O., S.P. 104/19. The folios of this item are not numbered.

[31] P.R.O., P.R.O. 31/3/169, fols. 205–6; Sir James Mackintosh, *History of the Revolution in England in 1688* (Philadelphia, 1835), 455.

Dijckvelt had more success in rallying internal opposition to James's religious and political measures. The government cannot have been entirely ignorant of what was happening: perhaps it thought best to overlook it. Middleton — probably on May 28, 1687 — wrote a letter to the States General — in answer to one Dijckvelt had brought from Holland — that assured that body of his desire to preserve peace between the English and Dutch nations. Dijckvelt's report to William apparently favored the opposition over King James, for the prince declared his unwillingness to consent to the removal of the tests.[32] Later in 1687, William's cousin, the Count of Nassau-Zuilesteyn, renewed the contact made by Dijckvelt.

Louis XIV welcomed the coldness between his chief enemy and that enemy's natural ally, and his emissary Bonrepaus sent Louis the names of Englishmen who built their hopes on the Prince of Orange. D'Avaux, reflecting his master's mind, wondered that James, being so provoked by William, did not form closer ties with France. Rumors of such a tie had circulated through Europe and had worsened Anglo-Dutch relations. The pregnancy of Queen Maria Beatrice, which alarmed the "Orangists" in England, also threatened to reduce the strength of the prince in Holland. The pregnancy could not be recognized as real; it would have undone too much.

The recall of the troops in Dutch service brought out the prince's attitude, for William was the Dutch commander and his opinion had weight. He refused to let loyal officers go home, saying that their debts must be paid — but James paid their debts. William refused to "bridle" the tongues of rebellious Englishmen, and he permitted, if he did not order, the arrest of sergeants and soldiers who "preached loyalty." Although he had personally signed the Convention of 1678 about the troops, he denied that it was binding without ratification. (Middleton asserted that William had been authorized to make a binding agreement, which was all that was necessary in such a case, "very different from national treaties.")[33] In the light of this record of obstruction, James's decision to mortify the Prince of Orange by setting a fleet out in the English Channel in the following summer is understandable enough.[34]

[32] B.M., Add. MS 17,677 HH, fol. 98; Mackintosh, *History*, 460.
[33] B.M., Add. MS 41,823, fol. 65.
[34] P.R.O., P.R.O. 31/3/175, fol. 393; see also Mackintosh, *History*, 496.

Albeville addressed a long dispatch to James II on March 23/April 2, 1687/88, begging the king to read another dispatch which he had written to Middleton. In England and in the Low Countries, he said, support of the Prince of Orange was now based on fears for the survival of the Protestant religion, and the princess was completely submissive to her husband, who was planning war in the coming summer. To learn all that he could of naval preparations, Albeville had secured (probably by bribery) an undersecretary of the Dutch "admiralties," who would give naval advices to Daniel Petit, English consul at Amsterdam, for transmission to Middleton. Albeville reported, however, that daily prayers were offered at The Hague for the safe delivery of the queen and for the birth of a boy.[35]

After the birth of the Prince of Wales, Albeville asked Middleton whether he should invite the Prince and Princess of Orange to the celebration at The Hague of the birth — the birth that nullified Mary's presumptive right to the English crown. Middleton conveyed the king's wish that the prince and princess not be invited on that or on any other occasion. D'Avaux knew, and perhaps James also knew, that William was attempting to rally support both on the continent and in England for action against the king of England.[36] In any case, the relations between the king and the prince were very bad. The Count of Nassau-Zuilesteyn then made a second journey to England, ostensibly to congratulate James on the birth of his son, but no one could have ignored that he conferred closely with the opposition.

Albeville's entertainment at The Hague — to which a princess of England and her husband were not invited — suffered from "the general defection of all the ladies, of all the courtiers [of the prince], and most of the men of quality." The Spanish envoy absented himself, pleading business, but the imperial envoy was present throughout. Two Danish diplomats dined with Albeville, and the Brandenburg envoy saw his fireworks, but no other representatives of Protestant states attended any part of the festivities; and Albeville, quite naturally, thought William was responsible.[37] In contrast to this sad rite of celebration, Skel-

[35] B.M., Add. MS 32,095, fols. 261–63.
[36] B.M., Add. MS 41,823, fol. 69; see, e.g., d'Avaux, *Négociations*, VI, 175–76. For the facts, see, e.g., P.R.O., S.P. 8/1, part 1, fol. 248, and part 2, fol. 85; B.M., Egerton MS 2,621, fol. 7.
[37] B.M., Add. MS 41,816, fols. 108–9, 123.

ton's *feux d'artifice* and *magnifique festin* at Paris were attended by the greatest of the nobility and by princes and princesses of the blood.

William, of course, had other affairs in hand. On July 1, 1688, he was reported to be in conference at Hoogstraeten with the Marquis Gastañaga, governor general of the Spanish Netherlands. On the same day, Albeville wrote in dismay to Middleton: "I am not at all dejected, but for what I would wish I could conceal even from your lordship, but it is impossible since it is the public discourse of everybody that his royal highness the Prince of Wales is no more prayed for in her royal highness's chappel." Albeville was using subterfuges to avoid going to the princess's court, where he had little to do and saw only disloyal Englishmen.[38] Middleton replied without delay that the king had written to his daughter and that Albeville should learn whether her chaplains had resumed the omitted prayers; if not, he was to protest to her.[39] The prayers were begun again. "This is looked upon with amazement," Albeville wrote, "as well as the former proceedings." Well they may have been, for they implied that the princess had doubts about the birth of her half brother but had been overawed. These doubts were spread in the Netherlands (and elsewhere) by Dutch prints in coarse words that needed no English translation.

> Hoe wonder, wonder is't geval!
> Dat nu de *Papen Bastaards maken:*
> Om zo het erfregt van de kroon,
> Te geven aan een Bastaard zoon.[40]

The supposed Anglo-French alliance, of which rumors had been set about by the French, was by now taken for granted by many; and the most convincing "evidence" was soon forthcoming. In August, d'Avaux delivered a memorial to the States General, proclaiming that an attack on England would be treated as an act against France, and the anti-Orangist party was convinced — despite James II's and Middleton's vigorous denials — that the alliance existed.[41] The Dutch were united

---

[38] *Ibid.*, fol. 133.
[39] B.M., Add. MS 41,823, fol. 70.
[40] *Den Engelschen Bokkum Gebraden op den France Rooster* (London, [?] 1688), p. 21.
[41] D'Avaux, *Négociations*, VI, 133; B.M., Add. MS 41,823, fols. 71–72.

against a king even more dangerous to them than Cardinal Fürstenberg; the house of Stuart, to which William had once looked for support, now gave him, as its enemy, an invaluable accession of strength.

D'Avaux, in the passage quoted at the beginning of this section, took only the French view, as one might expect. James never "delivered himself" to William; he attempted, rather, to deal with him as a fact of life and (after all) a member of the family. So things stood in 1685 and early 1686, until later that year a turning point was reached that is not clearly explained. Tentatively, we may attribute it to the rumors at the conferences before the conclusion of the League of Augsburg, to late revelations about the prince's dealings with Monmouth, the case of the officers who attacked Sir Robert Peyton, and to the continued presence of English fugitives in the United Netherlands. The mission of Dijckvelt was William's effort either to mend the breach or to build a party in England that would resist any change in the English succession. William had not taken a stand on the removal of the tests before Dijckvelt went to England; it was only later that religion became an issue, though of course the king and the prince disagreed about it. The Protestant Netherlanders were tolerant enough of their Catholics, as a rule, and William later proved to be fairly tolerant of Catholics in England. No doubt, Dijckvelt found that the Anglicans insisted that the prince declare himself against the repeal of the anti-Catholic acts and told the prince; then the prince gave in to their objections.

The Oranges' sponsorship of Dr. Gilbert Burnet was particularly roiling to King James. True, the States General's consent was necessary for Burnet's expulsion, but Burnet appeared often at the court of the Princess of Orange — and dramatically told his friends he expected to be kidnaped or assassinated by James's agents.[42] The refusal of the States General to return the British troops on the king's demand and the prince's obstruction of James's wishes (an obstruction that was at least in part intended to keep the Dutch army intact) brought the king and prince to a point at which the prince could cast doubt on his father-in-law's honesty and on his wife's half brother's legitimacy, and rid himself of the ties of kinship that ruling houses

---

[42] F. C. Turner, *James II*, p. 358. See also B.M., Add. MS 41,823, fol. 60.

used so variously. William was certainly no Duke of Modena or Elector Palatine, a protégé of the King of England; rather, he had been but in 1688 he was a protégé no longer.

Middleton was very friendly toward the Prince of Orange early in James's reign, and he rejoiced in the reconciliation that resulted from Ouwerkerk's mission. This attachment persisted for some time; in October, 1685, for instance, he wrote Skelton of his cousin Major Middleton: "I perceive my kinsman is ruined, but I do not know how to help him, for I will not do anything that may offend the Prince of Orange. . . ."[43] He attributed the failure of the States General to eject the English fugitives to other forces in the Netherlands.[44] Later, when this assumption of William's good intentions could not be kept up, Middleton's letters reveal no hostility against the prince.

Middleton was a monarchist, and one difficulty he found in dealing with the Dutch was their republican form of government. In January, 1684/85, he denied leave to the English envoy at The Hague, because "in most cases matters may be treated here [in London] with a king's ambassadors but not with a commonwealth's, who having so many masters of different minds there must be one upon the place to negociate with them."[45] James apparently agreed, for in the following July Middleton told Skelton that the king wished to have Dutch officers removed from the British regiments in the Dutch service, "though most of them out of a point of honour or interest, I believe, would fight for the king, yet those who are bred up in commonwealths are generally tainted with republican principles, of whom we have too many already. . . ."[46] Subsequent disputes with the republic did not improve the opinion of king or minister. The retention of the troops was "a thing unheard of"; and "one would think they studied to provoke the king"; it was pointless, Middleton wrote in April, 1688, to send Albeville fresh instructions, as the Dutch were "already resolved."[47]

Middleton says little by which we can know his opinion of the other governments in his province. He must have been well

---

[43] B.M., Add. MS 41,823, fol. 30.
[44] *Ibid.*, fol. 40.
[45] *Ibid.*, fol. 4.
[46] *Ibid.*, fol. 21.
[47] *Ibid.*, fols. 61, 67.

informed on the court of the emperor, but during most of his time as secretary there was no English minister in Vienna, and he did not express an opinion about the missions of Thun and Kaunitz.

Middleton's lapses from prompt correspondence with ministers abroad may to some extent be explained by his reliance on their discretion for many ordinary concerns. Sylvius, say, at Copenhagen, with all his experience of diplomacy and of the Danish court, knew what line to take on most questions; his requests for instructions have an air of pedantic correctness about them. Middleton wrote to Chudleigh once that he would leave a decision to the envoy's prudence, "for being upon the place and acquainted with those you have to deal with, you can best know how to manage them."[48] More important questions were apparently decided by Middleton from his knowledge of the situation and of the king's mind. Some few were reserved for consideration by the king, in or out of council: these might be postponed when the king was out of reach, as was a dispatch from Skelton in April, 1686, when James was on progress. There was apparently a "committee" which sometimes considered dispatches from English ministers abroad. This may have been the "camarilla" referred to by Barrillon, of which Middleton, Sunderland, Dartmouth, Godolphin, and Jeffreys were members, meeting on Sundays.[49]

In January, 1687/88, this committee heard Middleton read a dispatch from Albeville at The Hague.

When I read . . . the king's orders signed by the Lord Melfort concerning the Scotch privileges at Campheir [Camphere or Campvere in Zeeland], it was taken notice of as a thing very irregular and unfit, and all the lords present were of the same mind, in which his majesty had been surprised; if the king subscribed the letter, then you could do no otherwise, but by your instructions you are only to follow such directions as you receive from one of the principal secretaries of state, which cannot be understood of the Scotch secretaries; however, since the business is begun, you are to make an end of it; what I have said now is only to advise you for the future. . . .[50]

---

[48] B.M., Add. MS 41,823, fol. 2.
[49] P.R.O., P.R.O. 31/3/173, fol. 139.
[50] B.M., Add. MS 41,823, fol. 58.

Melfort may have taken advantage of the king's inattention to intrude into Middleton's sphere; or the intrusion may have been unintentional. What is interesting is that Middleton defended his (and Sunderland's) functions, and the other members of the committee supported him.

It was appropriate that secretaries should call upon experts and interested parties for advice and arguments to be used in relations with foreign states, and Middleton did so. Thus Raines gave his opinion on the Algerines and *Schermerhorn*, and the East India Company's statements of events at Bantam and elsewhere served to prepare representations to the Dutch government. Similarly, the Eastland Company, the Merchant Adventurers, and the merchants trading to Norway were solicited to help in the drawing up of a treaty of commerce with Denmark in 1685/86.[51] A counter-project of such a treaty made by the Danes was submitted to the three groups in 1687; their remarks were taken as a guide.[52] Lacking the assistance of consuls in the modern style, the government could hardly proceed otherwise.

Private persons often invoked their government's assistance in securing their rights. Middleton instructed Sylvius, for example, to intervene to help one Francis Stratford to collect a debt of thirteen thousand rix-dollars from inhabitants of Eyderstadt in Holstein in 1687. (Scottish business, where there was no Scottish agent, was sometimes handled by English diplomats.)[53]

Even when a debt was acknowledged and arrangements for payment made, a diplomat might be forced to watch for evasion. In 1687, Middleton directed Poley at Stockholm to labor for the payment of a debt by Charles XI of Sweden to two English merchants. The debt was to have been repaid out of the Swedish salt duty, but settlement had already been postponed for three years. "I cannot well imagine what the Swedish ministers can object against the satisfying of such a liquidated debt, which their king is pleased so freely to own and so earnestly to direct and order the payment of. . . ."[54] In an age when "international

---

[51] *Ibid.*, fols. 84–85.
[52] *Ibid.*, fols. 90–91.
[53] P.R.O., S.P. 104/119, fols. 40–41.
[54] B.M., Add. MS 41,823, fols. 97–98.

law" was unformed, even routine cases required diplomatic pressure to secure justice for a foreigner in a strange land.

With some envoys in his province Middleton was more friendly than with others, although he assured all of them at one time or another that he would protect their private interests while they were abroad on the king's service.[55] One of his friends was Thomas Chudleigh, at The Hague when Middleton became secretary and recalled in March, 1684/85. Informing Chudleigh that his successor (Skelton) would soon pass over to replace him, Middleton urged him to "hasten back to friendship and love, and I wish you all success . . . ,"[56] alluding, no doubt, to some love affair of Chudleigh's. Middleton's relations with Skelton, in contrast, were cool. Albeville, who followed Skelton, was an embarrassment — a man of good breeding with a high title, but of little reputation or wealth, given to extravagance against all orders; Albeville's accounts, Middleton suggested, were irregularly kept or worse.[57] The secretary was pleasant with Lord Carlingford, at Vienna in 1688:

Caesar dum magnus ad altum [he quoted] *fulminat Euphraten bello, victorque volentes per populos dat jura, viamque affectat Olympo.* Your friends here pursue the old sports, women a little, wine more, but whisk [whist] most. . . .[58]

Etherege, at Ratisbon, was his closest friend among the diplomats, and wrote the most lively personal letters, as on January 16/26, 1687/88: "I know you are Mr. Secretary still, but I know not whether you are the same Lord Middleton I left you. You may be grown as temperate as Sir Charles Sedley and as uxorious as my Lord Dorset; 'twould be a fine way then to make my court to you to talk of wine and women."[59] On his side, Middleton wrote to Etherege of London playgoing.

Probably Middleton enjoyed his foreign work more consistently than his domestic. His province (unlike Sunderland's) did not involve him in the religious intrigues of Louis XIV; rather, he had to execute a foreign policy which was innocuous, and

[55] See, e.g., P.R.O., S.P. 104/187/290.
[56] B.M., Add. MS 41,823, fol. 6.
[57] *Ibid.*, fol. 50; P.R.O., S.P. 104/237, fol. 131.
[58] B.M., Add. MS 41,823, fol. 103.
[59] Etherege, *Letterbook*, p. 317.

almost inevitable in the circumstances, though not conspicuously effectual. Here was no need for self-questioning or pangs of conscience, as in James's domestic actions. No doubt, also, Middleton resembled some other secretaries in preferring the work which dealt with kings to that which dealt with informers and petty patronage. A taste so common, though perhaps snobbish, escapes scorn. Many Englishmen desired his place and functions, but did not get them.

A few last words on this innocuous foreign policy will suffice to a reader who has studied the case histories given above. Harsh remarks have been made, and repeated from book to book, as to the subservience of English foreign policy to that of France. So far as the Northern Department was concerned, these remarks are not borne out by the facts. France was not directly involved in the East India Company disputes, although Louis XIV was certainly pleased that it damaged the good will which England and the United Netherlands might otherwise have felt for each other. Yet James wanted to end these disputes despite the inflexibility of the two companies. Had he been successful, not only would the English company's grievance have been redressed, but England would have been nearer the reconciliation with the Dutch which Louis XIV feared.

James labored earnestly for the restraint of France in Germany in the early part of his reign. He did so to maintain the peace. He changed his policy when alliance between German states and the United Netherlands appeared to be a grave danger to his own position: his approval of Cardinal Fürstenberg's cause in 1688 may be taken as self-defense.

The Holstein-Hamburg affair was strictly a matter of English commercial interests which depended on peace in the lower valley of the Elbe. Toward its end, English and French diplomats were working together to settle the dispute, but their objects were not the same, for France was concerned to free itself from an inconvenient commitment to Denmark, while England's commitment, if any, was to Hamburg. James II, be it said to his credit, could see the Duke of Holstein's side, even while he urged him to compromise. Louis XIV was neither sympathetic nor concerned with justice in the case of a prince who had caused him trouble.

It is difficult to connect either Russia or Poland with French policy. The English fugitives in the Netherlands, however, by exacerbating Anglo-Dutch relations, unwittingly conferred a benefit on Louis XIV, who desired that very object. Otherwise it hardly mattered to the king of France what became of these men. The same might be said of the Algerine corsairs.

Louis XIV was vitally interested in the alteration of the English succession to prevent William of Orange from becoming dominant there. For this reason he had collaborated in arranging the Duke of York's second marriage and hoped that a son might be born to it. Alternatively, the exclusion of the Princess Mary would have pleased him. Disagreements between the king and prince might have led James to attempt the exclusion; however that might be (improbable, in fact), disagreements could weaken the resistance of western Europe to French ambitions. Nothing could have been more acceptable to Louis than the recall of the regiments of British subjects — a reduction of the army of the States General, a cause of dissension in the Netherlands as well as in England, and a subject of quarrel between James and William. One cannot avoid believing that French representations (and rumors spread by the French) helped to widen the breach of which the recall was one cause. On the other hand, the easy belief of the prince, his friends, and his foreign allies in the supposed Anglo-French alliance was equally a cause of the breach, and these personages were as much duped by France as James could have been. The doubt cast upon the birth of the Prince of Wales was a final severance of the family tie which alone remained.

A study of the Northern Department is not the whole story. Case histories will probably be published on the disputes caused by the persecution and flight of the French Protestants, the position of English Protestants in France, the French encroachments upon the Spanish Netherlands (and other Franco-Spanish difficulties), the French attacks on English posts in the Hudson's Bay region, and the principality of Orange. Such case histories exist. This is not the place in which to publish them. A view of the whole world would be somewhat different from that of the Northern Department alone. Here I assert that the difference would not be great.

CHAPTER XI

The Revolution

James II, as we have seen, had caused his Protestant subjects distress and doubt by his removal of many Protestants from office, by his promotion of Catholics, by his extension of toleration, and by his suspension of parliamentary statutes. His army, disloyal though it later showed itself, had made many fearful of a future despotism. The remodeling of corporations gave James apparent, though not real or permanent, control of parliamentary elections in the boroughs, as well as of the choice of local magistrates. The birth of his son removed the hope that a Protestant would eventually succeed James — unless a restorative revolution could turn back the clock.

A number of well-connected and influential Protestants, having observed the general excitement at the trial of the seven bishops, the rejoicing at their acquittal, and the depression of spirits on the birth of the Prince of Wales, thought a revolt possible and favored it. Some had for months been corresponding with William. Seven, including the Tory Danby, the Whiggish Earl of Devonshire, and the mutinous Bishop Compton, on June 30, 1688, sent William a signed letter inviting him to come to England with an armed force to reestablish the English constitution and to assert his wife's right as heiress to the throne.

Ranke explains William's response to the invitation very charitably: revolution in England was inevitable, "even if he did not take part in it." If William did not take part, and James repressed the rebellion, the victorious king would treat the prince and his wife badly; if James suffered defeat, the rebels would "probably proclaim the Commonwealth and deprive him [William] of all that he claimed for the very reason that he had refused them his help." [1] Ranke strains credulity in this passage: Danby cannot be imagined as a republican, and his party was strong. The Princess Anne was present as an alternative monarch. Again, William's response to an invitation from the men on whom Dijckvelt and Zuilesteyn had been working was not doubtful. Actually, it is hard to see how a rebellion could have succeeded without William. The inviters must have been happy to receive a favorable reply from the prince, which spared them the grave risk of acting without Dutch support.

During the summer of 1688, William had interviews with princes and others who could help him (or hinder him), and Bentinck, his friend and agent, shared in the work of persuasion. Privy councillor Fuchs of Brandenburg; Fuchs's master, the Elector Frederick William III; Bernstorp, the chief minister of the Duke of Celle; the Landgrave Charles of Hesse-Cassel; and a minister representing the governor general of the Spanish Netherlands — all conferred either with William or with Bentinck. [2] Naval armament was carried out in Dutch ports. The first sign of an open breach between William and James was the suspension of prayers for the infant Prince of Wales, and Albeville thereafter watched English exiles and Dutch officials for corroborating evidence of hostile plans, while Sir Peter Wyche kept watch over the English colony at Hamburg.

Wyche reported a curious occurrence. The English Merchant Adventurers held a "court" on August 16, and Wyche had stood — with support from James and Middleton — for the position of deputy of the company. As Wyche had rendered good service in the crisis of 1686, he had strong claims, but the court had received a letter from the company at London "full of spite and malice against me." The London members had rejected Wyche because he was a Catholic, triumphing also because they had defeated the recommendation from James and the secretary of state. The Londoners, moreover, threatened to cut off trade with the company at Hamburg if it chose Wyche over their objections. [3] Such defiance was highly unusual, the letter was sure to be reported to King James, and merchants at

<hr />

[1] P.R.O., S.P. 8/2, part 2, fol. 85; Ranke, *History of England, Principally in the Seventeenth Century*, IV, 398–400.

[2] Ranke, *History of England*, IV, 411–13; P.R.O., S.P. 77/55, fol. 495.

[3] B.M., Add. MS 41,827, fol. 72.

London were within the king's reach. A few days later Wyche sent Middleton a paper he had received from The Hague, "containing so dire and frightful a design against his majesty and an unheard of inclination of so many of his subjects to take service against him." [4] Wyche had further word from other foreign ministers at Hamburg that he hesitated to send on, he said, because "the common report here seems to load too much a certain prince, that he should be contriving a manifesto against the Prince of Wales. . . ." [5]

Bevil Skelton sent similar rumors from Paris, but Sunderland replied:

[The king] is no stranger to the discourses and reports of some designs upon England, which you mention . . . though he cannot believe any such thing. . . . as to Mr. Herbert's opinion about our seamen being unwilling to fight against the Prince of Orange, Herbert is very much mistaken. . . . This his majesty would have you upon all fitting occasions say. . . . not only because it is proper for his ministers to act so, but because it is truth. Men are not to judge of Englishmen by their talk in coffee houses, nor by what idle beggarly knaves, that go into Holland, say (as they think) to make their court. All the Dissenters are satisfied, and the Church of England's principles will keep them loyal, though they may be indiscreet. In short, I believe, there never was in England less thoughts of rebellion. . . . [6]

Seldom has a prediction been proved so disastrously wrong by later events. On September 7 (N.S.), Albeville warned Middleton:

The people generally everywhere [are] mad for war both against England and France; those of Amsterdam more than any. . . . those conferences continue betwixt the pensioner [Fagel], Dijkvelt, Bentinck, Herbert, Burnet and others: frequent expresses come and go: a hundred thousand guineas have been sent last week out of England to the Prince of Orange, which arrived at Rotterdam, as I am informed. . . . [7]

Louis XIV knew as much of the Dutch plans as James II.

[4] *Ibid.*, fol. 74.
[5] *Ibid.*, fol. 76.
[6] P.R.O., S.P. 78/151, fol. 201; Sunderland to Skelton, Aug. 27, 1688, S.P. 104/19. (Folios in this item are not numbered.)
[7] B.M., Add. MS 41,816, fols. 170–71.

Perhaps he wished to seem to confirm the story of a secret alliance between himself and the King of England; perhaps he meant only to deter the United Netherlands from supporting William in the invasion attempt; whatever he intended, his minister at The Hague, d'Avaux, submitted a memorial (on September 9), stating that because of "ties of friendship and allegiance" Louis would regard a Dutch attack upon James as an open rupture with France.[8]

As we have remarked, the memorial caused a storm both in Holland and in England, for it seemed to verify Dutch suspicions of a secret alliance. Albeville wrote:

I had a long conference yesterday with pensioner Fagel in which he expressed the States' and his own surprise at Count d'Avaux's memorial, which has opened their eyes, and let them see what they are to stick to; that they could not believe the King of England was under his [Louis's] tutelage till now: that they did believe there was some engagement between both kings, but did not think it of this nature: that our king was the occasion of their setting a fleet to sea this summer, for suffering the Algerines (against the treaties) to come into the channel, and let them have the benefit of his ports; that it would soon appear how this declaration of the King of France would be relished in England . . . that he [Fagel] would represent it, and their danger to the States. . . .[9]

Fagel's remarks may be discounted; d'Avaux's memorial served only to unite the last dissidents with the prince.

The deputies of Amsterdam, Albeville wrote a few days later, stuck to the story that the naval preparations were intended against the Algerines. The Prince of Orange had returned from his conferences with the Elector of Brandenburg and the Landgrave of Hesse-Cassel and now was meeting constantly with members of the States General and those of the States of Holland. Bulstrode wrote from Brussels that all advices confirmed that the naval armament was intended against England, and that the malcontent former Admiral Herbert had entered the Dutch service.

Van Citters answered for his masters to James II at Windsor on September 11. The king told the envoy plainly that the

[8] For this memorial, see G. A. Ellis (ed.), *Letters Written during the Years 1686, 1687, and 1688, and Addressed to John Ellis*, II, 177–79.
[9] B.M., Add. MS 41,816, fol. 175.

preparations in Dutch ports were greater than were necessary for defense. As for d'Avaux's memorial, James had been as much surprised as the States General at its contents. Middleton then, in a private talk with Van Citters, said: "The king's power is too great to need a foreign protection, his spirit as well as his dignity is too high, to put himself in the balance with the Cardinal of Fürstenberg; and he is too wise to do a thing that might prejudice his affairs both at home and abroad. . . ." [10]

James's affairs were indeed much embarrassed at that time. He had long been pondering the calling of a new parliament, in which the recent remodeling would be reflected, and Sunderland had begun the work of recommending the king's candidates to the constituencies (the high incidence of later Jacobite conspirators among the known candidates is remarkable: for examples, Sir Theophilus Oglethorpe, Sir John Fenwick, Sir John Friend, and James Graham). To reassure the country, the king issued a proclamation on September 21, saying that parliament would meet in November and would confirm the Acts of Uniformity so that they could be altered only to remove the penalties inflicted on persons "not promoted or to be promoted to any ecclesiastical benefices or promotions within the meaning of the said acts, for using and exercising their religion" contrary to the provisions of the acts. [11] In plainer language, James would secure passage of an act or acts that would allow only Anglican clerics to be punished for failure to conform to the doctrines of the Anglican church.

The day after the issue of the proclamation, the Earl of Clarendon talked with Lord Chancellor Jeffreys about its authorship.

He [Jeffreys] then told me . . . that he had drawn it; that Sunderland, Middleton, Dartmouth and Godolphin had agreed with him in it; but he said there were alterations made in it at the [council] board by the influence of others; Godolphin had broken from them, by endeavouring to trim, and to find out softer words than he [Jeffreys] would have had. [12]

[10] B.M., Add. MS 41,823, fols. 71–72; Campana de Cavelli, *Les Derniers Stuarts à St.-Germain-en-Laye*, II, 256–60.

[11] *London Gazette*, Sept. 20–24, 1688; R. R. Steele (ed.), *Bibliotheca Lindesiana* (2 vols., Oxford, 1910), I, 469.

[12] B.M., Add. MS 22,578, fol. 31. The version given in Clarendon, *State Letters* (II, 219), is a careless paraphrase.

Evidently, this proclamation was considered by the "committee," which was acting here as a "cabinet." Middleton had agreed to the words originally used; but probably he was one of those who later yielded to Godolphin.

One of the intentions of the invitation to William of Orange had been to prevent the sitting of a parliament packed for James. This intention was achieved. A few days after the proclamation, the imminence of invasion compelled James to halt the issue of writs for elections.[13]

James's need to reassure his subjects was much increased by the news of d'Avaux's memorial, which linked him with the invader of the Palatinate and the Electorate of Cologne, the destroyer of European peace. Some British subjects, also, were observed to go to and from Holland with messages, although, late in September, James concluded from the stable price of gold that no large quantity could have been sent to William from England.[14] James undertook further steps of reassurance and self-defense. Middleton wrote Albeville, on September 28:

There is a general pardon in the press, the king has restored the Bishop of London, ten of that order [bishops] were with him this morning, whom he sent away mightily satisfied. I hope our fleet shall be ready time enough to oppose their landing: all the seamen and soldiers express their resolution of dying in doing their duty, so that I do not doubt but that I shall keep my place, and if you remove from yours, it shall be to a better. . . .[15]

Albeville wrote home the melancholy news that the prayers for the Prince of Wales had again been omitted.

Van Citters, maintaining that the Dutch fleet was not intended to act against England, on October 3/13 impudently protested the English seizure of the ship, *Arms of Amsterdam*, at Dover, and demanded that it be released "without any cost or expense." It was released. At that very time, Bulstrode wrote that the minister of the Spanish governor general in the Netherlands had endeavored to dissuade William from the attack on King James and was told that the prince

---

[13] Lucile Pinkham, *William III and the Respectable Revolution* (Cambridge, Mass., 1954), pp. 128–29.

[14] D'Avaux, *Négociations . . . en Hollande*, VI, 131.

[15] B.M., Add. MS 41,823, fol. 76.

intends nothing of ill against the king, queen, Prince of Wales or
government, and goes only to protect the Protestant religion, and
the people's liberties, and to have a free parliament and to oblige
the king to declare war against France, and many persons of the
first quality here [Brussels] believe the prince his intention to be
very just and reasonable and that all matters will be composed without fighting.[16]

Bulstrode also said he was "well assured" that the governor
general was "concerned and heartily angry at the Prince of
Orange's proceedings."[17] The intentions of Spain were a subject of speculation. John Stafford, the English envoy at Madrid,
thought "the people sufficiently inclined on our party, but what
measures the ministers may take I think is very doubtful."[18] One
of these, at least, wrote to Ronquillo at London that the Prince of
Orange followed a "diabolical policy" in spreading stories
of the illegitimacy of the Prince of Wales.[19]

The policy of reconciliation rapidly (within a month) went
into effect. On September 24, James asked all bishops con-
veniently near London to meet him at Whitehall the following
Friday, September 28, when Compton was reinstated. On September 30, Archbishop Sancroft met with the king alone, and
appointed Wednesday, October 3, for another meeting. Nine of
the bishops who remained in London took the opportunity to
present a petition for an explanation of the proclamation of
September 21 and made proposals as follows. The king should
put county government into the hands of legally qualified persons, abolish the Ecclesiastical Commission, and issue no dispensations from legal qualifications for holders of posts in
church, state, or universities. He should especially restore Magdalen College. He should set aside licenses to Roman Catholics
for teaching in "public schools" and should issue none in future.
He should desist from use of the dispensing power and should
allow it to be debated and settled in parliament. The Catholic
vicars apostolic should be inhibited from encroaching on Angli-

[16] B.M., Add. MS 41,832, fol. 291; P.R.O., S.P. 77/55, fol. 495.
[17] P.R.O., S.P. 77/55, fol. 497.
[18] P.R.O., S.P. 94/72, fol. 248.
[19] Montalto, "Cartas . . ." in *Colección de Documentos Inéditos para la
Historia de España*, LXXIX (Madrid, 1882), 457.

can ecclesiastical jurisdiction, and vacant Anglican bishoprics
should be filled with men of learning and piety. He should restore old charters — especially those of towns — should "super-
sede" further proceedings of *quo warranto* against corporations,
and should issue writs for election of a free and regular parliament. Moreover, James should permit the bishops to offer arguments for his return to the Anglican communion.[20]

A newswriter who apparently had good information tells us
the king said that he did not intend to nullify all the acts of uniformity, that he had instructed Sunderland, Middleton, and the
lord chancellor to draw the proclamation "as fully and amply in
favour of the Church of England as they could, which his
majesty resolves to maintain in all its rights and properties." [21]
James dissolved the ecclesiastical commission on October 5
and restored the charter of London on October 6. (According
to Barrillon, the people of the city kindled bonfires in celebration.) Sunderland convoked another conference with the bishops for October 8. The next day Middleton wrote Albeville that
Magdalen College had been restored and that the Earl of Danby
had "offered his services" to the king.[22] The Jesuit school in the
Savoy was shut up, the well-informed newswriter said, and a
master and ten scholars had already departed for Dover to go
"beyond sea." [23] The Modenese resident wrote that the king had
given the principal posts in five new regiments to Protestants.[24]
Sancroft saw the king alone on October 16, and on October 17
the old charters of other corporations were ordered restored,
as London's had been. James summoned the bishops to still another meeting, October 22.

The privy council also met on October 22, and some of the
king's Protestant councillors resolved to act against the Catholic members. Lord Clarendon had called on Lord Halifax
earlier, and had conferred with Lords Burlington and Weymouth. These later agreed with Lord Nottingham that he should
tell the king they would not sit in the council with Father Petre,

---

[20] Edmund Bohun, "The History of the Desertion . . . ," reprinted in *A
Collection of State Tracts, Publish'd on Occasion of the Late Revolution in
1688 and during the Reign of King William III* (3 vols.; London, 1705–7),
I, 38–125, especially pp. 46–47.
[21] B.M., Add. MS 38,175, fol. 138.
[22] B.L., Tanner MS 28, fol. 190; B.M., Add. MS 41,823, fol. 78.
[23] B.M., Add. MS 38,175, fol. 140.
[24] C.U.L., Add. MS 4,836, fols. 259–60.

though they would attend James as peers; the king told the five peers that Father Petre, though still a privy councillor, would not attend the council thereafter. Nottingham also pointed out that there were other unqualified (Catholic) councillors. The king seemed a little angry, but he took the five into the council chamber at the appointed time. Three peers took their seats as peers only. Also assembled were the Queen Dowager Catherine, the lord mayor and aldermen of London, the bishops, the judges, and members of the "Council Learned." It was announced that the object of the meeting was to answer doubts about the birth of the king's son, and all who had been present at the birth deposed what they could remember having seen and heard.[25]

The depositions were made by men of many sorts: Sancroft, Compton, and Mew of Winchester, among other bishops; Lords Belasyse and Castlemaine, among other Catholics; Halifax, the leading "trimmer"; Ormond, Nottingham, Churchill, Godolphin, Clarendon, and Rochester among English Tories; and Melfort, Hamilton, Preston, and (of course) Middleton among Scottish Tories; the Whigs were represented by Bishop Compton. In sum, the evidence was overwhelmingly in favor of the complete propriety (as distinguished from taste) of the birth of the young prince.

Middleton's deposition was among the most important. He had not, he said, seen the delivery, for the midwife was working with her hands beneath a cloth (which appears to have been the only concession to the queen's privacy), but he had seen the child "in a foul state" almost immediately after parturition, and had earlier heard the king describe the stage of labor at which the queen had arrived. He said he had heard doubts that the queen was pregnant and had therefore stood near the childbed to ascertain the truth. (Lord Ailesbury thought his deposition too intimate in its details.) Middleton's account was clear and pointed. The king ordered all the depositions printed to counter the rumors then current. The very next day, nevertheless, Lord Clarendon heard the Princess Anne ridicule the testimony.[26]

Shortly another step was taken which must have pleased

[25] B.M., Add. MS 22,578, fols. 37–38; Depositions on the birth of the Prince of Wales (London, 1688) [printed without title].
[26] B.M., Add. MS 22,578, fols. 38–39.

constant Anglicans. Sunderland, showing signs of exhaustion and deterioration — the results of the risks he had taken, the unpopularity of the cause he had espoused, and the danger of retaliation to which he was exposed — was reduced to a state in which he could no longer transact business for King James.[27] Reports of his fall circulated early in October,[28] but the king only dismissed him on October 27. Lord Middleton was removed to the Southern Department as senior secretary of state, and Lord Preston was made secretary for the Northern Department.[29] Preston, who had been an envoy to France and a member of parliament, was a Protestant. His loyal principles were beyond question, and his associates included such future Jacobites as John Ashton, David Lindsay, and Sir John Fenwick, as well as William Wake, a future Archbishop of Canterbury. He had shared the leadership of the House of Commons with Middleton in 1685, and since October, 1685, had served as chancellor to the queen dowager, Master of the Great Wardrobe, and Lord Lieutenant of Cumberland and Westmorland.

Middleton had already had some military business. He had deliberated with the council on such matters as impressment of sailors and victualing of ships, and sometimes he had conveyed the king's orders to commanders. He had ordered Lord Langdale, governor of Hull, to provision his garrison so as to withstand a siege if William landed in the North, and he had countersigned a warrant to Lord Dartmouth, master general of the ordnance, directing him to provide a train of artillery.[30]

The military duties increased with Middleton's promotion. On October 30, he renewed James II's orders that the Duke of Newcastle (at York) seize large bodies of recently acquired horses kept by their owners near the seacoast. He ordered the arrest of Lord Lumley, on suspicion of "divers practices dangerous to the peace of the government"[31] — and issued a warrant for the protection of the horses and house of his stepmother, the Dowager Countess of Middleton, in Kensington.

[27] Kenyon, *Sunderland*, pp. 220–21.
[28] G. A. Ellis (ed.), *Letters . . . Addressed to John Ellis*, II, 237–38.
[29] *Ibid.*, p. 266; Clarendon, *State Letters . . . during the Reign of K. James the Second*, vol. II, pp. 232–33.
[30] B.M., Add. 41,823, fol. 125; P.R.O., W.O. 55/335, fol. 89.
[31] H.M.C. *Various Collections*, vol. II, pp. 403–4.

On November 12 he countersigned James's order that Admiral Lord Dartmouth fight the Dutch on sight. He also received reports on the muster of militia against the expected invasion. (His task was not made easier by James's removal of Protestants from the lieutenancies of counties: the Earl of Derby, receiving a warrant to raise militia to keep the peace in Lancashire and Cheshire, replied that he would do what he could but that, as he had been dismissed some months before, he had no commission to act as lord lieutenant.)[32] Middleton also countersigned the commission of Lord Churchill to be lieutenant-general of James's army.

Sunderland had arranged the earlier meetings with the Anglican bishops. Middleton also absorbed that duty: on November 1, he sent Archbishop Sancroft notice that the king wished to see the bishops on the morning of the next day. The king had Preston read to the bishops, when they were gathered, the clause of William's declaration which said that he had been invited over by several of the lords spiritual and temporal.[33] All the bishops present denied having participated — including Compton, the only bishop who had in fact signed the invitation. On November 4, Preston urged Archbishop Sancroft to secure a declaration from the bishops that they opposed the prince's enterprise, and a conference took place on November 6, at which the bishops raised various objections. The king asserted that the temporal peers had worked up the bishops to change their minds. In argument the fundamental block was exposed: if the bishops could not meddle with affairs of state without being accused and tried, they would not meddle even on this occasion. The Bishop of Rochester reported that the king burst forth: "This is the last time, I will urge you no farther: If you will not assist me as I desire, I must stand upon my own legs, and trust to myself and my own arms." The bishops then promised to help with prayers and as peers of parliament, or, "if that should be thought too long [remote], by assembling together with us as many of the temporal peers as were about

[32] B.M., Add. MS 41,805, fols. 91–92.

[33] Clarendon, *State Letters*, II, 236. Copies of this declaration were seized in London on October 31. French Ministry of Foreign Affairs, Correspondance Politique, Angleterre, henceforth cited as A.E., Corr. Pol. Ang., Vol. 167, fols. 52–53.

the town. This was not hearkened to, and so we were dismissed." [34]

James had had a breathing space during this time. The Dutch fleet, which had sailed on October 19, had suffered storm damage at sea and had been forced to put back into port. Albeville remained at his post, although Dutch intentions were perfectly apparent. On October 20/30 he wrote Middleton: "Nothing will satisfy some great men of this court but the hanging of some of you lords of the king's council. . . . Your lordship writes of cultivating their friendship; that is never to be expected, but by being in a condition to make war upon them, and punishing them." [35] Some of the government's supporters faced the crisis with little confidence. The Duke of Norfolk wrote Middleton that it would be unwise to light the beacons of alarm, when the descent occurred, until after the lords lieutenant had been forewarned. "The rabble . . . are so unsteady and in some parts so ill affected, that it might as well guide them where we would not have them go." [36]

John Whitrow, of Dartmouth, sent to Middleton's office on November 5 the first "certain account" of the anchoring of the Dutch fleet in Torbay and the landing of the first troops at Brixham, with a copy of William's declaration. [37] Not far away was Exeter, where Lord Bath was to preside over the restoration of the city's old charter. Bath too wrote to Middleton before going to Plymouth, his appointed station if William landed in the west. Middleton's clerk Wynne must have received the news from Brixham soon after Lord Bath, for the messenger had galloped the 160 miles in "little more than 20 hours." [38]

Within a few days it was clear that the west could not or would not defend itself. Lord Bath wrote from Plymouth that the gentry there were loyal but "the common people are so prejudiced with the late regulations of corporations, and so much corrupted, that there can be no dependence at present

---

[34] Clarendon, *State Letters*, II, 465; B.L., Tanner MS 28, fols. 233–38, 241–42.
[35] B.M., Add. MS 41,815, fol. 300.
[36] B.M., Add. MS 41,805, fols. 109–10.
[37] *Ibid.*, fol. 117.
[38] B.M., Sloane MS 3,929, fol. 105; Add. MS 4,194, fols. 394–95.

on the militia, but only upon his majesty's standing forces." [39]
The Duke of Beaufort, lord lieutenant of several counties in
Wales and the west, wrote that one of the counties was disaffected and another was peaceable. If the king wished to hold
Bristol, Beaufort told Middleton, he should send a force to
defend it — "The militia is not in the present circumstances to
be built upon." [40] Middleton replied that help was coming. The
magistrates of Exeter, an exception to the lukewarmness of their
region, committed one of the Prince of Orange's recruiting officers for high treason. [41] As the prince's army was only a few
miles away, it was a very courageous action. For this and other
reasons, William's recruitment was not satisfactory; the postmaster of Kerton reported, on November 9, that not a single
gentleman of the neighborhood had joined the prince, although
many of the lower classes had — a result reminiscent of the
Monmouth fiasco.

The "mobile" (mob) was very turbulent in London. Hills, the
king's printer, was several times menaced in his own house
before James left London for the West, [42] and there were other
breaches of the peace. After James's departure, apparently,
preparation for the bombardment of the city was actually proposed, for Middleton wrote Preston on November 22:

As to Sir Edward Hales's project of mounting mortar-pieces, he
[the king] will by no means allow of it, nay though there were disorders in the city, he would not have them made use of, since they
could not destroy the rioters but the city itself in which principally
consists the wealth and strength of the nation, and consequently
his own; besides it might so far exasperate the people all over
England as to cause a general defection. . . . [43]

The peers in London also asserted themselves: on November 17 six spiritual and twelve temporal lords presented a petition to King James for the prompt assembly of a free parliament.
In his reply, November 20, James sharply pointed out that an
enemy was in the kingdom, in a position to return "near an
hundred voices," but he promised to call a parliament as soon

---

[39] B.M., Add. MS 41,805, fols. 129–30.
[40] *Ibid.*, fols. 156–57.
[41] *Ibid.*, fol. 160.
[42] P.R.O., S.P. 44/97, p. 15.
[43] *Ibid.*, p. 20.

as the prince should leave the country.[44] James had already departed to join his army when his reply was printed.

Before leaving, James sent his artillery train ahead. The prince was then moving generally eastward and recruiting more successfully. Lord Lovelace and some men he had raised were stopped and secured in Gloucester, on a warrant signed by Middleton, but Lords Wiltshire, Cornbury, Colchester, and others apparently reached the prince.

William had seized Exeter and four hundred pounds of excise money there — an incident which casts him in an interesting role. The mayor and aldermen refused to turn over the customs and hearth-tax money in their keeping, pleading their oaths of allegiance to James as an excuse. "So I hear," an informant wrote Middleton, "their charter has been examined by the prince's council and they [were] found out not [to have been] legally elected, and are (as I hear) all to be turned out and new chosen." [45] We have here a tantalizing glimpse of a crude *quo warranto* proceeding and a remodeling. And the bullying Gilbert Burnet ordered the clergy of Exeter cathedral not to pray for the Prince of Wales, "which they would not comply with till they were severely threatened." [46]

Ominously, leaders in other parts were rising and declaring for the prince, as Lord Delamere did at Manchester, and the king may have thought, as he made his way into the west, that there were few reliable men among his servants, ministers, and officers. He arrived in Salisbury on November 19, "in perfect health," accompanied by Middleton, who wrote Preston that the king had no troops to spare to deal with Delamere; indeed, Lord Tyrconnel, the lord deputy of Ireland, had been ordered to send a force to England. The king, no longer in perfect health, "was yesterday [November 20] taken three or four times with a bleeding at nose, for which he was let blood at night, and when he went to bed, took diascordium; he is this morning very well." [47] It is quite possible that this nosebleed was the

[44] B.L., Tanner MS 28, fol. 249; P.R.O., S.P. 31/4, fol. 196; Bohun, *History of the Desertion*, 62–63. Apparently, the Catholicizing Bishop of Oxford was not allowed to sign the petition. R. Steele (ed.), *Bibliotheca Lindesiana*, I, 471.

[45] B.M., Add. MS 41,805, fol. 207.

[46] Bohun, *History*, p. 61.

[47] P.R.O., S.P. 44/97, p. 19.

king's psychological reaction to the news of Delamere's revolt. When bleeding recurred on November 22, Middleton wrote Preston that "the physicians say it is only a ferment in his blood occasioned by too constant and anxious application to business."[48] Perhaps so. At York, meanwhile, Lords Danby and Fairfax had risen, and Delamere's force was said to have grown to 1,500 horse, and Lords Devonshire and Lumley had also rebelled in the Midlands and Northumberland. From Cornwall came news that Lord Radnor had gone over to the prince.

Preston, in London, forwarded accounts of rebellion received by the post office "from Coventry, Derby, and other places," and regretted that the king could not spare troops to deal with Delamere.[49] This was hardly reassuring to the overwrought king. Lord Langdale informed Middleton from Hull that many northern notables had joined Danby and Fairfax. Skirmishing had begun, and Lieutenant-General James Douglas reported eight killed on the king's side and eighteen on the other.[50] Because the western gentry were unfriendly to the court and the common people were spies for Orange, Middleton wrote on November 23: "His majesty has been prevailed with by the unanimous advice of his general officers to return with the army [toward London]; most of the foot and cannon march this day."[51] Lord Churchill, apparently alone, stood for a vigorous campaign, but as he soon went over to William, his motives are suspect. James arrived in London on November 26.

The officers and officials no doubt attempted to keep order in the army, but desertion and demoralization were common. Watchers in London, such as the Earl of Nottingham, observed the return of the army with foreboding. Nottingham wrote to Lord Hatton, "It looks as if London was to be the stage."[52] But of what? Battle? Negotiations? A *coup de main*? A council of forty English peers, convoked by James, recommended that the king summon a free parliament.[53] (The parties concerned

[48] *Ibid.*, p. 21.
[49] B.M., Add. MS 41,805, fols. 266–67.
[50] B.M., Add. MS 28,053, fols. 355–56.
[51] P.R.O., S.P. 44/97, p. 22; (see also B.M., Add. MS 28,053, fol. 357); P.R.O., W.O. 5/4, pp. 9–14, 17.
[52] B.M., Add. MS 29,594, fol. 135.
[53] B.M., Add. MS 15,397, fols. 474–75.

would by this time have found "free parliament" a phrase hard to agree upon.)

The news continued bad. Prince George and Princess Anne deserted, as did General Kirk and other officers; Lord Dunbarton, however, captured Kirk and sent him to Lord Feversham at Andover. Lord Bath had surrendered Plymouth; the Duke of Beaufort had fallen back from Bristol; Hull was "taken" by Danby — who actually bought that town for the prince from Sir John Hanmer for five thousand pounds.[54] Lord Lumley took Newcastle. On December 2 the Duke of Somerset, the Earl of Clarendon, and others left London to join the prince. A newswriter tells us that James said of them: "Let them go; they are not worth sending after."[55] And whom could he trust enough to send?

"The king's affairs being now reduced to a state as will oblige him to take other measures," Middleton sent orders to Tyrconnel countermanding the sending of troops from Ireland; instead, Tyrconnel held Ireland.[56] "Other measures" meant negotiation with the prince, to whom James now sent emissaries. Middleton must have favored that step. Even before the journey to Salisbury, Barrillon had written Louis XIV: "The secretaries of state and other ministers except some Catholics advise him [James] to treat and yield to necessity."[57] Now, on December 3/13, Barrillon wrote that some at court urged James to hold a free parliament and give security to the laws and the Protestant religion. Among these advisors was the Catholic Lord Belasyse. "Milord Halifax and Milord Godolphin are also of that opinion, as well as the secretaries of state, who hope in a compromise to be continued in their posts." But Melfort and other Catholics were "of a contrary opinion."[58]

On December 6, William Longueville wrote Lord Hatton: "The king was in Hyde Park today with some of his army. . . . 'Tis a very hard and pitiable condition that men of quality are now in; and another trial is like to be added to their many

[54] B.M., Add. MS 28,053, fols. 365, 369.
[55] B.M., Add. MS 41,805, fols. 283–84, 293; Add. MS 34,517, fol. 41; Add. MS 36,707 fol. 50; Add. MS 28,053, fol. 365; B.L., Ballard MS 45, fol. 19.
[56] P.R.O., S.P. 63/340, fol. 151.
[57] A.E., Corr. Pol. Ang. 167, fol. 113.
[58] *Ibid.*, fols. 179–80.

former nice ones." [59] The pitiable condition was of course uncertainty in choosing sides. James himself was in doubt as to future actions, and prominent Catholics were already running away.[60] The suggestion that the king withdraw had already been made by Catholics at Salisbury.[61] A person who appears to have been well informed wrote Lord Abingdon on December 8:

The king is much divided upon his three counsels. . . . The Protestant lords advised him to throw himself upon his parliament and discard his popish counsels and assured him the parliament would secure him and not hurt a hair of his head; and this advice he promised to take: But the queen and others advise him to fight though he has but 5000 men to stand by him, being infatuated that the Virgin Mary will give him the victory. And admit he be beaten, secondly that then it's time enough for him to think of flying into France afterwards and if he does that: they persuade him that he will leave the kingdom so embroiled and confused; that they [the rebels] will not know what to do: for there will be no legal way to call a parliament or give commissions and the Church of England men are so cautious that they will not then meddle and the Dissenters will [illegible word] the Church of England men and so they will cut one the other's throats and he will leave them in a distracted condition till the king can get a power [army] from France to come and assert his own right, and these counsels so distract his majesty that he knows not which to take; one while he is for the popish advice, and then he orders the drums to beat up for volunteers to supply vacancies. Another while he is full of fear, and then he orders the priests and Jesuits to be gone and says he must be advised by his parliament but is so confused that he looks pitifully, takes no rest and falls away [grows thin] strangely. I pray God direct him to see his own and the good of the nation.

The author was obviously a Protestant and a Tory; he was probably a gentleman.[62] That the leading Protestants advised

[59] E. M. Thompson (ed.), *Correspondence of the Family of Hatton* (2 vols., Camden Society, 1878), II, 119.

[60] "The Revolution Vindicated . . . ," reprinted in *A Collection of State Tracts Publish'd on Occasion of the Late Revolution in 1688 and during the Reign of King William III* (3 vols., London, 1705-7), III, 694–728, especially p. 710.

[61] *A Letter to a Bishop Concerning the Present Settlement and the New Oaths* (London, 1689), p. 14.

[62] B.M., Add. MS 18,675, fol. 48.

the king to yield is thoroughly proved. The stratagem of leaving the government to break down has the peculiar impress of Lord Melfort's mind, which would have ignored the example of the Convention of 1660, used as a substitute for a legal parliament. The more James gave in to advice from Melfort, the worse off he would be.

Whatever James intended to do, he wished to protect the royal family. After an unsuccessful attempt to send the Prince of Wales to France by way of Portsmouth, he entrusted Maria Beatrice and the child to the Count de Lauzun. Middleton wrote a pass for Lauzun on December 9, and the group apparently left the same day, for James announced on December 10 that he had sent the queen and the young prince to a place where they might be safe. His own decision may not yet have been final on December 10, for the king was still active in his control of the army and Middleton on that day actually issued a warrant for a grant of the archdeaconry of York to John Robinson. These actions were inconsistent with plans to abandon church and state to their own devices. Yet some (perhaps tentative) preparations must have been made during the day, and James took advantage of them that night. According to James's own account and others, he left Whitehall at one o'clock in the morning of December 11, crossed the Thames to Lambeth, and took horse with two other persons. About ten o'clock he boarded a boat at Elmley Ferry to go abroad.

James had concealed his decision from his courtiers and friends, but a few of them, shrewdly guessing what he would do, called a meeting of the lords then in London. One of these, Francis Turner, Bishop of Ely, in February, 1688/89, when the struggle for the crown was over, wrote to explain why he had acted as he had in December. He admitted that he stood in need of a pardon from King James (Turner never recognized William as king).

But abating our passions and human infirmities in this late great transaction, I cannot see wherein such as I have acted with, have done any thing unlawful by the law of God. . . . I will look no farther back (unless you bid me), than the king's first going away; some of us foresaw it two or three days beforehand, though we were never foretold it. Thereupon the E. [Earl] of R. [Rochester] and myself were the sole contrivers of the Guildhall meeting of the peers, with the lord mayor and the court of aldermen. That noble [the name scratched out, which undoubtedly was *Earl,* meaning the Earl of Rochester] and I drew a declaration ready: then went together privately to Lambeth, and engaged the archbishop: then writ a great many billets (to send forth as soon as his majesty should withdraw) to entreat the Lords as *Consiliarii Nati* that they would convene at Guildhall and take upon them the government for the preservation of the kingdom, and this great city: we had otherwise been a state of banditti and London had certainly been the spoil of the rabble. I could multiply instances from our English history, that this very course has been frequently taken by the peers, in the absence of our kings, and without their consent.[63]

(Brackets shown here are also present in the copy through which this letter survives.) The intention, Turner said, was to preserve the king's crown, though "we easily understood that many others had even then a secret purpose" to depose James, through an accord between the king and William on the basis of the prince's declaration "to get effectual securities for our religion and laws, in a free parliament of his majesty's calling, and to call the king home again with honour and safety." That intention was stated in the draft of the peers' declaration, by which they assumed responsibility for the government of the metropolis, but some of the peers forced revision.[64]

Thus the first assembly of peers at Guildhall arose from conservative instincts among James's Protestant followers, who, averse to leaving the country unsettled and "distracted," stepped into the gap to arrange a compromise. Turner and Rochester were of course agreed that their plan was better than the king's. It is no wonder that Turner, when both plans had failed, believed that he stood in need of a pardon from James.

At this first session, the lord mayor and aldermen of London agreed to the assumption of power by the lords.[65] Moreover, the principal army officers were convened (by the Bishop of Ely and Lord Rochester?) at Whitehall at the same hour as the meeting of the peers — that is, at ten o'clock in the morning of December 11. These commanders addressed a letter to the

---

[63] B.M., Add. MS 29,546, fol. 103.
[64] *Ibid.*, fols. 183–84.
[65] See, e.g., *Nouvelles uyt Engelandt, Nevens een Missive van den Koningh* (broadsheet), December 22 (N.S.), 1688; Bohun, *History*, p. 89.

Prince of Orange, promising to keep order in the forces and to obey the prince's commands.[66]

The lords in London who took part in the Guildhall meeting were naturally such as had not yet ventured to declare for the prince, or were not minded to do so. Twenty-seven were present (of whom six were bishops) at the outset. Of the bishops, Sancroft, Turner, and the Bishop of Rochester later refused allegiance to William and Mary; Mew of Winchester was a staunch Tory; only William Lloyd of St. Asaph was unsympathetic to James II. Of the lay peers, the Earls of Ailesbury and Rochester were absolutely committed to the king; Lord Berkeley was loyal; so was Mulgrave; and Lords Thanet, Burlington, Weymouth, Pembroke, and North were Tories.[67] The Earl of Kent, an obscure nobleman who had recently married the daughter of the Marquis of Halifax, may have followed his father-in-law's trimming course, but several others are not easy to place politically. Lord Wharton, on the other hand, was a Whig, and Lord Montagu, when a commoner, had distinguished himself as a supporter of the Exclusion Bill (See Appendix). The lords attacked their new responsibilities with a will, ordering Lords Feversham and Dartmouth to avoid engaging William's forces. As Middleton and Preston, who were not English peers, remained at Whitehall, the lords asked them to "attend their lordships."[68]

This attendance may have been desired to convey instructions — another order to Bevil Skelton, then at the Tower of London, was clearly for that purpose. Perhaps Middleton so understood it; however that may have been, Preston appeared before the lords the same day and was "asked by their lordships if the king had left any orders with him before his [the king's] going away; his lordship answered he had not seen his majesty since seven o'clock the night before; being asked concerning the great seal answered he knew nothing of it; the Earl of Middleton was not at home."[69]

The lords then approved a draft declaration of their resolu-

[66] "The Revolution Vindicated . . . ," p. 711; P.R.O., S.P. 31/4, fol. 203.
[67] John, Duke of Buckinghamshire [Mulgrave], *Works* (2 vols.; London, 1753), II, 71–77; K. G. Feiling, *A History of the Tory Party, 1640–1714* (Oxford, 1924), pp. 232, 240–41.
[68] B.M., Stowe MS 370, fol. 4; P.R.O. 30/25, fol. 22.
[69] B.M., Stowe MS 370, fol. 4.

tion (the king having gone) to apply to the Prince of Orange for the settlement of outstanding disputes in a free parliament. A delegation — a bishop (Turner of Ely), an earl (Pembroke), a viscount (Weymouth), and a baron (Culpepper) — was sent off with a letter to the prince. Here the very conservative (except Turner) evidently felt qualms, for the prince was at war with their sovereign; Sancroft, Mulgrave, Burlington, and the Earl of Rochester are among those who "omitted" to sign.[70] After the transaction of much business and, probably, a great deal of argument, the peers adjourned at eleven in the evening until ten in the morning of December 12, when they reassembled, in the council chamber at Whitehall. At that time, several new faces appeared, among them Halifax, who had abandoned James's cause after the flight, and who had just returned from William's camp. The conservatives were not, however, much diluted in strength by these accessions.

Halifax, the only marquis present, took the chair. (Lord Mulgrave said that Halifax's presidency had been approved by William beforehand.)[71] Then "the rest of the lords and others of the privy council were summoned and met the peers there." The "lords" were the Duke of Hamilton, the Earl of Middleton, and Viscount Preston — all Scottish peers; the "others" were Sir John Ernley, Sir John Trevor, and Colonel Silius Titus. It was now clear that the Protestant privy councillors were to reinforce the authority of the English lords. Perhaps also they were expected to supply knowledge of the situation. The lords and councillors began at once to act as a body (commanding the king's officers to keep their Protestant troops together, local officials to preserve order, and all persons to refrain from pulling down houses or buildings, "especially those of foreign ministers").[72] Middleton signed nothing, it would seem deliberately. After a recess, Middleton (and others) signed an order for the recovery of the Levant Company ship *Asia* from the hands of some Irish soldiers, but no other of the many orders emanating from the council chamber. After December 12, he attended only one session.

[70] *Ibid.*, fol. 6.
[71] *Ibid.*, fol. 7; Mulgrave, "Some Account of the Revolution," B.M., Add. MS 9,363, fols. 7–8.
[72] B.M., Stowe MS 370, fols. 8–9.

Because Middleton was fully aware of the king's intention in leaving Whitehall, he may have thought it disloyal to go counter to the plan. The author of James II's *Life,* William Dicconson, later wrote of those present at the sittings:

They looked upon the present situation of affairs as an interregnum, that the government was in a manner devolved upon them, and were in a great haste to make a present of it to the Prince of Orange: those who were most zealous in the matter took care to advertise, and even press the two secretaries of state, the Earl of Middleton and Lord Preston, to be there, to add a greater weight to their pretended authority; but the former absolutely refused, and soon after hearing the king was at Faversham went immediately down to him; the latter was prevailed with to meet, but when he saw what was aimed at refused to concur. . . .[73]

This is an unfair oversimplification, as we shall see.

In the meantime, James II, after boarding his little ship, ran aground in her; it only began to float at eleven o'clock in the evening of December 11. By that time, the men of Kent were out to stop the Catholics and other fugitives. To judge by the treatment of James, the first object of the mob was to strip the helpless of their valuables; the second was to earn rewards.

Some fifty or sixty men, James says in his story of the event, boarded his ship from three fishing boats and made the passengers prisoners. Taken ashore at Faversham, first Sir Edward Hales was recognized, then the king. James attempted to buy his freedom, but a local mob prevented his escape. Gentlemen of the neighborhood intervened to protect him, and two companies of militia assembled at Faversham the next morning. James wrote to London for money, clothes, and other things on December 12.

When the lords and privy councillors met at ten o'clock in the morning of December 13, Thomas Liniall, a servant of Archbishop Sancroft, appeared with a note from a man at Canterbury.

It was whispered that he had brought news of the king being stopped

---

[73] J. S. Clarke (ed.), *Life of James II, Collected out of Memoirs Writ of His Own Hand,* II, 259–60.

in Kent, whereupon he [Liniall] was ordered to withdraw alone, and that he might not discourse with any in the meantime.

Earl of Mulgrave some time afterwards acquainted the lords that there was a rumour that the king was at Faversham, and he thinks it his duty to move the lords to take off any restraint, if there is any upon him.[74]

And so, evidently much against their inclination, the lords and privy councillors called Liniall in to give his story. Mulgrave, who found the messenger at the door of the council chamber — "without anybody's being willing to take notice of him" — showed his indignation at "so mean a proceeding in the council"; Halifax hastily adjourned the meeting, but Mulgrave persuaded the lords to sit down again, and "represented to them what a barbarity it would be for such an assembly to connive at the rabble's tearing in pieces even any private gentleman, much more a great prince, who with all his popery was still their sovereign, so that mere shame obliged them to suspend their politics awhile, and to call in the messenger. . . ."[75] Perhaps Halifax did not intend to connive at mob violence, but he certainly tried to prevent the lords' concerning themselves with the king's plight. He was obviously William's man by December 12, but many of the peers and privy councillors were not.

Liniall gave the group a good description of the king's position. Mulgrave then moved that a "party of horse" should be sent to protect James; Lord Berkeley seconded, and added that persons of quality should go to attend him. Halifax countered "that there may be many reasons to doubt that this information may not be true, that therefore nothing may be done at present, but that they [i.e., the lords] meet again in the afternoon." Mulgrave suggested that Liniall be sworn, but action was postponed until a meeting at four o'clock, at which thirty-four persons were present. Sancroft, Middleton (who had been absent in the morning), Preston, Lord Rochester, Nottingham, Berkeley, and Feversham attended, and all remained loyal to King James. (Mulgrave was unaccountably absent.) The lords at first insisted on dealing with petty business. Lacking Mulgrave, the

[74] B.M., Stowe MS 370, fol. 18.
[75] B.M., Add. MS 9,363, fols. 8–9.

conservative cause fell to the sword bearer of the City of London, who had brought a seaman, Robert Clinton, with an independent account of the king's detention. After Berkeley moved that a guard be sent down to release the king, this exchange followed:

Marquis of Halifax [said] that neither of them [Liniall and Clinton] says he knows the king.

But the Earl of Rochester takes notice that the last described him with a patch on his lip, and said he [Clinton] had seen him before.

Earl of Middleton desires if any there doubts of the truth of this matter, he would demand an oath, but for his part he was satisfied of it this morning; and therefore he moves that all respects should be shown the king, and that such a number of guards should be sent to him as would secure him from the rabble, but that he should be left at entire liberty to go where he pleases, and that some lords should attend him and give him their advice.[76]

Bishop Mew of Winchester opined that the king would not have had to flee if he had waited for an answer to the proposals he had sent to the Prince of Orange. Lords Feversham and Montagu urged immediate action on Middleton's motion. Godolphin observed a general agreement and gave his support to Middleton, Feversham, and Montagu. Lords Carlisle and Rochester both said that the prince should be given this latest news. And Halifax, still determined to limit the help given by the lords to the fugitive,

agrees with sending some horse to the king, though no great number . . . that the Prince of Orange should be made acquainted with it, but no message or advice sent to the king by the lords with the guards, for it would look like restraint.

Earl Middleton that notwithstanding the guards the king may be at entire liberty, which all agree to.

Lord Ailesbury was sent to tell the king that the guard and a deputation of lords would soon be on the way, and Feversham was given command of the guard. Lords Yarmouth and Middleton were to attend the king with appropriate Protestant servants, and the keeper of the privy purse, Mr. Graham, was to go with them. Immediately after the drawing of passes for these

---

[76] B.M., Stowe MS 370, fols. 20–23.

and other persons, the lords notified the Prince of Orange of the actions they had taken.[77]

The prince was, no doubt, disturbed, for the flight had eased his position. He had already written that the recent change "obliges me to go to London with all the speed imaginable to prevent such disorders as may happen in this conjuncture,"[78] but he needed no "obliging." He also instructed Lord Danby to send the prince's friends home and have them "stand for to be chosen parliamentmen in their counties, and keeping their inclinations for me, of which they have given such evident proofs in this occasion, that they shall be always acknowledged by me."[79] The return of the king was precisely what he did not want; Halifax had probably been aware of that when he had opposed effectual steps to bring James back from Faversham. It is unlikely that Middleton would have agreed with Halifax, but it is significant that he had not been the first to speak for sending help in the meeting of the lords, and Ailesbury was later to criticize him for it. (Ailesbury incidentally misrepresented his own part in retrospect.) Did Middleton hesitate to cross the king's plans? Or did he fear that James would be murdered?

The four lords set out; the assembly at Whitehall later sent after them a request that they learn from the king what had become of the great seal and the writs for elections to parliament. (Both were missing.) Lord Feversham presented himself to James on December 15, and escorted the dejected king through the mob to the guards, who, to prevent a clash, had been left behind at Sittingbourne. James assumed command and sent Feversham to the Prince of Orange with a letter of credence and an invitation to a meeting at London on Monday, December 17; the king then set out with the guards for London. Ailesbury, Middleton, and Preston rode with the king in his coach.[80] Middleton had sent word ahead to Whitehall, ordering preparations for James's return to his palace, and as the coach and escort passed over London Bridge and through the city, officers pretending to be loyal warned James that he would not

[77] *Ibid.*; P.R.O., S.P. 8/2, part 2, fol. 87.
[78] B.M., Add. MS 18,675, fol. 49.
[79] B.M., Add. MS 28,053, fol. 375.
[80] Ailesbury, *Memoirs*, I, 214.

be safe at Whitehall. The people who saw the coach in the city greeted him with joy.[81] He reached Whitehall about five o'clock in the afternoon.

Hardly had James arrived when the Count of Nassau-Zuilesteyn appeared with a request that James remain at Rochester and not come on to London. This word came too late, but the king invited the prince to stay at St. James's Palace; the emissary said that William probably would not do so until the royal troops were withdrawn from the city. Upon hearing that Lord Feversham had been arrested on William's orders, James held a meeting of the privy council, his last. Only eight councillors were present: Middleton, Preston, the Duke of Hamilton, Berkeley, Craven, and Godolphin, Silius Titus, and the Master of the Rolls. Barrillon reported that the crowd at Whitehall was very great but that it consisted chiefly of obscure and inconsiderable people. After supper, which was in public, James spoke with Barrillon privately about his departure and capture, his concern for his wife and son in France, and his desire to escape again.[82]

December 17 was apparently a quiet day. In the evening, the Count of Solms, an officer of the prince, came to place Dutch guards in the usual posts about Whitehall. The king's English guards were already in place, but James ordered Lord Craven to withdraw them. After James had retired for the evening, Lords Delamere, Halifax, and Shrewsbury descended upon Whitehall with a message from William and insisted upon delivering it to the king, although it was one o'clock in the morning. Servants woke Middleton, who had been sleeping in the royal bedchamber, and Middleton woke the king. James had the messengers admitted, to learn that he was ordered to go to Ham House (once the Duke of Lauderdale's) "that very morning." [83] The king thought Ham House "unhealthy for a winter stay"; Middleton called the three messengers back and said that the king would prefer to go to Rochester, where he still had some of his own infantry. The three

[82] P.R.O., Privy Council Register, Vol. 71, entry for December 16; A.E., Corr. Pol. Ang., Vol. 167, fols. 237–38.

[83] J. S. Clarke (ed.), *Life of James II*, II, 265. Cf. Foxcroft, *Life and Letters of Sir George Savile, Bart., First Marquis of Halifax*, II, 41.

[81] B.M., Stowe MS 370, fols. 39–40; B.M., Add. MS 34,501, fol. 7.

lords said that they would consult the prince and would send
word of his decision by nine o'clock (James was to leave Whitehall before ten). The reply was that Rochester was acceptable
to the prince.[84]

A myth was spread about this brief stay at Whitehall. William
Lloyd, Bishop of St. Asaph, and no friend of James, on December 17 wrote Bentinck that Bishop Turner had heard from
Halifax that the king was willing to surrender almost all his
powers, even the appointment of officials and the making of war
and peace. Lloyd did not believe the report — he thought
"criminals that are in danger of the law" still had the king's
ear, "for as I am certainly informed, there was a throng of
papists about him last night, with Monsieur Barrillon in the
head of them: and this day there were thirty or forty at his
majesty's dinner, and no priest but a Jesuit to say grace." [85]

It is apparently true that there were still Catholics about
Whitehall. Except in the king's presence, well-known Catholics
could hardly feel safe in England. The lords and privy councillors had ordered the arrest of some; others had been abused
by mobs; for his own safety, the lords had invited the Spanish
ambassador to stay at Whitehall and had undertaken to provide
him with diet. It was thus no wonder that prominent Catholics
thronged around the king. Many would have gone abroad, but
were prevented from leaving the country by the closing of the
ports.[86] A number of familiar faces were missing: James's queen,
Melfort, Sunderland, d'Adda, and Powis were abroad; Jeffreys
and Bevil Skelton were in prison. Middleton was still at Whitehall, with some other Protestants; only Protestants had been
present at the privy council meeting on December 16. Yet the
myth spread rapidly, after James's departure for Rochester, that
Whitehall had been so "crowded with Irish men, priests, Jesuits,
and Roman Catholics" that "all things were returning apparently into the old channel." [87] Had the way been clear, most
of the terrified Catholics would have departed from Whitehall
instantly.

The king was now under pressure. Not only had he been

[84] B.M., Add. MS 34,501, fol. 9; Ailesbury, *Memoirs*, I, 317–18.
[85] P.R.O., S.P. 8/2, part 2, fol. 91.
[86] *Ibid.*, fols. 44–45; B.M., Add. MS 17,677 HH, fol. 543.
[87] Bohun, *History*, p. 93.

forced to leave his own palace on the demand of a foreigner, but he had received a plea from his wife to join her in France. He was also frightened. No doubt the best course for him to follow was much discussed at Whitehall and during the journey to Rochester.

The king expected to pass with his carriages through the city, as he had on his return, but Halifax objected "with heat" that this might arouse compassion in the people of London and cause disorder. In the morning of December 18, James left Whitehall in a barge, attended by the Earl of Arran and others, spent the night at Gravesend, and the next day went on to Rochester.

Middleton stayed behind, on the king's orders, but followed him on December 20.[88] Thus he was present at the end of James's reign as he had been at the beginning. James had other faithful friends: Lords Ailesbury, Dumbarton, Arran, Newburgh, Balcarres, Suffolk, Lichfield, and Dundee had gone to Rochester to be with him, as well as General Edward Sackville, Sir John Talbot, and the recently created Edward, Lord Griffin. Several officers waited on the king and surrendered their commissions to him, as others had already done at Whitehall. Middleton, a newswriter tells us, now gave up his secretaryship.[89]

Middleton took part in the discussions of the wisdom of a second flight. The guards at Rochester were obviously negligent, and the king had an opportunity which he might never have again. According to James's two accounts of these discussions, Dr. Brady, one of his physicians, argued that the king should remain in England, even if he had to go into hiding. James "argued the whole matter" with Middleton, who had the advantage of having observed "what occurred after the Prince of Orange's arrival." Middleton could not advise the king to stay, because of the danger to his person; he "only told the king he was very confident, that if his majesty went out of the kingdom, the door would immediately be shut upon him." Middleton's

[88] B.M., Add. MS 34,501, fol. 9; B.M., Add. MS 29,563, fol. 380; A.E., Corr. Pol. Ang., Vol. 167, fol. 245; *The English Currant*, December 14–19, 1688. For the compassion of the public, see also B.M., Egerton MS 2,621, fol. 83.

[89] B.M., Add. MS 34,501, fol. 10; P.R.O., S.P. 44/338, p. 143; P.R.O., Adm. 78/2, p. 291; F. A. J. Mazure, *Histoire de la révolution de 1688 en Angleterre* (3 vols.; Paris, 1825), III, 280–81.

son told Thomas Carte in 1739/40 that Lords Dundee and Dunbarton took Middleton's side in the argument. Dundee advised James to stay in England, and give him a commission; Dundee would gather ten thousand of the disbanded troops and defeat William; but James refused to precipitate a civil war.[90]

James recorded that he wrote two aldermen of London and offered to deliver himself to them, "if they would undertake to secure his person" until he had "given full satisfaction in all things relating to religion, liberty, etc.," but the common council of London, moved by Sir Robert Clayton, refused. Some Anglican bishops had advised James not to withdraw, or at least not to leave the country, but they refused a similar offer. It was fear of assassination that caused the king to decide to go to France.[91]

In the evening of December 22, after supper, James showed Middleton a paper giving reasons for his flight, which he intended to leave for the earl, to be delivered the next morning. He instructed Middleton to have it printed, and then entrusted it to Lord Dunbarton for delivery, so as to avoid letting it be known that Middleton was aware that the king was going. Lords Ailesbury and Lichfield were also in the secret. James went to bed at his usual hour, got up, dressed, and went down a back staircase to the garden of the house. There he met one of his officers, and the two went to a ship commanded by Captain Trevanion. He sailed at midnight, taking with him the Duke of Berwick (his illegitimate son) and only three other persons. He spent a short while aboard the fireship *Eagle*; after daylight he transferred to another ship, which had been waiting to carry him away.[92]

Some Jacobites, at least, believed that he had had a narrow escape. Charles Hornby, a pamphleteer, left a manuscript from which Thomas Carte made extracts in 1741, which shows (if it tells a true story) that James was in danger while he was at Whitehall and William at Windsor.

At Windsor a council was held about the disposal of the king's [James II's] person, where some, and even of those who did not

[90] Clarke (ed.), *James II*, II, 268; B.M., Add. MS 34,501, fol. 10; B.L., Carte MS 231, fol. 62.

[91] B.L., Carte MS 231, fol. 62.

[92] Clarke (ed.), *James II*, II, 273–75; B.M., Add. MS 34,501, fol. 12; Sloane MS 3,929, fols. 123–24.

afterwards seem enamoured with the revolution, were for confining him to the Tower, some for sending him to Holland, not without broad innuendos of something worse; nay, a near relation had so forgot that and his duty as a subject and a Christian as to insinuate there needed no further trouble, there being many convenient private places in St. James's house, but his daughter having exacted and even extorted the most solemn promise for the safety of his person, those shocking proposals were reject.[93]

In Rochester, the letter of explanation was duly delivered by Dunbarton to Middleton. As the king was gone, his servants were released. Middleton and Ailesbury returned to the capital with the others in coaches, Ailesbury says: "Our conversation in coach as well as at dinner, was equal to that which might have been at the king's funeral. Indeed two persons that sat at table, by each were never seen to be so merry, which gave the rest great scandal. They were the secretary of state, and Doctor Frasier the physician. . . ."[94] The "secretary of state" was Middleton. He had given up his seals. His authority was past, and so was his responsibility, greatly to his relief. The king had made his decision, over Middleton's objections, but he had got safely off, and a funereal air would have been inappropriate. There had already been far too much tension and gloom. Also Middleton was a stoic, or thought he was, and the emotions of Stoics are independent of the world's troubles. Ailesbury put the worst interpretation on a display of levity. He was not a good interpreter, for he disliked Middleton and had no sense of humor. Each, in his way, paid for being the man he was.

[93] B.L., Carte MS 104, fol. 23. The near relation may have been Cornbury, James's nephew by marriage, or one of Charles II's natural sons. Prince George and William of Orange were not James's subjects. It is inconceivable that Rochester or Clarendon could have made such a suggestion.

[94] Ailesbury, *Memoirs*, vol. I, pp. 225–26.

CHAPTER XII

"The Best Sort We Can Have"

On their return to London, Middleton went with Ailesbury to report James's departure to the Prince of Orange.[1] Word of the letter addressed to Middleton by James spread. The lords and privy councillors had ceased to meet on December 16, but on December 21 an assembly of English peers alone met on summons from William, which included neither Middleton nor Preston; many of its members had joined the prince before he arrived in London. On December 25, several Tory peers asked to have the letter shown to the assembly, but their opponents defeated them on a vote.[2] Lord Rochester obtained the letter, however, and Lord Clarendon took a copy. Widespread knowledge of the letter's contents may have been important in persuading Tories to vote against declaring the throne vacant.

It is probable that the prince made advances to Middleton for his support; William was practical about his quest for friends. All but a few (like Jeffreys) of James's important officeholders were welcome on the prince's side, and they could expect rewards. Middleton did not accept any such offers, if they were made. There is no evidence that he recognized the new government by taking the oaths of allegiance and supremacy. The prince, quite rightly, suspected him very early. On December 28, Philip Frowde, manager of the post office, was ordered in William's name to intercept all letters addressed to James, his queen, Middleton, or Preston.[3] Surveillance of the hardy remnant of James's friends was thus begun.

Middleton had family concerns in his retirement. Since the

---

[1] B.M., Sloane MS 3,929, fol. 123.
[2] B.M., Stowe MS 370, fols. 67–68.
[3] B.M., Add. 40,791, fol. 8.

birth of his eldest son, John, Lord Clermont, in 1683, a daughter and another son had been born: Katherine (August 10, 1685) and Charles (December 4, 1688, during the dismal period between the return from the west and the first flight of the king). Another daughter, Elizabeth, would be born on June 25, 1690. Middleton and his family continued to live in England; he had a house at Winchester, and perhaps leased Goodwood, a house on the Sussex site of the later house of the dukes of Richmond. Though suspect, he was not ill treated; his horses were exempted from impressment and his Winchester house from the quartering of troops. Lord Shrewsbury, his wife's nephew, was his successor as secretary of state for the Southern Department. Shrewsbury was on pleasant terms with Middleton and could use his position to ease his predecessor's relations with the government.

Middleton could thus have lived on in a pleasant, undemanding round of family life and care of his property, and to some extent he must have done so, but the attraction of politics was too strong. The sources tell us little of his everyday existence, but much of his political associations and actions as one of the best known and most respected of those who remained loyal to James, who were coming to be called "Jacobites."

From one point of view, these men — who opposed the government of William and Mary — brought troubles on themselves. The early years of the new reign were marked by a series of grave indiscretions among the Jacobites. William was temperate at first: his opponents were usually powerless and could not much endanger his position; and some of them were members of influential families and had other alliances as well. Sometimes, after a cautionary arrest, an obviously guilty conspirator was released without punishment, but the more vocal of the Jacobites neither learned prudence nor reconciled themselves to William. Their second and subsequent offenses tended to provoke harsher treatment, and even the death penalty.

On the other hand, William needed the Jacobites as foils. Opposition to James had united many Tories with the Whigs during the revolution; it might also unite them in the war against France, if other arguments failed. The continuance of Jacobite activities facilitated the grants of money which parliament made to William and justified the heavy loss of life during his mediocre and inconclusive military campaigns. It also kept the two parties which supported William from taking each other by the throats. There is no evidence that William deliberately encouraged Jacobite conspiracy for his own ends, but some contemporaries held that he used it from time to time to alarm the political classes and to work up popular fervor.[4] Thus even late in his life, William took no action against known Jacobites unless they were engaged in a dangerous conspiracy or unless a domestic event called for adroit use of the Jacobite menace.

Middleton either received no invitation or refused to appear at a meeting of Scottish noblemen at St. James's Palace on January 7 — or at another on January 8, at which the Earl of Arran suggested recalling James II and holding a free parliament. Nor did he present himself in the Scottish convention that made William and Mary rulers of Scotland in the spring, although other Jacobites were there.

Middleton, of course, corresponded with King James, who wrote to Lord Preston (January 8/18, 1688/89) approving the latter's intention of staying in London for the convention and parliament. Preston should correspond frequently, James said, and render all possible service.

I am sure that you will do it and you that are acquainted with members of both houses, may do me very much, by speaking and consulting with such of them as you can trust and considering of the best ways how you may do it the most effectually. I send by this bearer [Ralph] Sheldon, to Lord Middleton a letter to be delivered to my privy council, which I hope will be made public, as well as what I left on my table at Rochester when I came from thence; remember I must have great consideration for such of you as have stuck firm to me, so few so very few having done it.[5]

The letter James sent to Middleton was apparently given to Preston, who on January 19/29 showed it to Lord Clarendon. It was countersigned by Lord Melfort, and addressed to the privy council, but was not sealed with the great seal. Clarendon objected that the letter was harmful, and that James's privy council no longer had authority; Preston agreed, but insisted on consulting other councillors. Clarendon wrote, "In the evening

---

[4] See Charles Hornby, *A Third Part of the Caveat against the Whigs* . . . (London, 1712), pp. 94–95.

[5] B.M., Add. MS 34,516, fol. 44.

he told me they had resolved it should be quashed."[6] (Tran
scripts of James's letters to Preston survive — but nothing at a
of those to Middleton — from which we learn that the forme
king expected letters by every post on the actions of the conver
tion, with copies of the *London Gazette* "and such printed pa
pers as are worth reading.")[7]

Middleton observed the steps of the transfer of authority t
the new rulers. After debate, the convention did its duty by Wi
liam and offered the crown to him and to his wife, jointly
There was no consideration of the position of the former Princ
of Wales; as a newswriter tells us: "Here's no room for the ex
amination of the little gent title which perhaps will be hereafte
the best proof he has of his title that, after 'twas in their powe
to examine his birth, they durst not refer it to a free parliamen
as was pretended. . . ."[8] As the usual oaths of allegiance an
supremacy were tendered to officials, army and navy officer
and incumbent clergymen, agonizing choices were forced upc
the Tories. Middleton would have seen with what stoicism l
could command the conversion of Tories such as Danby, Roc
ester, and Nottingham into loyal subjects of the new goveri
ment. A formerly faithful subject, a schoolmaster, Edwa
Leedes, explained his submission to a friend in 1695:

For my own part I obeyed King James as long as I could, and I
thought fit to rule. But when he would stay no longer to defer
himself and those that would have obeyed him, but left us all
the mercy of the rabble and the Dutch, in whose power it was
have taken away our lives, and, if they had, all obligation of payin
allegiance any further to King James, I suppose, had been at a
end. And seeing they did not is not at all owing to him or anythii
that he did to preserve us, I do not see why our allegiance shou
any longer be thought due to him, to whom we owe nothing of th
remaining part of our lives, but may in reason be demanded
and paid to that person to whom we owe it, and the protectio
thereof.[9]

Middleton may have felt compassion for the troubles of me
like Leedes, but he shared the loyalist views of those who r

[6] Clarendon, *State Letters*, II, 304.
[7] James to Preston, Jan. 16/26, 1689, B.M., Add. MS 34,516.
[8] B.L., Ballard MS 45, fol. 27a.
[9] Trinity College Library, Cambridge, MS R. 4.44, fol. 18.

fused the oaths. Five bishops were deprived of their sees for this offense, and many clergymen and laymen also declined the oaths and thus barred themselves from office. Sir William Boothby asked Archbishop Sancroft — who himself refused to swear and lost his position — for advice. Boothby, who had been put out of public employments by James "for standing firm to our laws," was reinstated after the revolution. "I would neither be wanting in my duty on the one hand; nor yet do anything contrary to those steady principles which I have ever professed, on the other. An oath is a sacred thing, and I do with all humble submission beg your lordships help and advice. . . ." [10]

In the end, most took the oaths; but Lord Preston would not; nor would he abstain from politics. On March 11, 1688/89, Narcissus Luttrell wrote of news from the north "that some disturbances are likely to break out there; that the Lord Preston, Lord Griffin, Sir John Fenwick, Colonel Oglethorpe are there, fomenting the same on behalf of the late King James." [11] In May, the high sheriff of York and others wrote of meetings of Catholics with Preston and Lord Fairfax of Gilling. Preston was arrested, brought to London at the end of the month, and held in the Tower. Griffin was also arrested and was not released until December. When Preston had been bailed, he was committed to the Tower again for pretending to have been created a peer of England by King James after the revolution.

Although we hear less about him, Middleton also was active. In September, 1689, one Harry Cox deposed that he had heard from two witnesses that Middleton had received money to spend for the Jacobite cause. [12] James was then in Ireland at the head of an army; England was not firmly settled on its new foundation, and some Englishmen were restive. In January, 1689/90, a clerk of the Green Cloth had to be suspended by the lord steward for drinking the former king's health. That same month, "at a church in Friday Street a young man preached an inveter-

---

[10] B.L., Tanner MS 27, fols. 9–10.

[11] Narcissus Luttrell, *A Brief Historical Relation of State Affairs, 1678–1714* (6 vols.; Oxford, 1857), I, 509.

[12] H.M.C., *Finch MSS*, II, 242. The belief of Mr. David Ogg that Middleton was abroad for some time after the revolution and was sent back to England to deal with Lord Shrewsbury is an error. *England in the Reigns of James II and William III*, p. 363.

ate sermon against the government and prayed for King James, both in the common prayer and also in that before his sermon." [13] From Ireland, James promised his supporters help. Although the new government found it wise to arrest a number of suspects, it usually allowed them bail after short periods in custody.

In January, 1690/91, Captain John Ashton, formerly secretary to James II's queen, was apprehended on his way to France, carrying incriminating papers.[14] A Jacobite, Neville Payne, who had also fallen into the government's hands, was sent to Scotland and tortured to obtain evidence (under Scottish law), until his thumbs had been squeezed "as thin as the back of an ordinary knife." [15] Payne confessed nothing, eventually went free, and died at Paris in 1705, but Ashton suffered on the scaffold. Preston was tried and convicted, but pardoned in consideration of a full confession, and thereafter ceased to have the confidence of his party (he translated *The Consolation of Philosophy*, and died in 1693).

Middleton's position as a Jacobite leader was even greater after Preston's betrayal. Later in the year (1691), however, he was accused of being "well-affected" to King James by a debt prisoner (who also accused many others). In February, 1691/92, Middleton was listed as one of the persons who had subscribed an address to Louis XIV begging help in effecting James's restoration.[16] James had withdrawn from Ireland, where his supporters made terms for themselves in 1691, to France; he lived at St.-Germain in hope of a future return to England.

An invasion of England for that purpose was indeed planned in the spring of 1692. Lord Melfort, James's "secretary of state," was in full favor at St.-Germain, and appears to have originated the plan, which was practicable because the French fleet was unusually strong. The preparations became known in England; to prevent rebellion, orders went out in May for the arrest of prominent Jacobites — including Middleton, the Earl of Dun-

[13] B.M., Add. MS 11,043, fols. 140, 154.

[14] See B.M., Sloane MS 3,328, fols. 157–65.

[15] R.H.E., Leven and Melville Papers, sec. VII A, No. 60; newsletter of December 20/30, 1690, P.R.O., Adm. 78/4.

[16] B.L., Carte MS 130, fols. 333–34, 337–38; H.M.C., *Report VII*, p. 210.

more, and Sir Andrew Forrester (formerly Lauderdale's secretary) — "being charged with high treason in abetting and adhering to their majesties' enemies."[17] Middleton fled, but he was found — according to report — in a Quaker's house in Goodman's Fields, with Dunmore and Forrester; all three were sent to the Tower of London.[18] The Earl of Marlborough (formerly Lord Churchill), who had also been arrested, was released on June 15, but the three Scotsmen were remanded to custody on the oath of one Aron Smith that there was sufficient evidence of high treason for a trial. No proper excuse was made for not presenting the evidence at that time, and there was no trial, so that the accused were released.[19] Middleton was very busy in other Jacobite correspondence and planning before the end of 1692.

Exactly what Middleton was doing to warrant his arrest, if indeed anything, is still hidden by lack of evidence. He must have been aware of the planned invasion; that he took to his heels suggests that he expected it to succeed and therefore hoped to escape punishment by concealing himself for a short time. If so, he miscalculated James's chances, for on May 19 the English and Dutch fleets defeated the French, and on May 23 the victors destroyed the transports that were to have ferried French troops across the Channel. After this battle of La Hogue, the English fleet's power waxed and its rival's waned.

The affairs of the former king had reached a gloomy state: his supporters had capitulated everywhere in the British Isles. His high hopes before the defeat at La Hogue had encouraged him to deal haughtily with supporters who had urged him to "compound" or compromise with his subjects — to promise to preserve the constitution and to respect the privileges of the Church of England. Melfort was his spokesman; and a contemporary pamphleteer tells us that James had said "he would

[17] P.R.O., P.C. 2/74, pp. 388, 394. For Forrester's past, see B.M., Add. MS 35,125, fol. 296.

[18] P.R.O., P.C. 2/74, fol. 401; B.M., Add. MS 7,080, fol. 37; James Grant (ed.), *Seafield Correspondence from 1685 to 1708* (Edinburgh: Scottish History Society, 1912), p. 88.

[19] B.M., Add. MS 34,096, fol. 25; E. M. Thompson (ed.), *Hatton Correspondence*, II, 180; H.M.C., *Report XIV*, appendix VI (*Lords MSS* III), p. 91. For one account of Marlborough's imprisonment, see Sir Winston Churchill, *Marlborough*, I, 352–61, setting aside the author's evident bias.

rather never see England again, than come to treat or capitulate with his subjects again." [20] Under Melfort's influence, James had made a stiff, unconciliatory declaration shortly before the battle.

After the disaster at La Hogue, the former king changed his mind, and Melfort attempted to accommodate himself to the shift. As early as June 24/July 4, 1692, Melfort reopened negotiations with such men as Lords Clarendon, Montgomerie, and Orford ("Mr. Russell" in the correspondence),[21] and the friendly tone is apparent.

The encouragement you gave me to propose your being a partner in my friends' [James's] concerns, and the hopes I had from you of your joining a considerable stock [following(?)], in case I could assure you of such terms as might not destroy the manufacture [church(?) constitution(?)] of England, nor hinder any from that freedom he ought to have to pursue his own affairs without molestation, makes me thus address you. . . .

So Melfort wrote to Orford.[22] James was willing to come to terms, and Melfort was willing to serve as his agent.

It was evident, however, that the "Compounders" in England did not wish to deal with Melfort, who perceived this fact and introduced his former enemy Middleton into the correspondence. On September 23/October 3, he sent the former secretary this message:

I am well satisfied with your care of my concerns, and am sorry you should have met with such trouble upon my account. I shall ever be ready to requite your kindness with that affection I have always had for you. I am sorry that your affairs will not permit you to stay where my affairs principally are.[23]

This missive refers to James's rather than Melfort's affairs, and to Middleton's imprisonment; it was nevertheless a reopening of communication between the leader of the Drummond interest and James's most important Protestant minister of 1688. Once reopened, the correspondence continued. Middleton must have

[20] *A Short and True Relation of Intrigues Transacted, Both at Home and Abroad, to Restore the Late King James* (London, 1694), p. 8. The author of this pamphlet was very well informed.

[21] B.M., Add. MS 37,661, fols. 1–2.

[22] *Ibid.*, fols. 7–8.

[23] *Ibid.*, fol. 75.

replied to Melfort's letter, for the latter wrote again, on October 7/17, "As nothing could have suited more with my inclination there was not any one thing I did more heartily wish for, than an entire friendship with you. . . ." [24] But the communications from the Compounders were not as precise as James had hoped, as he wrote to former Major General Maxwell:

The bearer [David Lindsay] has given me an account of what you charged him with concerning the E. of M., and though I do in no manner doubt of what you say to me from him, and am fully satisfied of the loyalty and ability of the said earl, yet I can not enter further into that affair till by something from himself under his own hand, or some trusty person impowered by him, be speedily sent to me to give a full account of what is proposed by him, who the persons are, of what party and quality that he corresponds with, that I may the better know what measures I am to take. [25]

The "E. of M." was probably Middleton.

The association of Compounders, it seems, included Lords Orford, Godolphin, Marlborough, Rochester, Middleton, and Shrewsbury; Maxwell and Sackville, former generals in James's army; and perhaps Lord Torrington, who was in disgrace with William. More distant possibilities were Princess Anne and her husband, Prince George. It is certain that some of these persons were only "insuring" themselves against an unpredictable future: some, like Marlborough, Middleton, and Torrington, had suffered loss of office or had recently been imprisoned. Spite was undoubtedly another motive. Middleton, Maxwell, and Sackville, however, were sincere in their support of James, and Melfort could hardly avoid dealing with them. The "secretary of state" had at least two independent channels of correspondence with Middleton by October, 1692. [26]

The obvious method of reaching an agreement in a matter so secret and delicate was for the Compounders to send a trusted agent to St.-Germain with their terms. Middleton ("Mrs. Betty"), encouraged by Melfort, went to London to arrange a

[24] *Ibid.*, fol. 87.

[25] *Ibid.*, fols. 87–88.

[26] *Ibid.*, fols. 99–100; for Marlborough, see *ibid.*, fol. 31. Marlborough is identified as the person addressed by the contemporary index to the volume, fol. 196 ("The King to Ld. Ch:"). See also James II to Lord Churchill, fol. 91; for Orford, see fol. 110, also interpreted with the help of the index.

bargain and, as Sir John Fenwick later said, "to settle a correspondence," before going on to France.[27] In 1696 the Duke of Shrewsbury recalled that Middleton told him "one night at supper, when he was pretty well in drink," that he was going overseas, and he asked what favors Shrewsbury might wish of him there. Shrewsbury later, in a letter to William III,[28] denied that he had requested any favors, but as he had been accused of correspondence with St.-Germain, he may have concealed the answer he returned in 1692 or 1693. (At the time, he did not tell William that such an approach had been made.)

Rumors were circulated that autumn (1692) as to James's negotiation with the Compounders and the line he was taking. "I have seen letters from several parts that speak of a design King James has of going to England this winter; I am well informed he has condescended to all things that may tend to the security of the Church of England, the liberty and property of the subject, and will leave the rest to a free parliament. . . ."[29] The rumors were well grounded, and a number of prominent persons were engaged by James's assurances of willingness to make concessions. Using the guise of commercial correspondence, Melfort wrote Sackville, on October 31/November 10:

Since it begins now with the goods No. 338 [Lord Bath] and 573 [Plymouth], I must again repeat that my partner [King James] is satisfied with the price and only now desires to know the time and place of delivery; that you must secure for us there, with all that belongs thereto. We had the sample of the goods No. 668 [Admiral Russell, Lord Orford] and liked it well, believing that further in towards the middle of the parcel will be as we could wish it, the merchant having made as great advances as could have been expected before he knew our minds. . . . I am of opinion that the goods No. 461 [Middleton] is of the best sort we can have, and I in my particular like them best of all you can mix with these No. 668 [Russell]. . . . I am glad to know that the Hamborow Merchant [unidentified] is in good health. . . . I like it the better that he is of the same mind as to the goods No. 461 [Middleton].[30]

[27] H.M.C., *Buccleuch MSS*, II, 293.

[28] Charles, Duke of Shrewsbury, *Private and Original Correspondence*, ed. William Coxe (London, 1821), p. 148.

[29] B.L., Tanner MS 25, fol. 405.

[30] B.M., Add. MS 37,661, fols. 124–25. The key to Melfort's cipher is found in B.L., Carte MS 256, fols. 2–10.

Melfort wrote that the "merchant's" letter had been kindly received and acknowledged his debt to Sackville for proposing "the bargain for the goods No. 20," the Princess Anne, to the "merchant." There evidently was hope of securing the French fleet for use in the execution of the plan, for Melfort hoped to get the English fleet to take James's side, so that he might without misgivings encourage the French one. To please English opinion, Melfort pretended (truly or falsely) that he favored "the entire liberty and property of the subject" and that he opposed arbitrary government by the crown.[31]

But Middleton must cross the Channel to serve James. On November 21/December 1, Melfort sent Maxwell a message for Middleton:

I had yours [a letter] and one for your grandfather [James II] inclosed in it, and I am glad to find that you are inclined to come into those parts and that anything in my power can make that journey pleasing to you. . . . I do promise to you all the service in my power and that you shall have all my credit in these parts to support yours.

James added a postscript:

I can assure you your grandfather will be glad to see you. The sooner the better. I promise you shall find me tractable and ready to do anything which can clear the estate and that I shall be ready to take any course proposed by you whom I trust and to whom I am so obliged. Adieu.[32]

According to James's *Life*, some of Middleton's associates, unnamed lords, insisted that the former king agree to hard terms. "My Lord Middleton did not altogether approve of what these lords so positively insisted upon, however thought it his duty to give the king an account of their demands." He sent first a priest named Cary, who arrived at St.-Germain in January, 1692/93.[33] Melfort expected Middleton to follow. "I am glad that the goods 461 [Middleton] are packed up . . . for I have made way for them in the storehouse [at the exiled court (?)] and have treated of them so that if they answer expectation they

[31] B.M., Add. MS 37,661, fol. 121.
[32] *Ibid.*, fols. 152–53.
[33] J. S. Clarke (ed.), *Life of James II*, II, 501–2.

will bring us a double profit at this time. . . ." [34] Cary brought eight proposals; if they were accepted, Middleton would go to France with full instructions. Louis XIV and his foreign minister recommended acceptance, and on January 12 James wrote Middleton that he agreed to all of the proposals. Middleton then sent over a draft of a declaration, and — probably in March — made his way to France.[35]

The government learned of Middleton's departure on or shortly before April 11, when James Vernon wrote to Sir William Colt:

It is confidently reported that my Lord Middleton is gone for France. It is certain he has not been in town this fortnight. He has a house near Chichester and so may have contrived his getting away with safety from Sussex. It is the more taken notice because nobody believes he would go upon a slight errand. He is supposed to have taken with him my Lord Dunmore and Sir Andrew Forrester.[36]

A little later, William III wrote to Bentinck, whom he had made Earl of Portland: "I am not at all pleased that Lord Middleton has gone to France; that is not a man who would take such a step without some subject both important and well planned, on which I have made many reflections, which I reserve to tell you [in person]." [37]

The Jacobites and their opponents seem to have shared a high opinion of the Earl of Middleton. Doctor James Welwood, a supporter of William, confessed to "a just esteem" for Middleton's abilities, and the author of "A Reply" to Welwood referred to Middleton as "an excellent person [whom] I esteem just as much for his parts as Doctor Welwood . . . can, and yet more for his integrity than for his parts." [38] The Jacobites hoped for great changes as a result of Middleton's mission. Charlwood Lawton, a Jacobite pamphleteer, said:

[34] B.M., Add. MS 37,661, fol. 176.
[35] J. S. Clarke (ed.), *Life of James II*, II, 502; Fenwick's Informations, B.M., Egerton MS 2,618, fol. 184.
[36] B.M., Add. MS 34,096, fol. 334; see also H.M.C., *R.R. Hastings MSS*, II, 228.
[37] N. Japikse, *Correspondentie van Willem III en van Hans Willem Bentinck* (5 vols.; The Hague, 1927–37), I, 177.
[38] Welwood, *An Answer to the Late K. James's Last Declaration* (London [?], 1693); *A Reply to the Answer Doctor Welwood Has Made to King James's Declaration* . . . (1693 [?]), p. 15.

Can any man of sense believe that the Earl of Middleton, who could never during his whole ministry be drawn into any one irregular step, would go over upon any other errand? That great man is known to understand his duty to his country as well as his prince, and thinks he ought at the same time to be the minister of both, and his affection and firmness to Protestancy was never once suspected: he will neither betray our laws, nor his own religion, nor will he, to do the king but justice, be tempted to either; for all that we have misliked in the king's measures abroad, has proceeded from misrepresentations from hence; and my Lord Middleton is so fraughted with the genuine interest as well as sense of these nations that the most inveterate of our enemies will have hereafter no opportunities to clamor and exasperate. . . . The future acts of state that come from that court [St.-Germain] will prove he has discoursed many of the leading men, and compromised the grievances of all parties . . . there is so good an understanding between my Lord Middleton and those who had before entire credit with the king, that they don't only personally agree, but concur in sentiments. . . .[39]

This is really too much. To call Middleton a great man was a permissible exaggeration and accorded with contemporary usage, but to represent the Jacobites at St.-Germain and in England as fully agreed was glaring misrepresentation.

It may have suited Melfort's friends to yield to the pressure of Middleton and the Compounders for a change of policy; if it did not, they could not have resisted James's decision. The proposals taken over by Father Cary in January were used for writing a new declaration to be issued by James. Middleton arrived at St.-Germain in April, it seems, for on April 16 he presented himself at Versailles.[40] The new declaration was undoubtedly the subject of discussion with Louis XIV and his ministers at that time.

James also consulted with priests before he issued his new document which, by promising to preserve the position of the Church of England, was intended to bring sound Anglicans back into the Jacobite camp; but Melfort, for one, questioned whether the former king could issue it with a good conscience. Of several accounts of the discussions which followed, James's

---

[39] Charlwood Lawton, *A French Conquest Neither Desirable Nor Practicable. Dedicated to the King of England* (London, 1693), p. 23.

[40] Philippe, Marquis de Dangeau, *Journal* (19 vols.; Paris, 1854–60), IV, 266; H.M.C., Buccleuch MSS, II, 294.

seems to be the best. Four English and Scottish priests considered the clause "protect and defend the Church of England" and enjoined James to limit this promise to the members of that church and make no promise to the church as a body. This would have been noticed by readers trained in James's past words. The Compounders appealed for a fresh consideration by a body of French priests — who approved not only the promises to the Church of England but also a promise that James would not dispense with or violate the Test Act.[41] The declaration was signed on April 17, 1693, the day after Middleton's visit to Versailles, and printed copies were distributed in England and abroad. Both James and Middleton were now committed, the former to a new and more conciliatory policy, the latter to its execution, so that they might go home honorably to England.

[41] Thomas Sheridan, "Political Reflexions," Royal Archives, Windsor Castle, pp. 98–100; J. S. Clarke (ed.), *Life of James II*, II, 507–10. I have been forced by gross differences from all accounts of St.-Germain to discard the account given in *A Short and True Relation of Intrigues*, p. 9.

CHAPTER XIII

St. - Germain

Middleton found his master at St.-Germain-en-Laye, a gloomy palace west of Paris which Louis XIV had given (with six hundred thousand livres a year) to the former king of England. The place was convenient both to Paris and to Versailles, which by 1693 had taken on the magnificence so desired by the King of France.

Melfort, still the chosen minister, held the title "secretary of state," and was in fact responsible for almost everything, as most offices were unfilled. Melfort had adapted himself to James II's tractability, but neither the king nor his minister was easy in altering principles espoused and declared long years before. About this court clustered dozens of exiles, while elsewhere, in French convents and camps, were thousands of others who looked to James for commands and help, most of them Catholics. (Rumor in England had it that Protestants were persecuted. Certainly the king of France, who detested Protestantism, would permit no Anglican services at St.-Germain.)

When Middleton appeared as the spokesman of the Compounders, most of the exiles were opposed to the policy for which he stood. These men and women had given up their property and their peace to stand with legitimacy, and they formed a solid bloc of reactionaries; as they saw it, the king had lost his crown for his insistence on his right and on his subjects' duty, but God would restore that crown in his own time. If James compromised, he would weaken his moral position and that of his supporters; moreover, as most of the exiles had suffered some loss through their fidelity, would not compromise mean sacrifice of the loyal to the factious and rebellious? Were those who had offended the exiles to get off scot-free? In short, was there no true justice in the world?

A naïve question and a saddening state of affairs. Yet Middleton had his instructions from the Compounders, and he followed them faithfully. After securing the issue of the declaration of April 17, 1693, he took up the management of James's affairs to see that its terms were observed.

The reactionaries were not his only problem: his principals in England were not all trustworthy, and some of those who were reliable were politically inexperienced and without adequate plans. The king of France, on the other hand, would act only within the limits imposed by his resources and according to his own interests. When Middleton crossed the Channel, the Jacobites expected Louis XIV to lend ships and soldiers to assist a Jacobite rising. The invasion and the rebellion were scheduled for the end of May, 1693, but neither took place.

The circumstances of France in 1693 and Louis's assessment of the schemes of his cousin and pensioner were too clear for inordinate risk of men. France was at war with most of its neighbors; its fleet had been defeated at La Hogue and had no minister as capable as Seignelay had been to restore its efficiency and morale; money was scarce; troops were needed on several fronts. A diversion to England of even a small force must have some expectation of success: that is, the projected rising must be a strong one. Middleton could show no such prospect: the English Jacobites lacked a good general, arms, and unity. The invasion was canceled. The plotters hid their preparations and hoped for a more favorable opportunity.

William's government was fully aware of the plans. One Mackgill, who had been Melfort's page, returned to England, the authorities apprehended him, and he made "a considerable discovery if it may be credited. He says positively that some men are to land in the north of this kingdom about the end of May." The Jacobites, the Scottish secretary James Johnston wrote to William Carstares, "do not dissemble that, if May pass over without having a venture for it, they'll lose hopes." Viscount Tarbat was trying to sell his official place under William and Mary, Johnston wrote: "If he be in earnest . . . and to sell it so cheap, it is because he trusts to the success of the designs now in my Lord Middleton's hands." [1]

---

[1] R.H.E., Johnston's Letter Book, April 27 and May 4, 1693; *ibid.*, May 16, 1693.

Later, the government learned that in December, 1692, there had been an agreement for a French invasion in the spring of 1693. (This is supported by frequent references to the French fleet and troops in Melfort's letterbook.) In January and February, 1693, the French government cooled toward the project, raising various difficulties. In March, it was favorable once more, and asked for fresh assurances from Scotland, which were conveyed to Middleton in writing two days before his departure from London. Lords Arran and Home were reported to be the leaders of the plot. Johnston hoped for the confession of Neville Payne, who knew the secrets of Arran's and Home's faction, which had been in agreement with Melfort. Sir William Bruce was said to be the "manager" of Middleton's faction, presumably Scottish Compounders.[2] According to newsletters, ill-affected persons distributed seditious pamphlets and had a second edition of James's recent declaration actually in press when it was discovered. There were many arrests.

Middleton, now exposed to the full retaliation of the government, was summoned — as was Melfort — to answer charges of treason in Scotland. On July 2, 1694, the lord justice clerk and the Commissioners of Justiciary ordered Middleton and Melfort "put to the horn" (proclaimed outlaws) and declared their movables escheated. On July 23 they were declared fugitives,[3] and in July, 1695, they were declared forfaulted. A curious error occurred in the decree of forfaulture: throughout the document, Middleton was called by the Christian name of "John."[4] Apparently this error (perhaps deliberately inserted by friends) was never challenged by Middleton's sons, who could have used it to challenge the validity of the decree.

In England, Middleton was indicted for high treason on August 30, 1695, and was outlawed early in 1696.[5] Middleton's Scottish estates fell to King William, who disponed them on

[2] *Ibid.*, May 24, 1693; June 1, 1693.

[3] R.H.E., Justiciary Records, Process, Melfort and oʳˢ, July 23, 1694.

[4] T. Thomson and C. Innes (ed.), *Acts of the Parliament of Scotland*, VIII, 407 and appendix, 112–14.

[5] We know this from George I's orders to his attorney general, in February, 1726/27, directing that that official give consent to a writ of error in the proceedings, so that the outlawry might be reversed in favor of Middleton's elder son. B.M., Add. MS 36,126, fols. 153, 155.

August 14, 1695, to Charles Straton, who took sasine on July 21, 1696. This was a curious circumstance, for Straton was one of Middleton's good friends, and there is evidence that the earl received at least part of the income for many years — which agrees with the Duke de St.-Simon's later story that Middleton continued to receive money from his estates.[6] Did William, in bestowing these estates on Straton, know what the arrangement would be? If so, he must have conveyed them for some reason. The obvious reason would be that Middleton betrayed James to William, but William did not necessarily know. Such fictitious holding of property, in "trust" for a friend or relative who had got into trouble, was not rare in Scotland. It may be that the government avoided notice of remittances (as it avoided rigorous prosecution of Jacobites) because it had more important things to do and because it craved quiet.

In December, 1695, several months after the decree of forfaulture, Middleton instructed his wife that the remaining "apprisings" (debts) of the estates should be bought, but the earl must be secured against the government of William III. As his half brother John was now of age, his interests also must be cared for. Perhaps John Middleton would accept a reasonable composition for twelve thousand pounds to which he was entitled. The letter was evidently to be shown to him.[7] As John Middleton died without children in the next year, it is unlikely that he made the composition and certain that it made no difference.

In November, 1706, Middleton's son Lord Clermont gave a letter of procuration to John, Earl of Strathmore, authorizing Strathmore's entry into all Clermont's lands and estate, with power to let such lands, collect rents, go to law for payments not made, and pay Clermont's debts out of the revenue.[8] Thus a "trust" was confided to Strathmore, over and above that to Straton.

Later, Middleton seems to have been disturbed by the possibility that the trusts might be discovered or that some other mishap might hinder his son's collection of the income. He con-

---

[6] Louis de Rouvroy, Duke de St.-Simon, *Mémoires*, ed. A. de Boislisle (41 vols.; Paris, 1879–1928), XV, 417–18.

[7] B.L., Carte MS 208, fols. 124–25.

[8] B.L., Carte MS 180, fol. 462.

sulted a Scottish friend, James Forbes, probably in late 1712, and Forbes replied early in 1713 that he had in turn consulted a lawyer and the "accomptant."

All three [the lawyer, "the accomptant," and Forbes] have dili-gently revised [reread] and considered both *acts of parliament of Scotland and parliament of England,* for near twenty-four years past. . . . And we find nothing in *Scotch Acts of Parliament* that can any way make against Lord Clermont, even though he should after the peace [of Utrecht] join in copartnership with *the king* [the Pretender James], but indeed there is an article in *English parliament* that it is plain will be troublesome to evade. . . . I must tell you, that the *Princess* [Queen] *Anne's* doers [agents] should design the worst against *Lord Clermont,* it will be difficult (if possible) for them, with any colour of law to reach *his* effects (there being none alive infeft of the estate but *Charles Straton*) unless *Princess Anne's* agents discover *Strathmore's* and *Charles Straton's trust,* which I hope, and think I may be confident, never will be done. And as I have reason to believe, that *Charles Straton* never designed to discover any thing to the prejudice of *Earl Middleton,* I am persuaded he never will. But after all, if *Earl Middleton* apprehends any new danger from *his son's* being again partner with *the king,* then the only remedy that can be at present thought on, is, that Lord Clermont before he part [depart] *from England* [where Clermont was a prisoner of war] may assign or dispone the contract betwixt him the late *Strathmore* and *Charles Straton* to some trusty friend in England.[9]

The tone of this letter does not suggest that Middleton could or did rely on connivance by the government, although by 1713 some of Anne's ministers were corresponding with the Pretender and apparently favorable to his restoration. The evidence goes no further, but there is this to be said: John Caryll, Middleton's colleague as a Jacobite minister, also entrusted some of his family property to another person, and no one (at the time or since) has charged him with betrayal. Lord Melfort, too, dis-posed of some Irish lands through Sir William Wallace and Colonel Douglas of Spott. It is quite possible that Caryll's, Mel-fort's, and Middleton's property transactions were completely unknown to William or any of his sincere supporters. No act of betrayal has yet been traced to either Caryll or Middleton.

[9] B.L., Carte MS 211, fol. 85 (italics indicate contemporary decipherment).

Lady Middleton and her children had remained behind in England. She is known to have occupied a house on the site of 19, Buckingham Street (then a new and fashionable quarter) after her husband's departure. The countess may have enjoyed the income from the family property for a time, for the earl was only forfaulted in Scotland on July 2, 1695, and outlawed in England in February, 1696/97. It may have been these two events which forced her, in 1695 or after, to go to St.-Germain to join her husband.

Middleton kept in touch with his wife through Jacobite channels until she went over to France with their sons. Copies of his letters to her were entered in his letterbook in the midst of his more official correspondence. Thus it is that we have his only letters which speak of John Middleton, Lord Clermont, and the younger son, Charles, during their childhood. In May, 1695, he wrote to Lady Middleton:

I judge it absolutely necessary that Tatty [Charles] the sweet should go to his brother [presumably at school] next Michaelmas; John the discreet will take care of him. I should fear that this would be very grievous to you, but I know you are most pleased with doing what is for his good. Young master here [Prince James] who is but six months elder has begun to learn Latin above a year ago, and had been removed from women [nurses] already if our Hampshire neighbor [apparently the Earl of Perth, the prince's governor] had come sooner.[10]

In June he wrote again:

In my last I writ to you about sending Tatty the giant to his brother, but since I have thought better of it, and fearing they may be spoiled or neglected there, it is my earnest desire to have them both here, where they will be carefully observed and directed and by the fondest father alive. . . . I cannot imagine that a pass can be refused to them, to go by the ship that carries over the [exchanged?] prisoners to Calais.

He instructed his wife to sound Lord Godolphin herself for this pass and have friends solicit other persons.[11] A few months later, mother and sons were with the earl at St.-Germain.

[10] B.L., Carte MS 208, fol. 78.
[11] *Ibid.*, fol. 86.

Evidently Middleton was settling at St.-Germain, without any very definite prospect of returning to Great Britain. In June, 1694, Melfort was forced to resign as one of James II's secretaries of state. Middleton had that rank already; Melfort was replaced by John Caryll, a member of an old family of English Catholics.[12] Melfort left the court for the provinces, and Middleton assumed responsibility for most correspondence, but Caryll handled the correspondence with Rome and with various Catholic prelates.

In his main purpose — persuasion of Louis XIV and his ministers to undertake an invasion of Great Britain — Middleton had no success until 1695. He continued to correspond with English and Scottish Jacobites and to put his master's case at Versailles, but without undue reiteration. "I am glad to find by l'Abbe Rizzini that their majesties approve of my notion, which is that when a matter is fully explained importunity may do more hurt than good. . . . I must think that those who affect double diligence and repeating of conversations whether true or false do it more for their own sakes than for their master's. . . ."[13]

Middleton's opinions and practices show more clearly through his Jacobite correspondence than through his official papers written before the revolution. He had more leisure and he was compelled to appeal on personal grounds to men of different factions, as in December, 1694, to a pseudonymous correspondent:

I beg you would not think me so arrogant as to take upon me to tell people, where they are to like or dislike. . . . it is without consequence if we differ in opinion about one [probably Melfort] whom I have known long, and I believe you never saw. I desire to live well with everybody, that we may all concur in the main, to which nobody can contribute more than you; many defects observable in me are fully supplied by my partner [Caryll], but if that will not satisfy some, let them propose another that will be heard, and I shall join my entreaty with theirs, that he may be employed. . . .[14]

Some of the Jacobites required restraint from above. Middleton wrote to a merchant at Calais about the same time, asking him

[12] B.M., Add. MS 31,246, fol. 78; B.M., Add. MS 31,245, fol. 12.
[13] B.L., Carte MS 256, fols. 55–56.
[14] *Ibid.*, fol. 74.

to inquire about one Captain Vaughan, who was said to have boasted that he and his men had burned London Bridge and the town of Warwick, saying, "It would be very prejudicial to the king my master's service that it should be reported in England that he sends over incendiaries amongst them. . . ."[15] Sometimes Middleton allowed himself to expound a little of his stoic opinions to his correspondents, as he did late in 1694.

The *bona animi* can never shine forth, except as they have *bonae fortunae* to attend them: power and *richesse* are in themselves onerous, and only valuable as they are well used; in this corrupt age, 'tis very hard to distinguish betwixt sincerity and dissimulation, bragging and bravery, devotion and hypocrisy: many persons, with hearts full of revenge, pray for their enemies, and neglect their friends and, wallowing in luxury, see virtue clothed in rags, and only use their credit to depress merit by rendering it suspected.[16]

As the English and Scottish Jacobites were terrified of treachery, James allowed each to designate his own trusted correspondent at St.-Germain, so that only the king had full knowledge of affairs at home — an arrangement proposed by Middleton.[17]

He had a good deal of business to transact with the court of France, "for besides matters of moment, there are a great many little things occur constantly which nobody can think should be neglected, for there are few days in which I do not either go or write thither."[18]

Again and again Middleton stated his policy that detailed decisions must be made by the Jacobite leaders in England and Scotland. This policy was distinctly his: Melfort had been too rigid to yield such authority. For example, on the rumor of Queen Mary II's death, Middleton instructed a correspondent that the Jacobites should attempt to bring about the dissolution of parliament, then in being.[19] According to Croissy, the French secretary of state for foreign affairs, "If they [the Jacobites] were fortunate enough to prevent the Prince of Orange from

---

[15] *Ibid.*, fol. 76.

[16] *Ibid.*, fol. 78.

[17] *Ibid.*, fol. 68. For interpretation of this passage, see also fols. 101 and 79–80.

[18] *Ibid.*, fol. 79.

[19] *Ibid.*, fol. 85.

drawing large supplies from the parliament, they would very soon see the effects of their zeal for the service of the king their master strongly supported by His Majesty [of France]." [20] Middleton agreed, but he left details of breaking up a parliament to Jacobites on the spot. (Incidentally, Middleton, having no experience whatever of opposition, could not have given very useful instructions.) Parliament, however, resolved to assist William III against his domestic and foreign enemies. Middleton's comment reminds us of his method at Linz in 1680 and 1681.

Here then is an authentic confession of the two houses of parliament that there is a party opposed to that [William's] government, and that it must be formidable, since they think it necessary to offer themselves to help it [the government] against it [the party of opposition]: it seems to me that that proves more than all that we have been able to say on the subject. [21]

Middleton intended this argument for the French; no doubt he thought privately, *"Valeat tantum valere potest."* Let the king of France find the weakness.

Through the years 1694 and 1695 Middleton nursed the Jacobites at home and abroad, reconciling their differences, quieting their fears, and offering his good will. In May, 1695, for instance, he wrote one of his correspondents:

The person you write of I heartily forgive all he has done to me; but the injury he has done to his character, must needs give great offense, to all who are concerned in the honor of his family. . . . you cannot say too much from me to *Ely* and *Wells* [presumably Bishops Turner and Ken]: from all I beg a favorable construction, some allowance for frailties, and that they would not determine on malicious suggestions, or deceitful appearances. [22]

Late in 1695, Middleton wrote an agent for an inventory of the troops and garrisons in England and overseas. [23] To another he applauded the news "that most of the prodigals are returned and thereby the rent in the temple almost repaired, which must be attributed to your prudent conduct and indefatigable en-

---

[20] *Ibid.*, fol. 84.
[21] *Ibid.*, fol. 89.
[22] B.L., Carte MS 208, fols. 84–85.
[23] *Ibid.*, fol. 119 (for the necessary cipher key, see B.L., Carte MS 256, fols. 2–10).

deavours." [24] Once again he suggested using the animosities of Whigs and Tories in parliament to disturb the government.[25] He told a Jacobite, who evidently sat in the House of Commons, that the Church of England party should block proposals for a comprehension of dissenters in the church and for a general naturalization.[26] All this was designed to rock the government in advance of an armed attack.

Since the spring of 1695 a group of Non-Compounders had urged a French invasion in support of a rising in England. The moment would be a good one, and a number of faithful persons of that faction were ready to take part. Louis XIV had postponed action, but in October he was favorably disposed to a new proposal. At the end of the year the Count de Pontchartrain, minister of the navy, suggested Yarmouth as a landing place. Middleton proposed Newcastle. On January 6, 1696, a newswriter-spy wrote Lord Lexington, in England: "It is observed that a quite long conference of the two kings [Louis and James] was followed by another of M. de Pontchartrain with King James three hours long, and by a third of Lord Middleton of two hours; that gives rise to different conjectures." [27] Two weeks later Melfort reappeared in Paris, but James II refused him leave to return to St.-Germain. Apparently the Non-Compounding plotters had not secured his return to favor. In the first half of February it became known in Paris that many transport vessels in the French Atlantic ports were stopped, and rumor spread that

there is a party in England which they [the French court] wish to encourage by the hope of a descent, or at least that they wish to give cause for thought to King William, and to try in that manner to weaken his army in Flanders. It is certain that the consultations with the court of St.-Germain are more frequent than usual, and that they persuade themselves that the affair of the [recoinage of] moneys will cause some disorder in England. I also know that some Englishmen left St.-Germain about three weeks ago as if to come

---

[24] B.L., Carte MS 208, fols. 21–22.

[25] *Ibid.*, fols. 122–23.

[26] *Ibid.*, fol. 124.

[27] Newsletter, Paris, Jan. 6, 1696, B.M., Add. MS 46,544; see also George Hilton Jones, *The Main Stream of Jacobitism* (Cambridge, Mass., 1954), pp. 44–46.

to Paris, but in fact in order to pass in England, and that they are gone out of the kingdom with this intention.[28]

We know much of these Englishmen. About twenty English officers in the French army went over to England to join Sir George Barclay, formerly lieutenant-colonel of the Horse Guards, in a conspiracy to attack William III in person. Other conspirators from among the planners of the rising also joined. If necessary, this plot would envisage William's murder. The event is well known: the plot was betrayed, and most of the conspirators in England were arrested. The Duke of Berwick, who had visited England to concert the revolt and the invasion, left the country barely in time to escape capture.

Although Middleton had helped in the preparations for the invasion, his position as representative of the Compounders was weakened by the leadership the Non-Compounders had assumed in the plan for the rising. James, moreover, had considered himself released by lapse of time from promises he had made in 1693 — which had failed to win English support. He signed a much less conciliatory proclamation on February 28, 1696. Middleton succeeded in retaining in that document only a part of the promises which he had originally gone to France to secure. He was perhaps supported by French influence, for if the French army met determined resistance in England, conquest would be impossible.

The news of the detection of the plot arrived after James II and Middleton had left St.-Germain for Calais; Louis XIV decided to cancel the invasion plans and sent word on to James. Middleton wrote to Caryll on March 21: "The king goes next Friday to Boulogne where, free from crowds, I shall be able to entertain you with my melancholy speculations; in the meantime I must tell you that, next to the Bastille, I think St.-Germain the dreadfullest place in France." [29] James and Middleton stayed on until May 1; they then returned to the "dreadfullest place." [30]

Many of the conspirators lost their lives; others were imprisoned by act of parliament. Informers were responsible for much suffering. But some accused escaped, and at least one of these, a Mr. Birkenhead, who had once been one of Middleton's

---

[28] Newsletter, Paris, Feb. 13, 1696, *ibid.*
[29] B.L., Carte MS 208, fols. 67, 138.
[30] *Ibid.*, fol. 286a.

best correspondents, had his revenge: escaping from Newgate Prison and reaching the English coast, Birkenhead found and boarded a French vessel. The next night he landed again, went with eighteen men to the house of a smuggler named James Hunt, who had denounced Birkenhead and others to the government, and carried Hunt off to Calais. Middleton asked the Lieutenant of the Admiralty at Calais to send over for other escaped prisoners.[31] The kidnaping of Hunt was only a small consolation, but it reminded informers in England that Jacobites were neither forgiving nor helpless.

The peace of Ryswick was concluded in 1697. France recognized William III as king of England and agreed not to favor or assist conspirators against him; James II did not renounce his claim, but William promised to pay Queen Maria Beatrice her jointure of fifty thousand pounds a year. However, as James remained at St.-Germain, contrary to the general expectation, the jointure was not paid. Bentinck, the Earl of Portland, sent to Versailles as English ambassador, saw many of the English exiles at the French court, especially Lords Middleton and Melfort, "which was no very agreeable sight to him." Louis XIV therefore requested that Middleton avoid the court thereafter when Portland was present.[32] The position of James and his followers was very uneasy. Middleton wrote Lord Clancarty: "It would be no news to tell you that this is a melancholy place and if I should say otherwise, I am sure you would not believe me." [33] No doubt Princess Louise Marie, born to James and his wife in 1692, enlivened her father's court with her prattle, but what were her family's prospects or her own? Even very loyal supporters were shaken; some of them submitted and went home to England or Scotland.

There remained the work of detail, especially that of caring for individual Jacobites, keeping up contact with Great Britain, and dealing with the French ministers. The informer Hunt, who had been detained at Calais, threatened revenge on the exiles.

---

[31] *Ibid.*, fols. 148–49.
[32] B.M., Add. MS 9,088, fol. 27; N. Japikse, *Correspondentie van Willem III en van Hans Willem Bentinck, Eersten Graaf van Portland*, I, 224; Philippe, Marquis de Dangeau, *Journal*, VI, 297.
[33] B.L., Carte MS 208, fol. 157; see also B.M., Add. MS 40,771, fol. 239.

Middleton recommended that the man be transported to Canada or St.-Domingue and imprisoned. If questioned by the English government, "one can always reply truthfully that he is not in France."[34] The "sieur Crosby," a correspondent of Jacobites in England, was killed in the streets of Paris; Middleton requested that the dead man's papers be secured and delivered to an agent. The death of Crosby was fortunate for Middleton's friends, for Lord Portland had already concluded a bargain with Crosby for a denunciation of Jacobites known to him.[35] Indeed, the murder may have been perpetrated by survivors of the recent assassination plot, who had the most to lose by Crosby's treachery. These former conspirators were reported to be in Paris; a friend of William III's government said that "Lord Middleton's party and the honester sort of these people would not keep the villains company," but that King James ordered them to do so.[36]

Middleton continued to keep a sharp eye on British affairs, giving special attention to causes of discontent and agitation against the government of William III. He expressed sorrow in 1699, for example, on the misfortunes of the Scots who attempted to colonize Darien. He had foreseen its failure for lack of adequate "force or skill to manage it" and for another reason "too obvious to be mentioned," probably English opposition to the scheme.[37] Many Scotsmen resented William III's failure to protect his Scottish subjects for a long time thereafter.

The years 1700 and 1701 were full of hope, misleading and therefore soon dashed. As it was rumored that William intended to make provision for the royal succession in the eventuality that he and his sister-in-law Anne should die without children, Middleton, speaking for James, wrote to an anonymous correspondent:

It is desired from his friends that may be in or out of parliament to guard against anything that may be proposed relative to the succession at all: but if they find that they cannot obtain that, and then it will be taken into consideration, rather than any other

[34] B.L., Carte MS 208, fol. 173.
[35] *Ibid.*, fol. 176; Paul Grimblot, *Letters of William III and Louis XIV and of Their Ministers* (2 vols.; London, 1848), I, 403–4.
[36] B.M., Add. MS 40,771, fols. 242–44.
[37] B.L., Carte MS 208, fol. 180.

should be named to endeavour that the Prince of Wales have the preference.[38]

James had refused to consider the substitution of his son for himself during the negotiations of 1697,[39] but in 1700 he was willing to allow the subject to be mentioned, either as a last resort or as a ruse. (Boislisle, the editor of St.-Simon's *Memoirs*, tells us that Middleton advocated renunciation of the elder James's rights in favor of the younger.)[40] James was certainly conciliatory and hopeful of support from some influential group. He would agree, Middleton wrote an unidentified person, to meet anyone who might be sent over to represent the people, "and he does not doubt but to give them all the satisfaction they can expect; and if the thing be rightly understood they must see the great advantages that is upon their side; whereas he has nothing before his eyes but to have everything by *parliament* disposed of to the best advantage of the people. . . ."[41]

At this very time, in 1700 and 1701, Middleton's position as secretary was menaced by the temporary return of Lord Melfort to St.-Germain. Moreover, the safety of his correspondents was jeopardized and their arguments weakened by Melfort's intrigues, which culminated in an indiscreet letter foolishly (or treacherously) sent by ordinary mail to London, where it was opened and published by the government. The letter disclosed a plan for the reestablishment of Catholicism in England and for obtaining Middleton's dismissal. James sent Melfort away again, but the damage was already done. The former king suffered a stroke in the spring of 1701, possibly as a result of his favorite friend's blunder, and his followers were in consternation.

In April, James, his queen, and Middleton went to Bourbon, a watering place, where it was hoped the invalid would convalesce. Maria Beatrice wrote hopefully to Caryll, who had remained behind: "I thank God, the king grows better every day than other, his gout is quite gone, he eats well, sleeps well, and his hand and knee are much stronger than they were; if the wa-

[38] B.L., Carte MS 238, fol. 2.
[39] George Hilton Jones, *The Main Stream of Jacobitism*, p. 52.
[40] St.-Simon, *Mémoires*, XV, 417 n.
[41] B.L., Carte MS 237, fols. 4–5. Italics represent a deciphered word.

ters do but never so little good he must go back quite well." [42]
Middleton could not have shared the queen's optimism. James
was visibly paralyzed on one side of his body and never fully
recovered, though he returned to St.-Germain in June. On September 16, he died.

The king of France, on a visit to St.-Germain, had promised
the "Prince of Wales" and the stricken former king that he
would recognize "James III" as King of England whenever
James II might die. Many of the exiles were present; Middleton
was probably among them, for he had been with the king during
his entire illness and on September 8 had signed James's name
to his last will, because infirmity made it impossible for James
to sign it himself. [43] After Louis's visit, James "ordered quickly
that the prince go to Marly to thank His Most Christian Majesty; however the queen decided not to send him there, having
sent in his place Milord Middleton his first minister." [44]

At the last, when James was dying,

He was not content with having spoke to his children, he made a
sort of short exhortation to almost every one about him, with the
greatest fervour and pity imaginable, but particularly to my Lord
Middleton and his other Protestant servants, whom he persuaded
to embrace the Catholic faith, and did it with so much force and
energy, he made no small impression upon them. . . . [45]

James is said to have died smiling. Because Middleton followed
the body to the church of the English Benedictines at Paris, [46]
he was not present at the formal proclamation of the "Prince of
Wales" as king. [47]

The response of the English government to the sentimental
and dangerous recognition of "James III" was prompt: the Eng-

[42] B.M., Add. MS 28,224, fol. 35.

[43] B.M., Add. MS 31,244, fol. 30.

[44] B.M., Add. MS 16,454, fol. 214.

[45] J. S. Clarke (ed.), *Life of James II, Collected out of Memoirs Writ of
His Own Hand*, II, 594; St.-Simon, *Mémoires*, XV, 417–18.

[46] B.M., Add. MS 10,118, fol. 404; B.M., Add. MS 16,454, fol. 215; J. S.
Clarke (ed.), *Life of James II*, II, 603.

[47] Ranke (*History of England, Principally in the Seventeenth Century*, V,
277) points out that young James was given the title of "king of France,"
which English kings had used since the reign of Edward III, so that Middleton
may have absented himself deliberately. Yet it seems more plausible that he
was too busy with the arrangements for the funeral and with other work.

lish ambassador withdrew, breaking diplomatic relations. Although there were many reasons for war on the continent, the War of the Spanish Succession, which followed, was just as truly a "War of the English Succession." There was this difference: the powers allied against France were fighting in order to overthrow Philip V, the king of Spain and grandson of Louis XIV, who was in possession. Louis, on the other hand, had no settled intention of making "James III" king of England. He had recognized him as a gesture, and the course of the war might make it worthwhile to invade England and restore the male line of the family of Stuart, but unless he did so, Louis's recognition would mean nothing.

The thirteen-year-old James, now called the Pretender in England, was thus a pawn in the French game, but he was the fond hope of the Jacobites. Spasmodically other conservatives, disappointed in the post-revolutionary regime or out of favor with it, either joined him or thought of doing so. Potentially, of course, he was an independent agent, free to seek other sponsors if France failed him, but in 1701 he was too young to choose his own course. His dying father had instructed him to rely utterly on the king of France, and the son promised eternal gratitude to that king for his kindness and support.

Pope Clement XI recognized the Pretender in October. The papal nuncio at Paris, Filippo Antonio Gualtieri (or Gualterio), became an advisor of the "young king" and one of his closest friends. (Gualtieri was made a cardinal a few years later, then cardinal protector of England, and the British Museum eventually acquired his papers. Through them we are now made better acquainted with affairs at the exiled court.)

Middleton's future was not clear. He remained secretary and was created an English peer, with the title of Earl of Monmouth, and his wife was governess to Princess Louise Marie, but he was a Protestant, and Maria Beatrice was probably not happy that her son's chief minister should be so. Shortly after James's death, Middleton was made a member of a small council "for the direction of the most important affairs," with the Duke of Berwick, the Earl (called Duke) of Perth, and Caryll.[48] In August, 1702, the Middleton family passed through a crisis. One of the earl's sons was desperately ill of "*la malatia patita*,"

---

apparently a wasting disease, and Middleton shut himself up in his son's room. Gualtieri wrote:

God used this occasion to convert him [the son], and in fact the other [the father] declared to the queen yesterday that he also wished to abjure, and yesterday he moved into the English College here [at Paris] to have himself instructed. Her Britannic Majesty took an infinite joy in it, and wept with tenderness when the Cavaliere [the son] made the first declaration to her. She confessed that she had not had any consolation but this one since the death of the king her consort, and it is so much greater that she remembers that the event was predicted by him a little before passing to a higher life.[49]

Middleton settled at the English College for some weeks longer. Maria Beatrice spoke of his instructor, the superior of the house, as "a holy man." Gualtieri wrote to Rome that the earl wanted not only instruction but introduction to the practice of the devout life, "which he has undertaken very exemplarily, and not without austerity."[50] He asked to be allowed to resign as secretary of state. Because the queen was now entirely on his side, and the French court also wished him to continue,[51] Middleton did not resign but returned to St.-Germain in greater favor than ever. In January, 1703, by means of Gualtieri, he sent letters to the pope and the papal secretary of state on his conversion. In February, Clement XI sent him a cordial reply and a blessing.[52]

Middleton knew that he was a ruined man in British politics. In a manuscript (dated in August, 1702) giving the reasons for his withdrawal, he wrote that he had always held his seals of office with the understanding that he could return them if James II were restored. The secretary should be an Englishman of repute and capacity, well versed in the English constitution, and should possess large English estates. "All that told directly against me. . . ." An even more important reason for his wish to retire was the English dislike of converts to Catholicism — even stronger than their dislike of "old Catholics." It would be

[49] B.M., Add. MS 20,269, fol. 211.
[50] Falconer Madan (ed.), *Stuart Papers Relating Chiefly to Queen Mary of Modena and the Exiled Court of King James II* (2 vols.; London: Roxburghe Club, 1889), I, 100; B.M., Add. MS 20,269, fol. 218.
[51] *Ibid.*, fol. 245.
[52] B.M., Add. MS 20,274, fol. 9; B.M., Add. MS 20,251, fol. 61.

harmful to his young master's interests for him to remain at his post; moreover, he said, his weakness would be subjected to temptation at court. Because he had long lived in habitual sin, he should now do penance. He denied any worldly object in changing his religion.[53]

Middleton's political opinion was correct. Many Protestant Englishmen and Scotsmen never trusted him after his conversion, and his Catholic enemies, such as Melfort and Perth, did not like him better for it. He retained his position in future only as a stopgap, because there was no strong and united party in England supporting its own candidate for the secretaryship or determined to remove him. The event proved that when such a party appeared Middleton would be forced to go.

This fate was a hard one. To the end, Middleton had remained a spokesman of the moderates of his party and a conciliator of Anglicans. In March, 1702, after specific requests for reassurance had been made by nonjurors (Jacobite Anglicans) through Dr. Charles Leslie, "James III" issued a set of "Instructions," which Middleton countersigned. The "Instructions" represented the culmination of his favoring of religious conciliation, and there is no reason to believe that he changed his views on that subject in August, 1702, or thereafter;[54] but he was a Catholic convert and was marked for discard by the very Compounders whom he had served.

[53] B.L., Carte MS 209, fols. 194–96.
[54] *Ibid.*, fol. 481; see also George Hilton Jones, *The Main Stream of Jacobitism*, pp. 64–66.

CHAPTER XIV

Declining Fortunes

In 1702, the situation of Europe and England was very different from that of 1693. King Charles II of Spain, dissatisfied with the arrangements made by the other powers for the division of Spanish territories to take place after his death, had made a will disposing of his entire inheritance: the undivided Spanish kingdom was to be offered to a grandson of Louis XIV. If the bequest was refused, it was then to be offered to the second son of Emperor Leopold. Charles II did then die in November, 1700, and the offer was made to Louis for the Duke of Anjou.

Louis's position was difficult: he had recently bound himself to the terms of the Second Partition Treaty, and although the French share would be enormously increased if Anjou were allowed to accept, it would be at the expense of open violation of his word. On the other hand, the emperor had not ratified the Second Partition Treaty; thus, if Louis rejected the windfall, the emperor could and would accept it. Louis, a true dynast, accepted, and Philip, Duke of Anjou, went off to Madrid and was installed as King Philip V of Spain. With him went French advisors. Shortly after, French troops were admitted to the fortresses of the Spanish Netherlands, and French trading companies were granted commercial privileges in the Spanish colonies. The great powers of Europe at once took alarm. William III played a great part in organizing them for resistance to the resumed growth of French power. For the continental powers the fighting began in September, 1701, but England was on balance until the recognition of the Pretender by Louis XIV. Early in 1702, the English parliament supplied William with the money to fight the new war.

France and Spain, in combination, were dangerous enemies. With French troops in possession of Flanders and Brabant, it would be the task of the allies to displace them. With Philip enthroned at Madrid, the Austrian claimant, Charles, must wage a bloody war — using all allied resources — to secure that kingdom. William, the leader of the alliance, died of injuries sustained while riding in March, 1702. No one could then know that his successor, Queen Anne, would obtain the appointment as captain-general in the Low Countries of Marlborough, one of the great generals of the age.

Within Great Britain, other changes were important for the Jacobites. Queen Anne was childless and would probably have no children thereafter. Unlike William, she was given to second thoughts about the justice of the Revolution. Her close friends, Marlborough and Godolphin, were politically conservative, and with full faith in their loyalty and ability, Anne promoted them as quickly as possible to the highest positions. Tories of various stripes were put into other offices. Middleton's friend Mulgrave, now Marquis of Normanby, was lord privy seal, and Lord Nottingham was a secretary of state. New men in politics often rallied to the rising Tories, as did older politicians who courted the queen's favor.

Parliament had committed the succession to Anne by its Act of Settlement. Electress Sophia of Hanover, granddaughter of James I, was the nearest Protestant heir. Sophia and her descendants were designated as the new royal line, setting aside the many Catholics who were nearer according to the old rules of succession. So far as England was concerned, the matter was decided as clearly as parliament could decide it.

But in Scotland, there was no equivalent act. No doubt William, had he lived, would have obtained one, but William had left that task unfinished. Many Scots were opposed to its completion: some were resentful of the long-continued dependence of Scotland on a monarch in London; others held grudges against the government for the Glencoe massacre and for the collapse of the Darien trading colony; others were devoted Jacobites; still others sought personal advantage. It was therefore possible that various factions might unite to destroy the union of the Scottish and English crowns whenever Anne might die.

The plan to circumvent these factions was a legislative union of the two nations. In 1702 discussions took place between commissioners appointed for the purpose. They broke down over apparently insoluble problems. In the summer of 1703, indeed, the Scottish parliament passed an Act of Security, under which the successor to Queen Anne should be designated from among Protestant descendants of the Stuart house but should not, unless certain conditions were met, be the same as the successor in England. The royal assent was refused, but in 1704 the same act was passed once more and allowed to go into effect.

The development of the situation in Scotland was Middleton's immediate business after he left the English College. In March, 1703, Simon Fraser (called Lord Lovat) arrived at St.-Germain with a letter from the Duke of Hamilton that described the state of affairs. According to the pamphleteer Charles Hornby, the Earl of Perth was let into the secret, but Middleton was kept in ignorance for some months.[1] Hamilton feared that Queen Anne's ministers would effect a closer union of Scotland and England, which the Duke of Berwick thought would make restoration of the Pretender impossible. Hamilton expected that Hanoverian money would be available to influence members of the Scottish parliament; he asked for twenty-five thousand pounds to be used as a counterinfluence. Berwick hoped that the pope could find the money. Maria Beatrice reported that England and Scotland were full of malcontents and dissension. The court of Queen Anne was divided; the Scottish nobility was dissatisfied; and Ireland awaited an opportunity to rebel. The chiefs of Scottish clans had authorized Lovat to offer the Pretender ten thousand men to join Hamilton in rebellion. In May, Gualtieri reported that Lovat was leaving soon for Scotland with eight proposals to the Jacobites "in favor of religion and the royal cause." Gualtieri wrote to the papal secretary of state that he had good hopes of this mission.[2] Hornby tells us that Middleton, when he learned of Lovat's promises, knew that the Scots could not perform them. Never-

---

[1] [Hornby,] *The Fourth and Last Part of a Caveat against the Whiggs, &c. . . .* , 2d ed. (London, 1712), p. 49.

[2] B.M., Add. MS 20,270, fols. 81–83, 150; B.M. Add. MS 20,318, fols. 67–68.

theless, Louis XIV, whose minister, Torcy, was in the secret, gave the emissary a colonel's commission.

Middleton was subjected to various trials at about this time. In August, 1703, he excused himself from some business with Torcy on the plea of illness, a rare event. More serious were attacks made upon him by his enemies, so fierce that some important business, like Lovat's mission, was kept secret from him. He also had to defend Berwick from such attacks and to soothe the duke's irritation. On one occasion he wrote to Berwick:

I hope . . . that it will appear there has been no neglect nor delay in what regards you; humility is a great virtue, but you seem to carry yours too far; for without vanity you may believe your reputation too well established to be blasted by a scold who in a letter to the Comte de Brienne used me like a dog, and yet the king our master t'other day said I was fatter than Monseigneur [the Dauphin].[3]

Lovat's mission to Scotland was nearly a disaster for the Jacobites. Fortunately, James Murray, who already had one surreptitious visit to Scotland to his credit, went ahead with a warning from Middleton directed against Lovat, for the latter promptly revealed his errand to the Duke of Queensberry in Edinburgh. As Queensberry supported Queen Anne, Lovat's subsequent stay in the Highlands was nothing but entrapment of leading Jacobites, using for the purpose credential letters which Lovat brought from the court of St.-Germain. Lovat overreached himself when he addressed a previously unaddressed letter to the Marquis of Atholl, one of his own enemies, and betrayed it to Queensberry, who shared Lovat's hatred of Atholl. Fortunately Atholl learned of this plot against him and anticipated attack by personal appeal to Queen Anne. Atholl thus got off, as did some implicated by the Jacobite Sir John Maclean, who was in England without a pass. Two of these were Major Boucher, Berwick's aide de camp, and David Lindsay, Middleton's secretary; Boucher and Lindsay were actually condemned, but Queen Anne pardoned them.[4]

A memorial that Lindsay addressed to the Earl of Notting-

[3] B.L., Carte MS 238, fol. 40.
[4] George Hilton Jones, *The Main Stream of Jacobitism*, pp. 67–68; [Hornby,] *The Fourth and Last Part . . .* , pp. 55, 57.

ham, a secretary of state, found its way to France. Since King William's death, Lindsay said, there had been no plan to encourage a revolt against Anne. "Follies of that kind occurred by means of those [irresponsible] people and my Lord Middleton has always opposed them so long as it has been in his power to do so." The only design to go very far was Lovat's, which had been hidden from Middleton.[5]

Lindsay was in a position to know much of what went on in St.-Germain, but he was Middleton's friend and supporter and on this occasion he lied: Middleton did in fact learn enough of Lovat to send James Murray ahead. True, Lovat had been adopted by the Drummond faction at court, which opposed Middleton, but concealment from the earl was impossible.[6] The court of St.-Germain was like that. Lindsay's statement is consistent, however, with Middleton's habitual caution and dislike of ill-founded plans for rebellion.

Lovat very incautiously returned to France and submitted an account of his mission to the French ministers. Middleton had full opportunity then to show the seedy adventurer for what he was; he also vented some malice. On Lovat's relation he remarked:

He has not had the care in some places of the authors of romances, to observe likelihood, for besides the vanity which is diffused throughout, as if he were the foremost man in the world, he begins by a completely fabulous story at Durham; he confesses clearly to a plain disobedience, for he was forbidden to treat except with the Highlanders, and of that number only with those who had sent him: He told me that Queensberry, Argyle, and Leven were the greatest enemies of the king my master in that country, however he communicated to them his whole commission, which is a hanging matter all over the world. . . .

If the king [of France] thinks good to have him arrested, it ought to be done without noise, and so that it were no more heard of, and at the same time have his papers seized. . . .[7]

Lovat, perhaps not knowing of Middleton's attitude, wrote to the earl to felicitate him on the countess's recovery from an indisposition and to say that Lovat rejoiced that Middleton

[5] B.M., Add. MS 20,311, fols. 30–31.
[6] B.M., Add. MS 20,271, fol. 41.
[7] B.L., Carte MS 238, fol. 54.

was still a good friend. Nevertheless, Middleton made devastating remarks on Lovat's replies to interrogation.[8]

As a result, Lovat was arrested and confined for several years.

The plan for an invasion of Scotland was postponed in June, 1704. Torcy wrote to Middleton that the reports on the situation in Scotland were inadequate: the Scots should send an authorized person to France to make an agreement on the employment of French help.[9] Middleton did not abandon his attempts to persuade Louis XIV and his ministers of the necessity of a French-supported restoration. Once the Hanoverians were in possession, he wrote to Torcy and Chamillart, there would be a perpetual league of Holland, Austria, Hanover, and England, directed against France. If restored, the Pretender would be the Catholic king of a Protestant nation, who would always want support from France. The consensus, Middleton said, was that the restoration would settle all questions. The celebrated sea captain Jean Bart thought the plan practicable.[10] But in the autumn, when the campaign season's end released French troops, there was no attempt at invasion. The Pretender was seriously ill; moreover, the French army had suffered an almost crushing disaster at Blenheim in August.

That defeat was an English victory, for the Duke of Marlborough commanded the victorious army. The French lost their reputation for invincibility, and their army had to undergo reorganization. The Irish troops in French service distinguished themselves, but with great losses.[11] Middleton's son, Lord Clermont, was at Blenheim, serving in the regiment of Lee. In November, the earl requested for Clermont the colonelcy of a half-battalion at Douai which was to be filled up to make a regiment.

It is a very sad life to grow grey in subordinate positions, which would inevitably happen to M. de Clermont without some act of grace, of which examples are not lacking among the Irish troops. . . . The testimony of Monsieur Lee, with whom Milord

[8] B.L., Carte MS 180, fols. 430–35 (for Lovat's replies, see fols. 428–29).
[9] B.M., Add. MS 20,318, fol. 112.
[10] B.L., Carte MS 180, fols. 99–100.
[11] W. S. Churchill, *Life of Marlborough*, I, 857–58.

Clermont served last campaign in Bavaria, cannot be suspect, neither that of the officers of his regiment, who saw him in a terrible situation.

Yet Middleton excused himself for asking this favor, saying that he confided himself to paper because paper could not blush.[12] Clermont was promoted to a colonelcy in December, 1704.[13]

Middleton did solicit for other Jacobites as well. In September, 1705, for instance, he drew up a petition for the relief of the Viscountess of Dunkeld, widowed by the last battle in Italy. He had his hands so full relieving those already in distress that he discouraged Jacobites in England from going to France unless they had means to support themselves.

Through agents in Great Britain he obtained for France such intelligence as the destination of Admiral Shovel's fleet and Lord Peterborough's army in the spring of 1705. (In this case, Middleton's information was incorrect.) He also served as a source of information about British subjects in France. One occasion, at least, shows him in a pitiless light. An Englishman called Harcourt lived in Languedoc, and the French minister Chamillart asked Middleton to inquire about him. Middleton did so and replied to Chamillart that "Harcourt's" real name was Wigsted; he had once been a Franciscan of the *récolets* but had left the order to return to England, where he had married. Wigsted's wife was dead, and he had returned to France presuming himself unknown. In closing, Middleton advised Chamillart: "You will do a benevolent action, Monsieur, in having this wretch shut up in a house of his order, to do penance there for the rest of his days."[14] It was a usual solution to such a case at the time, but it shows a change in Middleton, whose tolerance had once been a happy characteristic.

The politics of Scotland remained the most favorable possibility of advancing the Pretender's cause. In December, 1704, the English House of Lords passed resolutions demanding steps to press Scotland to treat for a union; early in 1705 bills to embody these resolutions in law were passed by the House of

[12] B.L., Carte MS 238, fol. 130.
[13] Philippe, Marquis de Dangeau, *Journal,* X, 198.
[14] B.L., Carte MS 238, fol. 56.

Commons. Faced with denial to Scots of commercial privileges and the rights of English subjects, the Scottish parliament was indeed pressed.

In August, the French minister Torcy selected an English officer in the French service, Nathaniel Hooke, to visit Scotland and sound of the Scottish Jacobites. From first to last, Hooke was a French emissary, and he was close to the Drummond group. He returned to France on September 25 without any conclusive word from the Scots. His report showed the Jacobites as divided into factions; the Duke of Hamilton was playing a lone hand. Hamilton's support appeared to be essential, but he did not like either Middleton or Caryll. "The latter does not understand business; the other is very intelligent, but I will have no dealings with him." [15] Lords Erroll (nephew of the Earl of Perth) and Strathmore (nephew of Middleton) joined in beseeching the king of France not to tell secrets to the ministers at St.-Germain, "each of them distrusting in his own as well as in the other uncles." [16] It is not surprising that the French again postponed direct intervention in Scotland.

The Duke of Hamilton may have hoped to secure the Scottish crown for himself, for he was of Stuart descent in a female line. At last he abandoned both that hope and the Jacobite cause, proposing in the Scottish parliament that Queen Anne (or rather her ministry) should appoint the Scottish commissioners for the approaching negotiations. In February, 1706, the list of names was announced, and it was obvious that the treaty would be concluded. The commissioners met with their English counterparts in April. Articles were drawn more easily than had been expected, for the English adopted a liberal policy. These articles were signed in July. The Duke of Hamilton lent his support to the treaty, and in spite of determined Jacobite opposition the Scottish parliament approved it. The treaty then secured approval in the English parliament and went into effect in May, 1707. The opening presented by the Act of Security was closed. [17]

[15] B.M., Add. MS 20,858, fol. 19 (cf. H.M.C., *Portland MSS.*, IV, 307).
[16] B.M., Add. MS 20,858, fol. 59.
[17] Charles Hamilton, reputedly the son of the Duke of Hamilton's natural son, explains the duke's actions as inspired by Middleton at St.-Germain. Middleton, that writer says, asked the duke to withdraw his opposition to

In June, 1706, the Pretender was eighteen and began to manage his own affairs. "He imitates and grows very like the king his uncle [Charles II]," wrote Mme de Maintenon.[18] The Earl of Perth had completed his duties as governor; he received the post of first gentleman of the bedchamber. Middleton, however, remained the chief minister. In July, 1706, some of the Scots sent Captain Harry Straton to France to negotiate with the Pretender, not through Middleton's means but through Perth's. This mission resulted in Hooke's second visit to Scotland.

Middleton did not trust Hooke. He stood against a landing in Scotland, which would bring out the Pretender's friends and expose them to punishment, without adequate support from France. Perth and his supporters were more willing to take risks. Hooke naturally found the Drummond interest more in accord with the policy of France, and he relied upon it. After a series of defeats, Louis XIV was concerned with Scotland largely as a field into which England could be forced by a small French invasion to divert troops which would otherwise be used directly against France. This is not to say that the king of France wished the Jacobites ill; he could not afford to do otherwise. Middleton, who had seen the play of self-interest in European politics for more than a quarter of a century, discerned the danger to the Pretender and the Jacobites. He was careful not to draw unwelcome distinctions between the good of Scotland and that of France. Indeed, he encouraged the idea of a diversion, provided that it were an effectual stroke for young James.

If the affairs of the King [of France] are urgent here, that supports strongly the project of Scotland; if a small part of the troops and money which one uses here [on the continent] would finish the business there, one should not hesitate about it, and what would once have been prudent and glorious has become now absolutely necessary.

---

the union because the Pretender had "recent engagements" with Queen Anne's ministers "to procure a peace to the French King. . . ." This the duke must keep secret. *Transactions during the Reign of Queen Anne; from the Union to the Death of That Princess* (Edinburgh, 1790), p. 41. I discount this statement; by all other accounts, Middleton and Hamilton were on bad terms. There is a false ring to Charles Hamilton's whole account.

[18] B.M., Add. MS 20,918, fols. 73–74.

The king of France knew what it was to be incommoded by rebellion in the Cevennes, Middleton wrote, and the emperor was embarrassed by disturbances in Hungary.[19]

Hooke went to Scotland in April, 1707, and returned in July. He found some of the Scots Jacobites reluctant to deal with him. These preferred the usual channels, which included Middleton as "secretary of state." Others opened their minds, however, and offered to revolt if Louis XIV could send them eight thousand regular troops and arms for men to be raised, with a good general and the Pretender in person.

These demands were great. The Pretender was willing to participate, and the French army could supply a general, but eight thousand regulars were too many for so risky an enterprise. The French trimmed the estimate to six thousand and warned the Scots at the end of 1707 to expect the expedition in March, 1708. Middleton did not send this notification; instead, John Ogilvie was employed to convey it. As Ogilvie was a spy of the English minister, Robert Harley, he passed the information to the government.[20]

Preparations advanced and became public knowledge. Marshal de Matignon received the military command, and the Count de Forbin the naval one; departure was set for March 9. Mme de Maintenon wrote to the Princess Orsini (des Ursins) in Spain: "You think well, Madame, that if God wishes to bless this undertaking, it will make a great diversion and perhaps peace. If you have saints in Spain, set them to prayers." The Pretender was "transported with joy to be leaving."[21]

Middleton's influence is evident in a proclamation which the Pretender issued to Scotland on March 1, and the earl accompanied his master to Dunkirk, arriving March 9. There the young man succumbed to measles, so that departure was delayed until March 17. Only 5,100 soldiers were actually embarked for Scotland.

Followed by an English squadron under Admiral Byng, Forbin escorted the French troop transports to the eastern coast of Scotland. The weather was very bad, and many of the passengers

---

[19] B.L., Carte MS 238, fol. 189.

[20] For these negotiations, see George Hilton Jones, *The Main Stream of Jacobitism*, pp. 70–78.

[21] B.M., Add. MS 20,918, fol. 401.

were very sick. Finding no reply to his signals, the French admiral refused to allow any disembarkation. Over the protests of the Pretender, he sailed back to France. Three ships had already been forced to turn back on the outward journey, and another, *Salisbury*, formerly captured from the English, was recaptured by them while returning, with Middleton's two sons on board.

Middleton, who was aboard ship during the whole course of the expedition, suffered so from seasickness that he was unable to write with his own hand to the French minister of marine after landing. When the capture of *Salisbury* became known, he was even more uneasy. As both his sons had French commissions, they were entitled to treatment as prisoners of war. Unfortunately for them, the British government resented the refusal of such treatment to French Protestants, taken during an English attack on Brest, and threatened retaliation on Middleton's sons and on the elderly Lord Griffin, who had also been taken. Queen Maria Beatrice assumed the task of securing their liberty through the offices of French ministers, who proposed an exchange of British officer-prisoners for the young Middletons.[22] The earl himself went to Flanders, where the Pretender was to serve as a volunteer during the campaign of 1708.

Middleton's sons survived. After a period of strict confinement, they were allowed parole through the influence of their English relatives, among them the Duke of Shrewsbury. The Earl of Wharton, a Whig magnate, was one of the sureties for these Jacobites.[23] They were allowed to leave England in 1712, during the negotiations that led to the Peace of Utrecht.[24] The rejoicing on their arrival at St.-Germain was great indeed.

The Pretender James took part in three campaigns in the Low Countries from 1708 to 1710, but Middleton accompanied his master only during the first. Thereafter he remained at St.-Germain. In 1710, when the king of France was in

[22] B.L., Carte MS 180, fol. 460; John, Duke of Marlborough, *Letters and Dispatches . . . from 1702 to 1712*, ed. Sir George Murray (5 vols.; London: 1845), IV, 68.

[23] George Lipscomb, *The History and Antiquities of the County of Buckingham* (4 vols.; London: 1847), I, 553.

[24] B.L., Carte MS 238, fol. 229; Carte MS 211, fol. 170.

desperate financial condition, the young prince's suite was reduced to almost nothing, as Mme de Maintenon wrote to the Princess Orsini: "He will have only two or three men with him. I find that suite much more honorable in his present state than if he had a great equipage."[25] Charles Booth, who did attend, wrote to Middleton in May, 1710, from Péronne: "Mr. Tunstall was here. He had a long conference with my Lord Churchill [the Duke of Marlborough] who asked him several times what was the reason your lordship was not with the Prince of Wales [the Pretender.] He made answer it was to save charges."[26]

At St.-Germain, Middleton's position was high. As exiles went, he was well provided for; he had quarters in the chateau; his stipend as "secretary of state" was 471 French livres, 9 sous, 6 deniers each month in January, 1709, and was increased by 100 livres a month before December. No other functionary received more, though the Earl of Perth came close with 458 *l.* 6 *s.* 8 *d.*; (in January, 1709) Caryll received pay equal to Middleton's. Melfort held no office at court, but received a substantial pension, as did Berwick.[27] Middleton had also some money from his Scottish estates and therefore was one of the richest men at the Jacobite court.

He could do little for the Pretender in the years of these campaigns. Louis XIV's war was to all appearance lost, and the enemies of France insisted not only that French gains be surrendered and the French king of Spain deposed, but that France must abandon the Pretender. That young man sought on the battlefield a reputation as a soldier, which, after Malplaquet, was an accomplished fact. Mme de Maintenon summarized the reports:

They write very glorious things about the King of England [James]. The English saw him and are charmed by him. Marlborough drank that evening to the health of the Prince of Wales [as Marlborough called James]. His subjects encountered him for the first time in a very advantageous manner. Our sad queen [Maria Beatrice] is very moved by this joy, which is the first we have seen in her.[28]

[25] B.M., Add. MS 20,919, fol. 289.
[26] B.L., Carte MS 210, fol. 115.
[27] B.M., Egerton MS 2,517, fols. 5–10.
[28] B.M., Add. MS 20,919, fols. 213–16.

The great Archbishop Fénelon wrote in even more flattering terms at about the same time, and the Jacobites took care to have his letter printed. Marlborough, we may assume, was simply "insuring," as he had done at least since 1694, although he was Queen Anne's greatest commander and one of her closest confidants.[29]

In the peace negotiations which were near, Middleton concerned himself chiefly with saving something for his master's family — the jointure of Queen Maria Beatrice. Otherwise, loyal Jacobites in exile had to be assisted in finding a livelihood. David Lloyd, who had been an agent in the 1690's, was living very cautiously in England; Middleton wrote to him to give assurances that Lloyd's son would be looked after.

Middleton had his own family troubles. When he had left England, he was separated from his children. His sons joined him with their mother a few years later, but the two daughters did not. Disliking his resolution to bring up their children as Protestants, the Countess of Middleton sent the girls to Poissy, where they were given a Catholic education. The earl was persuaded by some means that his wishes were being carried out until after his conversion, when he was at last told where they really were. In the words of a biographer of Maria Beatrice, he then "praised the ingenuity which she had used toward him."[30] Thus from 1693 until 1702 he did not see his daughters at all, and they had grown up believing him to be a heretic.

The elder daughter, Lady Catherine, married Sir John Giffard in 1702, when she was sixteen years old and Giffard was forty. She bore him at least three children, one of whom died as a child. At some time between 1706 and 1708, Giffard himself died, leaving Catherine a widow of twenty-three at the most. In February, 1710, Middleton wrote the Cardinal de Noailles that he was having difficulty. His daughter, he said, was still a minor. (By English law she was not.) For more than a year she had been secretly planning to marry again, but Middleton had only learned of her intention in November, 1709, through servants. His wife had then questioned Lady Catherine and obtained a confession. The match was an un-

[29] See, e.g., B.L., Carte MS 238, fol. 97.
[30] Falconer Madan (ed.), *Stuart Papers Relating Chiefly to Queen Mary of Modena and the Exiled Court of King James II*, II, 432–33.

equal one, and unwelcome to the family. The earl did not want any legal proceedings or publicity; rather he called upon Noailles for help, saying, "It is for your eminence to decide whether there are here the inclinations required of those who wish to participate in the holy sacraments of the church. . . ." There were, he suggested, too many prodigals going unpunished.[31] His tone throughout his letter was angry; he had forgotten Mrs. Compton at Tangier.

Noailles, a prince by birth as well as by his rank in the hierarchy, was also a man of the world. He did not rise to Middleton's hint that Catherine should be bullied by withdrawal of the sacraments. Instead, he wrote that he would like to bring the young lady around and that the earl was quite right to tell her her fault in the matter; yet, he went on: "It is difficult to resist to the end in such a case, and the example of the father of the prodigal son is, after a certain period of refusal, good to follow."[32]

In the correspondence, Lady Catherine's suitor is not named. She was at all events married, by 1719, to Michael Rothe, an Irish brigadier in the French service, a commander of the French Order of St. Louis.[33]

Middleton's younger daughter, Lady Elizabeth, was a woman of charm. She danced well and pleased Louis XIV. She was married at nineteen (in 1709) to Lord Edward Drummond, a younger son of the Earl of Perth.[34] The marriage was equal as to rank but was in other ways inappropriate, for Middleton and Perth disliked and distrusted each other, leading bitterly opposed Jacobite factions; but perhaps that opposition helps to account for the marriage. Just as two royal houses confirmed a peace or a political alliance by a marriage, so apparently did the two earls. The Countess of Middleton proposed the match; the Countess of Perth gave it cordial consideration in memory of past favors which Middleton's father had done for her family; and the Pretender and his mother approved it. Lord Perth surrendered his post of first gentleman

[31] C. E. Lart, *Parochial Registers of St.-Germain-en-Laye*, I, 13; II, 70–71; B.L., Carte MS 210, fol. 385.
[32] B.L., Carte MS 210, fol. 385.
[33] Lart, *Parochial Registers*, II, 154.
[34] *Ibid.*, p. 9; Dangeau, XI, 36, 444; XII, 67.

of the bedchamber to his son, so as to help establish him at court. Perth retained the favor of the royal family.[35] He did not, however, give up his private opposition to Middleton, in spite of the fact that he showed some affection to his new daughter-in-law. "We will take all the care we can of our lass," he wrote to Middleton in June, 1713, "and that's the only service we can perform to your lordship or my lady. . . ."[36] Fifteen months later he was as disapproving as ever of Middleton's policy: "All his family is provided for twice as abundantly as any other, himself lazy and idle, and always he finds insurmountable obstacles when a vigorous counsel is put forward."[37]

The dowries of both daughters were paid in full before Middleton made his last will in July, 1719; no further provision was to be made for either of them.

The exact balance of influence between Middleton and Perth after (say) 1709 is hard to fix. Perth made much of the trust reposed in him by the Pretender and the former queen, but Prince James charged Middleton, not Perth, with correspondence with the papal nuncio on church affairs after Caryll's death in 1711.[38] (In January, 1713, for instance, Middleton countersigned his master's recommendation to the pope that Cardinal Bellarmine, the long-dead Jesuit theologian, be beatified.) In political affairs, Middleton handled the difficult negotiations for the queen's jointure and made an approach to the Dutch States General in 1710, when Louis XIV was apparently intent on making peace at any price.[39] He accompanied the Pretender, on a visit to Alsace and also on the campaign of 1711 in the army of the Duke of Savoy.[40] Perth shared in none of these things, though he had correspondence in Scotland; as he was one of the last defenders of Lovat, he must have lost much influence through his stubbornness or credulity.

Neither Perth nor Middleton could rely on much support from English Protestants. Both were converts and Scotsmen; the differences of opinion that had begun before the revolution and continued after were forgotten by a new generation to

[35] B.M., Add. MS 31,256, fols. 34–35.
[36] B.L., Carte MS 211, fol. 189.
[37] B.M., Add. MS 31,256, fol. 91.
[38] B.M., Add. MS 20,297, fols. 35–36; Add. MS 31,257, fol. 1.
[39] See, e.g., B.L., Carte MS 180, fols. 228–29, 231–32.
[40] B.L., Carte MS 238, fol. 218; Carte MS 212, fol. 20.

whom Middleton's "compounding" would seem old-fashioned; and the personal antipathies between the survivors of the old factions were a hindrance to effective action. That Perth and Middleton both had to be replaced transpired during the negotiations for the Peace of Utrecht.

The peace negotiations of 1709 and 1710 failed. Refusing to help the anti-French coalition drive his grandson out of Spain, Louis XIV resolved to continue to fight. In England, however, the cost in blood and money of the long war caused a reaction among the political classes against Queen Anne's ministers Marlborough and Godolphin and against the Whigs, who were now the chief support of the government's policy. At court, the Duchess of Marlborough lost favor; Queen Anne deprived her of her place, removed Godolphin from the treasury, and in August, 1710, replaced him with Robert Harley, a Tory who had gone into opposition and now returned to lead a new Tory ministry and a newly elected Tory House of Commons.

The new ministers were aware of their greatest weakness. Queen Anne favored them, but she was older than her years and very sickly, and her children were all dead. The succession was settled upon Electress Sophia of Hanover, so much older than Queen Anne that the electress's son, Elector George Louis of Hanover, was the probable heir. George Louis was loyal to the great alliance against France, while the Tory ministers intended to desert it and make a separate peace. Tories could expect little favor from him. Moreover, many Tories were still attached to the house of Stuart. James II was dead; could not his son, half brother of the reigning queen, be designated her successor? He was of age, had attracted some attention as a volunteer at war, and had made promises to respect the English constitution and the established Church of England. True, he was a Catholic, but he might be persuaded to accept Anglicanism or he might give such guarantees as Tories could accept.

The leaders of the ministry were not sentimental in their consideration of the problem; they were rather attempting to please their followers and protect themselves by finding an alternative to George Louis than following the dictates of the heart. They made their first advances to the Pretender shortly after Godolphin's fall. In the course of secret parleys through agents who could be disavowed, they only gradually and, as it were, involuntarily involved themselves with the Jacobites. Had the secret been well kept, they might later have made terms with the Elector of Hanover. Absolute secrecy, however, was not maintained, and the earlier advances became well enough known to force the Tory ministers to go still further, until reconciliation was impossible and a Jacobite restoration alone could protect the Tory party from political eclipse.[41]

In August, 1710, Middleton warned Torcy against Tory approaches for French friendship:

> It is indifferent to you whether the parliament be dissolved or not, or that the rigid [High Church] dominate over the moderates, you will find your enemies there, and I am very sorry, Monsieur, to tell you, that even our friends [the Jacobites] will do nothing for you so long as you do nothing for them: they do not believe you to be so inclined, and it is only a real landing which can cure them of their disbelief.[42]

In a memorial of the same date, the Pretender offered to lead an invasion of Scotland, "in order to procure for France a peace which it appears to need so much, provided that he be granted the Irish troops to accompany him. . . ."[43] Middleton still regarded, or pretended to regard, invasion as a more practicable way of forcing peace than any diplomatic negotiation.

Middleton's master had certain drawbacks as a prospective ruler of England; though certainly brave, well-behaved, and willing to make political concessions, James was absolutely unwilling to change his religion, and he was not blessed with a strong constitution. In 1708 (as we have seen) he suffered a very inconvenient attack of measles. This tendency continued all his life. Mme de Maintenon wrote of him in 1710: "The King of England has left [for the campaign] with much good will and very little health." Again, "He has not one day of health." In 1711, "The King [of England] is so languishing that he could only dance two *courantes:* he was dizzy as soon as he dared risk a third. He is sad and dejected without any

[41] See K. G. Feiling, *A History of the Tory Party, 1640–1714*, pp. 456–60.
[42] B.L., Carte MS 180, fol. 272.
[43] *Ibid.*, fols. 269–72.

ailment or any new cause that one can see." In 1712 the Pretender had smallpox but recovered. (His sister, Princess Louise Marie, died of it.) Thus he appeared unlikely to live long, and he had no heir; no enthusiasm could arise from either of those facts, and Jacobitism needed enthusiasm more than anything else.

As the war was to end, and with it any chance of French military support, it became Middleton's task to work for a peaceful restoration with the ministers of Queen Anne. His first document for the purpose was drawn up in December, 1711, to help Torcy frame instructions to the French plenipotentiaries then about to begin work at Utrecht. (Among other objectives, they were to attempt to persuade the English government to allow the succession of "James III" to Queen Anne.) The acts of parliament that had changed the succession must first be repealed. James could then go to England, where he would have the title of king. Queen Anne would continue to enjoy all her authority peacefully as long as she lived, and the new king could be relied on to reward those who contributed to his restoration.[44]

At the same time as the English ministers secretly gave so much encouragement, they insisted publicly that the Pretender leave France for a more distant place. It was believed by many that this was only a temporary step to gull the Whigs until the conclusion of the peace. Thus one John Scrimger wrote (apparently to the Pretender) that he hoped his correspondent and "E.M." (probably Middleton) would soon find a lodging "in a wholesome air until Queen Anne does business to provide better."[45] Henry St. John, Viscount Bolingbroke, who replaced the Catholic Lord Jersey in the secret negotiations with the Pretender, insisted to the English plenipotentiaries at Utrecht that James must withdraw not only because a treaty required it but also because notice had been taken in parliament that he was still in France.[46] The Pretender's attack of smallpox delayed his removal, but English diplomatic pressure for it never relaxed.

Yet Queen Anne and the Tory leaders were thought to be

[44] B.L., Carte MS 180, fols. 282–84.
[45] B.L., Carte MS 211, fol. 11.
[46] B.M., Add. 22,205, fol. 305.

serious in favoring the young exile. The aged Duke of Buckinghamshire, a favorite of Queen Anne and (as Lord Mulgrave) Middleton's old friend, took part in discussions of a peaceful restoration.[47] In July, 1712, the duke wrote to the Pretender under a pseudonym, advising "the King" to change his religion, to which alone (he said) the queen objected; she might be willing to allow her half brother to go to Scotland and inherit her other kingdoms on her death.[48] As late as February, 1713, an agent reported that Buckinghamshire and "the rest of his opinion, would be glad to have the king home as soon as possible, if they knew how to do it without running any hazard, and that Princess Anne is of the same mind, but timorous. . . ."[49] The same agent said that Harley (now Earl of Oxford) was jealous of Buckinghamshire and had him watched; the agent used Lord Yarmouth as a go-between and had given papers to Queen Anne's cabinet council which should be published to persuade the public to support the Pretender's claim. Buckinghamshire was for having them published, but Oxford thought publication not to his own interest, for (the agent wrote) he wished to be free to give the crown "to whom he pleases." The agent had much more to say — for instance, that Middleton was "not hated" in England.[50]

Other Jacobite agents, such as Thomas Sheridan and General Edward Sackville, were reopening long-lapsed correspondence. David Nairne, Middleton's clerk, wrote to one of these in August, 1712, to tell him that "the king did not approve of Sackville's proposal to Churchill [Marlborough]; that he had had no commission from him [the Pretender] upon that head, and that he [the Pretender] would not accept of such a small sum from a debtor who owed him so much."[51]

In August, the date of James's retirement from France was fixed; the English ministers learned that he was to go to Bar-le-duc, in the Duchy of Bar, belonging to the Duke of Lorraine. Middleton went with his master to Châlons-sur-Marne, where the disheartened little court stopped to await arrival of a gen-

[47] B.L., Carte MS 211, fols. 49–50.
[48] *Ibid.*, fols. 364–66.
[49] *Ibid.*, fol. 96.
[50] *Ibid.*, fols. 96–97, 100.
[51] *Ibid.*, fol. 81; B.L., Carte MS 212, fol. 38 b.

eral safe conduct.[52] At first the Bishop of Châlons entertained
James and his retinue, but thereafter, a witness reports, James
lived at his own expense. He lived simply and saved his hosts
embarrassment by allowing them to address him simply as
Monsieur.[53]

The safe conduct apparently arrived. Duke Leopold of Lorraine offered James the castle at Bar, and the court installed
itself there in February, 1712/13. Bolingbroke wrote to the
English plenipotentaries at Utrecht; "Her majesty is glad to
hear, that by the removal of the Pretender out of France one
topic of clamour is taken from those who are at this time so
much disposed to complain." [54]

The attitude of the English ministers was ambiguous at best.
Elsewhere the Jacobites found little hope. Louis XIV was steer-
ing his kingdom to the safe port of peace; he had no intention
of arousing his enemies again. The king of Spain was friendly
to James but could do nothing without France. Pope Clement
XI was disputing the Pretender's nomination of Catholic bishops
in the British Isles. Middleton spoke frankly to the Abbé Tamisier, one of Gualtieri's correspondents:

Milord avows that reflecting on the little account which the Pope
takes of this king [the Pretender], leaving him without help or
succor, contesting with him all prerogative, either those bishoprics,
or the nomination of the Abbé de Polignac to the [cardinal's] hat,
or the protection granted to your lordship [Gualtieri] he would
almost be of the opinion that His Britannic Majesty would no longer
have anything spoken of to the Pope any more, and would cease
to treat or have treated anything with our master [the pope], since
it is apparent that His Holiness does not treat this king as king . . .
that he knows well that the Pope is naturally irresolute . . . fearful
of the Germans [i.e., the emperor and his adherents] but that it is
notwithstanding a scandal that he sacrifice this matter to please
them. . . .

Despite the strong expressions which Middleton used, Tamisier
professed to esteem him highly.[55] When Polignac at last re-

[52] B.M., Add. MS 31,257, fol. 133.
[53] B.M., Add. MS 22,206, fols. 198–99; Add. MS 20,297, fol. 33; Add.
MS 20,372, fol. 230.
[54] B.M., Add. MS 22,206, fols. 198–99.
[55] B.M., Add. MS 20,372, fol. 177.

ceived his promotion, Middleton's master stipulated that the nomination must be recognized openly.

Middleton's position was crumbling. He was attacked not only by English Protestant Jacobites who could not trust a convert, not only by English Tory ministers who would do nothing for the Pretender until he had purged himself and his court of Catholicism, but by an important group at Versailles. He received the following report from one M. White.

It is my Lord Fingal that told me, that Monsieur Pontchartrain told him, if my Lord Middleton was faithful to the king, he was false to the King of France: and he that is here, I mean Duke d'Aumont, is of the same opinion. . . . but it was not Lord Fingal that told me that. The Duke of Powis told me, he did not speak or trust himself to my Lord Middleton's sons, and repeated only at large, that there were strange reports of my Lord Middleton.[56]

Fingal reported in August, 1713, three charges made against Middleton, at least two of them going back to the 1690's. Fingal was satisfied that the charges were false; he asked "that my Lord Middleton will be pleased to send him his instructions, what the king would have moved in parliament." [57] But there were too many opponents, and there was no time for the long correspondence necessary to convince them. Practical support was lacking: France paid its promised contributions of money to the Jacobites only irregularly, the English ministers paid theirs not at all. Pope Clement was more favorable than he had been; he sent Middleton a friendly letter late in 1713, to which the earl replied respectfully.[58] The pope's favor, however, would be of no use with Protestants. The old minister could not stand.

A pretense of voluntary resignation was made when Middleton surrendered his seals of office on December 2, 1713.[59] Queen Maria Beatrice made him her Master of the Horse, and the Pretender made Lord Clermont first Gentleman of the Bedchamber, "to show the consideration which I have for the long services and fidelity of the father, who in losing his charge has lost none of the friendship and esteem which I have for

[56] B.L., Carte MS 211, fol. 148.
[57] *Ibid.*, fol. 140.
[58] B.M., Add. MS 31,257, fol. 200.
[59] B.L., Carte MS 212, fol. 62; B.M., Add. 31,255, fol. 3; George Hilton Jones, *The Main Stream of Jacobitism*, p. 94.

him. . . ." [60] Lord Perth said sourly that Middleton had retired,

the loyal English not being able to trust him. But his son is first Gentleman of the Bedchamber to the king. He is himself Master of the Horse to the queen so that he gains by it on the side of self-interest and he is content because of his natural laziness.[61]

The queen, on the other hand, expressed her regret both to others and to Middleton himself early in 1714. As she wrote to the former minister: "The better you are with him [her son], the kinder he is to me. . . ." [62]

[60] H.M.C., *Stuart Papers*, I, 285; B.M., Add. MS 31,255, fol. 3.
[61] B.M., Add. MS 31,256, fol. 70.
[62] B.L., Carte MS 211, fol. 186 a.

Epilogue: A Dead Man

Middleton moved from Bar back to St.-Germain to take up his new post. In departing from his master, he requested to be allowed to drop correspondence with those actually charged with Jacobite business in order to "abstain from everything which would give the least offense to those who wished for his withdrawal."[1] Thus he had almost complete leisure. No doubt he chafed a little at being so idle. He wrote to Cardinal Gualtieri at Rome in March, 1714:

That persecution was drawn upon me by my conversion, Beati qui persecutionem patiuntur propter justitiam.[2] As I no longer take part in affairs, I know no news. . . . Senes repuerescunt, and I amuse myself in reading the things which I learned at school, and I do not hesitate to place here three lines of Horace, because they agree with my present inclination

O rus quando [ego] te aspiciam, quandoque licebit
nunc veterum libris nunc somno et inertibus horis
ducere sollicitae jucunda oblivia vitae.[3]

His sons and daughters were adult and independent. There remained his wife. She had been the governess of Princess Louise Marie before her death of smallpox, and the princess, we learn from memoirs written at Chaillot, had great respect for the

[1] B.M., Add. MS 31,259, fol. 9.
[2] Matthew 5:10, in the King James Version: "Blessed are they which are persecuted for righteousness' sake. . . ."
[3] B.M., Add. MS 31,257, fol. 179. The quotation is from Horace, *Sermones*, Book II, No. VI, lines 60–62. A modern translation reads: "O my country home, when shall I behold you? When will it be possible for me to live among my books, to sleep, and in hours of idleness to drink the sweet draughts that make us forget life's worries?" *The Complete Works of Horace* (New York: Modern Library, 1936), pp. 72–73.

countess, "a person of admirable gravity, wisdom, and piety." [4]

Piety, indeed, had become her chief characteristic. During her stay in England after the revolution,

her continued occupation was to succor poor Catholics or prisoners, or sick people and to go to carry priestly vestments into the houses of Catholics in order to give them the consolation of hearing Mass. As she walked in the streets in the night . . . she had reason to fear that people would insult her, but respect for her rank and her virtue always prevented it. [5]

The story is perhaps heightened by the nuns' friendship for the countess. She often visited the convent at Chaillot with Queen Maria Beatrice. On one occasion, the countess read to her mistress after dinner "a chapter of the Imitation [of Christ] which speaks of crosses and sufferings; the queen sighed and was profoundly sad." [6] The countess was at Chaillot when her sons returned from England.

In the evening, Cardinal Gualtieri entered; with him entered the sons of the Countess of Middleton who have been prisoners in England for five years. The Countess of Middleton, who had not seen them at all since 1707, hearing that they had arrived, got up before Complines from the choir, where she was, to go see them, but halfway through the cloister she turned back to the choir and did not see them until an hour later, after evensong and all the prayers had been said. [7]

At the end of July, she endowed an evening service to be said on August 1 every year in perpetuity in gratitude for the conversion of her husband and the deliverance of her sons from the Tower. (Both these occurrences had taken place on August 1.) It is no wonder the nuns thought the countess pious.

At St.-Germain, life had settled into a gloomy routine. The queen, the only member of the royal family left there, complained of its dullness, sadness, and constant cares. The countess, preoccupied with religion, may have found some consolation, but Middleton had not given up quite so much of the worldly life.

[4] Falconer Madan, *Stuart Papers Relating Chiefly to Queen Mary of Modena and the Exiled Court of King James II*, II, 483, 495.

[5] *Ibid.*, p. 433.

[6] *Ibid.*, p. 392.

[7] *Ibid.*, p. 417.

He must have heard of Melfort's death shortly after the return to St.-Germain, but probably had no intimate knowledge of the Pretender's later relations with the Tory ministers in England: with the demand of their agent Gaultier that James change his religion, with the resolute refusal of that demand, and with the subsequent divisions among the Tories which overthrew Harley. Perhaps he heard the public report that the Duke of Buckinghamshire (formerly Mulgrave) had solemnly defended in the House of Lords the authenticity of the Pretender's birth.[8] He would have had no word of Queen Anne's last illness until after her death.

When the Pretender learned that Queen Anne was dead, he made an effort to pass through France to Great Britain, but he was turned back by Louis XIV and compelled to return to Bar-le-duc. An air of crisis prevailed: surely something could be done. Middleton's replacement, Sir Thomas Higgons, was a worthy man, a Protestant, well connected, and loyal, but no one thought him especially able. Middleton was blamed for every reverse, even though he was not in office.[9] In November, 1714, the Pretender recalled Middleton to Bar for consultation, and the French government approved the recall. The principal reason for sending him away had been Oxford's objection to him, but as Oxford's unreliability was now known, the Pretender could use Middleton again.[10]

The Pretender had already drawn up and printed a new declaration, dated at Plombières in Lorraine. The English Jacobites had approved it.[11] Middleton would also have liked it, for it dwelt on the foreignness of the "Elector of Hanover" and repeated former promises for the protection of the Church of England.[12]

Middleton hoped, as did all good Jacobites, that James would marry; he began almost at once the quest for a suitable wife. Perhaps there is some connection between that quest and a proposal that Middleton be sent to Vienna to thwart the work of Lord Stanhope for an alliance between George I and the em-

---

[8] B.M., Add. MS 31,256, fols. 80–82.

[9] See B.M., Add. MS 31,256, fol. 91.

[10] B.M., Add. MS 31,259, fol. 85. The "Mr Olive" referred to in this document stands for "Oxford."

[11] *Ibid.*; B.M., Add. MS 31,257, fol. 203.

[12] See D. G. Forbes (ed.), *Culloden Papers* (London, 1815), p. 30.

peror, Charles VI.[13] A marriage with one of the emperor's daughters or nieces would have been a brilliant coup. It is tempting to imagine the possible consequences of an encounter between a typical Stuart diplomat and the brilliant builder of the Hanoverian dynasty's security, but the mission was countermanded.

In Lorraine, there was not much Middleton could do to attract foreign support. He did appeal to Clement XI. If the Pretender married a princess of rank he might build an alliance on the power of her relations, but most princesses were not to be considered. A serious approach was made for the hand of an unnamed princess palatine, through the good offices of her uncle, Prince Charles of Neuburg, but the emperor's consent was indispensable, and the emperor would not give it.[14]

The disgruntled English Tories had had to adjust to a new and much less favorable situation: some of them remained in touch with Jacobite agents. One agent reported that Bolingbroke would have no dealings with Middleton.[15] Prosecutions of the former ministers were threatened, especially of Oxford and Bolingbroke in England and of Lord Mar in Scotland. In both countries men talked of rebellion, and Scottish Jacobites made some preparations. Bolingbroke's nerve gave way, however, and he fled from England to France in April, 1715.

Middleton observed from Bar the changed conditions in Great Britain, though he confessed that only those lately arrived from there could be well informed. Bolingbroke was the obvious man to take his place, but Middleton remained with the Pretender until Bolingbroke was willing to commit himself in August, 1715. The delay in transfer of responsibility may have been in part responsible for the failure of the rebellion in Scotland which followed. The Duke of Ormond would have been very useful in England, and the Pretender reposed great hopes in him, but the duke followed Bolingbroke to France during the summer; the Pretender prepared for a voyage to Great Britain in July, but some of his followers persuaded him to post-

[13] B.M., Add. MS 20,305, fol. 332.

[14] B.M., Add. MS 31,259, fols. 139–40, 145–46, 153–54. "Colomban," referred to in these sources is Prince Charles, "M. Epinois" the emperor, according to Gualtieri's cipher.

[15] H.M.C., *Stuart Papers*, I, 359.

pone it;[16] the Earl of Mar reached an apparently firm understanding on the conditions necessary for rebellion in July, but he lost his head, ran away from arrest, and led a premature revolt in violation of the agreement a few weeks later. When Bolingbroke took office, many mistakes had already been made, mistakes which Middleton was not in a position to prevent.

"James III" left his household behind at Commercy in October, 1715, to go secretly to his followers in Scotland. Middleton had permission to return to St.-Germain; James said that he would send for him later.[17] As James spent the next three months seeking an opportunity to embark, however, Middleton probably remained at the court of Queen Maria Beatrice. Lord Clermont set out for Great Britain, but the Austrian authorities stopped him in Flanders. He was apparently given up to the British government, for he was imprisoned in the Tower of London from November, 1715, to May, 1716. Once more his French commission and powerful English relations saved him.[18] Lord Edward Drummond, Middleton's son-in-law, was still in the Highlands when the revolt collapsed, but he escaped and rejoined the French army.[19] Charles Middleton was also in Scotland during the rebellion, but got away to Bergen in Norway and so to France.[20]

Bolingbroke behaved unsatisfactorily in office, neither leaving France for Scotland nor seeing to it that the Scots were supplied with what they needed. The Pretender appointed the Earl of Mar to receive correspondence on March 1, 1716, ten days after his return. The later history of Jacobitism cannot be told here.

Lord Middleton lived on at St.-Germain, inactive and quiet. In June, 1716, he became Lord Chamberlain to the former queen.[21] He replied to a New Year's letter from Cardinal Gualtieri in February, 1717:

It is a miracle which your eminence has just performed to resuscitate a dead man, and to recall him to a function of which he would

---

[16] B.M., Add. MS 31,259, fol. 177.
[17] B.L., Carte MS 211, fol. 332.
[18] H.M.C., *Stuart Papers*, I, 459; B.M., Add. MS 34,195, fol. 149.
[19] C. E. Lart, *Parochial Registers of St.-Germain-en-Laye*, II, 151.
[20] H.M.C., *Stuart Papers*, II, 157.
[21] *Ibid.*, p. 218.

have been incapable, if your goodness had not excited him to thank
you for it. . . . the honor of carrying my compliments to your
eminence is reserved to my son [Lord Clermont, then going to
Italy with the Pretender], whom I recommend to the honor of your
protection; as I do not at all mix in affairs, I shall not be tempted
to write of them in a *lettre des bonnes fêtes;* that would be a mortal
sin, which your secretary and your *maestro di camera* would never
pardon. . . .[22]

Middleton could be satisfied that he had done his best for his
sons, but his plans were undone. The Pretender placed Clermont in charge of his household in Italy; in that character he
lived on a good footing until the spring of 1718, when he was
displaced by John Hay and sent away from court. When he left
Italy he returned to St.-Germain.[23] Another servant of the Pretender, David Nairne, complained at the time that he expected
his own dismissal, "for certainly I cannot pretend to the merit
either of Milord Middleton or of Mr. Inese, who are neglected
in a fashion of which I cannot approve. . . ."[24] Charles Middleton was a captain in the French service.

St.-Germain was as poor a place for the exiles as ever. There
was little money, for George I did not pay the former queen's
jointure; and the French government of the Regent of Orléans,
which succeeded Louis XIV in 1715 and promised the Pretender a pension in 1717, let it fall into arrears.[25] Middleton or
Clermont still probably received income from British estates
which they had certainly had in 1713. On these and some portion of his nominal pay as Lord Chamberlain he had to live.

In 1718, Queen Maria Beatrice died. James charged Middleton and others in May with responsibility for the proper disposal of her papers. The earl wrote to condole with his master
and took the opportunity to beg favor for his own family.

If six and thirty years service to three kings may merit anything,
I make it all over to the old woman and her children. I have nothing
else to leave them. Your majesty has promised them your favor
and protection. I depend on it and shall die quietly in praying for
your prosperity.[26]

[22] B.M., Add. MS 31,257, fol. 211.
[23] H.M.C., *Stuart Papers*, VI, 498; VII, 5, 242.
[24] B.L., Carte MS 212, fol. 58.
[25] B.M., Add. MS 21,505, fols. 57–58.
[26] H.M.C., *Stuart Papers*, VI, 463–64.

He wrote again in August:

Old men are twice children, and, to use an Irish phrase, I wish him I love and honour most was after having children. There never was such heat in these parts as now and, though you bear it well, yet I wish you in a colder climate. *"Tibi serviet ultima Thule* [Furthest Thule will obey thee]."[27]

When it was evident that James had made a match, Middleton wrote to Mar: "Since I cannot dance at the wedding, I am resolved to drink *Haus in Kellar* [the house into the cellar]."[28]

In November, there was a happy stroke of luck. The Regent of Orléans, seeing the late queen's household destitute, made provision for it. William Dicconson, the author of most of James II's *Life*, wrote to the Pretender that Middleton was offered a pension of three thousand French livres but that the earl hesitated to accept it without permission from his master. James wrote almost immediately ordering acceptance. Thus, if the pension were paid, Middleton could spend his last months more comfortably.

For they were his last months. On July 7, 1719, he drew up his last will, leaving all his property to his wife during her lifetime, and thereafter to Lord Clermont, who would be obliged to pay two hundred pounds sterling a year to his younger brother Charles Middleton. The estate was charged also with provision for Middleton's granddaughter Mary Giffard, Lady Catherine's daughter by her first husband. The will was perhaps written under the pressure of his last illness, for in early August the earl died. He was buried at St.-Germain on August 9, 1719.[29]

In truth, as Middleton had said to Gualtieri, he had already been "dead" for several years. And what he stood for was as dead as he, as well as the institutions he knew. A man like Middleton had fitted well into office under Charles II and James II, finding the ways and means to execute the kings' commands. Then men who wished to force a policy upon the king were unwelcome and seldom held office. Not so in 1719, in the reign of George. By right Middleton had been a Scottish peer and member of the Scottish parliament, and by election a member of the

---

[27] *Ibid.*, VII, 192. The quotation is altered from Virgil, *Georgics*, Book I, 1. 30.

[28] H.M.C., *Stuart Papers*, VII, 433.

[29] Lart, *Parochial Registers*, II, 153, 100.

English House of Commons. In 1719 no new Scottish peers were being created, there was no Scottish parliament, and a Scottish peer could no longer sit in the new "British" House of Commons. The Spanish monarchy was broken up, and the international scene was otherwise unfamiliar. Most novel of all was the final conversion of the English monarchy to a sequence of individuals governing on the sufferance of a parliament greedy of power, rather than an indefeasible royal line. And what individuals!

Middleton, dying in France, must have missed many of the nuances of the changes in course. He could not escape consciousness of the gaps death made so wide in his acquaintance. Danby, Sunderland, Monmouth, Godolphin, James II, Anne, Dryden, Etherege, Wycherley, and many other contemporaries were dead before him. And those who remained were as much changed by time as the English constitution or as Middleton himself: once a skeptic, now a Catholic; once a lenient compromiser, now thought unduly conservative; once esteemed for his honesty, now discredited by reports that he was a spy or a traitor. What men thought meant more to Middleton than he said. (Otherwise why did he say so frequently that it meant little?) Ironically, his change of religion went against the times and cost him his political future, while that of his wife's nephew to Anglicanism, in accord with the tendencies of contemporaries, was hardly noticed by them and carried no taint. Fashions in religion and their moral implications might have gone another way. The hard truth was that they had not, and Middleton had had his day. Rereading Horace in his last years, he may have stopped at these lines:

> Lusisti satis, edisti satis atque bibisti:
> tempus abire tibi est, ne potum largius aequo
> rideat et pulset lasciva decentius aetas.[30]

He had played, eaten, and drunk enough of public life. He had tried to leave the table before he was ridiculous. Had he stayed too late? or was dignity still intact? Will we, for ourselves, know the answer?

[30] Horace, *Epistulae*, Book II, No. II, 11. 214–16.

APPENDIX

Peers Present at Guildhall, December 11, 1688

Archbishop of Canterbury
Archbishop of York
Bishop of Ely
Bishop of Winchester
Bishop of Rochester
Bishop of St. Asaph
Earl of Pembroke
Earl of Dorset
Earl of Mulgrave
Earl of Thanet
Earl of Carlisle
Earl of Ailesbury
Earl of Burlington

Earl of Sussex
Earl of Rochester
Earl of Berkeley
Viscount Newport
Viscount Weymouth
Lord Wharton
Lord North and Grey
Lord Chandos
Lord Montagu
Lord Culpepper
Lord Vaughan
Lord Jermyn
Lord Crewe
Lord Ossulston

Secretary: Mr. Gwyn
Appeared late:

Bishop of Peterborough
Earl of Craven

Summoned to give information:

Viscount Preston (appeared)
Earl of Middleton (did not appear)

Morning Session at Council Chamber, Whitehall, December 12, 1688

Those listed above, less Ely, Weymouth, Pembroke, and Culpepper, sent to inform William of James II's flight, and Canterbury and Burlington, unaccounted for. Wharton and Carlisle arrived late, as did the Earl of Kent, who attended for the first time. Other peers who attended for the first time were the Marquis of Halifax, the Earls of Anglesey, Nottingham, and Feversham, the Bishop of Durham, and Lords Lucas and Godolphin.

Afternoon Session

Archbishop of York
Bishop of Winchester
Bishop of Peterborough
Bishop of Durham
Marquis of Halifax
Earl of Kent
Earl of Thanet
Earl of Craven
Earl of Anglesey

Earl of Berkeley
Earl of Carlisle
Earl of Nottingham
Earl of Rochester
Viscount Saye and Sele
Lord Montagu
Lord North and Grey
Lord Chandos
Lord Vaughan
Lord Godolphin

Scottish peers: Duke of Hamilton, Earl of Middleton, and Viscount
Preston

Arrived late: Earls of Ailesbury, Mulgrave, Lichfield, and Sussex,
and Lord Crewe

BIBLIOGRAPHY

I. Manuscript Sources

British Museum

Middleton Papers, Add. MSS 41,803–42

Also Add. MSS 4,194, 7,080, 8,936, 9,088, 9,363, 9,749, 10,118, 11,043, 11,606, 12,068, 15,395–97, 15,587, 15,643, 15,858, 15,892, 15,897–98, 16,454, 17,677, 18,675, 18,827, 20,251, 20,268–71, 20,273–74, 20,277, 20,292–94, 20,297, 20,305, 20,311–12, 20,318, 20,372, 20,858, 20,918–19, 21,-505, 21,947–48, 22,205–6, 22,578, 22,910, 23,114–20, 23,-130–32, 25,118, 25,123, 25,362, 25,366, 25,368, 25,370–71, 25,373–74, 26,657, 27,448, 27,962 T, 27,962 W, 28,042, 28,053–54, 28,103, 28,224, 28,227, 28,875–76, 28,896, 29,546, 29,553, 29,560–62, 29,594, 31,244–46, 31,255–57, 31,259–60, 32,010, 32,095, 33,923, 34,096, 34,195, 34,501, 34,516–17, 35,104, 35,125, 35,838, 36,126, 36,528, 36,707, 36,784, 37,661, 38,175, 38,493, 38,694, 40,771, 40,791, 46,544

Birch MS 4,156

Egerton MSS 1,633, 2,517, 2,534, 2,536, 2,597, 2,618, 2,621

Harleian MS 4,187

Lansdowne MSS 253, 1,163

Sloane MSS 1,470, 1,961, 3,299, 3,328, 3,929, 3,510–11

Stowe MSS 191, 199–201, 370

Public Record Office

Class No.	Volumes or Bundles
Adm. 1 Papers	5,139
Adm. 77 Newsletters	1, 2, 3
Adm. 78 Greenwich News-letters	1, 2, 4

C.O. 279	Tangier	13, 15
P.C. 2	Privy Council Register	56–61, 71, 74
S.P. 8	King William's Chest	1, 2, 3
S.P. 29	State Papers, Domestic, Charles II	359
S.P. 31	State Papers, Domestic, James II	3, 4
S.P. 44	Entry Books	53, 54, 56, 57, 69, 73, 92, 166, 338
S.P. 47	Channel Islands	1
S.P. 63	Ireland	340
S.P. 71	Barbary States	3
S.P. 77	Flanders	52, 54, 55
S.P. 78	France	126–27, 143–44, 147–48, 150–51
S.P. 80	Germany, Empire	16
S.P. 81	Germany, States	86
S.P. 82	Hamburg and Hanse Towns	16
S.P. 84	Holland	220
S.P. 85	Italian States	10
S.P. 86	Malta	2
S.P. 93	Sicily and Naples	3
S.P. 94	Spain	72
S.P. 95	Turkey	20
S.P. 98	Tuscany	11, 17
S.P. 101	Newsletters	6, 35, 55, 61, 79, 83
S.P. 103	Treaty Papers	1, 50
S.P. 104	Entry Books	2, 19, 56, 59, 66, 68, 119, 153, 185, 187, 189
S.P. 108	Treaties	320
W.O. 4	Secretary at War	1
W.O. 5	Marching Orders	4
W.O. 26	Miscellaneous Orders	3, 4
W.O. 55	Warrants	335
P.R.O. 30/24	Shaftesbury Papers	5
P.R.O. 30/25	Venetian MSS	31
P.R.O. 31/3	Baschet's Transcripts	131, 136–37, 150–51, 154, 158–76

Cambridge University Library
  MS Mm. 1.51
  Add. MSS 4,836, 4,880
Trinity College Library, Cambridge
  MS R. 4.44
Cambridge University Archives
  Royal Mandates, James 2nd — George 2nd, 1686–1760
Dr. Williams' Library, London
  Morrice MS P
Archivio di Stato, Modena
  Cancelleria Ducale, Oratori e Ambasciatori, Inghilterra, Busta IV
Bodleian Library, Oxford
  Ballard MSS 11, 12, 45
  Carte MSS 33, 35, 38–39, 47, 72, 79, 103–4, 117, 130, 180–81,
    208–12, 217, 219, 222, 228, 231, 237–38, 256
  Rawlinson MSS A. 266, A. 341, C. 353, D. 909, Letters 91
  Tanner MSS 25, 27–28, 30–32, 34
Archives of the Ministère des Affaires Étrangères, Paris
  Correspondance Politique, Angleterre, vols. 165–67
Register House, Edinburgh
  General Register of Sasines, 3d series, vols. 4, 6, 10, 14, 23, 51, 71
  Johnston's Letter Book
  Justiciary Records, Books of Adjournal, 1693–1699
  Justiciary Records, Process, Melfort and o^{rs}, July 23, 1694
  Leven and Melville Papers, Sec. VIIA
  Morton Papers, Boxes 20 and 100
  M.P. Bundle 280
  Particular Register of Sasines, Aberdeen, &c., vol. 13
  Register of Deeds, Dalrymple Office, 66; Dur., 22; Mackenzie
    Office, 46
  Registered Books of Council and Session, Mackenzie Office,
    May 8, 1675
  Registrum Magni Sigilli, Commissiones, 9
  Secretary's Warrant Books (S.P. 57), vols. 2, 7–9, 11
  Supplementary Parliamentary Papers, vol. 11

II. Printed Sources

Airy, Osmund (ed.), *The Essex Papers* (2 vols.; Westminster:
  Camden Soc., 1890, 1913)
Airy, Osmund (ed.), *The Lauderdale Papers* (3 vols.; London:
  Camden Soc., 1884–85)
Allen, Robert J., "Two Wycherley Letters," *Times* (London)
  Literary Supplement, April 18, 1935
Armytage, G. J. (ed.), *Allegations for Marriage Licenses Issued*

by the Vicar-General of the Archbishop of Canterbury, 1660 to
1679 (London: Harleian Soc., 1886)

Birch, Thomas (ed.), *A Collection of the State Papers of John Thurloe* (7 vols.; London, 1725)

Brown, P. Hume (ed.), *Register of the Privy Council of Scotland,* 3d
series, vols. IV–VIII (vols. IX–XIII edited by Henry Paton)
(Edinburgh, 1911–32)

Brown, T., *Miscellanea Aulica* (London, 1702)

Burnet, Gilbert, "Some Unpublished Letters," ed. H. C. Foxcroft,
Camden Soc. Miscellany, vol. XI (London: Camden Soc., 1907)

*Calendar of State Papers, Colonial Series, America and West Indies,
1685–1688* (London, 1899)

Calendar of State Papers, Domestic Series (London, 1858–)

Calendar of Treasury Books, 1660–1689, ed. W. A. Shaw (8 vols.;
London, 1904–23)

Campana de Cavelli, E., marquise, *Les Derniers Stuarts à St.-Germain-en-Laye* (2 vols.; Paris, 1871)

Cartwright, Thomas, *Diary,* ed. Joseph Hunter (London: Camden
Soc., 1843)

Chesterfield, Philip, Earl of, *Letters . . . to Several Celebrated
Individuals of the Time of Charles II . . .* (London, 1834)

Christie, W. D. (ed.), *Letters Addressed from London to Sir Joseph
Williamson* (2 vols.; London: Camden Soc., 1874)

Clarendon, Henry, Earl of, *State Letters . . . During the Reign of
K. James the Second: And His Lordship's Diary . . .* (2 vols.;
Oxford, 1765)

Cole, Christian (ed.), *Memoirs of Affairs of State; Containing Letters
Written by Ministers . . . from . . . 1697 . . . to 1708* (London, 1733)

Colenbrander, H. T., *Bescheiden uit Vreemde archieven omtrent
de groote Nederlandsche zeeoorlogen, 1652–1676* (2 vols.; The
Hague, 1919)

Dalton, Charles, *English Army Lists and Commission Registers,
1661–1714* (6 vols.; London, 1892–1904)

De Witt, Johan, *Brieven,* ed. R. Fruin, vol. I (Amsterdam: Historisch
Genootschap, 1906)

Duckett, Sir George, *Penal Laws and Test Act* (2 vols.; London and
Kendal, 1882–83)

Dumont, Jean (ed.), *Corps universel diplomatique du droit des gens*
(8 vols.; Amsterdam, 1726–31)

Dunn, John (ed.), *Letters to the Earl of Aberdeen* (Aberdeen: Spalding Club, 1851)

Edye, L., *The Historical Records of the Royal Marines . . .* (London, 1893)

Ellis, Henry (ed.), *Original Letters Illustrative of English History*, 2d series (4 vols.; London, 1827)

Erdmannsdorffer, B., *et al.* (eds.), *Urkunden und Aktenstücke zur Geschichte des Kurfürsten Friedrich Wilhelm von Brandenburg* (23 vols.; Berlin, 1864–1930)

Etherege, Sir George, *Letterbook*, ed. Sybil Rosenfeld (London, 1928)

Étienne-Gallois, A. A. (ed.), *Lettres inédites des Feuquières* (5 vols.; Paris, 1845–46)

Evelyn, John, *Diary*, ed. E. S. de Beer (6 vols.; Oxford, 1955)

Ferguson, James (ed.), *Papers Illustrating the History of the Scots Brigade* (3 vols.; Edinburgh: Scott. History Soc., 1899–1901)

Firth, Sir Charles, and R. S. Rait, *Acts and Ordinances of the Interregnum, 1642–1660* (3 vols.; London, 1911)

Forbes, D. G. (ed.), *The Culloden Papers* (London, 1815)

Gordon, Patrick, *Passage from the Diary . . . , A.D. 1635–A.D. 1699*, ed. Joseph Paterson (Aberdeen: Spalding Club, 1859)

Grant, James (ed.), *Seafield Correspondence from 1685 to 1708* (Edinburgh: Scott. History Soc., 1912)

Grimblot, Paul (ed.), *Letters of William III and Louis XIV and of Their Ministers* (2 vols.; London, 1848)

[Gutch, John,] *Collectanea Curiosa; or Miscellaneous Tracts, Relating to the History and Antiquities of England and Ireland . . .* (2 vols.; Oxford, 1781)

Historical Manuscripts Commission Publications
    Buccleuch Papers, vols. I–III (1899–1926)
    Drumlanrig (Buccleuch MSS), vols. I–II (1897–1903)
    Finch MSS, vol. II (1922)
    Portland MSS, vols. I–IX (1891–1923)
    R. R. Hastings MSS, vols. I–IV (1928–1947)
    Stuart MSS, vols. I–VII (1902–1923)
    Various Collections, vol. II (1903)
    Report VII (1879)
    Report IX, Appendix III (1883–84)
    Report XI, Appendix V (1887)
    Report XII, Appendices VI–IX (1889–91)
    Report XIV, Appendix VI (1894)
    Report XV, Appendix VIII (1897)

Innocent XI, Pope, *Epistolae ad principes*, ed. I. I. Berthier (2 vols.; Rome, 1891–95)

Japikse, N. (ed.), *Correspondentie van Willem III en van Hans Willem van Bentinck, Eersten Graaf van Portland* (5 vols.; The Hague, 1927–37)

Journals of the House of Commons, vol. IX, *1667–1687* (London, 1803)

Lart, C. E. (ed.), *The Parochial Registers of Saint-Germain-en-Laye* (2 vols.; London, 1910–12)

Laursen, L. R. (ed.), *Danmarks-Norges Traktater* (11 vols.; Copenhagen, 1907–49)

"Lists of Fees and Pensions Granted to the Officers of State and Other Servants of the Crown, etc. in Scotland, MDCLXVII–MDCXCIX," *Miscellany of the Maitland Club*, vol. III (Edinburgh: Maitland Club, 1842)

Macray, W. D. (ed.), *Notes Which Passed at Meetings of the Privy Council . . . 1660–1661* (London: Roxburghe Club, 1896)

Madan, Falconer (ed.), *Stuart Papers Relating Chiefly to Queen Mary of Modena and the Exiled Court of King James II* (2 vols.; London: Roxburghe Club, 1889)

Marlborough, John, Duke of, *Letters and Dispatches . . . from 1702 to 1712*, ed. Sir George Murray (5 vols.; London, 1845)

Montalto, Duke of, "Cartas . . . á Don Pedro Ronquillo," *Colleccion de Documentos Inéditos para la historia de España*, LXXIX (Madrid, 1882), 299–475

Morrison, Alfred (ed.), *The Bulstrode Papers* (privately printed, 1897)

Pepys, Samuel, *Diary*, ed. H. B. Wheatley (8 vols. in 3; London, 1928)

Sayle, R. T. D., *Lord Mayors' Pageants of the Merchant Taylors' Company in the 15th, 16th, & 17th Centuries* (privately printed, London, 1931)

[Sharpe, James,] "Excerpts from the Household Book of My Lord Archbishop of St. Andrews from 1663 to 1666," *Miscellany of the Maitland Club*, vol. II (Edinburgh: Maitland Club, 1840)

Shrewsbury, Charles, Duke of, *Private and Original Correspondence . . .* , ed. William Coxe (London, 1821)

Steele, R. R. (ed.), *Bibliotheca Lindesiana*, vols. V–VI, *Tudor and Stuart Proclamations* (Oxford, 1910)

Stevenson, J. H. (ed.), *The Register of the Great Seal of Scotland, A. D. 1660–1668* (Edinburgh, 1914)

Thompson, E. M. (ed.), *Correspondence of the Family of Hatton* (2 vols.; London: Camden Soc., 1878)

Thomson, Thomas, and Cosmo Innes (eds.), *Acts of the Parliament of Scotland* (11 vols.; Edinburgh, 1811–44)

Watson, Charles B.B. (ed.), *Roll of Edinburgh Burgesses, 1406–1700* (Edinburgh: Scott. Record Soc., 1929)

William III, King, *His Highness the Prince of Orange his Speech to the Scots, Lords and Gentlemen . . .* (London, 1689)

III. Contemporary Works

Ailesbury, Thomas, Earl of, *Memoirs*, ed. W. E. Buckley (2 vols.; Westminster: Roxburghe Club, 1890)

d'Avaux, J., Count, *Négociations . . . en Hollande, depuis 1679, jusqu'en 1688* (6 vols.; Paris, 1752–53)

Bohun, Edmund, "The History of the Desertion," reprinted in *A Collection of State Tracts, Publish'd on Occasion of the Late Revolution in 1688. And During the Reign of King William III* (3 vols.; London, 1705–7), I, 38–125.

Boyer, Abel, *Memoirs of the Life and Negotiations of Sir William Temple, Bar.* (London, 1714)

Bramston, Sir John, *Autobiography*, ed. Richard, Lord Braybrooke (London: Camden Soc., 1845)

Brandt, Geeraert, *Vie de Michel de Ruyter* (Amsterdam, 1698)

Buckinghamshire, John, Duke of, *Works* (2 vols.; London, 1753)

Chamberlayne, Edward, *Angliae Notitia*, various editions

Cholmley, Sir Hugh, *An Account of Tangier . . .* (London, privately printed, 1787)

Clarendon, Edward, Earl of, *Life . . . Written by Himself* (Oxford, 1759)

Clarke, J. S. (ed.), *Life of King James II Collected out of Memoirs Writ of His Own Hand* (2 vols.; London, 1816)

Coke, Roger, *A Detection of the Court and State of England* (2 vols.; London, 1694)

Dumont, Jean, and Jean Rousset, *Le Cérémonial diplomatique des cours de l'Europe* (Amsterdam and The Hague, 1739)

Faithful Register; or the Debates of the House of Commons in Four Several Parliaments (London [1689?])

Grey, Anchitel, *Debates in the House of Commons, 1667–1694* (10 vols.; London, 1763)

[Heylin, Peter,] *The Voyage of France . . .* (London, 1673)

Higgons, Bevil, *Historical Works* (2 vols.; London, 1736)

Higgons, Bevil, *A Short View of the English History* (London, 1723)

[Hornby, Charles,] *The Fourth and Last Part of a Caveat against the Whiggs, &c. . . . ,* 2d ed. (London, 1712)

[Hornby, Charles,] *A Second Part of the Caveat against the Whiggs, &c.,* 2d ed. (London, 1712)

[Hornby, Charles,] *A Third Part of the Caveat against the Whigs* (London, 1712)

Kirkton, James, *The Secret and True History of the Church of Scotland, from the Restoration to the Year 1678* (Edinburgh, 1817)

Lamont of Newton, John, *Diary . . . , 1649–1671*, ed. G. R. Kinloch (Edinburgh: Maitland Club, 1830)

Lauder of Fountainhall, Sir John, *Historical Notices of Scottish*

Affairs, ed. David Laing (2 vols.; Edinburgh: Bannatyne Club, 1848)

Lauder of Fountainhall, Sir John, *Historical Observes of Memorable Occurrents in Church and State . . . ,* ed. A. Urquhart and David Laing (Edinburgh: Bannatyne Club, 1840)

Lauder of Fountainhall, Sir John, *Journals . . . ,* ed. Donald Crawford (Edinburgh: Scott. History Soc., 1900)

Lonsdale, John, Lord, *Memoir of the Reign of James II* (York, privately printed, 1808)

Luke, John, *Tangier at High Tide: The Journal of John Luke,* ed. H. A. Kaufman (Paris and Geneva, 1958)

Luttrell, Narcissus, *A Brief Historical Relation of State Affairs, 1678–1714* (6 vols.; Oxford, 1857)

McCormick, Charles (ed.), *The Secret History of the Court and Reign of Charles the Second, by a Member of His Privy Council . . .* (2 vols.; London, 1792)

Mackenzie, Sir George, *Memoirs of the Affairs of Scotland from the Restoration of King Charles II* [ed. Thomas Thomson] (Edinburgh, 1821)

Meyer, Johan, *Newe Landesbeschreibung der zwei Herzogtümer Schleswick und Holstein* (n. pl., 1652)

Nicoll, John, *Diary of Public Transactions and Other Occurrences . . . ,* ed. David Laing (Edinburgh: Bannatyne Club, 1836)

[Philips, George,] *The Present State of Tangier* (n. pl., 1676)

Reresby, Sir John, *Memoirs,* ed. Andrew Browning (Glasgow, 1936)

Row, William, *Life of Robert Blair . . . with Supplement . . . and Continuation,* ed. Thomas McCrie (Edinburgh, 1848)

St.-Simon, Louis de Rouvroy, Duke de, *Mémoires,* ed. A. de Boislisle (41 vols.; Paris, 1879–1928)

Sandford, Francis, *The History of the Coronation of the Most High . . . Monarch, James II . . .* ([London,] 1687)

Short and True Relation of Intrigues Transacted, Both at Home and Abroad, to Restore the Late King James (London, 1694)

State Poems; Continued . . . to This Present Year 1697 ([London?] 1697)

Turner, Sir James, *Memoirs of My Own Time,* ed. Thomas Thomson (Edinburgh: Bannatyne Club, 1829)

IV. Pamphlets and Tracts

Den Engelschen Bokkum Gebraden op den France Rooster ("London," 1688)

A Full Answer to the Depositions: And to All Other the Pretences and Arguments Whatsoever, Concerning the Birth of the Prince of Wales (London, 1689)

[Lawton, Charlwood,] *A French Conquest Neither Desirable Nor Practicable. Dedicated to the King of England* (London, 1693)

A Letter to a Bishop Concerning the Present Settlement and the New Oaths (London, 1689)

Nouvelles uyt Engelandt, Nevens een Missive van den Koningh (broadsheet), Dec. 22 [N.S.], 1688

A Reply to the Answer Doctor Welwood Has Made to King James's Declaration . . . [1693?]

Revolution Politicks: Being a Compleat Collection of All the Reports, Lyes, and Stories . . . *in 1688* . . . (London, 1733)

"The Revolution Vindicated . . . ," reprinted in *A Collection of State Tracts, Publish'd on Occasion of the Late Revolution in 1688. And during the Reign of King William III* (3 vols.; London, 1705–7) III, 694–728

[Welwood, James,] *An Answer to the Late K. James's Last Declaration* ([London?] 1693)

V. Contemporary Newspapers

The English Currant
The Intelligencer
The Kingdomes Intelligencer
The London Gazette
Mercurius Publicus
The Observator
Publick Occurrences Truely Stated

VI. Secondary Works

Books

Auerbach, Bertrand, *La Diplomatie française et la cour de Saxe, 1648–1680* (Paris, 1887)

Auerbach, Bertrand, *La France et le Saint Empire Romain Germanique depuis la paix de Westphalie jusqu'à la révolution française* (Paris, 1912)

Barrington, Michael, *Grahame of Claverhouse, Viscount Dundee* (London, 1911)

Bieber, R. P., *The Lords of Trade and Plantations* (Allentown, Penna., 1919)

Bittner, Ludwig, *et al.*, *Repertorium der diplomatischen Vertreter aller Länder* (2 vols.; Berlin, 1936, 1950)

Browning, Andrew, *Thomas Osborne, Earl of Danby and Duke of Leeds, 1632–1712* (3 vols.; Glasgow, 1951)

Bruce, John, *Annals of the Honorable East-India Company* (3 vols.; London, 1810)

Bulard, Gustave, *Les Traités de St.-Germain, essai sur l'alliance étroite de Louis XIV et du Grand-Électeur après la guerre de Hollande* (Paris, 1898)

Burnet, Gilbert, *History of My Own Time*, ed. Osmund Airy (2 vols.; Oxford, 1897)

Campbell, John, *The Naval History of Great Britain* (8 vols.; London, 1818)

Churchill, Sir Winston, *Marlborough: His Life and Times*, new ed., (2 vols.; London, 1947)

Coxe, William, *Memoirs of John, Duke of Marlborough*, 2d ed. (6 vols.; London, 1820)

Cruden, R. P., *The History of the Town of Gravesend in the County of Kent and of the Port of London* (London, 1843)

Custis, Charles, *Jaer-boecken der stadt Brugge*, 2d ed. (3 vols.; Bruges, 1765)

Dalton, Charles, *The Scots Army, 1661–1688* (London, 1909)

Davis, John, *History of the Second Queen's Royal Regiment* (6 vols.; London, 1887–1906)

D'Oyly, George, *The Life of William Sancroft, Archbishop of Canterbury*, 2d ed. (London, 1840)

Elliott, Hugh, *The Life of Sidney, Earl of Godolphin, Lord High Treasurer of England, 1702–1710* (London, 1888)

Emerson, W. R., *Monmouth's Rebellion* (New Haven, 1951)

Ennen, Leonard, *Frankreich und Niederrhein, oder Geschichte von Stadt und Kurstaat Köln* (2 vols.; Köln and Neuss, 1855–56)

Evans, F. M. G. (Mrs. C. S. S. Higham), *The Principal Secretary of State* (Manchester, 1923)

Feiling, K. G., *A History of the Tory Party, 1640–1714* (Oxford, 1924)

Ferèt C. J., *Fulham, Old and New, Being an Exhaustive History* . . . (3 vols.; London, 1900)

Fester, Richard, *Die Augsburger Allianz von 1686* (Munich, 1893)

Fortescue, Sir John, *A History of the British Army* (13 vols.; London, 1899–1930)

Fox, Charles, *A History of the Early Part of the Reign of James the Second* (London, 1808)

Foxcroft, H. C., *The Life and Letters of Sir George Savile, Bart., First Marquis of Halifax* (2 vols.; London, 1898)

Foxcroft, H. C., and T. E. S. Clarke, *A Life of Gilbert Burnet, Bishop of Salisbury* (Cambridge, 1907)

Fraknoi, Wilhelm, *Papst Innocenz XI (Benedikt Odescalchi) und Ungarn's Befreiung des Türken Herrschaft*, trans. into German by Peter Jekel (Freiburg-in-Breisgau, 1902)

Fruin, R., and W. J. Knoop, *Willem III en de slag van St.-Dénis* (The Hague, 1881)

Gray, Arthur, and Frederick Brittain, *A History of Jesus College, Cambridge* (London, 1960)

Hamilton, Charles, *Transactions during the Reign of Queen Anne; From the Union to the Death of That Princess* (Edinburgh, 1790)

Harris, John, *History of Kent* (London, 1719)

Hart, A. Tindal, *William Lloyd, 1627–1717* (London, 1952)

Jones, George Hilton, *The Main Stream of Jacobitism* (Cambridge, Mass., 1954)

Jones, J. R., *The First Whigs* (London, 1961)

Kenyon, J. P., *Robert Spencer, Earl of Sunderland, 1641–1702* (London, 1958)

Klopp, Onno, *Der Fall des Hauses Stuart und die Succession des Hauses Hannover* . . . (14 vols.; Vienna, 1875–88)

Knight, H. R., *Historical Records of the Buffs, East Kent Regiment, 3rd Foot* (London [1905])

Levaë, A., *Essai historique sur les négociations de la trêve de vingt ans conclue à Ratisbonne en 1684* (Brussels, 1855)

Lipscomb, George, *The History and Antiquities of the County of Buckingham* (4 vols.; London, 1847)

Liubimenko, I., *Les Relations* . . . *l'Angleterre avec la Russie avant Pierre le Grand* (Paris: *Bibliothèque de l'École des Hautes Etudes*, 1933)

Lodge, Sir Richard, *History of England from the Restoration to the Death of William III* (London, 1918)

London County Council Survey of London:
Parish of St. Margaret Westminster
Parish of St. Martin-in-the-Fields

Macaulay, T. B., Lord, *History of England from the Accession of James II*, ed. Sir Charles Firth (6 vols.; London, 1913–15)

Mackintosh, Sir James, *History of the Revolution in England in 1688* (Philadelphia, 1835)

Mazure, F. A. J., *Histoire de la révolution de 1688 en Angleterre* (3 vols., Paris, 1825)

Ogg, David, *England in the Reign of Charles II*, 2d ed. (2 vols.; Oxford, 1955)

Ogg, David, *England in the Reigns of James II and William III* (Oxford, 1955)

Pagès, Georges, *Contributions à la politique française en Allemagne sous Louis XIV* (Paris, 1905)

Paul, Sir James (ed.), *The Scots Peerage* (9 vols.; Edinburgh, 1904–14)

Pinkham, Lucile, *William III and the Respectable Revolution* (Cambridge, Mass., 1954)

Ranke, Leopold von, *History of England, Principally in the Seventeenth Century*, trans. G. W. Kitchin *et al.* (6 vols.; Oxford, 1875)

Rapin de Thoyras, Paul, *History of England*, trans. N. Tindal (15 vols.; London, 1725–31)

Return of Members of Parliament, Part I, Parliaments of England, 1213–1702 (London, 1878)

Routh, E. M. G., *Tangier: England's Lost Atlantic Outpost, 1661–1684* (London, 1912)

Scott, Eva, *The Travels of the King: Charles II in Germany and Flanders, 1654–1660* (London, 1907)

Sykes, Norman, *William Wake, Archbishop of Canterbury* (2 vols.; Cambridge, 1957)

Terry, C. S., *John Graham of Claverhouse, Viscount Dundee, 1648–1689* (London, 1905)

Thomson, M. A., *The Secretaries of State, 1681–1782* (Oxford, 1932)

Turner, F. C., *James II* (London, 1948)

Venn, J. and J. A., *Alumni Cantabrigenses, Part I* (Cambridge, 1922)

Victoria County Histories
  Berkshire
  Buckinghamshire
  Hampshire

Vlekke, B. H. M., *Nusantara, A History of the East Indian Archipelago* (Cambridge, Mass., 1944)

Waldteufel, Édouard, *La Politique étrangere de Louis XIV, conquête de Hollande* (Paris, 1898)

Articles

Brinkmann, C., "England and the Hanse under Charles II," *English Historical Review*, XXIII (1908), 683–708

Brinkmann, C., "The Relations between England and Germany, 1660–1688," *English Historical Review*, XXIV (1909), 247–77, 448–69

Davies, Godfrey, and P. H. Hardacre, "The Restoration of the Scottish Episcopacy, 1660–1661," *Journal of British Studies*, I (1962), 32–51

Evans, F. M. G. (Mrs. C. S. S. Higham), "The Emoluments of the Principal Secretaries of State in the Seventeenth Century," *English Historical Review*, XXXV (1920), 513–24

George, R. H., "The Charters Granted to English Parliamentary Boroughs in 1688," *English Historical Review*, LV (1940), 47–56

George, R. H., "Parliamentary Elections and Electioneering in 1685," *Transactions of the Royal Historical Soc.*, 4th series, XIX (1936), 167–95

Grose, C. L., "The Anglo-Dutch Alliance of 1678," *English Historical Review*, XXXIX (1924), 349–72, 526–51

Grose, C. L., "Louis XIV's Financial Relations with Charles II and the English Parliament," *Journal of Modern History*, I (1929), 177–204

Guillot, Gaétan, "Léopold Ier et sa cour (1681–1684)," *Revue des questions historiques*, LXXXI (1907), 401–46

Hassenkamp, R., "Über die Versuche des Pfalzgrafen Philipp Wilhelm, König Karl II von England auf den Thron zurückzuführen," *Deutsche Zeitschrift für Geschichtswissenschaft*, Neue Folge, I (1896–97), 238–54

Samuel, Wilfred S., "Sir William Davidson, Royalist (1616–1689) and the Jews," *Transactions of the Jewish Historical Soc. of England*, XIV (1913), 39–75

Shaw, W. A., "The English Government and the Relief of Protestant Refugees," *English Historical Review*, IX (1894), 662–83

Steinman, G., "Memorials Preserved at Bruges of King Charles the Second's Residence . . . ," *Archaeologia*, XXXV (1853), 335–49

Wolf, Lucien, "The Jewry of the Restoration, 1660–1664," *Transactions of the Jewish Historical Society of England*, V (1904), 5–33

Wolf, Lucien, "The Status of the Jews in England after the Re-Settlement," *Transactions of the Jewish History Soc. of England*, IV (1903), 177–85

Index